Elwood Morris Wherry

A Comprehensive Commentary on the Qurán

Vol. 4

Elwood Morris Wherry

A Comprehensive Commentary on the Qurán
Vol. 4

ISBN/EAN: 9783337817572

Printed in Europe, USA, Canada, Australia, Japan

Cover: Foto ©Lupo / pixelio.de

More available books at **www.hansebooks.com**

TRÜBNER'S ORIENTAL SERIES.

"A knowledge of the commonplace, at least, of Oriental literature, philosophy, and religion is as necessary to the general reader of the present day as an acquaintance with the Latin and Greek classics was a generation or so ago. Immense strides have been made within the present century in these branches of learning; Sanskrit has been brought within the range of accurate philology, and its invaluable ancient literature thoroughly investigated; the language and sacred books of the Zoroastrians have been laid bare; Egyptian, Assyrian, and other records of the remote past have been deciphered, and a group of scholars speak of still more recondite Accadian and Hittite monuments; but the results of all the scholarship that has been devoted to these subjects have been almost inaccessible to the public because they were contained for the most part in learned or expensive works, or scattered throughout the numbers of scientific periodicals. Messrs. TRÜBNER & Co., in a spirit of enterprise which does them infinite credit, have determined to supply the constantly-increasing want, and to give in a popular, or, at least, a comprehensive form, all this mass of knowledge to the world."—*Times*.

Second Edition, post 8vo, pp. xxxii.—748, with Map, cloth, price 21s.

THE INDIAN EMPIRE:
ITS PEOPLE, HISTORY, AND PRODUCTS.

By the HON. SIR W. W. HUNTER, K.C.S.I., C.S.I., C.I.E., LL.D.

Member of the Viceroy's Legislative Council,
Director-General of Statistics to the Government of India.

Being a Revised Edition, brought up to date, and incorporating the general results of the Census of 1881.

"It forms a volume of more than 700 pages, and is a marvellous combination of literary condensation and research. It gives a complete account of the Indian Empire, its history, peoples, and products, and forms the worthy outcome of seventeen years of labour with exceptional opportunities for rendering that labour fruitful. Nothing could be more lucid than Sir William Hunter's expositions of the economic and political condition of India at the present time, or more interesting than his scholarly history of the India of the past."—*The Times*.

THE FOLLOWING WORKS HAVE ALREADY APPEARED:—

Third Edition, post 8vo, cloth, pp. xvi.—428, price 16s.

ESSAYS ON THE SACRED LANGUAGE, WRITINGS, AND RELIGION OF THE PARSIS.

BY MARTIN HAUG, PH.D.,

Late of the Universities of Tübingen, Göttingen, and Bonn; Superintendent of Sanskrit Studies, and Professor of Sanskrit in the Poona College.

EDITED AND ENLARGED BY DR. E. W. WEST.

To which is added a Biographical Memoir of the late Dr. HAUG by Prof. E. P. EVANS.

I. History of the Researches into the Sacred Writings and Religion of the Parsis, from the Earliest Times down to the Present.
II. Languages of the Parsi Scriptures.
III. The Zend-Avesta, or the Scripture of the Parsis.
IV. The Zoroastrian Religion, as to its Origin and Development.

"'Essays on the Sacred Language, Writings, and Religion of the Parsis,' by the late Dr. Martin Haug, edited by Dr. E. W. West. The author intended, on his return from India, to expand the materials contained in this work into a comprehensive account of the Zoroastrian religion, but the design was frustrated by his untimely death. We have, however, in a concise and readable form, a history of the researches into the sacred writings and religion of the Parsis from the earliest times down to the present—a dissertation on the languages of the Parsi Scriptures, a translation of the Zend-Avesta, or the Scripture of the Parsis, and a dissertation on the Zoroastrian religion, with especial reference to its origin and development."—*Times.*

Post 8vo, cloth, pp. viii.—176, price 7s. 6d.

TEXTS FROM THE BUDDHIST CANON
COMMONLY KNOWN AS "DHAMMAPADA."
With Accompanying Narratives.

Translated from the Chinese by S. BEAL, B.A., Professor of Chinese, University College, London.

The Dhammapada, as hitherto known by the Pali Text Edition, as edited by Fausböll, by Max Müller's English, and Albrecht Weber's German translations, consists only of twenty-six chapters or sections, whilst the Chinese version, or rather recension, as now translated by Mr. Beal, consists of thirty-nine sections. The students of Pali who possess Fausböll's text, or either of the above-named translations, will therefore needs want Mr. Beal's English rendering of the Chinese version; the thirteen above-named additional sections not being accessible to them in any other form; for, even if they understand Chinese, the Chinese original would be unobtainable by them.

"Mr. Beal's rendering of the Chinese translation is a most valuable aid to the critical study of the work. It contains authentic texts gathered from ancient canonical books, and generally connected with some incident in the history of Buddha. Their great interest, however, consists in the light which they throw upon everyday life in India at the remote period at which they were written, and upon the method of teaching adopted by the founder of the religion. The method employed was principally parable, and the simplicity of the tales and the excellence of the morals inculcated, as well as the strange hold which they have retained upon the minds of millions of people, make them a very remarkable study."—*Times.*

"Mr. Beal, by making it accessible in an English dress, has added to the great services he has already rendered to the comparative study of religious history."—*Academy.*

"Valuable as exhibiting the doctrine of the Buddhists in its purest, least adulterated form, it brings the modern reader face to face with that simple creed and rule of conduct which won its way over the minds of myriads, and which is now nominally professed by 145 millions, who have overlaid its austere simplicity with innumerable ceremonies, forgotten its maxims, perverted its teaching, and so inverted its leading principle that a religion whose founder denied a God, now worships that founder as a god himself."—*Scotsman.*

Second Edition, post 8vo, cloth, pp. xxiv.—360, price 10s. 6d.

THE HISTORY OF INDIAN LITERATURE.
By ALBRECHT WEBER.

Translated from the Second German Edition by JOHN MANN, M.A., and THÉODOR ZACHARIAE, Ph.D., with the sanction of the Author.

Dr. BUHLER, Inspector of Schools in India, writes:—"When I was Professor of Oriental Languages in Elphinstone College, I frequently felt the want of such a work to which I could refer the students."

Professor COWELL, of Cambridge, writes:—"It will be especially useful to the students in our Indian colleges and universities. I used to long for such a book when I was teaching in Calcutta. Hindu students are intensely interested in the history of Sanskrit literature, and this volume will supply them with all they want on the subject."

Professor WHITNEY, Yale College, Newhaven, Conn., U.S.A., writes:—"I was one of the class to whom the work was originally given in the form of academic lectures. At their first appearance they were by far the most learned and able treatment of their subject; and with their recent additions they still maintain decidedly the same rank."

"Is perhaps the most comprehensive and lucid survey of Sanskrit literature extant. The essays contained in the volume were originally delivered as academic lectures, and at the time of their first publication were acknowledged to be by far the most learned and able treatment of the subject. They have now been brought up to date by the addition of all the most important results of recent research."—*Times.*

Post 8vo, cloth, pp. xii.—198, accompanied by Two Language Maps, price 12s.

A SKETCH OF
THE MODERN LANGUAGES OF THE EAST INDIES.
By ROBERT N. CUST.

The Author has attempted to fill up a vacuum, the inconvenience of which pressed itself on his notice. Much had been written about the languages of the East Indies, but the extent of our present knowledge had not even been brought to a focus. It occurred to him that it might be of use to others to publish in an arranged form the notes which he had collected for his own edification.

"Supplies a deficiency which has long been felt."—*Times.*

"The book before us is then a valuable contribution to philological science. It passes under review a vast number of languages, and it gives, or professes to give, in every case the sum and substance of the opinions and judgments of the best-informed writers."—*Saturday Review.*

Second Corrected Edition, post 8vo, pp. xii.—116, cloth, price

THE BIRTH OF THE WAR-GOD.
A Poem. By KALIDASA.

Translated from the Sanskrit into English Verse by
RALPH T. H. GRIFFITH, M.A.

"A very spirited rendering of the *Kumárasambhava*, which was first published twenty-six years ago, and which we are glad to see made once more accessible."—*Times.*

"Mr. Griffith's very spirited rendering is well known to most who are at all interested in Indian literature, or enjoy the tenderness of feeling and rich creative imagination of its author."—*Indian Antiquary.*

"We are very glad to welcome a second edition of Professor Griffith's admirable translation. Few translations deserve a second edition better."—*Athenæum.*

Post 8vo, pp. 432, cloth, price 16s.

A CLASSICAL DICTIONARY OF HINDU MYTHOLOGY AND RELIGION, GEOGRAPHY, HISTORY, AND LITERATURE.

By JOHN DOWSON, M.R.A.S.,
Late Professor of Hindustani, Staff College.

"This not only forms an indispensable book of reference to students of Indian literature, but is also of great general interest, as it gives in a concise and easily accessible form all that need be known about the personages of Hindu mythology whose names are so familiar, but of whom so little is known outside the limited circle of *savants*."—*Times*.

"It is no slight gain when such subjects are treated fairly and fully in a moderate space; and we need only add that the few wants which we may hope to see supplied in new editions detract but little from the general excellence of Mr. Dowson's work."
—*Saturday Review*.

Post 8vo, with View of Mecca, pp. cxii.—172, cloth, price 9s.

SELECTIONS FROM THE KORAN.

By EDWARD WILLIAM LANE,
Translator of "The Thousand and One Nights;" &c., &c.
A New Edition, Revised and Enlarged, with an Introduction by
STANLEY LANE POOLE.

"... Has been long esteemed in this country as the compilation of one of the greatest Arabic scholars of the time, the late Mr. Lane, the well-known translator of the 'Arabian Nights.' ... The present editor has enhanced the value of his relative's work by divesting the text of a great deal of extraneous matter introduced by way of comment, and prefixing an introduction."—*Times*.

"Mr. Poole is both a generous and a learned biographer. ... Mr. Poole tells us the facts ... so far as it is possible for industry and criticism to ascertain them, and for literary skill to present them in a condensed and readable form."—*Englishman, Calcutta*.

Post 8vo, pp. vi.—368, cloth, price 14s.

MODERN INDIA AND THE INDIANS,

BEING A SERIES OF IMPRESSIONS, NOTES, AND ESSAYS.

By MONIER WILLIAMS, D.C.L.,
Hon. LL.D. of the University of Calcutta, Hon. Member of the Bombay Asiatic Society, Boden Professor of Sanskrit in the University of Oxford.
Third Edition, revised and augmented by considerable Additions, with Illustrations and a Map.

"In this volume we have the thoughtful impressions of a thoughtful man on some of the most important questions connected with our Indian Empire. ... An enlightened observant man, travelling among an enlightened observant people, Professor Monier Williams has brought before the public in a pleasant form more of the manners and customs of the Queen's Indian subjects than we ever remember to have seen in any one work. He not only deserves the thanks of every Englishman for this able contribution to the study of Modern India—a subject with which we should be specially familiar—but he deserves the thanks of every Indian, Parsee or Hindu, Buddhist and Moslem, for his clear exposition of their manners, their creeds, and their necessities."—*Times*.

Post 8vo, pp. xliv.—376, cloth, price 14s.

METRICAL TRANSLATIONS FROM SANSKRIT WRITERS.

With an Introduction, many Prose Versions, and Parallel Passages from Classical Authors.

By J. MUIR, C.I.E., D.C.L., LL.D., Ph.D.

"... An agreeable introduction to Hindu poetry."—*Times*.

"... A volume which may be taken as a fair illustration alike of the religious and moral sentiments and of the legendary lore of the best Sanskrit writers."—*Edinburgh Daily Review*.

Second Edition, post 8vo, pp. xxvi.—244, cloth, price 10s. 6d.

THE GULISTAN;

OR, ROSE GARDEN OF SHEKH MUSHLIU'D-DIN SADI OF SHIRAZ.

Translated for the First Time into Prose and Verse, with an Introductory Preface, and a Life of the Author, from the Atish Kadah,

By EDWARD B. EASTWICK, C.B., M.A., F.R.S., M.R.A.S.

"It is a very fair rendering of the original."—*Times.*

"The new edition has long been desired, and will be welcomed by all who take any interest in Oriental poetry. The *Gulistan* is a typical Persian verse-book of the highest order. Mr. Eastwick's rhymed translation . . . has long established itself in a secure position as the best version of Sadi's finest work."—*Academy.*

"It is both faithfully and gracefully executed."—*Tablet.*

In Two Volumes, post 8vo, pp. viii.—408 and viii.—348, cloth, price 28s.

MISCELLANEOUS ESSAYS RELATING TO INDIAN SUBJECTS.

By BRIAN HOUGHTON HODGSON, ESQ., F.R.S.,

Late of the Bengal Civil Service; Corresponding Member of the Institute; Chevalier of the Legion of Honour; late British Minister at the Court of Nepal, &c., &c.

CONTENTS OF VOL. I.

SECTION I.—On the Kocch, Bódó, and Dhimál Tribes.—Part I. Vocabulary.—Part II. Grammar.—Part III. Their Origin, Location, Numbers, Creed, Customs, Character, and Condition, with a General Description of the Climate they dwell in.—Appendix.

SECTION II.—On Himalayan Ethnology.—I. Comparative Vocabulary of the Languages of the Broken Tribes of Nepál.—II. Vocabulary of the Dialects of the Kiranti Language.—III. Grammatical Analysis of the Váyu Language. The Váyu Grammar.—IV. Analysis of the Báhing Dialect of the Kiranti Language. The Báhing Grammar.—V. On the Váyu or Háyu Tribe of the Central Himaláya.—VI. On the Kiranti Tribe of the Central Himaláya.

CONTENTS OF VOL. II.

SECTION III.—On the Aborigines of North-Eastern India. Comparative Vocabulary of the Tibetan, Bódó, and Gáró Tongues.

SECTION IV.—Aborigines of the North-Eastern Frontier.

SECTION V.—Aborigines of the Eastern Frontier.

SECTION VI.—The Indo-Chinese Borderers, and their connection with the Himalayans and Tibetans. Comparative Vocabulary of Indo-Chinese Borderers in Arakan. Comparative Vocabulary of Indo-Chinese Borderers in Tenasserim.

SECTION VII.—The Mongolian Affinities of the Caucasians.—Comparison and Analysis of Caucasian and Mongolian Words.

SECTION VIII.—Physical Type of Tibetans.

SECTION IX.—The Aborigines of Central India.—Comparative Vocabulary of the Aboriginal Languages of Central India.—Aborigines of the Eastern Ghats.—Vocabulary of some of the Dialects of the Hill and Wandering Tribes in the Northern Sircars.—Aborigines of the Nilgiris, with Remarks on their Affinities.—Supplement to the Nilgirian Vocabularies.—The Aborigines of Southern India and Ceylon.

SECTION X.—Route of Nepalese Mission to Pekin, with Remarks on the Water-Shed and Plateau of Tibet.

SECTION XI.—Route from Káthmándú, the Capital of Nepál, to Darjeeling in Sikim.—Memorandum relative to the Seven Cosis of Nepál.

SECTION XII.—Some Accounts of the Systems of Law and Police as recognised in the State of Nepál.

SECTION XIII.—The Native Method of making the Paper denominated Hindustan, Nepálese.

SECTION XIV.—Pre-eminence of the Vernaculars; or, the Anglicists Answered; Being Letters on the Education of the People of India.

"For the study of the less-known races of India Mr. Brian Hodgson's 'Miscellaneous Essays' will be found very valuable both to the philologist and the ethnologist."—*Times.*

Third Edition, Two Vols., post 8vo, pp. viii.—268 and viii.—326, cloth, price 21s.

THE LIFE OR LEGEND OF GAUDAMA,

THE BUDDHA OF THE BURMESE. With Annotations.

The Ways to Neibban, and Notice on the Phongyies or Burmese Monks.

BY THE RIGHT REV. P. BIGANDET,

Bishop of Ramatha, Vicar-Apostolic of Ava and Pegu.

"The work is furnished with copious notes, which not only illustrate the subject-matter, but form a perfect encyclopædia of Buddhist lore."—*Times.*

"A work which will furnish European students of Buddhism with a most valuable help in the prosecution of their investigations."—*Edinburgh Daily Review.*

"Bishop Bigandet's invaluable work."—*Indian Antiquary.*

"Viewed in this light, its importance is sufficient to place students of the subject under a deep obligation to its author."—*Calcutta Review.*

"This work is one of the greatest authorities upon Buddhism."—*Dublin Review.*

Post 8vo, pp. xxiv.—420, cloth, price 18s.

CHINESE BUDDHISM.

A VOLUME OF SKETCHES, HISTORICAL AND CRITICAL.

BY J. EDKINS, D.D.

Author of "China's Place in Philology," "Religion in China," &c., &c.

"It contains a vast deal of important information on the subject, such as is only to be gained by long-continued study on the spot."—*Athenæum.*

"Upon the whole, we know of no work comparable to it for the extent of its original research, and the simplicity with which this complicated system of philosophy, religion, literature, and ritual is set forth."—*British Quarterly Review.*

"The whole volume is replete with learning. . . . It deserves most careful study from all interested in the history of the religions of the world, and expressly of those who are concerned in the propagation of Christianity. Dr. Edkins notices in terms of just condemnation the exaggerated praise bestowed upon Buddhism by recent English writers."—*Record.*

Post 8vo, pp. 496, cloth, price 18s.

LINGUISTIC AND ORIENTAL ESSAYS.

WRITTEN FROM THE YEAR 1846 TO 1878.

BY ROBERT NEEDHAM CUST,

Late Member of Her Majesty's Indian Civil Service; Hon. Secretary to the Royal Asiatic Society;

and Author of "The Modern Languages of the East Indies."

"We know none who has described Indian life, especially the life of the natives, with so much learning, sympathy, and literary talent."—*Academy.*

"They seem to us to be full of suggestive and original remarks."—*St. James's Gazette.*

"His book contains a vast amount of information. The result of thirty-five years of inquiry, reflection, and speculation, and that on subjects as full of fascination as of food for thought."—*Tablet.*

"Exhibit such a thorough acquaintance with the history and antiquities of India as to entitle him to speak as one having authority."—*Edinburgh Daily Review.*

"The author speaks with the authority of personal experience. . . . It is this constant association with the country and the people which gives such a vividness to many of the pages."—*Athenæum.*

Post 8vo, pp. civ.—348, cloth, price 18s.

BUDDHIST BIRTH STORIES; or, Jataka Tales.

The Oldest Collection of Folk-lore Extant:

BEING THE JATAKATTHAVANNANA,

For the first time Edited in the original Pāli.

BY V. FAUSBOLL;

And Translated by T. W. RHYS DAVIDS.

Translation. Volume I.

"These are tales supposed to have been told by the Buddha of what he had seen and heard in his previous births. They are probably the nearest representatives of the original Aryan stories from which sprang the folk-lore of Europe as well as India. The introduction contains a most interesting disquisition on the migrations of these fables, tracing their reappearance in the various groups of folk-lore legends. Among other old friends, we meet with a version of the Judgment of Solomon."—*Times*.

"It is now some years since Mr. Rhys Davids asserted his right to be heard on this subject by his able article on Buddhism in the new edition of the 'Encyclopædia Britannica.'"—*Leeds Mercury*.

"All who are interested in Buddhist literature ought to feel deeply indebted to Mr. Rhys Davids. His well-established reputation as a Pali scholar is a sufficient guarantee for the fidelity of his version, and the style of his translations is deserving of high praise."—*Academy*.

"No more competent expositor of Buddhism could be found than Mr. Rhys Davids. In the Jātaka book we have, then, a priceless record of the earliest imaginative literature of our race; and . . . it presents to us a nearly complete picture of the social life and customs and popular beliefs of the common people of Aryan tribes, closely related to ourselves, just as they were passing through the first stages of civilisation."—*St. James's Gazette*.

Post 8vo, pp. xxviii.—362, cloth, price 14s.

A TALMUDIC MISCELLANY;

OR, A THOUSAND AND ONE EXTRACTS FROM THE TALMUD, THE MIDRASHIM, AND THE KABBALAH.

Compiled and Translated by PAUL ISAAC HERSHON,

Author of "Genesis According to the Talmud," &c.

With Notes and Copious Indexes.

"To obtain in so concise and handy a form as this volume a general idea of the Talmud is a boon to Christians at least."—*Times*.

"Its peculiar and popular character will make it attractive to general readers. Mr. Hershon is a very competent scholar. . . . Contains samples of the good, bad, and indifferent, and especially extracts that throw light upon the Scriptures."—*British Quarterly Review*.

"Will convey to English readers a more complete and truthful notion of the Talmud than any other work that has yet appeared."—*Daily News*.

"Without overlooking in the slightest the several attractions of the previous volumes of the 'Oriental Series,' we have no hesitation in saying that this surpasses them all in interest."—*Edinburgh Daily Review*.

"Mr. Hershon has . . . thus given English readers what is, we believe, a fair set of specimens which they can test for themselves."—*The Record*.

"This book is by far the best fitted in the present state of knowledge to enable the general reader to gain a fair and unbiassed conception of the multifarious contents of the wonderful miscellany which can only be truly understood—so Jewish pride asserts—by the life-long devotion of scholars of the Chosen People."—*Inquirer*.

"The value and importance of this volume consist in the fact that scarcely a single extract is given in its pages but throws some light, direct or refracted, upon those Scriptures which are the common heritage of Jew and Christian alike."—*John Bull*.

"It is a capital specimen of Hebrew scholarship; a monument of learned, loving, light-giving labour."—*Jewish Herald*.

Post 8vo, pp. xii.—228, cloth, price 7s. 6d.

THE CLASSICAL POETRY OF THE JAPANESE.

BY BASIL HALL CHAMBERLAIN,
Author of "Yeigo Heñkaku Shirañ."

"A very curious volume. The author has manifestly devoted much labour to the task of studying the poetical literature of the Japanese, and rendering characteristic specimens into English verse."—*Daily News.*

"Mr. Chamberlain's volume is, so far as we are aware, the first attempt which has been made to interpret the literature of the Japanese to the Western world. It is to the classical poetry of Old Japan that we must turn for indigenous Japanese thought, and in the volume before us we have a selection from that poetry rendered into graceful English verse."—*Tablet.*

"It is undoubtedly one of the best translations of lyric literature which has appeared during the close of the last year."—*Celestial Empire.*

"Mr. Chamberlain set himself a difficult task when he undertook to reproduce Japanese poetry in an English form. But he has evidently laboured con amore, and his efforts are successful to a degree."—*London and China Express.*

Post 8vo, pp. xii.—164, cloth, price 10s. 6d.

THE HISTORY OF ESARHADDON (Son of Sennacherib),

KING OF ASSYRIA, B.C. 681-668.

Translated from the Cuneiform Inscriptions upon Cylinders and Tablets in the British Museum Collection; together with a Grammatical Analysis of each Word, Explanations of the Ideographs by Extracts from the Bi-Lingual Syllabaries, and List of Eponyms, &c.

BY ERNEST A. BUDGE, B.A., M.R.A.S.,
Assyrian Exhibitioner, Christ's College, Cambridge.

"Students of scriptural archæology will also appreciate the 'History of Esarhaddon.'"—*Times.*

"There is much to attract the scholar in this volume. It does not pretend to popularise studies which are yet in their infancy. Its primary object is to translate, but it does not assume to be more than tentative, and it offers both to the professed Assyriologist and to the ordinary non-Assyriological Semitic scholar the means of controlling its results."—*Academy.*

"Mr. Budge's book is, of course, mainly addressed to Assyrian scholars and students. They are not, it is to be feared, a very numerous class. But the more thanks are due to him on that account for the way in which he has acquitted himself in his laborious task."—*Tablet.*

Post 8vo, pp. 448, cloth, price 21s.

THE MESNEVI

(Usually known as THE MESNEVIYI SHERIF, or HOLY MESNEVI)

OF

MEVLANA (OUR LORD) JELALU 'D-DIN MUHAMMED ER-RUMI.

Book the First.

Together with some Account of the Life and Acts of the Author, of his Ancestors, and of his Descendants.

Illustrated by a Selection of Characteristic Anecdotes, as Collected by their Historian,

MEVLANA SHEMSU-'D-DIN AHMED, EL EFLAKI, EL 'ARIFI.

Translated, and the Poetry Versified, in English,

BY JAMES W. REDHOUSE, M.R.A.S., &c.

"A complete treasury of occult Oriental lore."—*Saturday Review.*

"This book will be a very valuable help to the reader ignorant of Persia, who is desirous of obtaining an insight into a very important department of the literature extant in that language."—*Tablet.*

Post 8vo, pp. xvi.—280, cloth, price 6s.

EASTERN PROVERBS AND EMBLEMS
ILLUSTRATING OLD TRUTHS.

BY REV. J. LONG,

Member of the Bengal Asiatic Society, F.R.G.S.

"We regard the book as valuable, and wish for it a wide circulation and attentive reading."—*Record.*

"Altogether, it is quite a feast of good things."—*Globe.*

"It is full of interesting matter."—*Antiquary.*

Post 8vo, pp. viii.—270, cloth, price 7s. 6d.

INDIAN POETRY;

Containing a New Edition of the "Indian Song of Songs," from the Sanscrit of the "Gita Govinda" of Jayadeva; Two Books from "The Iliad of India" (Mahabharata), "Proverbial Wisdom" from the Shlokas of the Hitopadesa, and other Oriental Poems.

BY EDWIN ARNOLD, C.S.I., Author of "The Light of Asia."

"In this new volume of Messrs. Trübner's Oriental Series, Mr. Edwin Arnold does good service by illustrating, through the medium of his musical English melodies, the power of Indian poetry to stir European emotions. The 'Indian Song of Songs' is not unknown to scholars. Mr. Arnold will have introduced it among popular English poems. Nothing could be more graceful and delicate than the shades by which Krishna is portrayed in the gradual process of being weaned by the love of

'Beautiful Radha, jasmine-bosomed Radha,'

from the allurements of the forest nymphs, in whom the five senses are typified."—*Times.*

"No other English poet has ever thrown his genius and his art so thoroughly into the work of translating Eastern ideas as Mr. Arnold has done in his splendid paraphrases of language contained in these mighty epics."—*Daily Telegraph.*

"The poem abounds with imagery of Eastern luxuriousness and sensuousness; the air seems laden with the spicy odours of the tropics, and the verse has a richness and a melody sufficient to captivate the senses of the dullest."—*Standard.*

"The translator, while producing a very enjoyable poem, has adhered with tolerable fidelity to the original text."—*Overland Mail.*

"We certainly wish Mr. Arnold success in his attempt 'to popularise Indian classics,' that being, as his preface tells us, the goal towards which he bends his efforts."—*Allen's Indian Mail.*

Post 8vo, pp. xvi.—296, cloth, price 10s. 6d.

THE MIND OF MENCIUS;
OR, POLITICAL ECONOMY FOUNDED UPON MORAL PHILOSOPHY.

A SYSTEMATIC DIGEST OF THE DOCTRINES OF THE CHINESE PHILOSOPHER MENCIUS.

Translated from the Original Text and Classified, with Comments and Explanations,

By the REV. ERNST FABER, Rhenish Mission Society.

Translated from the German, with Additional Notes,

By the REV. A. B. HUTCHINSON, C.M.S., Church Mission, Hong Kong.

"Mr. Faber is already well known in the field of Chinese studies by his digest of the doctrines of Confucius. The value of this work will be perceived when it is remembered that at no time since relations commenced between China and the West has the former been so powerful—we had almost said aggressive—as now. For those who will give it careful study, Mr. Faber's work is one of the most valuable of the excellent series to which it belongs."—*Nature.*

A 2

Post 8vo, pp. 336, cloth, price 16s.

THE RELIGIONS OF INDIA.

By A. BARTH.

Translated from the French with the authority and assistance of the Author.

The author has, at the request of the publishers, considerably enlarged the work for the translator, and has added the literature of the subject to date; the translation may, therefore, be looked upon as an equivalent of a new and improved edition of the original.

"Is not only a valuable manual of the religions of India, which marks a distinct step in the treatment of the subject, but also a useful work of reference."—*Academy.*

"This volume is a reproduction, with corrections and additions, of an article contributed by the learned author two years ago to the 'Encyclopédie des Sciences Religieuses.' It attracted much notice when it first appeared, and is generally admitted to present the best summary extant of the vast subject with which it deals."—*Tablet.*

"This is not only on the whole the best but the only manual of the religions of India, apart from Buddhism, which we have in English. The present work . . . shows not only great knowledge of the facts and power of clear exposition, but also great insight into the inner history and the deeper meaning of the great religion for it is in reality any one, which it proposes to describe."—*Modern Review.*

"The merit of the work has been emphatically recognised by the most authoritative Orientalists, both in this country and on the continent of Europe. But probably there are few Indianists (if we may use the word) who would not derive a good deal of information from it, and especially from the extensive bibliography provided in the notes."—*Dublin Review.*

"Such a sketch M. Barth has drawn with a master-hand."—*Critic (New York).*

Post 8vo, pp. viii.—152, cloth, price 6s.

HINDU PHILOSOPHY.

THE SĀNKHYA KĀRIKA OF IS'WARA KRISHNA.

An Exposition of the System of Kapila, with an Appendix on the Nyāya and Vais'eshika Systems.

By JOHN DAVIES, M.A. (Cantab.), M.R.A.S.

The system of Kapila contains nearly all that India has produced in the department of pure philosophy.

"The non-Orientalist . . . finds in Mr. Davies a patient and learned guide who leads him into the intricacies of the philosophy of India, and supplies him with a clue that he may not be lost in them. In the preface he states that the system of Kapila is the 'earliest attempt on record to give an answer, from reason alone, to the mysterious questions which arise in every thoughtful mind about the origin of the world, the nature and relations of man and his future destiny,' and in his learned and able notes he exhibits 'the connection of the Sankhya system with the philosophy of Spinoza,' and 'the connection of the system of Kapila with that of Schopenhauer and Von Hartmann.'"—*Foreign Church Chronicle.*

"Mr. Davies's volume on Hindu Philosophy is an undoubted gain to all students of the development of thought. The system of Kapila, which is here given in a translation from the Sānkhya Kārikā, is the only contribution of India to pure philosophy. . . . Presents many points of deep interest to the student of comparative philosophy, and without Mr. Davies's lucid interpretation it would be difficult to appreciate these points in any adequate manner."—*Saturday Review.*

"We welcome Mr. Davies's book as a valuable addition to our philosophical library."—*Notes and Queries.*

Post 8vo, pp. x.—130, cloth, price 6s.

A MANUAL OF HINDU PANTHEISM. VEDÂNTASÂRA.

Translated, with copious Annotations,

BY MAJOR G. A. JACOB,

Bombay Staff Corps; Inspector of Army Schools.

The design of this little work is to provide for missionaries, and for others who, like them, have little leisure for original research, an accurate summary of the doctrines of the Vedânta.

"The modest title of Major Jacob's work conveys but an inadequate idea of the vast amount of research embodied in his notes to the text of the Vedantasara. So copious, indeed, are these, and so much collateral matter do they bring to bear on the subject, that the diligent student will rise from their perusal with a fairly adequate view of Hindû philosophy generally. His work . . . is one of the best of its kind that we have seen."—*Calcutta Review.*

Post 8vo, pp. xii.—154, cloth, price 7s. 6d.

TSUNI—||GOAM:

THE SUPREME BEING OF THE KHOI-KHOI.

BY THEOPHILUS HAHN, Ph.D.,

Custodian of the Grey Collection, Cape Town; Corresponding Member of the Geogr. Society, Dresden; Corresponding Member of the Anthropological Society, Vienna, &c., &c.

"The first instalment of Dr. Hahn's labours will be of interest, not at the Cape only, but in every University of Europe. It is, in fact, a most valuable contribution to the comparative study of religion and mythology. Accounts of their religion and mythology were scattered about in various books; these have been carefully collected by Dr. Hahn and printed in his second chapter, enriched and improved by what he has been able to collect himself."—*Prof. Max Müller in the Nineteenth Century.*

"It is full of good things."—*St. James's Gazette.*

In Four Volumes. Post 8vo, Vol. I., pp. xii.—392, cloth, price 12s. 6d., Vol. II., pp. vi.—408, cloth, price 12s. 6d., Vol. III., pp. viii.—414, cloth, price 12s. 6d., Vol. IV., pp. viii.—340, cloth, price 10s. 6d.

A COMPREHENSIVE COMMENTARY TO THE QURAN.

TO WHICH IS PREFIXED SALE'S PRELIMINARY DISCOURSE, WITH ADDITIONAL NOTES AND EMENDATIONS.

Together with a Complete Index to the Text, Preliminary Discourse, and Notes.

By Rev. E. M. WHERRY, M.A., Lodiana.

"As Mr. Wherry's book is intended for missionaries in India, it is no doubt well that they should be prepared to meet, if they can, the ordinary arguments and interpretations, and for this purpose Mr. Wherry's additions will prove useful."—*Saturday Review.*

Post 8vo, pp. vi.—208, cloth, price 8s. 6d.

THE BHAGAVAD-GÎTÂ.

Translated, with Introduction and Notes.

By JOHN DAVIES, M.A. (Cantab.)

"Let us add that his translation of the Bhagavad Gîtâ is, as we judge, the best that has as yet appeared in English, and that his Philological Notes are of quite peculiar value."—*Dublin Review.*

Post 8vo, pp. 96, cloth, price 5s.

THE QUATRAINS OF OMAR KHAYYAM.

Translated by E. H. WHINFIELD, M.A.,

Barrister-at-Law, late H.M. Bengal Civil Service.

Post 8vo, pp. xxxii.—336, cloth, price 10s. 6d.

THE QUATRAINS OF OMAR KHAYYAM.

The Persian Text, with an English Verse Translation.

By E. H. WHINFIELD, late of the Bengal Civil Service.

"Mr. Whinfield has executed a difficult task with considerable success, and his version contains much that will be new to those who only know Mr. Fitzgerald's delightful selection."—*Academy.*

"The most prominent features in the Quatrains are their profound agnosticism, combined with a fatalism based more on philosophic than religious grounds, their Epicureanism and the spirit of universal tolerance and charity which animates them."—*Calcutta Review.*

Post 8vo, pp. xxiv.—268, cloth, price 9s.

THE PHILOSOPHY OF THE UPANISHADS AND ANCIENT INDIAN METAPHYSICS.

As exhibited in a series of Articles contributed to the *Calcutta Review.*

By ARCHIBALD EDWARD GOUGH, M.A., Lincoln College, Oxford; Principal of the Calcutta Madrasa.

"For practical purposes this is perhaps the most important of the works that have thus far appeared in 'Trübner's Oriental Series.' . . . We cannot doubt that for all who may take it up the work must be one of profound interest."—*Saturday Review.*

In Two Volumes. Vol. I., post 8vo, pp. xxiv.—230, cloth, price 7s. 6d.

A COMPARATIVE HISTORY OF THE EGYPTIAN AND MESOPOTAMIAN RELIGIONS.

By DR. C. P. TIELE.

Vol. I.—HISTORY OF THE EGYPTIAN RELIGION.

Translated from the Dutch with the Assistance of the Author.

By JAMES BALLINGAL.

"It places in the hands of the English readers a history of Egyptian Religion which is very complete, which is based on the best materials, and which has been illustrated by the latest results of research. In this volume there is a great deal of information, as well as independent investigation, for the trustworthiness of which Dr. Tiele's name is in itself a guarantee; and the description of the successive religions under the Old Kingdom, the Middle Kingdom, and the New Kingdom, is given in a manner which is scholarly and minute."—*Scotsman.*

Post 8vo, pp. xii.—302, cloth, price 8s. 6d.

YUSUF AND ZULAIKHA.

A POEM BY JAMI.

Translated from the Persian into English Verse.

By RALPH T. H. GRIFFITH.

"Mr. Griffith, who has done already good service as translator into verse from the Sanskrit, has done further good work in this translation from the Persian, and he has evidently shown not a little skill in his rendering the quaint and very oriental style of his author into our more prosaic, less figurative, language. . . . The work, besides its intrinsic merits, is of importance as being one of the most popular and famous poems of Persia, and that which is read in all the independent native schools of India where Persian is taught."—*Scotsman.*

Post 8vo, pp. viii.—266, cloth, price 9s.

LINGUISTIC ESSAYS.

By CARL ABEL.

"An entirely novel method of dealing with philosophical questions and impart real human interest to the otherwise dry technicalities of the science."—*Standard.*

"Dr. Abel is an opponent from whom it is pleasant to differ, for he writes with enthusiasm and temper, and his mastery over the English language fits him to be a champion of unpopular doctrines."—*Athenæum.*

Post 8vo, pp. ix.—281, cloth, price 10s. 6d.

THE SARVA-DARSANA-SAMGRAHA;

OR, REVIEW OF THE DIFFERENT SYSTEMS OF HINDU PHILOSOPHY.

By MADHAVA ACHARYA.

Translated by E. B. COWELL, M.A., Professor of Sanskrit in the University of Cambridge, and A. E. GOUGH, M.A., Professor of Philosophy in the Presidency College, Calcutta.

This work is an interesting specimen of Hindu critical ability. The author successively passes in review the sixteen philosophical systems current in the fourteenth century in the South of India; and he gives what appears to him to be their most important tenets.

"The translation is trustworthy throughout. A protracted sojourn in India, where there is a living tradition, has familiarised the translators with Indian thought."—*Athenæum.*

Post 8vo, pp. lxv.—368, cloth, price 14s.

TIBETAN TALES DERIVED FROM INDIAN SOURCES.

Translated from the Tibetan of the KAH-GYUR.

By F. ANTON VON SCHIEFNER.

Done into English from the German, with an Introduction,

By W. R. S. RALSTON, M.A.

"Mr. Ralston, whose name is so familiar to all lovers of Russian folk-lore, has supplied some interesting Western analogies and parallels, drawn, for the most part, from Slavonic sources, to the Eastern folk-tales, culled from the Kahgyur, one of the divisions of the Tibetan sacred books."—*Academy.*

"The translation . . . could scarcely have fallen into better hands. An Introduction . . . gives the leading facts in the lives of those scholars who have given their attention to gaining a knowledge of the Tibetan literature and language."—*Calcutta Review.*

"Ought to interest all who care for the East, for amusing stories, or for comparative folk-lore."—*Pall Mall Gazette.*

Post 8vo, pp. xvi.—224, cloth, price 9s.

UDÂNAVARGA.

A COLLECTION OF VERSES FROM THE BUDDHIST CANON.

Compiled by DHARMATRÂTA.

BEING THE NORTHERN BUDDHIST VERSION OF DHAMMAPADA.

Translated from the Tibetan of Bkah-hgyur, with Notes, and Extracts from the Commentary of Pradjnavarman,

By W. WOODVILLE ROCKHILL.

"Mr. Rockhill's present work is the first from which assistance will be gained for a more accurate understanding of the Pali text; it is, in fact, as yet the only term of comparison available to us. The 'Udanavarga,' the Thibetan version, was originally discovered by the late M. Schiefner, who published the Tibetan text, and had intended adding a translation, an intention frustrated by his death, but which has been carried out by Mr. Rockhill. . . . Mr. Rockhill may be congratulated for having well accomplished a difficult task."—*Saturday Review.*

In Two Volumes, post 8vo, pp. xxiv.—566, cloth, accompanied by a Language Map, price 25s.

A SKETCH OF THE MODERN LANGUAGES OF AFRICA.

By ROBERT NEEDHAM CUST,

Barrister-at-Law, and late of Her Majesty's Indian Civil Service.

"Any one at all interested in African languages cannot do better than get Mr. Cust's book. It is encyclopædic in its scope, and the reader gets a start clear away in any particular language, and is left free to add to the initial sum of knowledge there collected."—*Natal Mercury.*

"Mr. Cust has contrived to produce a work of value to linguistic students."—*Nature.*

Third Edition. Post 8vo, pp. xv.-250, cloth, price 7s. 6d.

OUTLINES OF THE HISTORY OF RELIGION TO THE SPREAD OF THE UNIVERSAL RELIGIONS.

By C. P. TIELE,

Doctor of Theology, Professor of the History of Religions in the University of Leyden.

Translated from the Dutch by J. ESTLIN CARPENTER, M.A.

"Few books of its size contain the result of so much wide thinking, able and laborious study, or enable the reader to gain a better bird's-eye view of the latest results of investigations into the religious history of nations. As Professor Tiele modestly says, 'In this little book are outlines—pencil sketches, I might say—nothing more.' But there are some men whose sketches from a thumb-nail are of far more worth than an enormous canvas covered with the crude painting of others, and it is easy to see that these pages, full of information, these sentences, cut and perhaps also dry, short and clear, condense the fruits of long and thorough research."—*Scotsman.*

Post 8vo, pp. xii.—312, with Maps and Plan, cloth, price 14s.

A HISTORY OF BURMA.

Including Burma Proper, Pegu, Taungu, Tenasserim, and Arakan. From the Earliest Time to the End of the First War with British India.

By LIEUT.-GEN. SIR ARTHUR P. PHAYRE, G.C.M.G., K.C.S.I., and C.B.,
Membre Correspondant de la Société Académique Indo-Chinoise
de France.

"Sir Arthur Phayre's contribution to Trübner's Oriental Series supplies a recognised want, and its appearance has been looked forward to for many years. . . . General Phayre deserves great credit for the patience and industry which has resulted in this History of Burma."—*Saturday Review.*

Third Edition. Post 8vo, pp. 276, cloth, price 7s. 6d.

RELIGION IN CHINA.

By JOSEPH EDKINS, D.D., PEKING.

Containing a Brief Account of the Three Religions of the Chinese, with Observations on the Prospects of Christian Conversion amongst that People.

"Dr. Edkins has been most careful in noting the varied and often complex phases of opinion, so as to give an account of considerable value of the subject."—*Scotsman.*

"As a missionary, it has been part of Dr. Edkins' duty to study the existing religions in China, and his long residence in the country has enabled him to acquire an intimate knowledge of them as they at present exist."—*Saturday Review.*

"Dr. Edkins' valuable work, of which this is a second and revised edition, has, from the time that it was published, been the standard authority upon the subject of which it treats."—*Nonconformist.*

"Dr. Edkins . . . may now be fairly regarded as among the first authorities on Chinese religion and language."—*British Quarterly Review.*

Post 8vo, pp. x.-274, cloth, price 9s.

THE LIFE OF THE BUDDHA AND THE EARLY HISTORY OF HIS ORDER.

Derived from Tibetan Works in the Bkah-hgyur and Bstan-hgyur. Followed by notices on the Early History of Tibet and Khoten.

Translated by W. W. ROCKHILL, Second Secretary U.S. Legation in China.

"The volume bears testimony to the diligence and fulness with which the author has consulted and tested the ancient documents bearing upon his remarkable subject."—*Times.*

"Will be appreciated by those who devote themselves to those Buddhist studies which have of late years taken in these Western regions so remarkable a development. Its matter possesses a special interest as being derived from ancient Tibetan works, some portions of which, here analysed and translated, have not yet attracted the attention of scholars. The volume is rich in ancient stories bearing upon the world's renovation and the origin of castes, as recorded in these venerable authorities."—*Daily News.*

Third Edition. Post 8vo, pp. viii.-464, cloth, price 16s.

THE SANKHYA APHORISMS OF KAPILA,

With Illustrative Extracts from the Commentaries.

Translated by J. R. BALLANTYNE, LL.D., late Principal of the Benares College.

Edited by FITZEDWARD HALL.

"The work displays a vast expenditure of labour and scholarship, for which students of Hindoo philosophy have every reason to be grateful to Dr. Hall and the publishers."—*Calcutta Review.*

In Two Volumes, post 8vo, pp. cviii.-242, and viii.-370, cloth, price 24s.
Dedicated by permission to H.R.H. the Prince of Wales.

BUDDHIST RECORDS OF THE WESTERN WORLD,

Translated from the Chinese of Hiuen Tsiang (A.D. 629).

By SAMUEL BEAL, B.A.,

(Trin. Coll., Camb.); R.N. (Retired Chaplain and N.I.); Professor of Chinese, University College, London; Rector of Wark, Northumberland, &c.

An eminent Indian authority writes respecting this work:—"Nothing more can be done in elucidating the History of India until Mr. Beal's translation of the 'Si-yu-ki' appears."

"It is a strange freak of historical preservation that the best account of the condition of India at that ancient period has come down to us in the books of travel written by the Chinese pilgrims, of whom Hwen Thsang is the best known."—*Times*.

Post 8vo, pp. xlviii.-398, cloth, price 12s.

THE ORDINANCES OF MANU.

Translated from the Sanskrit, with an Introduction.

By the late A. C. BURNELL, Ph.D., C.I.E.

Completed and Edited by E. W. HOPKINS, Ph.D., of Columbia College, N.Y.

"This work is full of interest; while for the student of sociology and the science of religion it is full of importance. It is a great boon to get so notable a work in so accessible a form, admirably edited, and competently translated."—*Scotsman*.

"Few men were more competent than Burnell to give us a really good translation of this well-known law book, first rendered into English by Sir William Jones. Burnell was not only an independent Sanskrit scholar, but an experienced lawyer, and he joined to these two important qualifications the rare faculty of being able to express his thoughts in clear and trenchant English. . . . We ought to feel very grateful to Dr. Hopkins for having given us all that could be published of the translation left by Burnell."—F. MAX MÜLLER in the *Academy*.

Post 8vo, pp. xii.-234, cloth, price 9s.

THE LIFE AND WORKS OF ALEXANDER CSOMA DE KOROS,

Between 1819 and 1842. With a Short Notice of all his Published and Unpublished Works and Essays. From Original and for most part Unpublished Documents.

By THEODORE DUKA, M.D., F.R.C.S. (Eng.), Surgeon-Major H.M.'s Bengal Medical Service, Retired, &c.

"Not too soon have Messrs. Trübner added to their valuable Oriental Series a history of the life and works of one of the most gifted and devoted of Oriental students, Alexander Csoma de Koros. It is forty-three years since his decease, and though an account of his career was demanded soon after his decease, it has only now appeared in the important memoir of his compatriot, Dr. Duka."—*Bookseller*.

In Two Volumes, post 8vo, pp. xii.-318 and vi.-312, cloth, price 21s.

MISCELLANEOUS PAPERS RELATING TO INDO-CHINA.

Reprinted from "Dalrymple's Oriental Repertory," "Asiatic Researches," and the "Journal of the Asiatic Society of Bengal."

CONTENTS OF VOL. I.

I.—Some Accounts of Quedah. By Michael Topping.
II.—Report made to the Chief and Council of Balambangan, by Lieut. James Burton, of his several Surveys.
III.—Substance of a Letter to the Court of Directors from Mr. John Jesse, dated July 20, 1775, at Borneo Proper.
IV.—Formation of the Establishment of Poolo Peenang.
V.—The Gold of Limong. By John Macdonald.
VI.—On Three Natural Productions of Sumatra. By John Macdonald.
VII.—On the Traces of the Hindu Language and Literature extant amongst the Malays. By William Marsden.
VIII.—Some Account of the Elastic Gum Vine of Prince-Wales Island. By James Howison.
IX.—A Botanical Description of Urceola Elastica, or Caoutchouc Vine of Sumatra and Pulo-Pinang. By William Roxburgh, M.D.
X.—An Account of the Inhabitants of the Poggy, or Nassau Islands, lying off Sumatra. By John Crisp.
XI.—Remarks on the Species of Pepper which are found on Prince-Wales Island. By William Hunter, M.D.
XII.—On the Languages and Literature of the Indo-Chinese Nations. By J. Leyden, M.D.
XIII.—Some Account of an Orang-Outang of remarkable height found on the Island of Sumatra. By Clarke Abel, M.D.
XIV.—Observations on the Geological Appearances and General Features of Portions of the Malayan Peninsula. By Captain James Low.
XV.—Short Sketch of the Geology of Pulo-Pinang and the Neighbouring Islands. By T. Ware.
XVI.—Climate of Singapore.
XVII.—Inscription on the Jetty at Singapore.
XVIII.—Extract of a Letter from Colonel J. Low.
XIX.—Inscription at Singapore.
XX.—An Account of Several Inscriptions found in Province Wellesley. By Lieut.-Col. James Low.
XXI.—Note on the Inscriptions from Singapore and Province Wellesley. By J. W. Laidlay.
XXII.—On an Inscription from Keddah. By Lieut.-Col. Low.
XXIII.—A Notice of the Alphabets of the Philippine Islands.
XXIV.—Succinct Review of the Observations of the Tides in the Indian Archipelago.
XXV.—Report on the Tin of the Province of Mergui. By Capt. G. B Tremenheere.
XXVI.—Report on the Manganese of Mergui Province. By Capt. G. B. Tremenheere.
XXVII.—Paragraphs to be added to Capt. G. B. Tremenheere's Report.
XXVIII.—Second Report on the Tin of Mergui. By Capt. G. B. Tremenheere.
XXIX.—Analysis of Iron Ores from Tavoy and Mergui, and of Limestone from Mergui. By Dr. A. Ure.
XXX.—Report of a Visit to the Pakchan River, and of some Tin Localities in the Southern Portion of the Tenasserim Provinces. By Capt. G. B. Tremenheere.
XXXI.—Report on a Route from the Mouth of the Pakchan to Krau, and thence across the Isthmus of Krau to the Gulf of Siam. By Capt. Al. Fraser and Capt. J. G. Forlong.
XXXII.—Report, &c., from Capt. G. B. Tremenheere on the Price of Mergui Tin Ore.
XXXIII.—Remarks on the Different Species of Orang-utan. By E. Blyth.
XXXIV.—Further Remarks. By E. Blyth.

MISCELLANEOUS PAPERS RELATING TO INDO-CHINA—continued.

CONTENTS OF VOL. II.

XXXV.—Catalogue of Mammalia inhabiting the Malayan Peninsula and Islands. By Theodore Cantor, M.D.
XXXVI.—On the Local and Relative Geology of Singapore. By J. R. Logan.
XXXVII.—Catalogue of Reptiles inhabiting the Malayan Peninsula and Islands. By Theodore Cantor, M.D.
XXXVIII.—Some Account of the Botanical Collection brought from the Eastward, in 1841, by Dr. Cantor. By the late W. Griffith.
XXXIX.—On the Flat-Horned Taurine Cattle of S.E. Asia. By E. Blyth.
XL.—Note, by Major-General G. B. Tremenheere.
General Index.
Index of Vernacular Terms.
Index of Zoological Genera and Sub-Genera occurring in Vol. II.

"The papers treat of almost every aspect of Indo-China—its philology, economy, geography, geology—and constitute a very material and important contribution to our accessible information regarding that country and its people."—*Contemporary Review*.

Post 8vo, pp. xii.-72, cloth, price 5s.

THE SATAKAS OF BHARTRIHARI.

Translated from the Sanskrit

By the Rev. B. HALE WORTHAM, M.R.A.S.,

Rector of Eggesford, North Devon.

"A very interesting addition to Trübner's Oriental Series."—*Saturday Review*.
"Many of the Maxims in the book have a Biblical ring and beauty of expression."—*St. James' Gazette*.

Post 8vo, pp. xii.-180, cloth, price 6s.

ANCIENT PROVERBS AND MAXIMS FROM BURMESE SOURCES;

OR, THE NITI LITERATURE OF BURMA.

By JAMES GRAY,

Author of "Elements of Pali Grammar," "Translation of the Dhammapada," &c.

The Sanscrit-Pâli word Nîti is equivalent to "conduct" in its abstract, and "guide" in its concrete signification. As applied to books, it is a general term for a treatise which includes maxims, pithy sayings, and didactic stories, intended as a guide to such matters of every-day life as form the character of an individual and influence him in his relations to his fellow-men. Treatises of this kind have been popular in all ages, and have served as a most effective medium of instruction.

Post 8vo, pp. xxxii. and 330, cloth, price 7s. 6d.
MASNAVI I MA' NAVI:
THE SPIRITUAL COUPLETS OF MAULANA JALALU-'D-DIN MUHAMMAD I RUMI.

Translated and Abridged by E. H. WHINFIELD, M.A.,
Late of H.M. Bengal Civil Service.

Post 8vo, pp. viii. and 346, cloth, price 10s. 6d.
MANAVA-DHARMA-CASTRA:
THE CODE OF MANU.

ORIGINAL SANSKRIT TEXT, WITH CRITICAL NOTES.

BY J. JOLLY, Ph.D.,

Professor of Sanskrit in the University of Wurzburg ; late Tagore Professor of Law in the University of Calcutta.

The date assigned by Sir William Jones to this Code—the well-known Great Law Book of the Hindus—is 1250-500 B.C., although the rules and precepts contained in it had probably existed as tradition for countless ages before. There has been no reliable edition of the Text for Students for many years past, and it is believed, therefore, that Prof. Jolly's work will supply a want long felt.

Post 8vo, pp. 215, cloth, price 7s. 6d.
LEAVES FROM MY CHINESE SCRAP-BOOK.
BY FREDERIC HENRY BALFOUR.

Author of "Waifs and Strays from the Far East," "Taoist Texts," "Idiomatic Phrases in the Peking Colloquial," &c. &c.

THE FOLLOWING WORKS ARE IN PREPARATION:—

In Two Vols., post 8vo.
ALBERUNI'S INDIA:
AN ACCOUNT OF ITS RELIGION, PHILOSOPHY, LITERATURE, GEOGRAPHY, CHRONOLOGY, ASTRONOMY, CUSTOMS, LAW, AND ASTROLOGY (ABOUT A.D. 1031).

TRANSLATED INTO ENGLISH.

With Notes and Indices by Prof. EDWARD SACHAU,
University of Berlin.

₊* The Arabic Original, with an Index of the Sanskrit Words, Edited by Professor SACHAU, is in the press.

TRÜBNER'S ORIENTAL SERIES.

In Two Volumes, post 8vo.
MISCELLANEOUS PAPERS RELATING TO INDO-CHINA.

Edited by R. ROST, Ph.D., &c. &c.,
Librarian to the India Office.

SECOND SERIES.

Reprinted for the Straits Branch of the Royal Asiatic Society from the Malayan "Miscellanies," the "Transactions and Journal" of the Batavian Society," and the "Journals" of the Asiatic Society of Bengal, and the Royal Geographical and Royal Asiatic Societies.

Post 8vo.
THE LIFE OF HIUEN TSIANG.
BY THE SHAMANS HWUI LI AND YEN-TSUNG.

With a Preface containing an account of the Works of I-TSING.

By SAMUEL BEAL, B.A.

(Trin. Coll., Camb.); Professor of Chinese, University College, London; Rector of Wark, Northumberland, &c.

Author of "Buddhist Records of the Western World," "The Romantic Legend of Sakya Budda," &c.

When the Pilgrim Hiuen Tsiang returned from his travels in India, he took up his abode in the Temple of "Great Benevolence;" this convent had been constructed by the Emperor in honour of the Empress, Wen-te-hau. After Hiuen Tsiang's death, his disciple, Hwui Li, composed a work which gave an account of his illustrious Master's travels; this work when he completed he buried, and refused to discover its place of concealment. But previous to his death he revealed its whereabouts to Yen-tsung, by whom it was finally revised and published. This is "The Life of Hiuen Tsiang." It is a valuable sequel to the Si-yu-ki, correcting and illustrating it in many particulars.

Post 8vo.
A SKETCH OF THE MODERN LANGUAGES OF OCEANIA.
BY R. N. CUST, LL.D.

Author of "Modern Languages of the East," "Modern Languages of Africa," &c.

Post 8vo.
ESSAYS ON THE INTERCOURSE OF THE CHINESE WITH WESTERN COUNTRIES IN THE MIDDLE AGES AND ON KINDRED SUBJECTS.
BY E. BRETSCHNEIDER, M.D.,

Formerly Physician of the Russian Legation at Pekin.

LONDON: TRÜBNER & CO., 57 AND 59 LUDGATE HILL.

250—16/7/87.

TRÜBNER'S
ORIENTAL SERIES.

A COMPREHENSIVE COMMENTARY

ON

THE QURÁN:

COMPRISING SALE'S TRANSLATION

AND

PRELIMINARY DISCOURSE,

WITH ADDITIONAL NOTES AND EMENDATIONS.

TOGETHER WITH

A Complete Index to the Text, Preliminary Discourse, and Notes,

BY THE REV. E. M. WHERRY, M.A.

VOL. IV.

LONDON:
TRÜBNER & CO., LUDGATE HILL.
1886.
[*All rights reserved.*]

Ballantyne Press
BALLANTYNE, HANSON AND CO.
EDINBURGH AND LONDON

CONTENTS.

CHAP.	PAGE
XLI.—Entitled Surat al Fussilat (Explanation)	1
XLII.—Entitled Surat al Shorí (Consultation)	11
XLIII.—Entitled Surat al Zukhráf (The Ornaments of Gold)	20
XLIV.—Entitled Surat al Dukhan (Smoke)	31
XLV.—Entitled Surat al Jásíyah (Kneeling)	37
XLVI.—Entitled Surat al Ahqáf (The Sandhill)	42
XLVII.—Entitled Surat Muhammad	51
XLVIII.—Entitled Surat al Fatah (Victory)	58
XLIX.—Entitled Surat al Hujrát (The Inner Apartments)	68
L.—Entitled Surat al Qáf (Q.)	73
LI.—Entitled Surat al Záriyát (The Dispersing)	79
LII.—Entitled Surat al Túr (The Mountain)	84
LIII.—Entitled Surat al Najm (The Star)	89
LIV.—Entitled Surat al Qamr (The Moon)	95
LV.—Entitled Surat al Rahmán (The Merciful)	102
LVI.—Entitled Surat al Wáqía (The Inevitable)	108
LVII.—Entitled Surat al Hadíd (Iron)	115
LVIII.—Entitled Surat al Mujádalah (She who Disputed)	122
LIX.—Entitled Surat al Hashr (The Emigration)	128

CHAP.	PAGE
LX.—Entitled Surat al Mumtahina (She who is Tried)	134
LXI.—Entitled Surat al Saf (Battle-Array) .	140
LXII.—Entitled Surat al Juma (The Assembly)	144
LXIII.—Entitled Surat al Munáfiqún (The Hypocrites)	147
LXIV.—Entitled Surat al Taghabún (Mutual Deceit)	150
LXV.—Entitled Surat al Taláq (Divorce) .	154
LXVI.—Entitled Surat al Tahrím (Prohibition)	158
LXVII.—Entitled Surat al Mulk (The Kingdom)	164
LXVIII.—Entitled Surat al Qalam (The Pen) .	168
LXIX.—Entitled Surat al Háqqat (The Infallible)	174
LXX.—Entitled Surat al Maárij (The Steps) .	178
LXXI.—Entitled Surat Núh (Noah) . .	182
LXXII.—Entitled Surat al Jinn (The Genii) .	186
LXXIII.—Entitled Surat al Muzzammil (Wrappéd Up)	190
LXXIV.—Entitled Surat al Muddassir (The Covered)	194
LXXV.—Entitled Surat al Qíyámat (The Resurrection)	199
LXXVI.—Entitled Surat al Insán (Man) . .	203
LXXVII.—Entitled Surat al Mursalát (The Messengers)	207
LXXVIII.—Entitled Surat al Nabá (The News) .	211
LXXIX.—Entitled Surat al Náziát (Those who Tear Forth)	214
LXXX.—Entitled Surat al Abas (He Frowned) .	218
LXXXI.—Entitled Surat al Takwír (The Folding Up)	221
LXXXII.—Entitled Surat al Infitár (The Cleaving in Sunder)	224

CONTENTS.

CHAP.		PAGE
LXXXIII.—Entitled Surat al Tatfíf (Those who Give Short Measure)	. . . .	226
LXXXIV.—Entitled Surat al Inshiqáq (The Rending in Sunder)	. . . .	230
LXXXV.—Entitled Surat al Burúj (The Celestial Signs)	. . . .	232
LXXXVI.—Entitled Surat al Táriq (The Star which Appeared by Night)	. . .	235
LXXXVII.—Entitled Surat al Álá (The Most High)		237
LXXXVIII.—Entitled Surat al Gháshiya (The Overwhelming)	. . . . .	239
LXXXIX.—Entitled Surat al Fajr (The Daybreak)		242
XC.—Entitled Surat al Balad (The Territory)	. . . . .	246
XCI.—Entitled Surat al Shams (The Sun)	.	249
XCII.—Entitled Surat al Lail (The Night)	.	251
XCIII.—Entitled Surat al Zuhá (The Brightness)		253
XCIV.—Entitled Surat al Inshiráh (Have we not Opened?)	. . . . .	255
XCV.—Entitled Surat al Tín (The Fig)	. .	257
XCVI.—Entitled Surat al Alaq (The Congealed Blood)	. . . . .	259
XCVII.—Entitled Surat al Qadr (Night of Power)		263
XCVIII.—Entitled Surat al Baiyana (The Evidence)	. . . .	265
XCIX.—Entitled Surat al Zilzál (The Earthquake)	. . . .	268
C.—Entitled Surat al Adiyát (The War-Horses which Run Swiftly)	. . .	270
CI.—Entitled Surat al Qáriá (The Striking)		272
CII.—Entitled Surat al Takásur (The Emulous Desire of Multiplying)	. . .	274
CIII.—Entitled Surat al Asar (The Afternoon)		276
CIV.—Entitled Surat al Hamza (The Slanderer)		277

CONTENTS.

CHAP.	PAGE
CV.—Entitled Surat al Fíl (The Elephant)	279
CVI.—Entitled Surat al Quraish (The Quraish)	282
CVII.—Entitled Surat al Máún (Necessaries)	284
CVIII.—Entitled Surat al Kauthar (Abundance)	286
CIX.—Entitled Surat al Káfirún (The Unbelievers)	288
CX.—Entitled Surat al Nasr (Assistance)	290
CXI.—Entitled Surat al Abu Lahab	292
CXII.—Entitled Surat al Ikhlás (Declaration of God's Unity)	294
CXIII.—Entitled Surat al Falaq (The Daybreak)	296
CXIV.—Entitled Surat al Nás (Men)	299
Index	301

THE QURÁN.

CHAPTER XLI.

ENTITLED SURAT AL FUSSILAT (EXPLANATION).

Revealed at Makkah.

INTRODUCTION.

In some manuscripts this chapter is entitled *Worship* or *Adoration*, "because," says Sale, "the infidels are herein commanded to forsake the worship of idols and to worship God; but the thirty-second chapter bearing the same title, that which we have here prefixed is, for distinction, generally used."

According to Hishám, 186 (Coussin de Perc, i. 375 *seq.*), the design of Muhammad in enunciating the revelations of this chapter was the conversion of Utba bin Rábia to Islám. This story accords well enough with the teaching of the chapter, but there is nothing in it to bar the idea of a more general application.

There is little in this chapter to distinguish it from other Makkan Suras, unless it be the vehemence with which Muhammad asserts his own prophetic claims and the inspired character of the Qurán. The Qurán is declared to be the Word of God (vers. 1–3, 41, 42), which has been revealed in the Arabic language (vers. 2 and 44) in order that the Quraish might have no good excuse for rejecting it (ver. 44). The Quraish are, however, charged with having rejected it (vers. 3 and 4); but this was not to be regarded as affording any evidence of the falsity of its claims, but rather of the contrary, inasmuch as the writings of Moses had met with similar treatment (ver. 45). The unbelievers are therefore threatened with the fate of the

Ádites and of the Thamúdites (vers. 13-15), while believers are assured of protection in this life and of glorious rewards in Paradise (vers. 17 and 30-32). The folly of the worship of the idolaters is exposed by reference to the fact that God is the Creator of all things, especially of the objects of Makkan worship.

Throughout the chapter Muhammad appears as a prophet of God, yet a simple preacher of Islám, a "warner" of the people of Arabia.

Probable Date of the Revelations.

Granting that this chapter was written in order to convert Utba bin Rábia to Islám, yet, as Noëldeke points out, this gives us no certain data wherewith to fix the date of the writing of it. True, Ibn Hishám gives the narrative of this attempt at conversion immediately after that of the conversion of Hamza, yet, when we remember that, in relating the events prior to the Hijra, this writer pays little attention to exact chronological order, we cannot infer that this attempt was really made at that time; moreover, nothing certain is known as to the time of Hamza's conversion. It therefore follows that nothing certain can be learned from tradition as to the date of this chapter.

Having regard, however, to the style and contents of the chapter, we may fix the date approximately at about B.H. 8, a time when there was offered to the Muslims a sturdy opposition at Makkah, but as yet without violence to the person of the Prophet or his followers.

Principal Subjects.

	VERSES
The Qurán declared to be given by inspiration	1-3
The people generally reject it	3, 4
Muhammad only a man, yet a prophet	5
The woe of the wicked and the blessedness of the righteous	6, 7
God's power manifested in the creation of earth and heaven	8-11
The Quraish are threatened with the fate of Ád and Thamúd	12-16
Believers among the Ádites and Thamúdites were saved	17
In the judgment the unbelievers shall be condemned by the members of their own bodies	18-22
The fate of the genii to befall the infidels	23, 24
Unbelievers counsel blasphemous levity—their punishment	25-28
False teachers to be trodden under foot by their own followers in hell	29
The glorious rewards of the faithful	30-32
The consistent Muslim commended	33
Evil to be turned away by good	34, 35
God the refuge of the Prophet against Satan's suggestions	36

	VERSES
God's works testify to himself as alone worthy of worship	37–39
Unbelievers shall not escape in the resurrection	40
The Qurán a revelation of God	41, 42
The infidels offer no new objections to Muhammad and the Qurán	43
Why the Qurán was revealed in the Arabic language	44
The books of Moses at first rejected by his people	45
God rewardeth according to works	46
The hour of the judgment known only to God	47
The false gods will desert their worshippers in the judgment	47, 48
The perfidy of hypocrites	49–51
Rejecters of God's Word exposed to awful punishment	52–54

IN THE NAME OF THE MOST MERCIFUL GOD.

‖ (1) H. M. *This is* a revelation from the most Merciful; (2) a book the verses whereof are distinctly explained, an Arabic Qurán, for *the instruction of* people who understand; (3) bearing good tidings and denouncing threats; but the greater part of them turn aside, and hearken not *thereto.* (4) And they say, Our hearts are veiled from *the doctrine* to which thou invitest us; and *there is* a deafness in our ears, and a curtain between us and thee: wherefore act thou *as thou shalt think fit;* for we shall act *according to our own sentiments.* (5) Say, Verily I am only a man like you. It is revealed unto me that your GOD is one GOD: wherefore direct your way straight unto him; and ask pardon of him *for what is past.* And woe *be* to the idolaters; (6) who give not the appointed alms, and believe not in the life to come! (7) But *as to* those who believe and work righteousness, they shall receive an everlasting reward.

SULS.

R $\frac{1}{15}$.

---

(1) *H. M.* See Prelim. Disc., pp. 100–102.

(2, 3) See notes on chap. xi. 2 and 3.

Arabic Qurán. This is said in order to prove to the Arabs that Muhammad is their Prophet and his Qurán the Word of God. See chap. xiv. 4. Observe the wide sense in which the word *Qurán* is here used.

(6) *Alms.* See notes on chap. ii. 42, 219, and ix. 60.

R $\frac{2}{16}$.

|| (8) Say, Do ye indeed disbelieve in him who created the earth in two days; and do ye set up equals unto him? He is the LORD of all creatures. (9) And he placed in *the earth mountains* firmly rooted, *rising* above the same: and he blessed it; and provided therein the food *of the creatures designed to be the inhabitants* thereof, in four days; equally, for those who ask. (10) Then he set his mind to *the creation of* heaven, and it was smoke; and he said unto it, and to the earth, Come, either obediently, or against your will. They answered, We come, obedient *to thy command*. (11) And he formed them into seven heavens, in two days; and revealed unto every heaven its office. And we adorned the lower heaven with lights, and *placed therein* a guard *of angels*. This *is* the disposition of the mighty, the wise God. (12) If *the Makkans* withdraw *from these instructions*, say, I denounce unto you a sudden destruction, like the destruction of Ád and Thamúd. (13) When the apostles came unto them before them and behind them,

---

(8) *Two days.* "The two first days of the week."—*Sale, Jaláluddín*. Comp. chaps. vii. 55, x. 3, and xi. 8.

(9) *Mountains firmly rooted.* See chaps. xv. 19, and xvi. 15 notes.

Four days. "That is, including the two former days wherein the earth was created."—*Sale.* I would say, with the two former days making six days. The *two* of ver. 11 are only reckoned among the six to escape the discrepancy otherwise apparent.

For those who ask. "For all, in proportion to the necessity of each, and as their several appetites require. Some refer the word *sawáan*, here translated *equally*, and which also signifies *completely*, to the four days; and suppose the meaning to be, that God created these things in just so many *entire* and *complete* days."—*Sale, Jaláluddín.*

(10) *Smoke.* "Or darkness. Al Zamakhsharí says this smoke proceeded from the waters under the throne of God (which throne was one of the things created before the heavens and the earth), and rose above the water; that the water being dried up, the earth was formed out of it, and the heavens out of the smoke which had mounted aloft."—*Sale.*

(11) *Two days,* viz., "On the fifth and sixth days of the week. It is said the heavens were created on Thursday, and the sun, moon, and stars on Friday; in the evening of which last day Adam was made."—*Sale, Baidháwi, Jaláluddín.*

See note above on ver. 9.

A guard of angels. See note on chap. xv. 17.

(13) *Apostles . . . before and behind.* "That is, on every side, per-

saying, Worship GOD alone; they answered, If our LORD had been pleased *to send messengers,* he had surely sent angels; and we believe not *the message* with which ye are sent. (14) As to *the tribe of* Ád, they behaved insolently in the earth, without reason, and said, Who *is* more mighty than we in strength? Did they not see that GOD, who had created them, was more mighty than they in strength? And they knowingly rejected our signs. (15) Wherefore we sent against them a piercing wind, on days of ill luck, that we might make them taste the punishment of shame in this world: but the punishment of the life to come will be more shameful; and they shall not be protected *therefrom.* (16) And as to Thamúd, we directed them: but they loved blindness better than the *true* direction: wherefore the terrible noise of an ignominious punishment assailed them, for that which they had deserved; (17) but we delivered those who believed and feared *God.*

|| (18) And *warn them of* the day on which the enemies R $\frac{3}{17}$. of GOD shall be gathered together unto *hell-*fire, and shall march in distinct bands; (19) until, when they shall arrive thereat, their ears, and their eyes, and their skins shall bear witness against them of that which they shall have wrought. (20) And they shall say unto their skins, Wherefore do ye bear witness against us? They shall answer, GOD hath caused us to speak, who giveth speech unto all things: he created you the first time; and unto

---

suading and urging them continually, and by arguments drawn from past examples and the expectation of future rewards and punishments."—*Sale.*

(14) *A'd.* See Prelim. Disc., pp. 20–22, and notes on chaps. vii. 66, and xi. 50–60.

(15) *Days of ill luck.* "It is said that this wind continued from Wednesday to Wednesday inclusive, being the latter end of the month Shawwál; and that a Wednesday is the day whereon God sends down his judgments on a wicked people."—*Sale, Baidháwi.*

(16) *Thamúd.* See Prelim. Disc., p. 22 *seq.,* and notes on chap. xi. 61–68.

(18) *Distinct bands.* Comp. chap. xxxix. 71.

him are ye returned. (21) Ye did not hide yourselves *while ye sinned*, so that your ears, and your eyes, and your skins could not bear witness against you; but ye thought that GOD was ignorant of many things which ye did. (22) This *was* your opinion, which ye imagined of your LORD: it hath ruined you, and ye are become lost *people*. (23) Whether they bear *their torment, hell*-fire *shall be* their abode; or whether they beg for favour, they shall not obtain favour. (24) And we will give them *the devils to be their* companions; for they dressed up for them *the false notions which they entertained of* this present world, and *of* that which is to come: and the sentence justly fitteth them, which was formerly pronounced on the nations of genii and men who were before them; for they perished.

|| (25) The unbelievers say, Hearken not unto this Qurán, but use vain discourse during *the reading* thereof; that ye may overcome *the voice of the reader by your scoffs and laughter*. (26) Wherefore we will surely cause the unbelievers to taste a grievous punishment, (27) and we will certainly reward them for the evils which they shall have wrought. (28) This *shall be* the reward of the enemies of GOD, *namely, hell-*fire; therein *is prepared* for them an everlasting abode, *as* a reward for that they have wittingly rejected our signs. (29) And the infidels shall say *in hell*, O LORD, show us the two that seduced us, of the genii and men, and we will cast them under our feet,

---

(21) *i.e.*, "Ye hid your crimes from men, little thinking that your very members, from which you could not hide them, would rise up as witnesses against you."—*Sale.* See note on chap. xxxvi. 65.

(24) *Companions.* See notes on chaps. vii. 39, 180, and x. 19, &c.

(25) *Vain discourse.* "Or loud talk."—*Sale.* The practice here animadverted on is very common among modern Muslims whenever the Gospel is preached among them.

(29) *The two, &c, i.e.,* "Those of either species who drew us into sin and ruin. Some suppose that the two more particularly intended here are Iblís and Cain, the two authors of infidelity and murder."—*Sale, Baidháwi.*

By *the two* is probably meant the false god and the human teacher. See chaps. x. 29-31, and xxv. 18-20, &c.

that they may become most base *and despicable.* (30) *As for* those who say, Our LORD *is* GOD, and who behave uprightly; the angels shall descend unto them, *and shall say,* Fear not, neither be ye grieved; but rejoice in the hopes of Paradise which ye have been promised. (31) We *are* your friends in this life, and in that which is to come: therein shall ye have that which your souls shall desire, and therein shall ye obtain whatever ye shall ask for; (32) *as* a gift from a gracious *and* merciful *God.*

|| (33) Who speaketh better than he who inviteth unto $R \frac{5}{19}$. GOD, and worketh righteousness, and saith, I *am* a Muslim? (34) Good and evil shall not be held equal. Turn away *evil* with that which is better; and behold, the *man* between whom and thyself *there was* enmity *shall become,* as it were, *thy* warmest friend: (35) but none shall attain to this *perfection* except they who are patient; nor shall any attain thereto except he who is endued with a great happiness *of temper.* (36) And if a malicious suggestion be offered unto thee from Satan, have recourse unto GOD; for *it is* he who heareth *and* knoweth. (37) Among the signs *of his power are* the night and the day, and the sun and the moon. Worship not the sun, neither the moon: but worship GOD, who hath created them; if ye serve him. (38) But if they proudly disdain *his service,* verily the *angels,* who are with thy LORD, praise him night and

---

(30) *The angels shall descend.* "Either while they are living on earth, to dispose their minds to good, to preserve them from temptations, and to comfort them; or at the hour of death, to support them in their last agony; or at their coming forth from their graves at the resurrection."—*Sale, Jaláluddín.*

Comp. Ps. xxxiv. 7, and Heb. i. 14.

(35) *Endued with a great happiness of temper.* Rodwell translates *the most highly favoured.*

(36) See chap. cxiv.

(37) *Worship God.* Comp. Rev. xix. 10. Passages like this illustrate the superiority of Muhammad over his countrymen as well as his power as a preacher.

(38) Comp. Rev. iv. 8.

day, and are not wearied. (39) And among his signs *another is*, that thou seest the land waste; but when we send down rain thereon, it is stirred and fermenteth. And he who quickeneth *the earth* will surely quicken the dead; for he is almighty. (40) Verily those who impiously wrong our signs are not concealed from us. *Is* he, therefore, better who shall be cast into *hell*-fire, or he who shall appear secure on the day of resurrection? Work that which ye will: he certainly beholdeth whatever ye do. (41) Verily they who believe not in the admonition *of the Qurán*, after it hath come unto them, *shall one day be discovered.* It *is* certainly a book of infinite value: (42) vanity shall not approach it, either from before it, or from behind it: *it is* a revelation from a wise *God*, whose praise is justly to be celebrated. (43) No other is said unto thee *by the infidels of Makkah* than what hath been formerly said unto the apostles before thee: verily thy LORD *is* inclined to forgiveness, and *is also* able to chastise severely. (44) If we had revealed *the Qurán* in a foreign language, they had surely said, Unless the signs thereof be distinctly explained, *we will not receive the same: is the book written in* a foreign tongue, and *the person unto whom it is directed* an Arabian? Answer, It is, unto those who believe, a sure guide, and a remedy *for doubt and uncertainty:* but unto those who believe not, *it is* a thickness of hearing in their ears, and it is a darkness which covereth them; these are *as they who are* called unto from a distant place.

R $\frac{6}{1}$.

|| (45) We heretofore gave the book *of the law* unto

---

(42) *Either from before, &c.* "That is, it shall not be prevailed against, or frustrated by any means or in any respect whatever."—*Sale.*

(44) See note on chap. xvi. 105.

A sure guide. See chap. xvii. 84, 85.

These are as they, &c. "Being so far off that they hear not, or understand not the voice of him who calls to them."—*Sale.*

(45) Here again we see Muhammad likening himself to the former prophets. See Introd. chap. xi. The allusion probably is to the unbelief of the Israelites in the wilderness.

Moses; and a dispute arose concerning the same: and if a previous decree had not proceeded from thy LORD, *to respite the opposers of that revelation,* verily *the matter* had been decided between them *by the destruction of the infidels;* for they were in a very great doubt as to the same. (46) He who doth right, *doth it* to *the advantage of* his own soul; and he who doth evil, *doth it* against the same: for thy LORD *is* not unjust towards *his* servants. (47) Unto him is reserved the knowledge of the hour *of judgment:* and no fruit cometh forth from the knops which involve it; neither doth any female conceive *in her womb,* nor is she delivered *of her burden,* but with his knowledge. On the day whereon he shall call them to him, *saying,* Where *are* my companions *which ye ascribed unto me?* they shall answer, We assure thee *there is* no witness *of this matter* among us: (48) and *the idols* which they called on before shall withdraw themselves from them; and they shall perceive that *there will be* no way to escape. (49) Man is not wearied with asking good; but if evil befall him, he despondeth and despaireth. (50) And if we cause him to taste mercy from us after affliction hath touched him, he surely saith, This *is due* to me *on account of my deserts:* I do not think the hour *of judgment* will *ever* come: and if I be brought before my LORD, I shall surely attain, with him, the most excellent *condition.* But we will *then* declare unto those who shall not have believed that which they have wrought; and we will surely cause them to taste a most severe punishment. (51) When we confer favours on man, he turneth aside, and departeth *without returning thanks;* but when evil toucheth him, he *is* frequent at prayer. (52) Say, What think ye? if *the Qurán* be from GOD, and ye believe not

---

(46) Comp. chap. xlv. 14.
(47) *No witness.* "For they shall disclaim their idols at the resurrection."—*Sale.* See above in note on ver. 29.
(48) See chap. xxviii. 62–66 and 74.
(50) See chap. xvii. 69.

therein; who will lie under a greater error than he who dissenteth widely *therefrom?* (53) Hereafter we will show them our signs in the regions *of the earth,* and in themselves; until it become manifest unto them that *this book* is the truth. Is it not sufficient *for thee* that thy LORD is witness of all things? (54) Are they not in a doubt as to the meeting of their LORD *at the resurrection?* Doth not he encompass all things?

---

(53) *We will show them our signs . . . in themselves.* "By the surprising victories and conquests of Muhammad and his successors." —*Sale, Baidháwi.* A better interpretation, and one in accord with the spirit of the chapter, is that the unbelievers would recognise the truth of Muhammad's teaching in the resurrection and the judgment. See vers. 41 and 52. Many years subsequent to the date of this chapter Muhammad disclaimed the ability to foretell future events. See chap. vi. 49, and note there.

CHAPTER XLII.

ENTITLED SURAT AL SHORÍ (CONSULTATION).

Revealed at Makkah.

INTRODUCTION.

THIS chapter receives its title from what is said in ver. 36 of the believers, " Whose affairs are directed by *consultation* among themselves." The five single letters at the beginning are used by some as a title of the chapter. Rodwell and Palmer call it the *Chapter of Counsel.* It might have been called the *Chapter of Apology* but for the fact that the laboured effort of the Prophet to establish his prophetic claims and to vindicate his Qurán from the accusation of forgery brought against it by his enemies is by no means limited to this chapter.

The feature of the chapter just alluded to reveals to us the main design of the author in writing it, while a careful reading of the contents will reveal the following circumstances of the Prophet at this time. (1) He was strongly opposed by his townsmen, and his prophetic pretensions were rejected, especially by the Jewish and Christian portion of his hearers. (2) Though he professed to attest the doctrines of the Bible, and declared himself a believer in all the prophets from Adam to Jesus (vers. 11–14), yet both Jews and Christians hesitated not to call him an impostor (ver. 23), insinuating that their opinion was attested by the fact that no one had ever seen him receive a revelation from God or Gabriel (vers. 50, 51). (3) Some of the people, however, had believed in him (vers. 5 and 25), while others, once believers, had become apostates (ver. 15).

Throughout the chapter Muhammad represents himself as simply a preacher, holding himself in no way responsible for the unbelievers, satisfied to vindicate his prophetic claims before the people of Makkah and "to direct them into the right way."

Probable Date of the Revelations.

From what has been said above, it will appear that this chapter belongs to Makkah. Its date is fixed by Noëldeke somewhat later than that of the preceding chapter.

Some writers, as Baidháwi and Umr bin Muhammad, have regarded vers. 22-25 as Madínic, and Jaláluddín, as Syúti (Itqán 35), regards vers. 35-37 as also belonging to Madína. The reasons given, however, do not carry conviction, being based upon the assumption that there could be no reference to *almsgiving* and *prayer* in passages revealed before the Hijra.

Principal Subjects.

	VERSES
The Almighty reveals his will to Muhammad	1, 2
Angels intercede with God on behalf of sinful man	3
Muhammad not a steward over the idolaters	4
The Qurán revealed in the Arabic language to warn Makkah	5
God the only helper, creator, and preserver, the all-knowing	6-10
Islám the religion of all the former prophets	11-13
Muhammad commanded to declare his faith in the Bible	14
Disputers with God shall be severely punished	15
God only knows the hour of the judgment	16, 17
The Almighty will reward the righteous and the wicked according to their deeds	18, 19
Sinners only spared through God's forbearance	20
Rewards of the just and of the unjust	21, 22
Muhammad charged with imposture	23
The sovereign God forgives and blesses whom he will	24-27
God's power manifested in his works	28-33
A true believer's character decided	34-41
The miserable fate of those whom God causes to err	42-45
Sinners exhorted to repent before it is too late	46
Muhammad only a preacher	47
God controls all things	48, 49
Why God reveals himself by inspiration and through apostles	50, 51
Muhammad himself ignorant of Islám until he had received the revelation of the Qurán	52, 53

IN THE NAME OF THE MOST MERCIFUL GOD.

‖ (1) H. M. A. S. Q. Thus doth the mighty, the wise R ½ God reveal *his will* unto thee; and *in like manner did he reveal it* unto the *prophets* who *were* before thee. (2) Unto him *belongeth* whatever *is* in heaven and in earth; and he is the high, the great *God*. (3) It wanteth little but that the heavens be rent in sunder from above *at the awfulness of his majesty*: the angels celebrate the praise of their LORD, and ask pardon for those who *dwell* in the earth. Is not GOD the forgiver *of sins* the merciful? (4) But *as to* those who take *other gods for their* patrons, besides him, GOD observeth their *actions:* for thou art not a steward over them. (5) Thus have we revealed unto thee an Arabic Qurán, that thou mayest warn the metropolis *of Makkah*, and the *Arabs* who *dwell* round about it; and mayest threaten *them* with the day of the *general* assembly, of which there is no doubt: *one* part *shall then be placed* in Paradise, and *another* part in hell. (6) If GOD had pleased, he had made them *all* of one religion; but he leadeth whom he pleaseth into his mercy; and the unjust shall have no patron or helper. (7) Do they take *other* patrons, besides him? whereas GOD is the *only true* patron: he quickeneth the dead, and he *is* almighty.

(8) Whatever matter ye disagree about, the decision R ⅔. thereof *appertaineth* unto GOD. This is GOD my LORD: in him do I trust, and unto him do I turn me: (9) the Creator of heaven and earth: he hath given you wives of your own species, and cattle both male and female; by which means he multiplieth you: there is nothing like

---

(1) *H. M. A. S. Q.* See Prelim. Disc., pp. 100–102.
Reveal . . . unto thee. Comp. chap. xxxix. 1. "The Korán was not revealed in the same way as the Law or the Gospel. Neither of them were brought by Gabriel."—*Brinckman*.
(3) *Angels . . . ask pardon for, &c.* See note on chap. xl. 7.
(5) See note on chaps. xxi. 105, and xli. 44. As yet Muhammad conceived of himself as merely the prophet of Arabia.
(9) *Wives of your own species.* See notes on chap. xvi. 74.

him; and *it is* he who heareth *and* seeth. (10) His are the keys of heaven and earth; he bestoweth provision abundantly on whom he pleaseth, and he is sparing *unto whom he pleaseth;* for he knoweth all things. (11) He hath ordained you the religion which he commanded Noah, and which we have revealed unto thee, *O Muhammad,* and which we commanded Abraham, and Moses, and Jesus: *saying,* Observe *this* religion, and be not divided therein. (12) The *worship of one God,* to which thou invitest them, is grievous unto the unbelievers: GOD will elect thereto whom he pleaseth, and will direct unto the same him who shall repent. (13) *Those who lived in times past* were not divided among themselves, until after that the knowledge *of God's unity* had come unto them; through their own perverseness: and unless a previous decree had passed from thy LORD, *to bear with them* till a determined time, verily *the matter* had been decided between them *by the destruction of the gainsayers.* They who have inherited the scriptures after them *are* certainly in a perplexing doubt concerning *the same.* (14) Wherefore invite *them to receive the sure faith,* and be urgent *with them,* as thou hast been commanded; and follow not their *vain* desires: and say, I believe in *all* the scriptures which GOD hath sent down; and I am commanded to

---

(11) In this passage Muhammad claims that his religion is the one true religion revealed from the beginning to all true prophets. This claim is fatal to his own prophetic pretensions; nothing is clearer than this, since Islám contradicts the whole plan of salvation revealed in the scriptures of the Old and New Testaments. See notes on chaps. ii. 40, 90, 100, iii. 2, iv. 44, 45, 162, v. 48–50, &c. For other similar passages, see Index under the word QURÁN. See also Prelim. Disc., chap. iv.

(13) *They who have inherited, &c.* "The modern Jews and Christians."—*Sale.*

In a perplexing doubt, &c. "Not understanding the true meaning nor believing the real doctrines thereof."—*Sale.* This is the interpretation of the commentators. The allusion is to the controversies relative to the doctrines of the Sonship of Christ and the Trinity.

(14) *I believe in all the scriptures.* See above under ver. 11.

establish justice among you: GOD is our LORD and your LORD: unto us *will* our works *be imputed*, and unto you *will* your works *be imputed:* let there be no wrangling between us and you; for GOD will assemble us *all at the last day*, and unto him shall we return. (15) *As to* those who dispute concerning GOD, after obedience hath been paid him *by receiving his religion*, their disputing *shall be* vain in the sight of their LORD; and wrath *shall fall* on them, and they shall suffer a grievous punishment. (16) *It is* GOD who hath sent down the scripture with truth; and the balance *of true judgment:* and what shall inform thee whether the hour *be* nigh at hand? (17) They who believe not therein wish it to be hastened *by way of mockery:* but they who believe dread the same, and know it to be the truth. Are not those who dispute concerning the *last* hour in a wide error?

|| (18) GOD is bounteous unto his servants: he provideth for whom he pleaseth; and he is the strong, the mighty. (19) Whoso chooseth the tillage of the life to come, unto him will we give increase in his tillage: and whoso chooseth the tillage of this world, we will give him *the fruit* thereof; but he shall have no part in the life to come. (20) Have *the idolaters* deities which ordain them a religion which GOD hath not allowed? But *had it* not *been* for the decree of *respiting their punishment to the day of* separating *the infidels from the true believers*, judgment had been *already* given between them: for the unjust shall surely suffer a painful torment. (21) *On that day* thou shalt see the unjust in great terror, because of their demerits; and *the penalty thereof* shall fall upon them: but they who believe and do good works *shall dwell* in the delightful meadows of Paradise; they shall obtain whatever they shall desire, with their LORD. This *is* the

R $\frac{3}{4}$.

---

(19) *Whoso chooseth, &c.* "Labouring here to obtain a reward hereafter; for what is sown in this world will be reaped in the next."—*Sale.*

Comp. Gal. vi. 8.

greatest acquisition. (22) This *is* what GOD promiseth unto his servants who believe and do good works. Say, I ask not of you, for this *my preaching*, any reward, except the love of *my* relations: and whoever shall have deserved well by *one* good action, unto him will we add *the merit of another* action thereto; for GOD *is* inclined to forgive *and* ready to reward. (23) Do they say *Muhammad* hath blasphemously forged a lie concerning GOD? If GOD pleaseth, he will seal up thy heart: and GOD will absolutely abolish vanity, and will establish the truth in his words; for he knoweth the innermost part of *men's* breasts. (24) *It is* he who accepteth repentance from his servants, and forgiveth sins, and knoweth that which ye do. (25) He will incline his ear unto those who believe and work righteousness, and will add unto them *above what they shall ask or deserve*, of his bounty: but the unbelievers shall suffer a severe punishment. (26) If GOD should bestow abundance upon his servants, they would certainly behave insolently in the earth: but he sendeth down by measure *unto every one* that which he pleaseth; for he well knoweth *and* seeth *the condition of his* servants. (27) *It is* he who sendeth down the rain, after *men* have despaired *thereof*, and spreadeth abroad his

---

(22) Comp. chap. xxv. 58, 59.
(23) See chaps. iii. 185, vii. 85 and 203, x. 39, and xi. 14, &c.

He will seal up thy heart. The translation should be *He could seal*, &c. "The meaning of these words is somewhat obscure. Some imagine they express a detestation of the forgery charged on the Prophet by the infidels; because none could be capable of so wicked an action but one whose heart was close shut, and knew not his Lord: as if he had said, 'God forbid that thou shouldst be so void of grace, or have so little sense of thy duty!' Others think the signification to be, that God might strike all the revelations which had been vouchsafed to Muhammad out of his heart at once; and others, that God would strengthen his heart with patience against the insults of the believers."—*Sale, Baidháwi.*

And God will absolutely abolish vanity, &c. The translation should be, *But God, &c.* "Wherefore if the doctrine taught in this book be of man, it will certainly fail and come to nothing; but if it be of God, it can never be overthrown."—*Sale, Baidháwi.*

mercy; and he is the patron, justly to be praised. (28) Among his signs *is* the creation of heaven and earth, and of the living creatures with which he hath replenished them both; and he *is* able to gather them together *before his tribunal* whenever he pleaseth.

‖ (29) Whatever misfortune befalleth you *is sent unto you by God*, for that which your hands have deserved; and *yet* he forgiveth many things: (30) ye shall not frustrate *the divine vengeance* in the earth; neither shall ye have any protector or helper against GOD. (31) Among his signs *also are* the *ships* running in the sea, like high mountains: if he pleaseth, he causeth the wind to cease, and they lie still on the back of *the water:* (verily herein *are* signs unto every patient *and* grateful person): (32) or he destroyeth them *by shipwreck*, because of that which *their crews* have merited; though he pardoneth many things. (33) And they who dispute against our signs shall know that *there will be* no way for them to escape *our vengeance*.

‖ (34) Whatever things are given you, *they are* the provision of this present life; but the *reward* which is with GOD is better, and more durable, for those who believe, and put their trust in the LORD; (35) and who avoid heinous and filthy crimes, and when they are angry, forgive; (36) and who hearken unto their LORD, and are constant at prayer, and whose affairs *are directed by* consultation among themselves, and who give *alms* out of what we have bestowed on them; (37) and who, when an injury is done them, avenge themselves, (38) (and the retaliation of evil *ought to be* an evil proportionate thereto): but he who forgiveth and is reconciled *unto his enemy* shall receive his reward from GOD; for he loveth not the unjust doers. (39) And whoso shall avenge himself, after he

---

(28) Comp. John ix. 1–3. Muhammad seems to have entertained the error of Job's friends.

(37–39) *Avenge themselves.* "Using the means which God has put into their hands for their own defence. This is added to com-

hath been injured; as to these, it is not lawful to punish them *for it:* (40) but it is only lawful to punish those who wrong men, and act insolently in the earth, against justice; these shall suffer a grievous punishment. (41) And whoso beareth *injuries* patiently and forgiveth, verily this *is* a necessary work.

R ⅝. ‖ (42) Whom GOD shall cause to err, he shall afterwards have no protector. And thou shalt see the ungodly, (43) who shall say, when they behold the punishment *prepared for them, Is there* no way to return back *into the world?* (44) And thou shalt see them exposed unto *hell-fire;* dejected, because of the ignominy *they shall undergo:* they shall look *at the fire* sideways and by stealth; and the true believers shall say, Verily the losers are they who have lost their own souls, and their families, on the day of resurrection: *shall* not the ungodly *continue* in eternal torment? (45) They shall have no protectors to defend them against GOD; and whom GOD shall cause to err, he shall find no way *to the truth.* (46) Hearken unto your LORD before the day come, which GOD will not keep back: ye shall have no place of refuge on that day; neither shall ye be able to deny *your sins.* (47) But if *those to whom thou preachest* turn aside *from thy admonitions,* verily we have not sent thee *to be* a guardian over them: thy duty is preaching only. When we cause man to taste mercy from us, he rejoiceth thereat; but if evil befall them, for that which their hands have formerly committed, verily man *becometh* ungrateful. (48) Unto GOD *appertaineth* the kingdom of heaven and earth: he createth that which he pleaseth; (49) he giveth females unto whom he pleaseth, and he giveth males unto whom

---

plete the character here given; for valour and courage are not inconsistent with clemency, the rule being, *Parcere subjectis et debellare superbos."—Sale.*

See note on chap. ii. 194.

Who forgiveth, &c. See chap. v. 49.

(45) *Whom God shall cause to err, &c.* See notes on chaps. vii. 179, 180, xvi. 95, and xx. 87.

he pleaseth; or he giveth them males and females jointly: and he maketh whom he pleaseth to be childless; for he *is* wise *and* powerful. (50) It is not *fit* for man that GOD should speak unto him otherwise than by *private* revelation, or from behind a veil, (51) or by his sending of a messenger to reveal, by his permission, that which he pleaseth; for he *is* high *and* wise. (52) Thus have we revealed unto thee a revelation, by our command. Thou didst not understand *before this* what the book *of the Qurán* was, nor *what* the faith *was;* but we have ordained the same *for* a light; we will thereby direct such of our servants as we please; and thou shalt surely direct *them* into the right way, (53) the way of GOD, unto whom *belongeth* whatever *is* in heaven and in earth. Shall not *all* things return unto GOD?

(50-51) This was said in answer to those who objected that no one ever saw Muhammad when *receiving* his revelations from God.

Messenger. See note on chap. ii. 96.

(52) *A revelation.* "Or, as the words may also be translated, 'Thus have we sent the Spirit Gabriel unto thee with a revelation.'"—*Sale.*

Thou didst not understand before this, &c. See note on chap. x. 17.

CHAPTER XLIII.

ENTITLED SURAT AL ZUKHRÁF (THE ORNAMENTS OF GOLD).

Revealed at Makkah.

INTRODUCTION.

ALTHOUGH the faith of Christians is alluded to in this chapter, the contents seem to have been solely intended for the instruction and warning of the idolaters of Makkah. The exposure of their idolatry is clear and convincing, while the truth of the new religion is everywhere assumed. The worship of female deities, who were called by the Arabs "daughters of God," is visited with scathing irony. "When one of them," says the revelation, "hath the news brought of the birth of a child of that sex, which they attribute unto the Merciful as his similitude, his face becometh black, and he is oppressed with sorrow!"

The allusion made to the Christian faith, though intended to be a reply to the Quraish, who had compared the worship of their deities with the Christian worship of Jesus, yet contains a distinct denial of the divinity of the Son of Mary. The Gospel of Jesus, according to Muhammad, was "Fear God and obey me: verily God is my Lord and your Lord; wherefore worship him: this is the right way."

The close of the chapter indicates that while Muhammad had no doubt about the triumph of God's cause, yet he despaired of the conversion of his townsmen (vers. 39–41, 88, 89). They have ears, but they hear not. He cries out, "O Lord, verily these are people who believe not." To which the Lord replies, "Therefore turn aside from them; and say, Peace." They are now rejected of God and his Prophet as reprobates.

Probable Date of the Revelations.

There can be no doubt that the whole of this chapter must be referred to Makkah. The imagination of the traditionists that ver.

44 was enunciated at Jerusalem during the celebrated night-journey (Rodwell, *note in loco*), is refuted by the absence of any proof that such a journey was ever performed.

As to the date, aside from the general style of the contents, we have, in the last verse, a distinct allusion to a breach between Muhammad and the Quraish. That this was not the final breach, when Muhammad determined to leave Makkah and go to Madína, is evident from the absence of any allusion to persecution of the Muslims. It is probable, therefore, that the allusion here refers to Muhammad's withdrawal with his followers to the house of Arqám to escape the taunts and threatened violence of the Quraish. This understanding of this passage would relegate this chapter to the fourth year of Muhammad's ministry (B.H. 9), with which the style of the contents very well agrees. Noëldeke, however, places it somewhat later, about the beginning of the fifth year of Muhammad's call.

Principal Subjects.

	VERSES
The Arabic Qurán copied from a divine original	1-3
Former nations, like the Quraish, rejected the prophets	4-7
Idolaters acknowledge God to be creator, yet worship the creature	8-14
The Arabs hate female offspring, and yet attribute such to God	15-18
Idolaters vainly excuse their unbelief by saying they will follow the religion of their fathers	19-24
Abraham rejected the idolatry of his fathers	25-27
God prospered the idolatrous Quraish until a prophet came, and now they reject him	28, 29
The unbelievers rebuked for saying they would have received the Qurán from some great man	30, 31
Poverty only permitted to save men from idolatry	32-34
Devils are constituted the companions of infidels, who lead them to destruction	35-38
Muhammad exhorted to remain steadfast in faith notwithstanding the unbelief of his countrymen	39-44
Moses rejected with contempt by Pharaoh and the Egyptians, who were drowned	45-56
The Arab idolaters justified their idolatry by reference to the Christian worship of Jesus	57, 58
But Jesus did not say he was a god, but was a servant and a prophet of God	59-64
Unbelievers warned of approaching judgment	65-67
The joys of Paradise reserved for Muslims and their wives	68-73

	VERSES
The damned shall vainly seek relief in annihilation	74-78
Angels record the secret plottings of infidels	79, 80
If God had a son, Muhammad would be the first to worship him	81, 82
God knoweth the folly of idolaters	83-87
Muhammad commanded to turn aside from the unbelieving Quraish	88, 89

IN THE NAME OF THE MOST MERCIFUL GOD.

R ½

|| (1) H. M. By the perspicuous book; (2) verily we have ordained the same an Arabic Qurán that ye may understand: (3) and it *is* certainly *written* in the original book, *kept* with us, *being* sublime and full of wisdom. (4) Shall we therefore turn away from you the admonition, and deprive *you thereof*, because ye are a people who transgress? (5) And how many prophets have we sent among those of old? (6) and no prophet came unto them but they laughed him to scorn: (7) wherefore we destroyed *nations who were* more mighty than these in strength; and the example of those who were of old hath been already *set before them*. (8) If thou ask them who created the heavens and the earth, they will certainly answer, The mighty, the wise *God* created them: (9) who hath spread the earth *as* a bed for you, and hath made you paths therein, that ye may be directed: (10) and who sendeth down rain from heaven by measure, whereby we quicken a dead country; (so shall ye be brought forth *from your graves:*) (11) and who hath created all the *various* species *of things*, and hath given you ships and cattle, whereon ye are carried; (12) that ye may sit firmly on the backs thereof, and may remember the favour of your LORD, when ye sit thereon, and may say, Praise be

---

(1) *H. M.* See Prelim. Disc., pp. 100-102.
(2) See chaps. xi. 2, 3, xvi. 105, xli. 2, and notes there.
(3) *Original book.* The Preserved Table. Prelim. Disc., p. 108.
(5, 6) Comp. chaps. xxiii. 24-26, and xxv. 5-10.

unto him, who hath subjected these unto our service! for we could not have mastered them *by our own power:* (13) and unto our LORD shall we surely return. (14) Yet have they attributed unto him some of his servants *as his* offspring: verily man is openly ungrateful. (15) Hath *God* taken daughters out of *those beings* which he hath created, and hath he chosen sons for you? (16) But when one of them hath the news brought of *the birth of a child of that sex,* which they attribute unto the Merciful as *his* similitude, his face becometh black, and he is oppressed with sorrow.

|| (17) Do they therefore *attribute unto God female issue,* R $\frac{2}{8}$. which are brought up among ornaments, and are contentious without cause? (18) And do they make the angels, who are the servants of the Merciful, females? Were they present at their creation? Their testimony shall be written down, and they shall be examined *concerning the same on the day of judgment.* (19) And they say, If the Merciful had pleased, we had not worshipped them. They have no knowledge herein: they only utter a vain lie. (20) Have we given them a book *of revelations* before this; and do they keep the same in their custody? (21) But they say, Verily we found our fathers practising a religion, and we *are* guided in their footsteps. (22) Thus we sent no preacher before thee unto *any* city, but the inhabitants thereof, who lived in affluence, said, Verily we found our fathers practising a religion, and we tread in their footsteps. (23) *And the preacher* answered, What, although I bring you a more right *religion* than that which ye found your fathers to practise? *And* they replied, Verily we believe not that which ye are sent *to preach.* (24) Wherefore we took vengeance on them:

(14–17) See notes on chap. iv. 116, 169.
(16) See chap. xvi. 60.
(21) See note on chap. ii. 171.
(24) See the *Histories* of the former prophets in chap. xi., &c.

and behold what hath been the end of those who accused *our apostles* of imposture.

R 3/9.

‖ (25) *Remember* when Abraham said unto his father and his people, Verily I am clear of *the gods* which ye worship, (26) except him who hath created me; for he will direct me *aright*. (27) And he ordained this *to be* a constant doctrine among his posterity, that they should be turned *from idolatry to the worship of the only true God*. (28) Verily I have permitted these *Makkans* and their fathers to live in prosperity, until the truth should come unto them, and a manifest apostle; (29) but now the truth is come unto them, they say, This *is* a piece of sorcery, and we believe not therein. (30) And they say, Had this Qurán been sent down unto some great man of *either of* the two cities, *we would have received it*. (31) Do they distribute the mercy of thy LORD? We distribute the necessary provision among them in this present life, and we raise some of them *several* degrees above the others, that the one of them may take the other to serve him: and the mercy of thy LORD is more valuable than the *riches* which they gather together. (32) If *it were* not that mankind would have become one sect *of infidels*, verily we had given unto those who believe not in the Merciful roofs of silver to their houses, and stairs *of silver* by which they might ascend *thereto*, (33) and doors *of*

---

(29) See notes, chaps. x. 39, and xi. 14.

(30) *Some great man, i.e.,* "To one of the principal inhabitants of Makkah or of Tayif, such as al Walíd, Ibn al Mughaira, or Urwa Ibn Masúd the Thakífite."—*Sale, Baidháwi.*

"This verse is worth marking. Many hold that half of Mohammed's first success is to be attributed to his rank and influence among the Meccans. The story of his being chosen to put the black stone in its place shows, at all events, that he was respected for his moral character."—*Brinckman* in *Notes on Islám.* However this may be, he had long since lost his prestige among the Quraish. His early successes were due entirely to the superiority of his religion to that of the Arabs, as he claims in ver. 23 of this chapter.

(31) *Do they distribute, &c.* "By this expression the prophetic office is here particularly intended."—*Sale.*

(32-34) But comp. chap. xxxv. 30.

silver to their houses, and couches *of silver* for them to lean on; (34) and ornaments of gold: for all this *is* the provision of the present life; but the next *life* with thy LORD shall be for those who fear *him*.

¶ (35) Whoever shall withdraw from the admonition of the Merciful, we will chain a devil unto him, and he shall be his inseparable companion: (36) (and *the devils* shall turn them aside from the way *of truth*; yet they shall imagine themselves *to be* rightly directed;) (37) until, when he shall appear before us *at the last day*, he shall say *unto the devil*, Would to GOD that between me and thee *there was* the distance of the east from the west! (38) Oh how wretched a companion *art thou!* But *wishes* shall not avail you on this day, since ye have been unjust; for ye shall be partakers of the *same* punishment. (39) Canst thou, *O Prophet*, make the deaf to hear, or canst thou direct the blind, and him who is in a manifest error? (40) Whether we take thee away, we will surely take vengeance on them; (41) or whether we cause thee to see *the punishment* with which we have threatened them *executed*, we will certainly prevail over them. (42) Wherefore hold fast *the doctrine* which hath been revealed unto thee; for thou *art* in a right way; (43) and it is a memorial unto thee and thy people, and hereafter shall ye be examined *concerning your observance thereof*. (44) And ask our apostles whom we have sent before thee whether we have appointed gods for them to worship besides the Merciful.

¶ (45) We formerly sent Moses with our signs unto Pharaoh and his princes, and he said, Verily I am the apostle of the LORD of all creatures. (46) And when he came unto them with our signs, behold, they laughed him

---

(35) *A devil, &c.* See chap. xix. 69, 86.
(40) This verse intimates that Muhammad was in doubt as to the ultimate success of his mission.
(44) "That is, Ask those who profess the religions which they taught, and their learned men."—*Sale, Baidháwi, &c.*

to scorn; (47) although we showed them no sign, but it was greater than the other: and we inflicted a punishment on them, that peradventure they might be converted. (48) And they said *unto Moses*, O magician, pray unto thy LORD for us, according to the covenant which he hath made with thee; for we *will* certainly *be* directed. (49) But when we took the plague from off them, behold, they brake their promise. (50) And Pharaoh made proclamation among his people, saying, O my people, is not the kingdom of Egypt mine, and these rivers which flow beneath me? Do ye not see? (51) Am not I better than this *Moses*, who is a contemptible person, (52) and can scarce express himself intelligibly? (53) Have bracelets of gold, therefore, been put upon him; or do the angels attend him in orderly procession? (54) And *Pharaoh* persuaded his people to light behaviour; and they obeyed him: for they were a wicked people. (55) And when they had provoked us to wrath, we took vengeance on them: and we drowned them all: (56) and we made them a precedent, and an example unto others.

∥ (57) And when the son of Mary was proposed for an example, behold, thy people cried out *through excess of joy*

---

(47) *No sign but it was greater*, &c. "Literally, *than its sister*. The meaning is, that the miracles were *all very great and considerable*, or as the French may express it, by a phrase nearly the same, *les uns plus grands que les autres*."—*Sale.*

A punishment, viz., "the successive plagues which they suffered previous to their final destruction in the Red Sea."—*Sale.*

That peradventure, &c. This contradicts Exod. iii. 19, 20.

(50-56) See notes, chap. vii. 104-136.

These rivers. "The Nile and its branches."—*Sale.*

Can scarce express himself intelligibly. See chap. xx. 28.

(53) *Have bracelets*, &c. "Such bracelets were some of the insignia of royalty; for when the Egyptians raised a person to the dignity of a prince, they put a collar or chain of gold about his neck (Gen. xli. 42), and bracelets of gold on his wrists."—*Sale, Baidháwi.*

(57) *Thy people cried out*, &c. "This passage is generally supposed to have been revealed on occasion of an objection made by one Ibn al Zabári to those words in the twenty-first chapter (ver. 92) by which all in general who were worshipped as deities besides God are doomed to hell: whereupon the infidels cried out, 'We are content that our gods should be with Jesus; for he also is worshipped

thereat; (58) and they said, *Are* our gods better, or he? They have proposed this *instance* unto thee no otherwise than for an occasion of dispute; yea, they are contentious men. (59) *Jesus* is no other than a servant, whom we favoured *with the gift of prophecy;* and we appointed him for an example unto the children of Israel: (60) (if we pleased, verily we could from ourselves produce angels, to succeed *you* in the earth;) (61) and he *shall be* a sign of the *approach of the last* hour; wherefore doubt not thereof. And follow me: this *is* the right way. (62) And let not

---

as God.' Some, however, are of opinion it might have been revealed in answer to certain idolaters, who said that the Christians, who received the Scriptures, worshipped Jesus, supposing him to be the son of God; whereas the angels were more worthy of that honour than he."—*Sale, Baidháwi.*

(59) *Jesus is no other than a servant, &c.* Muir says: "This was ... the only position which, at the present advanced period of his mission, Mahomet could consistently fall back upon; and it was ever after carefully maintained. Some terms of veneration in use among Christians are indeed applied to Jesus, as 'the Word of God,' and 'His Spirit which he breathed into Mary' (chap. iii. 39, iv. 16, xxi. 91, &c.) But the Divine Sonship was constantly denied."—*Life of Mahomet,* vol. ii. pp. 287, 288.

See also notes on chaps. iii. 39, and iv. 169.

An example. "Or an instance of our power, by his miraculous birth."—*Sale.* See chap. xxi. 91, where he is called "a sign unto all creatures."

(60) *We could . . . produce angels, &c.* "As easily as we produced Jesus without a father. The intent of the words is to show how just and reasonable it is to think that the angels should bear the relation of children to men, rather than to God; they being his creatures as well as men, and equally in his power."—*Sale, Baidháwi.*

(61) *A sign . . . of the last hour.* "For some time before the resurrection Jesus is to descend on earth, according to the Muhammadans, near Damascus (Prelim. Disc., pp. 132-133), or, as some say, near a rock in the Holy Land named Afik, with a lance in his hand wherewith he is to kill Antichrist, whom he will encounter at Ludd, or Lydda, a small town not far from Joppa. They add that he will arrive at Jerusalem at the time of morning prayer; that he shall perform his devotions after the Muhammadan institution, and officiate instead of the Imám, who shall give place to him; that he will break down the cross and destroy the churches of the Christians, of whom he will make a general slaughter, excepting only such as shall profess Islám," &c.—*Sale, Baidháwi, Jaláluddín.*

See also Prelim. Disc., p. 133.

(62) See note on chaps. iv. 116, and vi. 112.

Satan cause you to turn aside: for he *is* your open enemy. (63) And when *Jesus* came with evident *miracles*, he said, Now am I come unto you with wisdom, and to explain unto you part of *those things* concerning which ye disagree; wherefore fear God and obey me. (64) Verily GOD is my LORD and your LORD; wherefore worship him: this *is* the right way. (65) And the confederated sects among them fell to variance: but woe unto those who have acted unjustly, because of the punishment of a grievous day. (66) Do *the unbelievers* wait for any other than the hour *of judgment;* that it may come upon them suddenly, while they foresee it not? (67) The intimate friends on that day *shall be* enemies unto one another; except the pious.

R $\frac{7}{13}$.
‖ (68) O my servants, *there shall* no fear *come* on you this day, neither shall ye be grieved, (69) who have believed in our signs and have been Múslims; (70) enter ye into Paradise, ye and your wives, with great joy. (71) Dishes of gold shall be carried round unto them, and cups without handles: and therein *shall they enjoy* whatever *their* souls shall desire, and *whatever their* eyes shall delight in: and ye shall remain therein for ever. (72) This is Paradise, which ye have inherited *as a reward* for that which ye have wrought. (73) Therein shall ye have fruits in abundance, of which ye shall eat. (74) But the wicked

---

(63) *Wisdom.* "That is, with a book of revelations and an excellent system of religion."—*Sale.*

Part of those things, &c. "Muhammad again is careful only to allow that Jesus only came to explain '*part* of those things,' &c."— *Brinckman* in *Notes on Islám.* He, however, refers to *the things* about which *the Jews* differed in his time. The Christians having departed from the true faith, as he believed, a new prophet was needed to witness to and establish the doctrine of the Divine unity.

(65) "This may be understood either of the Jews in the time of Jesus, who opposed his doctrine, or of the Christians since, who have fallen into various opinions concerning him, some making him to be God, others the Son of God, and others one of the persons of the Trinity, &c."—*Sale, Baidháwi.* I think the reference is clearly to the Christians only.

(70) *Your wives.* Who are presumed to be true believers.

(71–73) See note on chap. iii. 15.

shall remain for ever in the torment of hell: (75) it shall not be made lighter unto them; and they *shall* despair therein. (76) We deal not unjustly with them, but they deal unjustly *with their own souls*. (77) And they shall call aloud, *saying*, O Málik, *intercede for us* that thy LORD would end us *by annihilation*. He shall answer, Verily ye shall remain *here for ever*. (78) We brought you the truth heretofore, but the greater part of you abhorred the truth. (79) Have *the infidels* fixed on a method *to circumvent our Apostle?* Verily we will fix *on a method to circumvent them*. (80) Do they imagine that we hear not their secrets and their private discourse? Yea, and our messengers who attend them write down *the same*. (81) Say, If the Merciful had a son, verily I *would be* the first of those who should worship *him*. (82) Far be the LORD of heaven and earth, the LORD of the throne, from that which they affirm *of him!* (83) Wherefore let them wade *in their vanity*, and divert themselves until they arrive at their day with which they have been threatened. (84) He who is GOD in heaven is GOD on earth also; and he *is* the wise, the knowing. (85) And blessed be he unto whom *appertaineth* the kingdom of heaven and earth, and of whatever is between them; with whom *is* the knowledge of the *last* hour; and before whom ye shall be assembled. (86) They whom they invoke besides him have not the privilege to intercede *for others;* except those who bear

---

(77) *O Málik.* "This the Muhammadans suppose to be the name of the principal angel who has charge of hell."—*Sale.* See chap. lxxiv. 30.

He shall answer. "Some say that this answer will not be given till a thousand years after."—*Sale.*

(80) *Our messengers, i.e.,* "the guardian angels."—*Sale.* But see chap. l. 16.

(81) *If the Merciful had a son, &c.* Comp. chap. xxxix. 6.

(86) *Except those who bear witness, i.e.,* "to the doctrine of God's unity. The exception comprehends Jesus, Ezra, and the angels, who will be admitted as intercessors, though they have been worshipped as gods."—*Sale, Baidháwi, Jaláluddín.* But see notes on chaps. ii. 47, 123, vi. 50, and xxxix. 45.

witness to the truth, and know *the same.* (87) If thou ask them who hath created them, they will surely answer, GOD. How therefore are they turned away *to the worship of others?* (88) *God also heareth* the saying of *the Prophet,* O LORD, verily these *are* people who believe not: (89) *and he answereth,* Therefore turn aside from them; and say, Peace: hereafter shall they know *their folly.*

---

(88) *The saying* Rodwell translates *And one saith.* Of this passage Noëldeke says a few words must have been lost here, as the words وقيله, even if the diacritical points are changed, cannot be satisfactorily connected with the preceding verse.

(89) *Say, Peace, &c.* See note on chap. xxv. 64.

CHAPTER XLIV.

ENTITLED SURAT AL DUKHAN (SMOKE).

Revealed at Makkah.

INTRODUCTION.

THIS is a distinctively Makkan chapter. Its title is found in ver. 9, where a visible smoke is mentioned. The subject of the preacher is the necessity of accepting Islám. The Qurán, he declares, is a revelation from the only true God. This revelation the people had rejected, especially its teaching concerning the resurrection and the judgment. They had even charged their Prophet with forgery and with being a madman. They are now warned of coming calamity of Divine vengeance, unless they immediately repent and accept Islám. This instruction is enforced by reference to the destruction of Pharaoh and his hosts, and of the people of Tubbá, for their unbelief, and for their ignominious treatment of the prophets of God. To this is added a description of the horrors of hell and the joys of Paradise. The chapter ends with a notice of the Divine condescension in giving the Arab people his Word in their own language.

Probable Date of the Revelations.

All agree that the revelations of this chapter are of Makkan origin. Some have thought, without good reason, that vers. 14 and 15 are Madínic, because of the supposition that the *plague* alluded to in ver. 14 refers to a famine which visited Makkah after the Hijra, and that the *vengeance* of ver. 15 was taken at Badr. The reference in these verses, however, is to the plague and vengeance of God to be visited upon the unbelievers in the judgment-day, and in the perdition to follow.

We learn from ver. 13 that while some of the people of Makkah charged their Prophet with forgery, others, moved by either more charitable or more contemptuous feelings, merely called him a madman. These charges, in the absence of any show of violence towards the preacher or followers of the new faith, point to an early period as the date of this chapter. Muir places it in the early part of the fourth stage, *i.e.*, at a period extending from the sixth to the tenth years of Muhammad's mission. Noëldeke places it in his second Makkan period, or the fifth and sixth years of Muhammad's mission.

Principal Subjects.

	VERSES
The Qurán sent down on the Blessed Night	1–6
God the only source of life	7
Unbelievers threatened with the tormenting smoke of the judgment-day	8–15
Pharaoh and his people destroyed for rejecting Moses	16–32
The people of Makkah threatened with the fate of the people of Tubbá	33–37
God did not create the universe in jest	38, 39
The judgment-day a day when none shall be helped	40–42
Punishment of the wicked in hell	43–50
Rewards of the righteous in Paradise	51–57
The Qurán revealed in Arabic as an admonition	58

IN THE NAME OF THE MOST MERCIFUL GOD.

‖ (1) H. M. By the perspicuous book *of the Qurán;* (2) verily we have sent down the same on a blessed night (for we had engaged *so to do*), (3) *on the night* wherein is distinctly sent down the decree of every determined thing, (4) *as a* command from us. Verily we have *ever* used to send *apostles with revelations at proper intervals,* (5) *as a*

---

(1) *H. M.* See Prelim. Disc., pp. 100–102.

(2) *A blessed night.* "Generally supposed to be that between the twenty-third and twenty-fourth of Ramadhán. See Prelim. Disc., p. 108, and chap. xcvii. and the notes there."—*Sale.*

(3) "For annually on this night, as the Muhammadans are taught, all the events of the ensuing year, with respect to life and death and the other affairs of this world, are disposed and settled. Some, however, suppose that these words refer only to that particular night on which the Qurán, wherein are completely contained the Divine determinations in respect to religion and morality, was sent down; and, according to this exposition, the passage may be rendered, 'The night whereon every determined *or* adjudged matter was sent down.'" —*Sale, Baidháwi, and Jaláluddín.*

mercy from thy LORD; for it is he who heareth *and* knoweth: (6) the LORD of heaven and earth, and of whatever *is* between them; if ye are *men* of sure knowledge. (7) There *is* no GOD but he: he giveth life, and he causeth to die; *he is* your LORD, and the LORD of your forefathers. (8) Yet do they amuse themselves with doubt. (9) But observe *them* on the day *whereon* the heaven shall produce a visible smoke, (10) which shall cover mankind: this *will be* a tormenting plague. (11) *They shall say,* O LORD, take *this* plague from off us: verily we *will become* true believers. (12) How *should* an admonition *be of avail* to them *in this condition;* when a manifest apostle came unto them, (13) but they retired from him, saying, *This man is* instructed *by others, or is* a distracted person? (14) We will take the plague from off *you*, a little: *but* ye will certainly return *to your infidelity*. (15) On the day whereon we shall fiercely assault *them* with great power, verily we will take vengeance *on them*. (16) We made

---

(9) *Smoke.* The commentators differ in their expositions of this passage. Some think it spoke of a smoke which seemed to fill the air during the famine which was inflicted on the Makkans in Muhammad's time, and was so thick that, though they could hear, yet they could not see one another. But, according to a tradition of Ali, the smoke here meant is that which is to be one of the previous signs of the day of judgment, and will fill the whole space from east to west, and last for forty days. This smoke, they say, will intoxicate the infidels, and issue at their noses, ears, and posteriors, but will very little inconvenience the true believers."—*Sale, Jaláluddín.*

(13) *This man is instructed by others, &c.* See note on chap. xvi. 105.

(14) *The plague.* "If we follow the former exposition, the words are to be understood of the ceasing of the famine upon the intercession of Muhammad, at the desire of the Quraish, and on their promise of believing on him, notwithstanding which, they fell back to their old incredulity; but if we follow the latter exposition, they are to be understood of God's taking away the plague of the smoke, after the expiration of the forty days, at the prayer of the infidels, and on their promise of receiving the true faith, which being done, they will immediately return to their wonted obstinacy."—*Sale.* See also chap. xxiii. 65, note.

(15) "Some expound this of the slaughter at Badr, and others of the day of judgment."—*Sale.*

VOL. IV. C

trial of the people of Pharaoh before them, and an honourable messenger came unto them, (17) *saying*, Send unto me the servants of GOD; verily I *am* a faithful messenger unto you: (18) and lift not yourselves up against GOD; for I come unto you with manifest power. (19) And I fly for protection unto my LORD, and your LORD, that ye stone me not. (20) If ye do not believe me, *at least* depart from me. (21) And *when they accused him of imposture*, he called upon his LORD, *saying*, These are a wicked people. (22) *And God said unto him*, March forth with my servants by night; for ye *will be* pursued: (23) and leave the sea divided, *that the Egyptians may enter the same;* for they are a host *doomed* to be drowned.

Sul⁸.

|| (24) How many gardens, and fountains, (25) and fields of corn, and fair dwellings, (26) and advantages which they enjoyed, did they leave behind them! (27) Thus *we dispossessed them thereof;* and we gave the same for an inheritance unto another people. (28) Neither heaven nor earth wept for them; neither were they respited *any longer*.

$R_{1\frac{2}{5}}$.

|| (29) And we delivered the children of Israel from a shameful affliction; (30) from Pharaoh; for he was haughty, and a transgressor: (31) and we chose them, knowingly, above *all* people; (32) and we showed them *several* signs, wherein was an evident trial. (33) Verily

---

(17) *Send unto me, &c., i.e.,* "Let the Israelites go with me to worship their God."—*Sale.*

(19) *Stone me not.* "Or that ye injure me not, either by word or deed."—*Sale, Baidhāwi.*

(20) *Depart from me.* Without opposing me, or offering me any injury, which I have not deserved from you."—*Sale.*

(27) *We gave the same, &c.* See chap. xxvi. 57–59, and note on chap. vii. 137.

(28) *Wept.* "That is, none pitied their destruction."—*Sale.*

(31) *We chose them knowingly, i.e.,* "knowing that they were worthy of our choice; or notwithstanding we knew they would, in time to come, fall into idolatry, &c."—*Sale.*

(32) *Signs.* "As the dividing of the Red Sea; the cloud which shaded them; the raining on them of manna and quails, &c."—*Sale, Baidhāwi.*

these *Makkans* say, (34) Assuredly *our final end* will be no other than our first *natural* death; neither shall we be raised again: (35) bring now our forefathers *back to life*, if ye speak truth. (36) Are they better, or the people of Tubbá, (37) and those who *were* before them? we destroyed them, because they wrought wickedness. (38) We have not created the heavens and the earth, and whatever *is* between them, by way of sport: (39) we have created them no otherwise than in truth; but the greater part of them do not understand. (40) Verily the day of separation *shall be* the appointed term of them all: (41) a day whereon the master and the servant shall be of no advantage to one another, neither shall they be helped; (42) excepting those on whom GOD shall have mercy; for he *is* the mighty, the merciful.

|| (43) Verily, *the fruit of* the tree of az Zaqqúm (44) R $\frac{3}{16}$ *shall be* the food of the impious; (45) as the dregs of oil shall it boil in the bellies *of the damned*, (46) like the boiling of the hottest water. (47) *And it shall be said to the tormentors*, Take him, and drag him into the midst of hell: (48) and pour on his head the torture of boiling water, (49) *saying*, Taste *this;* for thou art that mighty *and* honourable person. (50) Verily this is the *punish-*

---

(36) *The people of Tubbá*, viz., "the Hamyárites, whose kings had the title of Tubbá (Prelim. Disc., p. 26). The commentators tell us that the Tubbá here meant was very potent, and built Samarcand, or, as others say, demolished it; and that he was a true believer, but his subjects were infidels.

"This prince seems to have been Abu Qaríb Asad, who flourished about seven hundred years before Muhammad, and embraced Judaism, which religion he first introduced into Yaman (being the true religion at that time, inasmuch as Christianity was not then promulgated), and was, for that cause probably, slain by his own people."—*Sale, Baidháwi, al Jannábi.*

(39) *In truth.* See notes on chaps. xxi. 16, 17, and xxxviii. 26.

(40) *The day of separation, i.e.,* "the day of judgment, when the wicked shall be separated from the righteous, &c."—*Sale.*

(43) *Az Zaqqúm.* See chap. xxxvii. 60. "Jaláluddín supposes this passage to have been particularly levelled at Abu Jahl."—*Sale.*

(44-50) See note and references at chap. ii. 38.

ment of which you doubted. (51) But the pious *shall be lodged* in a place of security, (52) among gardens and fountains: (53) they shall be clothed in fine silk, and in satin; *and they shall sit* facing one another. (54) Thus *shall it be:* and we will espouse them to fair damsels, having large black eyes. (55) In that place shall they call for all *kinds of* fruits, in full security: (56) they shall not taste death therein, after the first death; and *God* shall deliver from the pains of hell: (57) through the gracious bounty of thy LORD. This will be great felicity. (58) Moreover we have rendered *the Qurán* easy *for thee, by revealing it* in thine own tongue; to the end that they may be admonished; (59) wherefore do thou wait *the event;* for they wait *to see some misfortune befall thee.*

(51–57) See notes on chaps. iii. 15, and 196–198, and xxxvii. 39–48.

(58) *Thine own tongue.* See note on chap. xli. 2, 3.

CHAPTER XLV.

ENTITLED SURAT AL JÁSÍYAH (KNEELING).

Revealed at Makkah.

INTRODUCTION.

THE title of this chapter is derived from verse 27, where it is said that in the judgment every nation shall be seen *kneeling* before God. The general outline of the teaching of this chapter differs little from that of other chapters enunciated at Makkah. God is declared to have revealed himself to Muhammad in the Qurán. Before this he had revealed himself to men in his works of creation and providence, and to the children of Israel in the Law and the Prophets. Infidels may reject this new revelation, but they shall realise, only too late for repentance to avail, that they have committed a fatal error.

The main point of interest to the Christian is the plain recognition of the Jewish Scriptures as the Word of God, preceding in date of revelation the Qurán. Muslims are, therefore, bound to receive the Bible as the Word of God.

Probable Date of the Revelations.

Noëldeke places the date of this chapter immediately after that of chap. xli. This agrees very well with the circumstances of the Muslims revealed in this chapter. Much depends upon what is implied in the exhortation of vers. 13 and 14. If the exhortation is intended to restrain the Muslims from violent resentment of the insults poured upon them, the date assigned above may be regarded as pretty correct. If, however, the exhortation implies actual persecution of Muslims, the date must be fixed at a later day.

Principal Subjects.

	VERSES
The Qurán a revelation from God	1
God revealed in his works	2–5
Punishment of those who reject the Qurán	6–10

	VERSES
God's mercy seen in his works of providence	11, 12
Muslims exhorted to forgive the unbelievers	13, 14
The Book of the law, wisdom, and prophecy given to the Israelites	15, 16
Muhammad received the Qurán	17–19
The wicked and just not rewarded alike	20
Unbelievers and idolaters threatened	21, 22
God the author of life, therefore may raise the dead	23–25
Contrasted condition of believers and unbelievers in the judgment	26–34
Praise to the Lord of the universe	35, 36

IN THE NAME OF THE MOST MERCIFUL GOD.

|| (1) H. M. The revelation of *this* book *is* from the mighty, the wise GOD. (2) Verily *both* in heaven and earth *are* signs of *the divine power* unto the true believers: (3) and in the creation of yourselves, and of the beasts which are scattered *over the face of the earth are* signs unto people of sound judgment; (4) and *also in* the vicissitude of night and day, and the rain which GOD sendeth down from heaven, whereby he quickeneth the earth after it hath been dead: in the change of the winds also *are* signs unto people of understanding. (5) These *are* the signs of GOD; we rehearse them unto thee with truth. In what revelation therefore will they believe, after *they have*

---

(1) *H. M.* See Prelim. Disc., pp. 100–102.

This book is, &c. See note on chap. xi. 2.

(3) "By the days of God, in this place, are meant the prosperous successes of his people in battle against the infidels. The passage is said to have been revealed on account of Omar, who being reviled by one of the tribes of Ghafár, was thinking to revenge himself by force. Some are of opinion that this verse is abrogated by that of War."—*Sale, Baidháwi.*

Since, according to Muslim belief, God will not pardon those who, having injured their fellow-men, have failed to secure pardon from them, this precept would amount to a refusal to allow enemies to escape the Divine wrath. See Prelim. Disc., pp. 145, 146. The forbearance towards enemies inculcated here was, however, dictated by policy. See note on chap. ii. 108.

rejected GOD and his signs? (6) Woe unto every lying *and* impious person; (7) who heareth the signs of GOD, which are read unto him, and afterwards proudly persisteth *in infidelity,* as though he heard them not: (denounce unto him a painful punishment:) (8) and who, when he cometh to the knowledge of any of our signs, receiveth the same with scorn. For these *is prepared* a shameful punishment: (9) before them *lieth* hell; and whatever they shall have gained shall not avail them at all, neither *shall* the *idols* which they have taken for *their* patrons besides GOD; and they shall suffer a grievous punishment. (10) This *is* a *true* direction; and for those who disbelieve the signs of their LORD, *is prepared* the punishment of a painful torment.

|| (11) *It is* GOD who hath subjected the sea unto R $\frac{2}{18}$. you, that the ships may sail therein, at his command; and that ye may seek *advantage unto yourselves by commerce,* of his bounty; and that ye may give thanks: (12) and he obligeth whatever *is* in heaven and on earth to serve you; the whole *being* from him. Verily herein *are* signs unto people who consider. (13) Speak unto the true believers, that they forgive those who hope not for the days of GOD, that he may reward people according to what they shall have wrought. (14) Whoso doeth that which is right *doth it* to *the advantage of* his own soul; and whoso doeth evil *doth it* against the same: hereafter shall ye return unto your LORD. (15) We gave unto the children of Israel the book *of the law,* and wisdom, and prophecy; and we fed them with good things, and preferred them above all nations: (16) and we gave them plain *ordinances* concerning the business *of religion;* neither do they fall to variance, except after that knowledge had come unto them, through envy among themselves: but thy LORD will decide the controversy between them on the day of resurrection, concerning that wherein

---

(16) See notes on chap. xliii. 63.

they disagree. (17) Afterwards we appointed thee, *O Muhammad*, to *promulgate* a law concerning the business *of religion:* wherefore follow the same, and follow not the desires of those who are ignorant. (18) Verily they shall not avail thee against GOD at all; the unjust *are* the patrons of one another; but GOD *is* the patron of the pious. (19) This *Qurán* delivereth evident *precepts* unto mankind; and *is* a direction and a mercy unto people who judge aright. (20) Do the workers of iniquity imagine that we will deal with them as with those who believe and do good works, *so that* their life and their death *shall be* equal? An ill judgment do they make.

R $\frac{3}{19}$.

|| (21) GOD hath created the heavens and the earth in truth, that he may recompense every soul according to that which it shall have wrought; and they shall not be treated unjustly. (22) What thinkest thou? He who taketh his own lust for his God, and whom GOD causeth knowingly to err, and whose ears and whose heart he hath sealed up, and over whose eyes he hath cast a veil; who shall direct him, after GOD *shall have forsaken him?* Will ye therefore not be admonished? (23) They say, *There* is no *other life*, except our present life: we die, and we live; and nothing but time destroyeth us. But they have no knowledge in this *matter;* they only follow a *vain* opinion. (24) And when our evident signs are rehearsed unto them, their argument *which they offer against the same* is no other than that they say, Bring *to life* our fathers *who have been dead;* if ye speak truth. (25) Say, GOD giveth you life; and afterwards causeth you to die: hereafter will he assemble you together on the day of resurrection; there is no doubt thereof; but the greater part of men do not understand.

---

(17) *Of those who are ignorant.* "That is, of the principal Quraish, who were urgent with Muhammad to return to the religion of his forefathers."—*Sale.*

(22) *Whom God causeth knowingly to err.* See note and references in chap. vii. 179, 180.

‖ (26) Unto GOD *appertaineth* the kingdom of heaven R $\frac{4}{20}$. and earth; and the day whereon the hour shall be fixed, on that day shall those who charge *the Qurán* with vanity perish. (27) And thou shalt see every nation kneeling: every nation shall be called unto its book *of account; and it shall be said unto them*, This day shall ye be rewarded according to that which ye have wrought. (28) This our book will speak concerning you with truth; *therein* have we written down whatever ye have done. (29) As to those who shall have believed and done good works, their LORD shall lead them into his mercy: this shall be manifest felicity. (30) But as to the infidels, *it shall be said unto them*, Were not my signs rehearsed unto you? but ye proudly rejected *them*, and became a wicked people! (31) And when it was said *unto you*, Verily the promise of GOD *is* true: and as to the hour *of judgment, there is* no doubt thereof: ye answered, We know not what the hour *of judgment is:* we hold an *uncertain* opinion only; and we are not well assured *of this matter*. (32) But *on that day* the evils of that which they have wrought shall appear unto them; and that which they mocked at shall encompass them: (33) and it shall be said *unto them*, This day will we forget you, as ye did forget the meeting of this your day: and your abode *shall be hell*-fire; and ye shall have none to deliver you. (34) This *shall ye suffer*, because ye turned the signs of GOD to ridicule; and the life of the world deceived you. On this day, therefore, they shall not be taken forth from thence, neither shall they be asked *any more* to render themselves well-pleasing *unto God*. (35) Wherefore praise be unto GOD, the LORD of the heavens, and the LORD of the earth; the LORD of all creatures: (36) and unto him be glory in heaven and earth; for he *is* the mighty, the wise *God*.

---

(27) *Every nation.* "The original word, *ummat*, properly signifies a people who profess one and the same law or religion."—*Sale.* The followers of each of the great prophets constitute an *ummat.*

This day shall ye be rewarded, &c. See Prelim. Disc., pp. 144, 145.

CHAPTER XLVI.

ENTITLED SURAT AL AHQÁF (THE SANDHILLS).

Revealed at Makkah.

INTRODUCTION.

IN this chapter the dwelling-place of the Ádites is called al Ahqáf; hence the title. Sale says, "Al Ahqáf is the plural of *haqf*, and signifies *sands which lie in a crooked or winding manner*, whence it became the name of a territory in the province of Hadhramaut."

Rodwell locates the *sandhills* at Tayif. This is in accordance with Sprenger's theory of the Ádites, adopted by Muir in his *Life of Mahomet*, vol. i., Introd., p. cxxxviii. note.

The object of this chapter was to warn the people of Makkah of the impending judgments of God on account of their sin of rejecting Muhammad and the Qurán. They had charged their Prophet with being an impostor, who had forged a book which he called the Qurán. In this they were encouraged by certain Jews. On the other hand, certain other Jews, probably adherents from Madína, upheld the claims of Muhammad, declaring that the teaching of the Qurán was confirmatory of the doctrine of their own Scriptures. Thus encouraged, Muhammad answers the charges of his enemies by a solemn warning. He can now afford to be patient and calmly await the destruction of the unbelievers.

It is here specially noteworthy how Muhammad likens himself to the former prophets (vers. 20-31), putting his own message to the Quraish, with their taunting reply, into the mouths of Húd and the Ádites, yea, even into the mouths of the believing genii. But on this point see introduction to chapter xi.

Probable Date of the Revelations.

Ver. 9 of this chapter is supposed by some to be Madínic, because of the Jews being mentioned; but this reason is not valid, since the Jews mentioned here were no doubt Jews of Madína visiting

Makkah, with whom Muhammad was now in close correspondence, if indeed they were not his adherents. The "*witness*" surely does not refer to any particular person, as Baidháwi and others suppose, when referring it to Abdullah Ibn Salám.

On similarly weak grounds, vers. 14–17, and 34, 35, have been regarded as Madínic. We may therefore safely regard the whole chapter as Makkan. Vers. 30–31 were not, however, originally in this place (see notes), but they nevertheless belong to the same period.

As to the date of the revelations, we have the mention of the discourse of Muhammad to the genii, which occurred on his return from Tayif, just before the Hijra. This agrees with the allusion to the fate of the people of al Ahqáf, who inhabited the region about Tayif, and with the attitude of Muhammad (ver. 34) toward the unbelievers, and also with the mention made of the Jews of Madína, with whom Muhammad was now in correspondence. Noëldeke places this chapter immediately after chap. vii.

Principal Subjects.

	VERSES
The Qurán a revelation from God	1
Creation a witness for God against idolaters and idolatry	2–5
Muhammad charged with forging the Qurán	6, 7
Muhammad, like other apostles, only a warner	8
Believing Jews confirm the Qurán; unbelieving Jews call it an antiquated lie	9, 10
The Qurán confirms the Book of Moses	11
True believers, their happy condition	12, 13
Obedient sons and true believers, their life here and hereafter	14, 15
The conduct and fate of the disobedient son	16, 17
Rewards and punishments bestowed in accordance with works	18, 19
The fate of the people of al Ahqáf, &c., a warning to Makkah	20–27
The genii converted by hearing Muhammad recite the Qurán	28–31
God able to raise the dead; Muhammad exhorted to patience and forbearance	32–35

IN THE NAME OF THE MOST MERCIFUL GOD.

TWENTY-SIXTH SIPARA.

R ¼.

|| (1) H. M. The revelation of *this* book *is* from the mighty, the wise GOD. (2) We have not created the heavens and the earth, and whatever is between them, otherwise than in truth and for a determined period; but the unbelievers turn away from the warning which is given them. (3) Say, What think ye?· Show me what *part* of the earth *the idols* which ye invoke, besides GOD, have created? Or had they any share in the *creation of* the heavens? Bring me a book *of scripture revealed* before this, or some footstep of *ancient* knowledge, *to countenance your idolatrous practices;* if ye are men of veracity. (4) Who is in a wider error than he who invoketh, besides GOD, that which cannot return him an answer, to the day of resurrection; and *idols* which regard not their calling *on them;* (5) and which, when men shall be gathered together *to judgment,* will become their enemies, and will ungratefully deny their worship? (6) When our evident signs are rehearsed unto them, the unbelievers say of the truth, when it cometh unto them, This *is* a manifest piece of sorcery. (7) Will they say, *Muhammad* hath forged it? Answer, If I have forged it, verily ye shall not obtain for me any *favour* from GOD: he well knoweth the *injurious language* which ye utter concerning it: he is a sufficient witness between me and you; and he *is* gracious *and* merciful. (8) Say, I am not singular among the apostles;

---

(1) *H. M.* See Prelim. Disc., pp. 100-102.
This book. See note on chap. xi. 2.
(2) *In truth.* See notes on chaps. xxi. 16, 17, and xxxviii. 26.
A determined period. "Being to last for a certain space of time, and not for ever."—*Sale.*
(3) *The idols.* This should be *the gods* or *the angels.*
(4) *To the day, &c., i.e.,* until the day of the resurrection, when they will repudiate their worshippers.
(6) *The truth, i.e.,* the Qurán.
A manifest piece of sorcery. See chaps. iii. 48, x. 39, and xxi. 5.
(8) *I am not singular among the apostles.* "That is, I do not teach a doctrine different from what the former apostles and prophets

neither do I know what will be done with me or with you *hereafter:* I follow no other than what is revealed unto me; neither am I any more than a public warner. (9) Say, What is your opinion? If *this book* be from GOD, and ye believe not therein; and a witness of the children of Israel bear witness to its consonancy *with the law,* and believeth therein; and ye proudly reject *the same: are ye not unjust doers?* Verily GOD directeth not unjust people.

|| (10) But those who believe not say of the true be- R 2/2. lievers, If *the doctrine of the Qurán* had been good, they had not embraced the same before us. And when they are not guided thereby they say, This *is* an antiquated lie. (11) Whereas the Book of Moses *was revealed* before *the Qurán, to be* a guide and a mercy: and this *is* a book confirming

---

have taught, nor am I able to do what they could not, particularly to show the signs which every one shall think fit to demand."—*Sale, Baidhāwi.*

The meaning seems to me to be, that his being called a sorcerer and an impostor is not wonderful, inasmuch as other prophets were treated in like manner. See chap. xxi. 26–100.

A public warner. See notes on chaps. ii. 119, iii. 184, and vi. 109.

(9) *A witness.* "This witness is generally supposed to have been the Jew Abdullah Ibn Salám, who declared that Muhammad was the prophet foretold by Moses. Some, however, suppose the witness here meant to have been Moses himself."—*Sale, Baidhāwi, Jaláluddín.*

See notes on chaps. vi. 20 and x. 93. "Whether the 'witness' and other Jewish supporters of Mahomet were among his professed followers, slaves perhaps, at Mecca, or were casual visitors there from Israelitish tribes, or belonged to the Jewish residents of Medina (with the inhabitants of which city the Prophet was on the point of establishing friendly relations), we cannot do more than conjecture."—*Muir* in *Life of Mahomet,* vol. ii. p. 185.

(10) *If . . . the Qurán, &c.* "These words were spoken, as some think, by the Jews, when Abdullah professed Islám; or, according to others, by the Quraish, because the first followers of Muhammad were for the most part poor and mean people; or else by the tribes of Amar, Ghatfán, and Asad, on the conversion of those of Juhainah, Muzainah, Aslam, and Ghifár."—*Sale, Baidhāwi.*

An antiquated lie. See chaps. x. 39, and xxi. 5.

(11) *A book confirming, &c.* See notes and references at chap. ii. 40.

the same, delivered in the Arabic tongue; to denounce threats unto those who act unjustly, and to bear good tidings unto the righteous doers. (12) *As to* those who say, Our LORD *is* GOD; and who behave uprightly, on them *shall* no fear *come*, neither shall they be grieved. (13) These *shall be* the inhabitants of Paradise, they shall remain therein for ever: in recompense for that which they have wrought. (14) We have commanded man *to show* kindness to his parents: his mother beareth him *in her womb* with pain, and bringeth him forth with pain: and *the space of* his being carried *in her womb*, and *of* his weaning, *is* thirty months; until, when he attaineth his age of strength, and attaineth *the age of* forty years, he saith, O LORD, excite me, by thy inspiration, that I may be grateful for their favours, wherewith thou hast favoured me and my parents; and that I may work righteousness, which may please thee: and be gracious unto me in my issue; for I am turned unto thee, and am a Muslim. (15) These *are* they from whom we accept the good work which they have wrought, and whose evil *works* we pass by; *and they shall be* among the inhabitants of Paradise: this *is* a true promise, which they are promised *in this world.* (16) He who saith unto his parents, Fie on you! Do ye promise me that I shall be taken

---

Arabic tongue. See note on chap. xli. 2, 3.

(14) *Thirty months.* "At the least; for if the full time of suckling an infant be two years (chap. ii. 233), or twenty-four months, there remain but six months for the space of his being carried in the womb, which is the least that can be allowed."—*Sale, Baidháwi.*

Forty years, &c. "These words, it is said, were revealed on account of Abu Baqr, who professed Islám in the fortieth year of his age, two years after Muhammad's mission, and was the only person, either of the Muhájjirín or the Ansárs, whose father and mother were also converted; his son Abdurrahmán and his grandson Abu Atik likewise embracing the same faith."—*Sale, Baidháwi.*

Rodwell thinks this interpretation was invented by the Muslims after the accession of Abu Baqr to the khalífat.

(16) *Fie on you.* "The words seem to be general; but it is said they were revealed particularly on occasion of Abdurrahmán, the son

forth *from the grave, and restored to life;* when *many* generations have passed away before me, *and none of them have returned back?* And *his parents* implore GOD's assistance, *and say to their son,* Alas for thee! Believe! for the promise of GOD *is* true. But he answereth, This *is* no other than silly fables of the ancients. (17) These *are they* whom the sentence *passed* on the nations which have been before them, of genii and of men, justly fitteth; they shall surely perish. (18) For every one *is prepared* a certain degree *of happiness or misery,* according to that which they shall have wrought: that *God* may recompense them for their works: and they shall not be treated unjustly. (19) On a certain day the unbelievers shall be exposed before the fire *of hell; and it shall be said unto them,* Ye received your good things in your lifetime, *while ye were* in the world; and ye enjoyed yourselves therein: wherefore this day ye shall be rewarded with the punishment of ignominy; for that ye behaved insolently in the earth, without justice, and for that ye transgressed.

|| (20) Remember the brother of Ád, when he preached R $\frac{3}{3}$. unto his people in al Ahqáf (and there were preachers before him and after him), *saying,* Worship none but GOD: verily I fear for you the punishment of a great day. (21) They answered, Art thou come unto us that thou mayest turn us aside from *the worship of* our gods? Bring on us now *the punishment* with which thou threatenest us, if thou art a man of veracity. (22) He said, Verily the knowledge *of the time when your punishment will be inflicted* is with GOD; and I *only* declare unto you that which I am sent *to preach;* but I see ye are an ignorant people. (23) And when they saw *the preparation made for their*

---

of Abu Baqr, who used these expressions to his father and mother before he professed Islám."—*Sale, Baidháwi.*

Silly fables, &c. See chap. xxi. 5.

(17) *Shall surely perish.* "Unless they redeem their fault by repentance and embracing the true faith, as did Abdurrahmán."—*Sale.*

(20) *The brother of A'd, i.e.,* the prophet Húd. See chap. xi. 50.

punishment, namely, a cloud traversing *the sky, and* tending towards their valleys, they said, This *is* a traversing cloud, which bringeth us rain. *Húd answered,* Nay; it is what ye demanded to be hastened: a wind wherein *is* a severe vengeance: (24) it will destroy everything, at the command of its LORD. And in the morning nothing was to be seen besides their *empty* dwellings. Thus do we reward wicked people. (25) We had established them in the *like flourishing condition* wherein we have established you, *O men of Makkah;* and we had given them ears, and eyes, and hearts: yet neither their ears, nor their eyes, nor their hearts profited them at all, when they rejected the signs of GOD; but the *vengeance* which they mocked at fell upon them.

R $\frac{4}{4}$.

|| (26) We heretofore destroyed the cities which *were* round about you; and we variously proposed *our* signs unto them, that they might repent. (27) Did those protect them whom they took for gods, besides GOD, *and imagined to be* honoured with his familiarity? Nay; they withdrew from them: yet this *was* their false opinion *which seduced them,* and *the blasphemy* which they had devised. (28) *Remember* when we caused certain of the genii to turn aside unto thee, that they might hear the Qurán; and when they were present at *the reading of* the

---

(24) *It will destroy everything.* "Which came to pass accordingly; for this pestilential and violent wind killed all who believed not in the doctrine of Húd, without distinction of sex, age, or degree, and entirely destroyed their possessions."—*Sale.* See notes to chaps. vii. 66–73, and xi. 50 *seq.*

Observe how Húd is represented as speaking in the language of Muhammad. See Introd., chap. xi.

(26) *Cities . . . round about you.* "As the settlements of the Thamúdites, Midianites, and the cities of Sodom and Gomorrah, &c."—*Sale.*

(28) *Certain . . . genii.* "These genii, according to different opinions, were of Nisibín, or of Yaman, or of Nineveh; and in number nine or seven. They heard Muhammad reading the Qurán by night, or after the morning prayer, in the valley of al Nakhlah, during the time of his retreat to al Tayif, and believed on him."—*Sale, Baidháwi, Jaláluddín.* Comp. chap. lxxii. 1–19.

same, they said *to one another*, Give ear: and when it was ended, they returned back unto their people, preaching *what they had heard*. (29) They said, Our people, verily we have heard a book *read unto us*, which hath been revealed since Moses, confirming the *scripture* which *was delivered* before it, *and* directing unto the truth and the right way. (30) Our people, obey GOD's preacher; and believe in him; that he may forgive you your sins, and may deliver you from a painful punishment. (31) And whoever obeyeth not GOD's preacher shall by no means frustrate *God's vengeance* on earth; neither shall he have any protectors besides him. These *will be* in a manifest error. (32) Do they not know that GOD, who hath created the heavens and the earth, and was not fatigued with the creation thereof, *is* able to raise the dead to life? Yea, verily; for he *is* almighty. (33) On a certain day the unbelievers shall be exposed unto *hell*-fire; *and it shall be said unto them*, Is not this really *come to pass?* They shall answer, Yea, by our LORD. *God* shall reply, Taste, therefore, the punishment *of hell*, for that ye have been unbelievers. (34) Do thou, *O Prophet*, bear *the insults of thy people* with patience, as *our* apostles, who were endued with constancy, bear *the injuries of their people;* and require not *their punishment* to be hastened unto them. On the day whereon they shall see the *punishment* wherewith

---

(29) *Revealed since Moses*. " Hence the commentators suppose those genii, before their conversion to Muhammadanism, to have been of the Jewish religion."—*Sale*.

See this incident described in Muir's *Life of Mahomet*, vol. ii. pp. 203-205.

(31) *God's preacher, i.e.,* Muhammad. See note on chap. ii. 119. Noëldeke thinks vers. 20–31 misplaced here, as they break the connection between vers. 19 and 32.

(34) *Bear* . . . *with patience*. " But his biography is full of instances of Mohammed not bearing insults with patience, and having those who spoke against him killed. When at Mecca he is patient, being powerless; when at the head of an army at Medina, he kills those who oppose him with words only."—*Brinckman* in *Notes on Islám*. This is true; but the Muslim reply is that in both cases he acted in accordance with the command of God.

they have been threatened, (35) it shall seem as though they had tarried *in the world* but an hour of a day. *This is a fair* warning. Shall they perish except the people who transgress?

---

(35) *But an hour.* See chap. xxiii. 114.

CHAPTER XLVII.

ENTITLED SURAT MUHAMMAD.

Revealed at Madína.

INTRODUCTION.

THIS chapter is also entitled WAR, because of the command enjoining the Muslims to fight in the cause of religion, which is certainly a more appropriate title than that of *Muhammad*.

Every student of Islám has observed the wondrous change which came over Muhammad and his religion at the time of the flight to Madína. Nothing could illustrate this change better than a comparison between this chapter and the one just preceding it. In chap. xlvi. we have Muhammad the warner of Makkah. There Islám is peaceable. Its Prophet is exhorted to bear the insults of the unbelievers with patience. In this chapter we have Muhammad the general of armies. Here Islám is warlike. Muslims are now required to lay aside the emblems of peace and to draw the sword. They are now enjoined to "strike off the heads" of their enemies. All must be prepared not only to spend their substance in the cause, but to fight to the death.

As yet but petty expeditions were sent forth from Madína to harass the caravans of the Quraish. Yet even this required courage and self-denial. Some of the Muslims were timorous. The "hypocrites" of Madína, begrudging the cost of this warfare, and perhaps fearing the consequences of a war with Makkah, were busy dissuading the Muslims from carrying out the war policy of Muhammad. Both these parties are attacked in this chapter. Cowards and hypocrites are alike threatened with the horrors of hell; while rivers of pure water, rivers of milk, rivers of wine, rivers of clarified butter, and all kinds of fruits are set before the eyes of the faithful as the sure reward of those who fight valiantly the battles of the Lord.

Probable Date of the Revelations.

Some Muslim writers have regarded this chapter as Makkan, but the best authorities, Baidháwi, Zamakhshari, Jaláluddín as Syútí, &c., agree that it is Madínic. One writer, Umar bin Muhammad, Itqan 43, maintains that ver. 14 was revealed during the flight from Makkah, when Muhammad with tearful eyes looked back towards his birthplace.

Noëldeke fixes the date of this chapter at a period some time after the victory of Badr. The reason for this opinion is his interpretation of ver. 37, which, he thinks, alludes to the efforts of some of Muhammad's people to conclude peace with the Quraish after the success of the Muslims at Badr. This date is, however, too late to account for the fear of the Muslims rebuked in this chapter. After the victory of Badr the fears of the faithful were all dispelled, so that at the battle of Ohod we find Muhammad himself obliged to assume an offensive rather than a defensive policy, owing to the impetuosity of his followers. It is better to follow Muir here, and to place the date of this chapter before the battle of Badr, say the latter part of A.H. I. See Muir's *Life of Mahomet*, vol. iii. pp. 79–81.

Principal Subjects.

	VERSES
The works of those who oppose Islám shall come to naught .	1
True believers shall receive the expiation of their sins . .	2, 3
How enemies of Islám are to be treated in war . . .	4, 5
God will reward those who fight for Islám	6–8
God will utterly destroy the unbelievers	9–12
The final condition of believers and infidels contrasted .	13–17
Hypocrites reproved and warned	18–20
Muhammad commanded to ask pardon for his sins . .	21
Cowardly Muslims and hypocrites rebuked and warned .	22–33
Those who would dissuade Muslims from their duty warned	34–36
Muslims exhorted to boldness in warring for their faith .	37
Muslims exhorted to liberality in contributing towards the expenses of holy war	38–40

IN THE NAME OF THE MOST MERCIFUL GOD.

R ⅛. ‖ (1) *God* will render of none effect the works of those who believe not, and *who* turn away *men* from the way of GOD; (2) but as to those who believe, and work righteousness, and believe *the revelation* which has been sent down unto Muhammad (for it is the truth from their LORD), he will expiate their evil deeds from them, and will dispose their heart aright.

‖ (3) This *will he do,* because those who believe not follow vanity, and because those who believe follow the truth from the LORD. Thus GOD propoundeth unto men their examples. (4) When ye encounter the unbelievers, strike off *their* heads, until ye have made a great slaughter among them; and bind *them* in bonds; (5) and either *give them* a free dismission afterwards, or *exact* a ransom; until the war shall have laid down its arms. This *shall ye do.* Verily if God pleased he could take vengeance on them *without your assistance;* but *he commandeth you to fight his battles,* that he may prove the one of you by the other. And *as to* those who fight in defence of God's true religion, *God* will not suffer their works to perish; (6) he will guide them, and will dispose their heart aright; (7) and he will lead them into Paradise, of which he hath told them. (8) O true believers, if ye assist GOD *by fighting for his religion,* he will assist you *against your enemies;*

RUBA.

---

(2) *Will expiate.* See note on chap. iii. 194.

(4) *Unbelievers, i.e.,* the Makkan and other enemies of Islám.

Strike off their heads, &c. "This law the Hanifites judge to be abrogated, or to relate particularly to the war of Badr, for the severity here commanded, which was necessary in the beginning of Muhammadism, they think too rigorous to be put in practice in its flourishing state. But the Persians and some others hold the command to be still in full force; for, according to them, all the men of full age who are taken in battle are to be slain, unless they embrace the Muhammadan faith; and those who fall into the hands of the Muslims after the battle are not to be slain, but may either be set at liberty gratis or on payment of a certain ransom, or may be exchanged for Muhammadan prisoners, or condemned to slavery, at the pleasure of the Imám or prince."—*Sale, Baidháwi.*

See notes on chap. viii. 40, 59, 68.

(5) *Those who fight, &c.* "Some copies, instead of *qátilu,* read *qûtilu,* according to which latter reading it should be rendered, 'who are slain' or 'suffer martyrdom,' &c."—*Sale.*

The text is correct. The object of the exhortation is to encourage the faithful to fight for their religion. The promise is not only to the martyrs, but to all who fight for Islám.

and will set your feet fast: (9) but *as for* the infidels, let them perish; and their works shall *God* render vain. (10) This *shall befall them,* because they have rejected with abhorrence that which GOD hath revealed: wherefore their works shall become of no avail. (11) Do they not travel through the earth, and see what hath been the end of those who *were* before them? GOD utterly destroyed them: and the like *catastrophe* awaiteth the unbelievers. (12) This *shall come to pass,* for that GOD is the patron of the true believers, and for that the infidels have no protector.

R 2/6. ‖ (13) Verily GOD will introduce those who believe and do good works into gardens beneath which rivers flow: but the unbelievers indulge themselves in pleasures, and eat as beasts eat; and their abode *shall be hell*-fire. (14) How many cities were more mighty in strength than thy city which hath expelled thee; *yet* have we destroyed them, and *there was* none to help them? (15) Shall he therefore, who followeth the plain declaration of his LORD *be* as he whose evil works have been dressed up for him *by the devil,* and who follow their own lusts? (16) The description of Paradise, which is promised unto the pious: therein *are* rivers of incorruptible water; and rivers of milk, the taste whereof changeth not; and rivers of wine, pleasant unto those who drink; (17) and rivers of clarified honey: and therein shall they have *plenty* of all *kinds* of fruits; and pardon from their LORD. *Shall the man for whom these things are prepared be* as he who must dwell for ever in *hell*-fire; and will have the boiling water given

---

(13) See note on chap. iii. 15.
(14) *Which hath expelled thee.* Muhammad here predicts the destruction of Makkah and its idolatrous inhabitants. There should be "none to help them." The leniency which afterward led him to spare the city and its people was dictated by circumstances which made forbearance more politic than the fulfilment of his own prophecy. See Muir's *Life of Mahomet,* vol. iv. pp. 120–122 note.
(16) *Rivers of wine.* The word here translated *wine* is *khamr,* which all Muslims admit to be the word used specially to indicate intoxicating drinks. See notes on chaps. ii. 218, iv. 42, and v. 92.

him to drink which shall burst their bowels? (18) Of the *unbelievers there are* some who give ear unto thee, until, when they go out from thee, they say, *by way of derision* unto those to whom knowledge hath been given, What hath he said now? These *are they* whose hearts GOD hath sealed up, and who follow their own lusts; (19) but *as to* those who are directed, *God* will grant them a more ample direction, and he will instruct them what to avoid. (20) Do *the infidels* wait for any other than the *last* hour, that it may come upon them suddenly? Some signs thereof are already come; and when it shall actually overtake them, how can they *then* receive admonition? (21) Know therefore that there is no god but GOD; and ask pardon for thy sin, and for the true believers, both men and women. GOD knoweth your busy employment *in the world*, and the place of your abode *hereafter*.

|| (22) The true believers say, Hath not a Sura been revealed *commanding war against the infidels?* But when a Sura without any ambiguity is revealed, and war is mentioned therein, thou mayest see those in whose hearts is an infirmity look towards thee with the look of one whom death overshadoweth. But obedience *would be*

R $\frac{3}{7}$.

---

(18) *Those to whom knowledge hath been given, i.e.,* "the more learned of Muhammad's companions, such as Ibn Masúd and Ibn Abbás."—*Sale, Jaláluddín.*

(19) *He will instruct them, &c.* "These words may also be translated, He will reward them for their piety."—*Sale.*

(20) *Some signs, &c.* "As the mission of Muhammad, the splitting of the moon, and the smoke mentioned in the 44th chapter."—*Sale.*

(21) *Ask pardon for thy sin, &c.* "Though Muhammad here and elsewhere acknowledges himself to be a sinner, yet several Muhammadan doctors pretend he was wholly free from sin, and suppose he is here commanded to ask forgiveness, not that he wanted it, but that he might set an example to his followers: wherefore he used to say of himself, if the tradition be true, ' I ask pardon of God an hundred times a day.' "—*Sale.*

See notes on chaps. iv. 105, ix. 43, xl. 57, xlviii. 1–3, lxvi. 1, &c.

(22) These words were uttered previous to the battle of Badr, when as yet there were many timorous ones among the faithful. See Muir's *Life of Mahomet*, vol. iii. p. 79.

more eligible for them, and to speak that which is convenient. (23) And when the command is firmly established, if they give credit unto GOD, it will be better for them. (24) Were ye ready, therefore, if ye had been put in authority, to commit outrages in the earth and to violate the ties of blood? (25) These *are they* whom GOD hath cursed and hath rendered deaf, and whose eyes he hath blinded. (26) Do they not therefore attentively meditate on the Qurán? Are there locks upon their hearts? (27) Verily they who turn their backs, after the *true* direction is made manifest unto them, Satan shall prepare *their wickedness* for them, and *God* shall bear with them for a time. (28) This *shall befall them*, because they say *privately* unto those who detest what GOD hath revealed, We will obey you in part of the matter. But GOD knoweth their secrets. (29) How therefore *will* it *be with them* when the angels shall cause them to die, *and* shall strike their faces and their backs? (30) This *shall they suffer*, because they follow that which provoketh GOD to wrath, and are averse to what is well-pleasing unto him: and he will render their works vain.

R $\frac{4}{8}$. ‖ (31) Do they in whose hearts is an infirmity imagine that God will not bring their malice to light? (32) If we pleased, we could surely show them unto thee, and thou shouldest know them by their marks; but thou shalt certainly know them by *their* perverse pronunciation of *their* words. GOD knoweth your actions; (33) and we will try

---

(23) This verse contains an implied threat against the timorous and hypocritical followers of Muhammad, referred to in ver. 22.

(24) *If ye had been put in authority.* "Or, as the words may also be translated, 'If ye had turned back,' and apostatised from your faith."—*Sale.*

(28) *Obey in part, i.e.,* "Obey in part of what ye desire of us, by staying at home and not going forth with Muhammad to war, and by private combination against him."—*Sale.*

(31) *In whose hearts is an infirmity,* "as hypocrisy, cowardice, or instability in their religion."—*Sale.*

(32) *Perverse pronunciation of words.* Either by playing upon the words of the Qurán to pervert its meaning (see chaps. ii. 57, 58, and vii. 163), or the uttering of vain excuses to escape from the duty of

you, until we know those among you who fight valiantly, and who persevere with constancy: and we will try the reports of your behaviour. (34) Verily those who believe not, and turn away *men* from the way of GOD, and make opposition against the Apostle, after the *divine* direction hath been manifested unto them, shall not hurt GOD at all; but he shall make their works to perish. (35) O true believers, obey GOD; and obey the apostle: and render not your works of no effect. (36) Verily those who believe not, and who turn away *men* from the way of GOD, and then die, being unbelievers, GOD will by no means forgive. (37) Faint not, therefore, neither invite *your enemies* to peace, while ye *are* the superior: for GOD *is* with you, and will not defraud you of *the merit of* your works. (38) Verily this present life *is* only a play and a vain amusement; but if ye believe, and fear *God*, he will give you your rewards. He doth not require of you your *whole* substance; (39) if he should require the whole of you, and earnestly press you, ye would become niggardly, and it would raise your hatred *against his Apostle*. (40) Behold, ye *are* those who are invited to expend *part of your substance* for the support of GOD's true religion; and *there are* some of you who are niggardly. But whoever shall be niggardly shall be niggardly towards his own soul; for GOD wanteth nothing, but ye *are* needy: and if ye turn back, he will substitute *another* people in your stead, who shall not be like unto you.

---

fighting for their religion; the meaning in this case being *perverse speeches* calculated to discourage others. See ver. 34.

(40) *He will substitute people . . . not like you, i.e.*, "In backwardness and aversion to the propagation of the faith. The people here designed to be put in the place of these lukewarm Muslims are generally supposed to be the Persians, there being a tradition that Muhammad, being asked what people they were, at a time when Salmán was sitting by him, clapped his hand on his thigh and said, 'This man and his nation.' Others, however, are of opinion the Ansárs or the angels are intended in this place."—*Sale, Baidháwi.*

CHAPTER XLVIII.

ENTITLED SURAT AL FATAH (VICTORY).

Revealed at Madína.

INTRODUCTION.

THIS chapter takes its name from the statement in the first verse. A similar statement in ver. 27 would give the same title.

This chapter is composed of two parts, written at different times. I am not certain as to the precise point of division, whether at the beginning of ver. 20 or of ver. 25: on the whole, I prefer the former. According to this plan, the first portion of the chapter consists of vers. 1–19, which relates to the victory of the Muslims over the Jews at Khaibar, and to the expedition previously made to Makkah, which ended in the truce of Hudaibiyah. This truce, though a deep humiliation to the Muslims at the time, turned out to be a master-stroke of policy, and might therefore be termed a victory.

The second portion of this chapter, consisting of vers. 20–29, was added on here, perhaps, by the compilers of the Qurán, because it related also to a victory—*the* victory of the Muslims over the sacred city of Makkah. The reasons for this division will appear from a perusal of the notes. The chapter as a whole is well named. Arabia was not yet conquered, but the final victory of the Muslims was now so well assured as to require no prophetic vision to foretell it.

Probable Date of the Revelations.

Nöldeke assigns vers. 1–17 to a period immediately after the expedition to Hudaibiyah, in the month of Zul Q'ada, A.H. 6. The remainder of the chapter he places after the victory of the Muslims over the Jews of Khaibar, in the early part of A.H. 7.

I am unable to follow Nöldeke here, for reasons expressed in the notes on the chapter. I would assign vers. 1–19 to a period immediately following the victory at Khaibar, A.H. 7, a victory which restored the prestige of the Muslims, lost in a measure at Hudaibiyah, and at the same time afforded an opportunity to punish the Bedouin Arabs for their previous disloyalty. Vers. 20-29 I would assign to a period immediately following the conquest of Makkah, but preceding the battle of Hunain, A.H. 8.

Principal Subjects.

	VERSES
The victory (at Khaibar) the earnest of the pardon of the sins of the Prophet	1-3
The mighty God the comforter of true believers, but the punisher of hypocrites	4-7
Loyalty to Muhammad is loyalty to God	8-10
Bedouin Arabs denounced for their treachery at Hudaibiyah and their subsequent hypocrisy	11-14
The Bedouin Arabs refused a share of the booty taken at Khaibar, but encouraged with promises	15, 16
Those alone excused from going to war who are incapacitated	17
Muslim fidelity at Hudaibiyah rewarded by the victory at Khaibar and much spoil taken there	18, 19
Many spoils assured to the believers though God had prevented the plunder of Makkah	20-24
God spared Makkah in the expedition to Hudaibiyah out of compassion	25, 26
The conquest of Makkah the divine attestation to Muhammad's apostleship and the religion of Islám	27-29

IN THE NAME OF THE MOST MERCIFUL GOD.

‖ (1) Verily we have granted thee a manifest victory, R $\frac{1}{9}$ (2) that GOD may forgive thee thy preceding and thy

---

(1) *A manifest victory.* "This victory, according to most received interpretation, was the taking of the city of Makkah. The passage is said to have been revealed on Muhammad's return from the expedition of al Hudaibiyah, and contains a promise or prediction of this signal success, which happened not till two years after; the preterite tense being therein used, according to the prophetic style, for the future.

"There are some, notwithstanding, who suppose the advantage here intended was the pacification of al Hudaibiyah, which is here called a *victory*, because the Makkans sued for peace and made a truce with Muhammad, their breaking of which occasioned the taking of Makkah. Others think the conquest of Khaibar, or the

subsequent sin, and may complete his favour on thee, and direct thee in the right way; (3) and that GOD may assist thee with a glorious assistance. (4) It is he who sendeth down secure tranquillity into the hearts of the true believers, that they may increase in faith beyond their *former* faith; (the hosts of heaven and earth are GOD'S; and GOD is knowing *and* wise): (5) that he may lead the true believers of both sexes into gardens beneath which rivers flow, to dwell therein for ever; and may expiate their evil deeds from them: (this will be great felicity with GOD:) (6) and that he may punish the hypocritical men, and the hypocritical women, and the idolaters, and the idolatresses, who conceive an ill opinion of GOD. They shall experience a turn of evil fortune; and GOD shall be angry with them, and shall curse them, and hath prepared hell for them: an ill journey shall it be *thither!*

NISF. ‖ (7) Unto GOD *belong* the hosts of heaven and earth;

---

victory over the Greeks at Muta, &c., to be meant in this place."—*Sale, Baidháwi, Zamakhshari.*

There is not the slightest reason for believing that Muhammad intended to foretell any future event. The preponderance of Muslim authority favours the reference to a past event. See also Muir's *Life of Mahomet,* vol. iv. pp. 36, 37, and note there. The conquest of Khaibar, which occurred soon after the treaty of Hudaibiyah, is probably intended here.

(2) *That God may forgive thee.* "That is to say, that God may give thee an opportunity of deserving forgiveness by eradicating of idolatry, and exalting his true religion, and the delivering of the weak from the hands of the ungodly, &c."—*Sale.*

Thy preceding and thy subsequent sin, i.e., "whatever thou hast done worthy of reprehension, or thy sins committed as well in the time of ignorance as since. Some expound the words more particularly, and say the *preceding* or *former* fault was his lying with his handmaid Mary (chap. lxvi. notes), contrary to his oath; and the *latter* his marrying of Zainab, the wife of Zaid, his adopted son (chap. xxxiii. notes)."—*Sale, Zamakhshari.*

Nothing could more clearly disprove the Muslim pretension that the prophets were sinless. See notes on chaps. iv. 105, ix. 43, xl. 57, and xlvii. 21.

It is hardly possible that the allusion here should be to the affairs of Zainab and Mary, for in these he professed to have the sanction of Divinity.

(5) *Expiate their evil deeds.* See note on chap. iii. 194.

and GOD is mighty *and* wise. (8) Verily we have sent thee *to be* a witness, and a bearer of good tidings, and a denouncer of threats; (9) that ye may believe in GOD and his Apostle; and may assist him, and revere him, and praise him morning and evening. (10) Verily they who swear fealty unto thee, swear fealty unto GOD: the hand of GOD *is* over their hands. Whoever shall violate *his oath* will violate *the same* to the hurt only of his own soul: but whoever shall perform that which he hath covenanted with GOD, he will surely give him a great reward.

‖ (11) The Arabs of the desert who were left behind will say unto thee, Our substance and our families employed us, *so that we went not forth with thee to war;* wherefore, ask pardon for us. They speak that with their tongues which *is* not in their hearts. Answer, Who shall be able *to obtain* for you anything from GOD *to the contrary,* if he is pleased to afflict you, or is pleased to be gracious unto you? Yea, verily, GOD is well acquainted with that which ye do. (12) Truly ye imagined that the Apostle and the true believers would never return to their families: and this was prepared in your hearts: but ye imagined an evil imagination; and ye are a corrupt people. (13) Whoso believeth not in GOD and his Apostle, verily we have prepared burning fire for the unbelievers.

R $\frac{2}{10}$.

---

(10) *Who swear fealty, &c.* "The original word signifies publicly to acknowledge or inaugurate a prince by swearing fidelity and obedience to him."—*Sale.*

The hand . . . over their hands. "That is, he beholdeth from above, that is, witness to the solemnity of your giving your faith to his Apostle, and will reward you for it. The expression alludes to the manner of their plighting their faith on these occasions."—*Sale, Jalâluddin.*

(11) *The Arabs of the desert, &c.* "These were the tribes of Aslam, Juhainah, Muzainah, and Ghifár, who, being summoned to attend Muhammad in the expedition of al Hudaibiyah, stayed behind, and excused themselves by saying their families must suffer in their absence, and would be robbed of the little they had (for these tribes were of the poorer Arabs); whereas in reality they wanted firmness in the faith and courage to face the Quraish."—*Sale, Baidhâwi.*

(14) Unto GOD *belongeth* the kingdom of heaven and earth: he forgiveth whom he pleaseth, and he punisheth whom he pleaseth: and GOD is inclined to forgive, *and* merciful. (15) Those who were left behind will say, When ye go forth to take the spoil, Suffer us to follow you. They seek to change the word of GOD. Say, Ye shall by no means follow us: thus hath GOD said heretofore. They will reply, Nay: ye envy us *a share of the booty.* But they are men of small understanding. (16) Say unto the Arabs of the desert who were left behind, Ye shall be called forth against a mighty *and* a warlike nation; ye shall fight against them, or they shall profess Islám. If ye obey, GOD will give you a glorious reward: but if ye turn back, as ye turned back heretofore, he will chastise you with a grievous chastisement. (17) It shall be no crime in the blind, neither shall it be a crime in the

---

(15) *Those . . . left behind,* viz., "in the expedition of Khaibar. The Prophet returned from al Hudaibiyah in Dhu'l Hajja, in the sixth year of the Hijra, and stayed at Madina the remainder of that month and the beginning of Muharram, and then set forward against the Jews of Khaibar with those only who had attended him to Hudaibiyah; and having made himself master of the place, and all the castles and strongholds in that territory, took spoils to a great value, which he divided among those who were present at that expedition, and none else."—*Sale, Baidháwi.*

Note that all these military orders, these arrangements for the campaign against the enemies of Islám, are here set forth as matters of Divine revelation. Not only is fealty to Muhammad now become fealty to God (ver. 10), but it would appear that the very thoughts of Muhammad have become to him as the thoughts of God.

They seek to change the word of God. "Which was his promise to those who attended the Prophet to al Hudaibiyah, that he would make them amends for their missing of the plunder of Makkah at that time by giving them that of Khaibar in lieu thereof. Some think the *word* here intended to be that passage in the ninth chapter (ver. 84), *Ye shall not go forth with me for the future,* &c., which yet was plainly revealed long after the taking of Khaibar, on occasion of the expedition of Tabúq."

(16) *A warlike nation.* "These were Banu Hunífa, who inhabited al Yamáma, and were the followers of Musailama, Muhammad's competitor; or any other of those tribes which apostatised from Muhammadanism; or, as others rather suppose, the Persians or the Greeks."—*Sale, Jaláluddín.*

lame, neither shall it be a crime in the sick, *if they go not forth to war:* and those who shall obey GOD and his Apostle, he shall lead them into gardens beneath which rivers flow; but whoso shall turn back, he will chastise him with a grievous chastisement.

|| (18) Now GOD was well pleased with the true believers when they sware fidelity to thee under the tree; and he knew that which *was* in their hearts; wherefore he sent down on them tranquillity of mind, and rewarded them with a speedy victory, (19) and many spoils which they took: for GOD is mighty *and* wise. (20) GOD promised you many spoils which ye should take; but he

R $\frac{3}{11}$.

---

(18) *When they sware fidelity, &c.* "Muhammad, when at al Hudaibiyah, sent Jawwás Ibn Umaiya the Khudháïte to acquaint the Makkans that he was come with a peaceable intention to visit the temple; but they, on some jealousy conceived, refusing to admit him, the Prophet sent Othmán Ibn Affán, whom they imprisoned, and a report ran that he was slain: whereupon Muhammad called his men about him, and they took an oath to be faithful to him, even to death; during which ceremony he sat under a tree, supposed by some to have been an Egyptian thorn, and by others a kind of lote-tree."—*Sale, Baidháwi.*

Tranquillity. The original word is *Sakínat,* and is found also in ver. 4. See note on chap. ii. 248.

A speedy victory. Sale says, "The success at Khaibar, or, as some others rather imagine, the taking of Makkah, &c."

Muhammad regarded the treaty at Hudaibiyah as "a manifest victory" (ver. 1), as indeed it was when viewed in the light of the interests of Islám. It was mainly on account of this treaty that the victory at Khaibar became possible, and to the same cause was due the alliance between Muhammad and the Bani Khudháah. See Muir's *Life of Mahomet,* vol. iv. p. 41.

(20) *God promised you many spoils, &c.* "These words, which point to the rule (chap. viii. and notes there) that all the spoils, save the Prophet's fifth, should be distributed among the Muslims, are a sufficient refutation of the statement made by Mr. Bosworth Smith (*Muhammad and Muhammadanism,* p. 231), that "in his capacity even of temporal ruler, Muhammad rarely gave material rewards to his followers." The fact is, that at this stage, and ever afterwards, the chief attraction of Islám was the hope of conquest and rich booty.

As we have seen, the punishment of the treacherous "Arabs of the desert" was that they were forbidden a share in the booty of Khaibar (ver. 15). Yet these very same people are encouraged to remain faithful to Islám by the assurance that they should partake in the "glorious reward" of future conquest (ver. 16).

gave you these by way of earnest; and he restrained the hands of men from you: that the same may be a sign unto the true believers; and that he may guide you into the right way. (21) And *he also promiseth you* other *spoils,* which ye have not *yet* been able *to take:* but now hath GOD encompassed them *for you;* and GOD is almighty. (22) If the unbelieving *Makkans* had fought against you, verily they had turned *their* backs; and they would not have found a patron or protector: (23) *according to* the ordinance of GOD, which hath been put in execution heretofore *against opposers of the prophets;* for thou shalt not find any change in the ordinance of GOD. (24) *It was* he who restrained their hands from you, and your hands from them, in the valley of Makkah; after that he had given you the victory over them: and GOD saw that

---

He restrained the hands of men from you, i.e., "the hands of those of Khaibar, or of their successors of the tribes of Asad and Ghatfán, or of the inhabitants of Makkah, by the pacification of al Hudaibiyah."
—*Sale, Baidháwi.*

(22) Rodwell translates, *If the infidels shall fight against you, they shall assuredly turn their backs.* The Hindustání and Persian translations agree with Sale.

(24) *He restrained, &c.* Jaláluddín says that fourscore of the infidels came privately to Muhammad's camp at al Hudaibiyah, with an intent to surprise some of his men, but were taken and brought before the Prophet, who pardoned them and ordered them to be set at liberty; and this generous action was the occasion of the truce struck up by the Quraish with Muhammad; for thereupon they sent Suhail Ibn Amrú and some others (and not Arwá Ibn Masúd, as is said by mistake in another place (Prelim. Disc., p. 89), for his errand was an actual defiance) to treat of peace.

Baidháwi explains the passage by another story, telling us that Akrima Ibn Abi Jahl marching from Makkah at the head of five hundred men to al Hudaibiyah, Muhammad sent against him Khálid Ibn al Walid with a detachment, who drove the infidels back to the innermost part of Makkah (as the word here translated *valley* properly signifies), and then left them, out of respect to the place."—*Sale.*

This story of Baidháwi could only apply on the hypothesis that the passage alludes to the clemency of Muhammad at the capture of Makkah. I confess that what follows in the text would well describe the feelings of Muhammad at that time. The allusion to secret followers of Islám in ver. 25, points to that event rather than to the affair at Hudaibiyah.

which ye did. (25) These *are they* who believed not, and hindered you from *visiting* the holy temple, and *also hindered* the offering being detained, that it should not arrive at the place where it ought to be sacrificed. Had it not been that ye might have trampled on *divers* true believers, *both* men and women, whom ye know not, *being promiscuously assembled with the infidels*, and that a crime might therefore have lighted on you on their account, without *your* knowledge, *he had not restrained your hands from them: but this was done* that GOD might lead whom he pleased into his mercy. If they had been distinguished from one another, we had surely chastised such of them as believed not with a severe chastisement. (26) When the unbelievers had put in their hearts an affected preciseness, the preciseness of ignorance, and GOD sent down his

---

(25) *The place where, &c.* "Muhammad's intent, in the expedition of al Hudaibiyah, being only to visit the temple of Makkah in a peaceable manner, and to offer a sacrifice in the valley of Mina, according to the established rites, he carried beasts with him for that purpose; but was not permitted by the Quraish either to enter the temple or to go to Mina."—*Sale.*

We had surely chastised, &c. It seems to me best to refer these words to a time subsequent to the conquest of Makkah. They explain the ground of Muhammad's leniency towards those who had so frequently been threatened with destruction. If, however, they be referred to the treaty of Hudaibiyah, they would express an idle boast on the part of those who at the time felt their lives to be in jeopardy. See note on vers. 18. It is probable that a subsequent revelation referring to the victory at Makkah has been added on here by the compilers of the Qurán.

(26) *God sent down his tranquillity, &c.* "This passage was occasioned by the stiffness of Suhail and his companions in wording the treaty concluded with Muhammad; for when the Prophet ordered Ali to begin with the form, *In the name of the most merciful God*, they objected to it, and insisted that he should begin with this, *In thy name, O God;* which Muhammad submitted to, and proceeded to dictate, *These are the conditions on which Muhammad, the Apostle of God, has made peace with those of Makkah;* to this Suhail again objected, saying, 'If we had acknowledged thee to be the Apostle of God, we had not given thee any opposition:' whereupon Muhammad ordered Ali to write, as Suhail desired, *These are the conditions which Muhammad, the son of Abdallah,* &c. But the Muslims were so disgusted thereat, that they were on the point of breaking off the

tranquillity on his Apostle and on the true believers; and firmly fixed in them the word of piety, and they were the most worthy of the same, and the most deserving thereof: for GOD knoweth all things.

R ${}_{12}^{4}$ ‖ (27) Now hath GOD in truth verified unto his Apostle the vision *wherein he said*, Ye shall surely enter the holy temple *of Makkah*, if GOD please, in full security; having your heads shaved and your hair cut: ye shall not fear: for *God* knoweth that which ye know not; and he hath appointed *you*, besides this, a speedy victory. (28) *It is* he who hath sent his Apostle with the direction, and the religion of truth; that he may exalt the same above

---

treaty, and had fallen on the Makkans, had not God appeased and calmed their minds; as it follows in the text.

"The terms of this pacification were, that there should be a truce for ten years; that any person might enter into league, either with Muhammad or with the Quraish, as he should think fit; and that Muhammad should have the liberty to visit the temple of Makkah the next year for three days."—*Sale, Baidhāwi.*

Fixed in them the word of piety, i.e., "the Muhammadan profession of faith, or the *Bismillah*, and the words, *Muhammad, the Apostle of God*, which were rejected by the infidels."—*Sale.*

(27) *The vision.* "Or dream which Muhammad had at Madīna, before he set out for al Hudaibiyah, wherein he dreamed that he and his companions entered Makkah in security, with their heads shaven and their hair cut. This dream, being imparted by the Prophet to his followers, occasioned a great deal of joy among them; and they supposed it would be fulfilled that same year: but when they saw the truce concluded, which frustrated their expectation for that time, they were deeply concerned; whereupon this passage was revealed for their consolation, confirming the vision, which was not to be fulfilled till the year after, when Muhammad performed the visitation, distinguished by the addition of *al Qadá*, or *completion*, because he then *completed* the visitation of the former year, when the Quraish not permitting him to enter Makkah, he was obliged to kill his victims, and to shave himself at al Hudaibiyah."—*Sale.*

The positive way in which this dream is here declared to be fulfilled confirms what we have already said as to the date of this portion of this chapter; see above in vers. 24, 25.

Hair cut, i.e., "some being shaved, and others having only their hair cut."—*Sale.*

A speedy victory, viz., "the taking of Khaibar."—*Sale.* I should say the conquest of Makkah and the establishment of Islám instead of the national religion.

(28) *Exalt the same above every religion.* Islám, being the only true religion, the religion of all the prophets, is now to be exalted,

every religion: and GOD is a sufficient witness *hereof*. (29) Muhammad *is* the Apostle of GOD: and those who are with him *are* fierce against the unbelievers, *but* compassionate towards one another. Thou mayest see them bowing down, prostrate, seeking a recompense from GOD, and *his* good-will. Their signs *are* in their faces, being marks of *frequent* prostration. This *is* their description in the Pentateuch, and their description in the Gospel: they - are as seed which putteth forth its stalk and strengtheneth it, and swelleth in the ear, and riseth upon its stem; giving delight unto the sower. *Such are the Muslims described to be:* that the infidels may swell with indignation at them. GOD hath promised unto such of them as believe and do good works pardon and a great reward.

---

through the instrumentality of Muhammad, above every other religion. Makkah having now fallen, he considers his religion as triumphant in Arabia, and may be in the world.

(29) *Muhammad is the Apostle of God.* The speaker being God, this form is peculiar, if Muhammad be the person addressed. unless, indeed, we regard these words as the *witness-bearing* of God. The passage would then read, "God is a sufficient witness *hereof; for he declareth that* Muhammad is the Apostle of God," &c.

The Pentateuch . . . the Gospel. Both books are spoken of as in existence in Muhammad's time.

They are seed, &c. Compare Mark iv. 28.

Such . . . as believe . . . and do good, &c. See note on chap. iii. 31.

CHAPTER XLIX.

ENTITLED SURAT AL HUJRÁT (THE INNER APARTMENTS).

Revealed at Madína.

INTRODUCTION.

THIS chapter receives its title from words contained in the fourth verse. It might have appropriately been styled the *Chapter of Rebuke*, inasmuch as it is made up of a variety of passages reprehending the Muslims for various offences. The faults for which the Muslims are rebuked are, too great familiarity in addressing the Prophet, rude calling to the Prophet when in retirement, false accusation, quarrelling among themselves, scornful laughing and taunting, evil speaking and use of opprobrious names, unjust suspicions, meddling, backbiting, and hypocrisy. The circumstances under which, and the parties for whose special instruction, these exhortations were originally uttered are described in the notes.

Probable Date of the Revelations.

All authorities agree that this chapter is Madínic. Vers. 1-5, referring to the envoys of the Bani Tamím, were revealed in A.H. 9 or 10. Vers. 6-8 must be referred to about the same period. Vers. 9-13 probably refer to the Quraish, and were enunciated soon after the occupation of the sacred city in A.H. 8. The remaining verses may be referred to about the year A.H. 9.

Principal Subjects.

	VERSES
The Prophet of God to be treated with honour and respect	1-5
Believers warned against misrepresenting any matter to the Prophet	6-8
The duty of peacemaking enjoined	9-11
Sundry faults of the Muslims exposed	11-13
Bedouin Arabs rebuked and warned on account of hypocrisy	14-18

IN THE NAME OF THE MOST MERCIFUL GOD.

|| (1) O true believers, anticipate not *any matter* in the R $\frac{1}{13}$. sight of GOD and his Apostle: and fear GOD; for GOD *both* heareth *and* knoweth. (2) O true believers, raise not your voices above the voice of the Prophet; neither speak loud unto him in discourse, as ye speak loud unto one another, lest your works become vain, and ye perceive *it* not. (3) Verily they who lower their voices in the presence of the Apostle of GOD *are* those whose hearts GOD hath disposed unto piety: they shall obtain pardon and a great reward. (4) *As to* those who call unto thee from without the inner apartments, the greater part of them do not understand *the respect due to thee*. (5) If they wait with patience until thou come forth unto them, it will certainly be better for them: but GOD *is* inclined to forgive, *and* merciful. (6) O true believers, if a wicked man come unto you with a tale, inquire strictly *into the truth thereof;* lest ye hurt people through ignorance, and afterwards repent of what

---

(1) *Anticipate not, &c.* "That is, do not presume to give your own decision in any case, before ye have received the judgment of God and his Apostle."—*Sale.*

(2) *Raise not your voices, &c.* "This verse is said to have been occasioned by a dispute between Abu Baqr and Omar concerning the appointment of a governor of a certain place, in which they raised their voices so high, in presence of the Apostle, that it was thought proper to forbid such indecencies for the future."—*Sale, Baidháwi, Jaláluddín.*

Others make the occasion to have been the rude and boisterous address of a representative of the Bani Tamím. See Rodwell *in loco*, and Muir's *Life of Mahomet*, vol. iv. pp. 173-175.

(4) *Those who call . . . without the inner apartments.* "These, they say, were Uyayna Ibn Husain and al Akrá Ibn Hábís, who, wanting to speak with Muhammad when he was sleeping at noon in his women's apartment, had the rudeness to call out several times, 'Muhammad, come forth to us.'"—*Sale, Baidháwi.*

(6) *Lest ye hurt people, &c.* "This passage was occasioned, it is said, by the following accident. Al Walíd Ibn Uqba being sent by Muhammad to collect the alms from the tribe of al Mustaliq, when he saw them come out to meet him in great numbers, grew apprehensive they designed him some mischief, because of past enmity between him and them in the time of ignorance, and immediately

ye have done; (7) and know that the Apostle of GOD *is* among you: if he should obey you in many things, ye would certainly be guilty of a crime *in leading him into a mistake.* But GOD hath made the faith amiable unto you, and hath prepared the same in your hearts; and hath rendered infidelity, and iniquity, and disobedience hateful unto you. These are they who walk in the right way; (8) through mercy from GOD and grace: and GOD *is* knowing *and* wise. (9) If two parties of the believers contend with one another, do ye *endeavour to* compose the matter between them: and if the one of them offer an insult unto the other, fight against that *party* which offered the insult, until they return unto the judgment of GOD; and if they do return, make peace between them with equity: and act with justice; for GOD loveth those who act justly. (10) Verily the true believers are brethren; wherefore reconcile your brethren; and fear GOD, that ye may obtain mercy. (11) O true believers, let not men laugh *other* men to scorn; who peradventure may be better than themselves: neither *let* women *laugh other* women *to scorn;* who may possibly be better than themselves. Neither

---

turned back, and told the Prophet they refused to pay their alms and attempted to kill him; upon which Muhammad was thinking to reduce them by force; but on sending Khálid Ibn al Walíd to them, he found his former messenger had wronged them, and that they continued in their obedience."—*Sale, Baidhāwi, Jalāluddīn.*

(9) *Two parties.* "This verse is supposed to have been occasioned by a fray which happened between the tribes of al Aus and al Khazraj. Some relate that the Prophet one day riding on an ass, as he passed near Abdullah Ibn Ubbai, the ass chanced to stale, at which Ibn Ubbai stopped his nose; and Ibn Rawáha said to him, 'By God, the piss of his ass smells sweeter than thy musk;' whereupon a quarrel ensued between their followers, and they came to blows, though they struck one another only with their hands and slippers, or with palm-branches."—*Sale, Baidhāwi, Jalāluddīn.*

(11) "It is said that this verse was revealed on account of Safía Bint Huyai, one of the Prophet's wives, who came to her husband and complained that the women said to her, 'O thou Jewess, the daughter of a Jew and of a Jewess;' to which he answered, 'Canst thou not say, Aaron is my father, and Moses is my uncle, and Muhammad is my husband?'"—*Sale, Baidhāwi.*

defame one another; nor call one another by *opprobrious* appellations. An ill name *it is to be charged with* wickedness after *having embraced* the faith: and whoso repenteth not, they will be the unjust doers.

|| (12) O true believers, carefully avoid *entertaining* a $R \frac{2}{14}$. suspicion *of another:* for some suspicions *are* a crime. Inquire not too curiously *into other men's failings;* neither let the one of you speak ill of another in his absence. Would any of you desire to eat the flesh of his dead brother? Surely ye would abhor it. And fear GOD; for GOD *is* easy to be reconciled, *and* merciful. (13) O men, verily we have created you of a male and female; and we have distributed you into nations and tribes, that ye might know one another. Verily the most honourable of you, in the sight of GOD, *is* the most pious of you: and GOD is wise *and* knowing. (14) The Arabs of the desert say, We believe. Answer, Ye do by no means believe; but say, We have embraced Islám: for the faith hath not yet entered into your hearts. If ye obey GOD and his Apostle, he will not defraud you of any part *of the merit* of your works: for GOD *is* inclined to forgive, *and* merciful. (15) Verily the true believers *are* those only who believe in GOD and his Apostle, and afterwards doubt not; and who employ their substance and their persons in the defence of GOD'S true religion: these are they who speak sincerely. (16) Say, Will ye inform GOD concerning your religion?

---

(12) *Would any of you desire, &c.* Slander is here likened to feasting upon the corpse of a dead man.

(14) *The Arabs of the desert.* " These were certain of the tribe of Asad, who came to Madína in a year of scarcity, and having professed Muhammadism, told the Prophet that they had brought all their goods and their families, and would not oppose him, as some other tribes had done; and this they said to obtain a part of the alms, and to upbraid him with their having embraced his religion and party."—*Sale, Baidháwi.*

We have embraced Islám. "That is, ye are not sincere believers, but outward professors only of the true religion."—*Sale.*

(16) *Will ye inform God, &c., i.e.,* "will ye pretend to deceive him by saying ye are true believers?"—*Sale.*

But GOD knoweth whatever *is* in heaven and in earth! for GOD *is* omniscient. (17) They upbraid thee that they have embraced Islám. Answer, Upbraid me not with your having embraced Islám: rather GOD upbraideth you, that he hath directed you to the faith; if ye speak sincerely. (18) Verily GOD knoweth the secrets of heaven and earth; and GOD beholdeth that which ye do.

---

(17) *Rather God upbraideth you, &c.* "The obligation being not on God's side, but on yours, for that he has favoured you so far as to guide ye into the true faith, if ye are sincere believers."—*Sale.*

CHAPTER L.

ENTITLED SURAT AL QÁF (Q).

Revealed at Makkah.

INTRODUCTION.

THE letter placed at the beginning of this chapter has been chosen as its title. The contents relate throughout to the doctrine of the resurrection and a future life. To the idolaters of Makkah the doctrine of the resurrection of the dead seemed impossible, and on this account they rejected Muhammad and his Qurán. Muhammad is called an impostor. In reply to his traducers, Muhammad appeals to the power of God as seen in his works of creation and providence. He tells them that other prophets were in like manner with himself charged with forgery, but their calumniators were miserably destroyed. They are accordingly warned of the coming judgment, for which they will be ill prepared. As usual, however, all this warning and instruction is represented as coming from the mouth of God.

Probable Date of the Revelations.

There can be no doubt about the Makkan origin of this chapter. One author, Umar bin Muhammad, however, maintains that ver. 37 was revealed in answer to the blasphemous talk of the Jews at Madína (see Sale's notes), but this is certainly a mistake. The passage is connected in thought with ver. 14. As to the date of the chapter, Noëldeke places it immediately after chap. xliv.

Principal Subjects.

	VERSES
The unbelievers wonder at the doctrine of the resurrection	1–3
This wonder due to their unbelief	4, 5
God's works a proof of his power to raise the dead	6–11
The Quraish warned by the fate of other nations who rejected their prophets	12, 13

	VERSES
God not so exhausted by the creation that he cannot raise the dead	14
God nearer man than his jugular vein	15
Angels record all human thoughts and actions	16, 17
Death and judgment shall overtake all men	18–20
The testimony of the two angels shall condemn the unbelievers	21, 22
God shall cast the wicked into hell	23–25
The devils shall disclaim the idolaters in hell	26–28
Hell shall be filled with the wicked	29
Paradise shall receive the true believers	30–34
Former generations destroyed as a warning to the people of Makkah	35, 36
The heavens and the earth created in six days	37
Muhammad exhorted to patience with unbelievers	38–43
Muhammad not sent to compel men to believe, but only to warn them	44, 45

IN THE NAME OF THE MOST MERCIFUL GOD.

SEVENTH MUNZIL.
SULS.
R $\frac{1}{15}$.

|| (1) Q. By the glorious Qurán; (2) verily they wonder that a preacher from among themselves is come unto them; and the unbelievers say, This *is* a wonderful thing; (3) after we shall be dead and become dust, *shall we return to life?* This *is* a return remote *from thought*. (4) Now we know what the earth consumeth of them; and with us *is* a book which keepeth an account *thereof*. (5) But they charge falsehood on the truth, after it hath come unto them: wherefore they *are plunged* in a confused business.

---

(1) Q. "Some imagine that this letter is designed to express the mountain Qáf, which several Eastern writers fancy encompasses the whole world. Others say it stands for *Qadr al amr, i.e.*, 'The matter is decreed,' viz., the chastisement of the infidels. See Prelim. Disc., pp. 100–102."—*Sale, Baidháwi, Jaláluddín*.

The glorious Qurán. In the Arabic, *Qurán al Majíd*. This is a term commonly applied to the Qurán by Muslims. It includes the idea of a complete Divine revelation—a book—and may here refer to the *Luh i Mahfúz*, or Preserved Table, from which the revelations delivered to Muhammad are said to have been copied.

(5) *They are plunged in a confused business.* "Not knowing what

(6) Do they not look up to the heaven above them, *and consider* how we have raised it and adorned it; and that *there are* no flaws therein? (7) We have also spread forth the earth, and thrown thereon *mountains* firmly rooted: and we caused every beautiful kind *of vegetables* to spring up therein; (8) for a subject of meditation, and an admonition unto every man who turneth *unto us.* (9) And we send down rain as a blessing from heaven, whereby we cause gardens to spring forth, and the grain of harvest, (10) and tall palm-trees having branches laden with dates hanging one above another, (11) as a provision for mankind; and we thereby quicken a dead country: so *shall be* the coming forth *of the dead from their graves.* (12) The people of Noah, and those who dwelt at Al Rass, and Thamúd, (13) and Ád, and Pharaoh, accused *the prophets* of imposture before *the Makkans;* and also the brethren of Lot, and the inhabitants of the wood *near Midian,* and the people of Tubba: all *these* accused the apostles of imposture; wherefore *the judgments* which I threatened were justly inflicted *on them.* (14) Is our power exhausted by the first creation? Yea; they are in a perplexity, because of a new creation *which is foretold them, namely, the raising of the dead.*

|| (15) We created man, and we know what his soul whispereth within him; and we *are* nearer unto him than $R \frac{2}{16}$.

---

certainly to affirm of the Qurán, calling it sometimes a piece of poetry, at other times a piece of sorcery, and at other times a piece of divination, &c."—*Sale.*

(7) Comp. chaps. xvi. 15, and xxxi. 9.

(10) *Dates.* "The date-tree produces three or four large clusters, which rise from the summit of the tree, and hang round. They are formed of small branches, long and flexible, from which hang the dates. These clusters will sometimes weigh as much as 120 pounds. The date is at first of a deep green; as it ripens it turns red, and it becomes blackish when it is ripe. This fruit, which is of a sugary and agreeable taste, loses much by drying."—*Savary.*

(12) *Who dwelt at Al Rass, &c.* See on chaps. xxv. 40, xi. 26–100, and notes there.

Tubba. See note on chap. xliv. 36.

his jugular vein. (16) When the two *angels* deputed to take account *of a man's behaviour* take an account *thereof*, one sitting on the right hand and *the other* on the left, (17) he uttereth not a word but *there is* with him a watcher ready *to note it.* (18) And the agony of death shall come in truth: this, *O man, is* what thou soughtest to avoid. (19) And the trumpet shall sound: this *will be* the day which hath been threatened. (20) And every soul shall come; *and* therewith *shall be* a driver and a witness. (21) *And the former shall say unto the unbeliever,* Thou wast negligent heretofore of this *day:* but we have removed thy veil from off thee; and thy sight *is become* piercing this day. (22) And his companion shall say, This *is* what *is* ready with me *to be attested.* (23) *And God shall say,* Cast into hell every unbeliever, *and* perverse person, (24) *and every one* who forbade good, *and every* transgressor, and doubter *of the faith,* (25) who set up another god with *the true* GOD; and cast him into a grievous torment. (26) His companion shall say, O LORD,

---

(16, 17) "The intent of the passage is to exalt the omniscience of God, who wants not the information of the guardian angels, though he has thought fit, in his wisdom, to give them that employment; for if they are so exact as to write down every word which falls from a man's mouth, how can we hope to escape the observation of him who sees our inmost thoughts?

"The Muhammadans have a tradition that the angel who notes a man's good actions has the command over him who notes his evil actions; and that when a man does a good action, the angel of the right hand writes it down ten times, and when he commits an ill action, the same angel says to the angel of the left hand 'Forbear setting it down for seven hours; peradventure he may pray, or may ask pardon.'"—*Sale, Baidháwi.*

(20) *A driver and a witness, i.e.,* "two angels, one acting as a serjeant, to bring every person before the tribunal; and the other prepared as a witness, to testify either for or against him. Some say the former will be the guardian angel who took down his evil actions, and the other angel who took down his good actions."—*Sale, Baidháwi.*

(26) *His companion,* viz., "the devil which shall be chained to him."—*Sale.* See also notes on chaps. vii. 39, 180, and x. 19, &c.

I did not seduce him, &c. "This will be the answer of the devil, whom the wicked person will accuse as his seducer: for the devil

I did not seduce him; but he was in a wide error. (27) *God* shall say, Wrangle not in my presence: since I threatened you beforehand *with the torments which ye now see prepared for you.* (28) The sentence is not changed with me: neither do I treat *my* servants unjustly.

|| (29) On that day we will say unto hell, Art thou R $\frac{3}{17}$. full? and it shall answer, *Is there* yet any addition? (30) And Paradise shall be brought near unto the pious; (31) *and it shall be said unto them,* This *is* what ye have been promised; unto every one who turned himself *unto God,* and kept *his commandments;* (32) who feared the Merciful in secret, and came *unto him* with a converted heart: (33) enter the same in peace: this *is* the day of eternity. (34) Therein shall they have whatever they shall desire; and *there will be* a superabundant addition *of bliss* with us. (35) How many generations have we destroyed before the *Makkans,* which were more mighty than they in strength? Pass, therefore, through the regions *of the earth, and see* whether *there be* any refuge *from our vengeance.* (36) Verily herein *is* an admonition unto him who hath a heart *to understand,* or giveth ear, and is present *with an attentive mind.* (37) We created the heavens and the earth, and whatever *is* between them, in six days, and no

---

hath no power over a man to cause him to do evil, any otherwise than by suggesting what is agreeable to his corrupt inclinations."—*Sale.*

Comp. chap. xiv. 26, 27.

(29) *Is there yet any addition?* *i.e.,* "are there yet any more condemned to this place, or is my space to be enlarged and rendered more capacious to receive them?

"The commentators suppose hell will be quite filled at the day of judgment, according to that repeated expression in the Qurán, *Verily I will fill hell with you,* &c."—*Sale.*

See chaps. xi. 119, xxxii. 13, 14. Comp. Prov. xxx. 15.

(34) See Prelim. Disc., p. 154.

(37) *Six days.* See note on chap. vii. 55.

No weariness, &c. "This was revealed in answer to the Jews, who said God rested from his work of creation on the seventh day, and reposed himself on his throne, as one fatigued."—*Sale, Baidháwi, Jalálnddín.*

Better, with Rodwell, to connect with ver. 14.

weariness affected us. (38) Wherefore patiently suffer what they say; and celebrate the praise of thy LORD before sunrise and before sunset, (39) and praise him *in some part* of the night: and *perform* the additional parts of worship. (40) And hearken unto the day whereon the crier shall call *men to judgment* from a near place: (41) the day whereon they shall hear the voice *of the trumpet* in truth: this *will be* the day of *men's* coming forth *from their graves:* (42) we give life, and we cause to die; and unto us *shall be* the return *of all creatures:* (43) the day whereon the earth shall suddenly cleave in sunder over them. This *will be* an assembly easy for us *to assemble.* (44) We well know what *the unbelievers* say; and thou *art* not sent to compel them forcibly *to the faith.* (45) Wherefore warn, by the Qurán, him who feareth my threatening.

---

(38) *What they say*, what the idolaters say in denying the resurrection.

(39) *The additional parts of worship.* "These are the two inclinations used after the evening prayer, which are not necessary or of precept, but voluntary and of supererogation, and may therefore be added or omitted indifferently."—*Sale.*

The *additional parts* of worship are *commanded* here, and therefore cannot be regarded by Muslims as indifferent. It is better to apply these words to other hours of prayer not mentioned here.

(40) *A new place.* "That is, from a place whence every creature may equally hear the call. This place, it is supposed, will be the mountain of the temple of Jerusalem, which some fancy to be nigher heaven than any other part of the earth; whence Israfl will sound the trumpet, and Gabriel will make the following proclamation: 'O ye rotten bones, and torn flesh, and dispersed hairs, God commandeth you to be gathered together to judgment.'"—*Sale, Baidháwi.*

(44) *Thou art not sent to compel, &c.* This is the spirit of the Makkan preacher, but compare that of the prophet-general of Madina, chaps. ix. 29, 74, and xlvii. 4, 5.

CHAPTER LI.

ENTITLED SURAT AL ZÁRIYÁT (THE DISPERSING).

Revealed at Makkah.

INTRODUCTION.

As in nearly all the earlier chapters of the Qurán, this one begins with a number of oaths, wherewith God, swearing by various natural objects, attests the truth of his Prophet's message. In this chapter the occasion of these vehement oaths was the rejection of the doctrine of a final judgment by the people of Makkah.

It is generally agreed that the latter portion of this chapter, consisting of vers. 24-60, was added on by the compilers of the Qurán, or during its recension under Othmán. The subject of discourse being similar, it was perhaps thought to belong to what precedes. While, however, it is true that the subject is the same, yet the circumstances under which it was enunciated were very different. In the first section the unbelievers simply reject the Prophet as an impostor and his message as incredible, but in this they threaten violent treatment (ver. 59), and the Prophet is in consequence told to withdraw from them (ver. 54).

Probable Date of the Revelations.

Noëldeke places this chapter near the end of his first period, *i.e.*, about the fourth year of Muhammad's mission.

This date will do very well for the first portion of the chapter, but vers. 24-60 must be assigned a much later date. Muir places it near the end of the fourth stage of Muhammad's ministry, when the ban against the Háshamites had interfered with his public preaching.

The date of this portion would therefore be about B.H. 6.

Principal Subjects.

	VERSES
Numerous oaths that the judgment will come	1-6
Oaths and curses relating to unbelievers	7-11
Doom of infidels and reward of true believers	12-16
The piety and charity of Muslims	17-19
God reveals himself in his work of providence	20-22
Muhammad swears by the Lord that the Qurán is true	23
The story of Abraham's entertaining angels	24-30
Story of the destruction of Sodom	31-37
Pharaoh, Ád, Thamúd, and the people of Noah destroyed for rejecting their prophets as impostors	38-46
God reveals himself to men in his works of creation	47-49
Makkans warned to leave their idols and to fly to God	50, 51
Every apostle of God called a magician or madman	52, 53
Muhammad to withdraw from idolaters and yet to admonish them for the sake of true believers	54, 55
Men and genii created to serve God	56, 58
Woe to unbelievers who injure the apostles of God	59, 60

IN THE NAME OF THE MOST MERCIFUL GOD.

R $\frac{1}{18}$. ‖ (1) By the *winds* dispersing and scattering *the dust;* (2) and by the *clouds* bearing a load *of rain;* (3) by the *ships* running swiftly *in the sea;* (4) and by the *angels* who distribute things *necessary for the support of all creatures;* (5) verily that wherewith ye are threatened is certainly true; (6) and the *last* judgment will surely come. (7) By the heaven furnished with paths; (8) ye widely differ in what ye say. (9) He will be turned

---

(1-4) The particles being in the feminine, *Sale* gives an alternate rendering as follows, "By the *women* who bring forth *or* scatter *children*, and by the *women* bearing a burden *in their wombs* (or the *winds* bearing *the clouds*); by the *winds* passing swiftly *in the air* (or *the stars* moving swiftly *in their courses*), and by *the winds* which distribute *the rain*, &c."

(7) *Paths.* "The paths or orbs of the stars, or the streaks which appear in the sky like paths, being thin and extended clouds."—*Sale.*

(8) *Ye widely differ.* "Concerning Muhammad or the Qurán, or

aside from *the faith* who shall be turned aside *by the divine decree.* (10) Cursed be the liars, (11) who *wade* in deep waters *of ignorance,* neglecting *their salvation.* (12) They ask, When *will* the day of judgment *come?* (13) On that day shall they be burned in *hell*-fire; (14) *and it shall be said unto them,* Taste your punishment; this *is* what ye demanded to be hastened. (15) But the pious *shall dwell* among gardens and fountains, (16) receiving that which their LORD shall give them; because they were righteous doers before this *day.* (17) They slept but a small part of the night; (18) and early in the morning they asked pardon *of God;* (19) and a due portion of their wealth *was given* unto him who asked, and unto him who was forbidden *by shame to ask.* (20) *There are* signs *of the divine power and goodness* in the earth, unto *men* of sound understanding; (21) and also in your own selves: will ye not therefore consider? (22) Your sustenance *is* in the heaven; and also that which ye are promised. (23) Wherefore by the LORD of heaven and earth *I swear* that this *is* certainly the truth; according to what ye yourselves speak.

|| (24) Hath not the story of Abraham's honoured guests R $\frac{2}{1}$. come to thy knowledge? (25) When they went in unto him, and said, Peace: he answered, Peace; *saying within himself, These are* unknown people. (26) And he went privately unto his family, and brought a fatted calf. (27) And he set it before them, *and when he saw they touched it*

---

the resurrection and the day of judgment, speaking variously and inconsistently of them."—*Sale.*

(17) *A small part.* "Spending the greater part in prayer and religious meditation."—*Sale.*

(22) "That is, your food cometh from above, whence proceedeth the change of seasons and rain ; and your future reward is also there, that is to say, in Paradise, which is situate above the seven heavens." —*Sale.*

(23) *According to what ye yourselves speak.* "That is, without any doubt or reserved meaning, as ye affirm a truth unto one another." —*Sale.*

(24) See chaps. xi. 69, and xv. 51, and notes there.

VOL. IV.   F

not, he said, Do ye not eat? (28) And he began to entertain a fear of them. They said, Fear not: and they declared unto him the promise of a wise youth. (29) And his wife drew near with exclamation, and she smote her face, and said, *I am* an old woman *and* barren. (30) The *angels* answered, Thus saith the LORD: verily he is the wise, the knowing.

TWENTY-SEVENTH SIPARA.

|| (31) *And Abraham* said *unto them,* What is your errand, therefore, O messengers *of God?* (32) They answered, Verily we are sent unto a wicked people, (33) that we may send down upon them stones of *baked* clay, (34) marked from thy LORD, for *the destruction of* transgressors. (35) And we brought forth the true believers who were in *the city;* (36) but we found not therein more than one family of Muslims. (37) And we *overthrew the same, and* left a sign therein unto those who dread the severe chastisement *of God.* (38) In Moses also *was a sign,* when we sent him unto Pharaoh with manifest power. (39) But he turned back with his princes, saying, *This man is* a sorcerer or a madman. (40) Wherefore we took him and his forces and cast them into the sea; and he was one worthy of reprehension. (41) And in *the tribe of* Ád *also was a sign,* when we sent against them a destroying wind; (42) it touched not aught whereon it came, but it rendered the same as a thing rotten, *and reduced to dust.* (43) In Thamúd *likewise was a sign,* when it was said unto them, Enjoy *yourselves* for a time. (44) But they insolently transgressed the command of their LORD: wherefore a terrible noise from heaven assailed them while they looked on; (45) and they were not able to stand *on their feet,*

---

(28) *Fear not.* "Some add, that, to remove Abraham's fear, Gabriel, who was one of these strangers, touched the calf with his wing, and it immediately rose up and walked to its dam; upon which Abraham knew them to be the messengers of God."—*Sale, Baidhâwi.*

(33) See note on chap. xi. 81.

(38-40) See notes on chaps. xii. 104-136, and xi. 26-60.

neither did they save themselves *from destruction.* (46) And the people of Noah *did we destroy* before *these;* for they were a people who enormously transgressed.

|| (47) We have built the heaven with might; and we have given *it a* large extent; (48) and we have stretched forth the earth beneath; and how evenly have we spread *the same!* (49) And of everything have we created two kinds, that peradventure ye may consider. (50) Fly, therefore, unto GOD: verily I *am* a public warner unto you from him. (51) And set not up another god with *the true* GOD: verily I *am* a public warner unto you from him. (52) In like manner there came no apostle unto their predecessors, but they said, *This man is* a magician or a madman. (53) Have they bequeathed this *behaviour* successively the one to the other? Yea; they are a people who enormously transgress. (54) Wherefore withdraw from them; and thou *shalt not be* blameworthy *in so doing.* (55) Yet continue to admonish; for admonition profiteth the true believers. (56) I have not created genii and men *for any other end* than that they should serve me. (57) I require not any sustenance from them; neither will I that they feed me. (58) Verily GOD is he who provideth *for all creatures;* possessed of mighty power. (59) Unto those who shall injure *our Apostle shall be given* a portion like unto the portion of those who behaved like them *in times past;* and they shall not wish *the same* to be hastened. (60) Woe, therefore, to the unbelievers, because of their day with which they are threatened!

R $\frac{3}{2}$.

---

(49) *Two kinds.* "As, for example, male and female, the heaven and the earth, the sun and the moon, light and darkness, plains and mountains, winter and summer, sweet and bitter, &c."—*Sale.*

(52) Comp. chap. xxii. 44, 45.

(54) *Withdraw from them.* This instruction points to Muhammad's flight to Madína.

(56) Compare with chap. xi. 119.

(57) *That they feed me.* Alluding to the food offerings presented to the idols.

CHAPTER LII.

ENTITLED SURAT AL TÚR (THE MOUNTAIN).

Revealed at Makkah.

INTRODUCTION.

THE earlier portion of this chapter is occupied with the doctrine of future rewards and punishments, and closely resembles the first part of chap. li. The violence of the opposition of the Quraish to this doctrine is illustrated by the vehemence of the oaths by which that doctrine is asserted. Unbelievers are assured that the fires of hell shall overtake them; but, on the other hand, believers are encouraged by a description of the sensual delights of Paradise. This marks the introduction of the houris or black-eyed maidens of Paradise into the descriptions of the heaven of Islám.

The latter part of this chapter reveals to us a more active opposition of the Quraish. They no longer simply deny the doctrine of his Qurán, but declare him to be an impostor and plot his destruction (ver. 42). Muhammad, however, is undisturbed. Believing the eye of God to be upon him (ver. 48), he calmly waits, trusting in God for deliverance.

Probable Date of the Revelations.

Noëldeke, in his chronological list of suras, places this chapter immediately after chap. li. He, however, maintains that vers. 21 and 29 *seq.* are of later date, because the use of certain expressions, *e.g.,* سبحان الله and شرك point clearly to the later style of Muhammad. Muir places the whole Sura in the early part of his fourth stage, *i.e.,* at a period extending from the sixth to the tenth year of Muhammad's ministry.

Principal Subjects.

	VERSES
Oaths by various objects that the judgment-day will come	1–8
The terrors of the unbelievers in that day	9–16
The bliss of Paradise described	17–28
Muhammad not a soothsayer, madman, poet, or impostor	29–34
Unbelievers reproved for their ignorance and idolatry	35–47
Plots of the enemies of Muhammad exposed	42, 43
Muhammad to leave the idolaters to their fate	44–47
Muhammad exhorted to praise and trust the Lord	48, 49

IN THE NAME OF THE MOST MERCIFUL GOD.

|| (1) By the mountain *of Sinai;* (2) and by the book R $\frac{1}{3}$. (3) written in an expanded scroll; (4) and by the visited house; (5) and by the elevated roof *of heaven;* (6) and by the swelling ocean; (7) verily the punishment of thy LORD will surely descend; (8) *there shall be* none to withhold it. (9) On that day the heaven shall be shaken and shall reel, (10) and the mountains shall walk and pass away. (11) And on that day woe be unto those who accused *God's apostles* of imposture; (12) who amused themselves in wading *in vain disputes!* (13) On that day shall they be driven and thrust into the fire of hell; (14) *and it shall be said unto them,* This *is* the fire which ye denied as a fiction. (15) *Is* this a magic illusion? Or do ye not see? (16) Enter the same to be scorched: whether ye bear *your torments* patiently or impatiently, *it will be* equal unto you: ye shall surely receive the reward of that

---

(3) *An expanded scroll.* "The book here intended, according to different opinions, is either the book or register wherein every man's actions are recorded; or the *preserved table* containing God's decrees; or the book of the law, which was written by God, Moses hearing the creaking of the pen; or else the Qurán."—*Sale, Baidháwi, Zamakhsharí.*

(4) *The . . . house, i.e.,* "the Kaabah, so much visited by pilgrims; or, as some rather think, the original model of that house in heaven, called al Duráh, which is visited and compassed by the angels, as the other is by men."—*Sale, Baidháwi.*

(11) See note on chap. iii. 185.

which ye have wrought. (17) But the pious *shall dwell* amidst gardens and pleasures, (18) delighting themselves in what their LORD shall have given them; and their LORD shall deliver them from the pains of hell. (19) *And it shall be said unto them*, Eat and drink with easy digestion, because of that which ye have wrought; (20) leaning on couches disposed in order: and we will espouse them unto virgins having large black eyes. (21) And unto those who believe, and whose offspring follow them in the faith, we will join their offspring *in Paradise;* and we will not diminish unto them aught of *the merit of* their works. (Every man *is* given in pledge for that which he shall have wrought.) (22) And we will give them fruits in abundance, and flesh of the *kinds* which they shall desire. (23) They shall present unto one another therein a cup *of wine*, wherein there shall be no vain discourse, nor any incitement unto wickedness. (24) And youths *appointed* to *attend* them shall go round them, *beautiful* as pearls hidden *in their shell*. (25) And they shall approach unto one another, and shall ask mutual questions. (26) *And* they shall say, Verily we were heretofore, amidst our family, in great dread *with regard to our state after death;* (27) but GOD hath been gracious unto us, and hath delivered us from the pain of burning fire: (28) for we called on him heretofore; and he is the beneficent, the merciful.

R ⅔. ‖ (29) Wherefore do thou, *O Prophet*, admonish *thy people*. Thou *art* not, by the grace of thy LORD, a sooth-

---

(17-25) See note on chap. iii. 15.

(20) *Virgins having large black eyes.* "This is the earliest mention of the hûries or black-eyed girls of Paradise, so famous in the Mahometan system, and which other creeds have singled out as the distinguishing feature of Islâm. They were not thought of, at least not *introduced into the revelation*, till four or five years after Mahomet had assumed the office of prophet."—Muir's *Life of Mahomet*, vol. ii. pp. 141, 142, note.

(21) *Every man, &c., i.e.,* "every man is pledged unto God for his behaviour; and if he does well, he redeems his pledge; but if evil, he forfeits it."—*Sale.*

sayer or a madman. (30) Do they say, *He is* a poet; we wait, concerning him, some adverse turn of fortune? (31) Say, Wait ye *my ruin:* verily I wait, with you, *the time of your destruction.* (32) Do their mature understandings bid them *say* this; or *are* they people who perversely transgress? (33) Do they say, He hath forged *the Qurán?* Verily they believe not. (34) Let them produce a discourse like unto it, if they speak truth. (35) Were they created by nothing; or were they creators *of themselves?* (36) Did they create the heavens and the earth? Verily they are not firmly persuaded *that God hath created them.* (37) Are the stores of thy LORD in their hands? Are they the supreme dispensers *of all things?* (38) Have they a ladder whereby they may *ascend to heaven, and* hear *the discourses of the angels?* Let one, therefore, who hath heard them produce an evident proof *thereof.* (39) Hath *God* daughters, and have ye sons? (40) Dost thou ask them a reward *for thy preaching?* but they are laden with debts. (41) Are the secrets of futurity with them; and do they transcribe *the same from the tables of God's degrees?* (42) Do they seek *to lay* a plot *against thee?* But the unbelievers are *they who shall be* circumvented. (43) Have they *any* god besides GOD? Far be GOD exalted above the *idols* which they associate *with him!* (44) If they should see a fragment of the heaven falling down *upon them,* they would say, *It is only* a thick cloud. (45) Wherefore leave

---

(30) See chap. xxi. 5.
(33) See notes on chaps. xi. 14, and xvi. 105.
(36) *They are not . . . persuaded, &c.* " For though they confess this with their tongues, yet they deny it by their averseness to render him his due worship."—*Sale.*
(38) *Have they a ladder, &c.* Compare chap. vi. 34, where this taunt is raised against Muhammad by the Quraish.
(39) See notes on chap. xvi. 59-61.
(42) See chap. viii. 30.
(44) *A thick cloud.* "This was one of the judgments which the idolatrous Makkans defied Muhammad to bring down upon them; and yet, says the text, if they should see a part of the heaven falling

them until they arrive at their day, wherein they shall swoon for fear: (46) a day in which their subtle contrivances shall not avail them at all, neither shall they be protected. (47) And those who act unjustly shall surely suffer *another* punishment besides this: but the greater part of them do not understand. (48) And wait thou patiently the judgment of thy LORD *concerning them;* for thou *art* in our eye: and celebrate the praise of thy LORD when thou risest up; (49) and praise him in the night-season, and when the stars begin to disappear.

---

on them, they would not believe it till they were crushed to death by it."—*Sale, Baidháwi.*

(45) *Their day, &c.* "At the first sound of the trumpet."—*Sale.* See Prelim. Disc., p. 135.

(47) *Another punishment.* "That is, besides the punishment to which they shall be doomed at the day of judgment, they shall be previously chastised by calamities in this life, as the slaughter at Badr and the seven years' famine, and also after their death by the examination of the sepulchre."—*Sale, Baidháwi.*

CHAPTER LIII.

ENTITLED SURAT AL NAJM (THE STAR).

Revealed at Makkah.

INTRODUCTION.

THIS chapter receives its title from the object by which Muhammad is commanded to swear, mentioned in the first verse. Like chapters li. and lii., this one consists of an earlier and a later portion, or may be, as Noëldeke suggests, fragments of one or two lost Suras have been added to the original revelation of this one by the compilers.

The earlier portion of this chapter presents two items of special interest. The first is the declaration of the Qurán itself that Muhammad was merely a passive instrument of revelation (ver. 6), and that, therefore, the words of the Qurán are in no sense whatever the words of Muhammad himself. The second item of special interest is the description of the angelic vision vouchsafed to Muhammad, and which was to him the proof of his apostleship. See the subject discussed in note on ver. 11.

The latter portion of the chapter contains the passage which records, in its amended form, a revelation said to have been suggested by Satan at the time of the lapse of the Prophet. The question of the lapse will be found discussed in notes on chap. xxii. 53.

Probable Date of the Revelations.

Guided by the traditions relating to the lapse alluded to in vers. 19-23, the date of this portion of the chapter would be the months of Ramadhán and Shawwál of the fifth year of the Call. Vers. 26-33 are probably of a somewhat later origin, while vers. 58-62 seem to form a little Sura by themselves. This portion, with the first eighteen verses, were the earliest revelations of this chapter.

Principal Subjects.

	VERSES
Oath that Muhammad received the Qurán from the Angel Gabriel	1–5
Description of the angelic visions vouchsafed to Muhammad	6–18
The revelation concerning Al Lát, Al Uzzah, and Manáh, &c.	19–23
The vanity of trusting to the intercession of female deities	24–31
God almighty and omniscient	32, 33
Rebuke of a man who employed another to bear his punishment on the judgment-day	34–56
Muhammad a preacher like other prophets	57
The judgment-day approacheth, therefore prepare for it	58–62

IN THE NAME OF THE MOST MERCIFUL GOD.

R $\frac{1}{5}$. ‖ (1) By the star when it setteth, (2) your companion *Muhammad* erreth not, nor is he led astray, (3) neither doth he speak of *his own* will. (4) It is no other than a revelation, (5) which hath been revealed *unto him*. (6) One mighty in power, endued with understanding, taught *it* him: (7) and he appeared in the highest part of the horizon. (8) Afterwards he approached *the Prophet*,

---

(1) *By the star.* "Some suppose the stars in general, and others the Pleiades in particular, to be meant in this place."—*Sale.*
When it setteth. "Or, according to a contrary signification of the verb here used, *when it riseth.*"—*Sale.*
(6) *One mighty in power.* "The Angel Gabriel."—*Sale.* "The commentators say that the terms Ruh-ul-Amín (Faithful Spirit) and Shadíd-ul-Quá (Mighty in Power) refer to no other angel or spirit."—Sell's *Faith of Islám*, p. 4.
Taught it him. "The use of the word 'taught' . . . and the following expression in Sura lxxv. 18, 'when we have *recited it,* then follow thou the recital,' shows that the Qurán is entirely an objective revelation, and that Muhammad was only a passive medium of communication."—Sell's *Faith of Islám*, p. 4.
(7) *And he appeared, &c.* "In his natural form, in which God created him, and in the eastern part of the sky. It is said that this angel appeared in his proper shape to none of the prophets except Muhammad, and to him only twice: once when he received the first revelation of the Qurán, and a second time when he took his night journey to heaven; as it follows in the text."—*Sale.*
(8) *He approached.* "In a human shape."—*Sale.*

and near *unto him*, (9) until he was at the distance of two bows' length *from him*, or yet nearer; (10) and he revealed unto his servant that which he revealed. (11) The heart *of Muhammad* did not falsely represent that which he saw. (12) Will ye therefore dispute with him concerning that which he saw? (13) He also saw him another time, (14) by the lote-tree beyond which there is no passing: (15) near it is the garden of *eternal* abode.

(9) *Two bows' length.* "Or, as the word also signifies, *two cubits length.*"—*Sale.*

(11) *The heart . . . did not falsely represent, &c.* That is, Muhammad was not the subject of any illusion, but saw it in reality. He was not mistaken as to what he saw.

We have here then the distinct and positive assertion on the part of Muhammad that he had personal intercourse with the Angel Gabriel. Now was he sincere and truthful in this statement? Did he see something, or did he see nothing? Did he report what he saw in truth, or did he utter a deliberate falsehood? It seems to me clear that the theory of deliberate falsehood is *in this case* untenable. That he was the subject of *some kind* of vision must be admitted, whether due to Divine or Satanic influence must be determined by *the result.* Judged by its fruits, Islám cannot have had God for its author. It is the most powerful of all the opposing influences to the religion of Jesus which have arisen in the world since the day of Pentecost.

Believing that Muhammad had intercourse with some being whom he believed to be Gabriel, and seeing that the effect of these revelations, vouchsafed to Muhammad through this being, or due to the influence which this being wrought upon his mind, was, and still is, to overthrow the faith of the Bible, I, as a Christian, must therefore hold that these visions were due to Satanic influence—Satan, however, revealing himself as an angel of light. This view is not only consistent with what the Bible teaches concerning the character of Satan's policy in this dispensation (Matt. iv. 1–11, xxiv. 24; 2 Thess. ii. 8–12, and Revelation throughout), but it is the theory which best accounts for the strange history and character of Muhammad himself. See note on chap. iv. 116. See the whole question of *the belief of Muhammad in his own inspiration* discussed at length in Muir's *Life of Mahomet,* vol. ii., CHAPTER THIRD.

(13) *Another time.* Comp. chap. vi. 8, where there is an apparently contradictory statement.

(14) *The lote-tree, &c.* "This tree, say the commentators, stands in the seventh heaven, on the right hand of the throne of God, and is the utmost bounds beyond which the angels themselves must not pass; or, as some rather imagine, beyond which no creature's knowledge can extend."—*Sale.*

See Rodwell's note *in loco.*

(16) When the lote-tree covered that which it covered, (17) *his* eyesight turned not aside, neither did it wander: (18) and he really beheld *some* of the greatest signs of his LORD. (19) What think ye of Al Lát, and Al Uzza, (20) and Manáh, that other third *goddess?* (21) Have ye male children, and *God* female? (22) This, therefore, *is* an unjust partition. (23) They are no other than *empty* names, which ye and your fathers have named *goddesses.* GOD hath not revealed concerning them anything to authorise *their worship.* They follow no other than a vain opinion, and what *their* souls desire: yet hath the *true* direction come unto them from their LORD. (24) Shall man have whatever he wisheth for? (25) The life to come and the present life *are* GOD'S.

R 2/8 || (26) And how many angels soever *there be* in the heavens, their intercession shall be of no avail, (27) until after GOD shall have granted permission unto whom he shall please and shall accept. (28) Verily they who believe not in the life to come give unto the angels a female appellation. (29) But they have no knowledge herein: they follow no other than a bare opinion; and a bare

---

(16) *That which is covered.* "The words seem to signify that what was under this tree exceeded all description and number. Some suppose the whole host of angels worshipping beneath it are intended, and others, the birds which sit on its branches."—*Sale, Baidháwi, Jaláluddín.*

(18) *He really beheld, &c.* "Seeing the wonders both of the sensible and the intellectual world."—*Sale, Baidháwi.*

(19, 20) *Al Lát, and Al Uzza, and Manáh* "Those were three idols of the ancient Arabs, of which we have spoken in the Preliminary Discourse, pp. 38–41.

"As to the blasphemy which some pretend Muhammad once uttered, through inadvertence, as he was reading this passage, see chap. xxii. 53, notes."—*Sale.*

See also notes on chaps. iv. 116, and xxii. 74–76.

(21) See chap. xvi. 59, notes.

(24) "That is, shall he dictate to God, and name whom he pleases for his intercessors or for his prophet; or shall he choose a religion according to his own fancy, and prescribe the terms on which he may claim the reward of this life and the next?"—*Sale, Baidháwi, Jaláluddín.*

(26) *Their intercession.* See chap. xxi. 28, 29.

opinion attaineth not anything of truth. (30) Wherefore withdraw from him who turneth away from our admonition and seeketh only the present life. (31) This *is* their highest pitch of knowledge. Verily thy LORD well knoweth him who erreth from his way; and he well knoweth him who is *rightly* directed.

|| (32) Unto GOD *belongeth* whatever *is* in heaven and earth, that he may reward those who do evil according to that which they shall have wrought, and may reward those who do well with the most excellent *reward*. (33) *As to* those who avoid great crimes and heinous sins, *and are guilty* only *of* lighter faults, verily thy LORD *will be* extensive in mercy *towards them.* He well knew you when he produced you out of the earth, and when ye *were* embryos in your mothers' wombs: wherefore justify not yourselves: he best knoweth *the man* who feareth *him.*

|| (34) What thinkest thou of him who turneth aside *from following the truth,* (35) and giveth little, and covetously stoppeth his hand? (36) *Is* the knowledge of futurity with him, so that he seeth *the same*? (37) Hath he not been informed of that which *is contained* in the books of Moses, (38) and of Abraham, who faithfully performed *his engagements?* (39) *To wit,* that a burdened *soul* shall not bear the burden of another; (40) and that nothing *shall be imputed* to a man *for righteousness* except

---

(33) *Heinous sins . . . lighter faults.* See note on chap. iv. 30.
(35) *Stoppeth his hand.* "This passage, it is said, was revealed on account of Al Walíd Ibn al Mughaira, who, following the Prophet one day, was reviled by an idolater for leaving the religion of the Quraish and giving occasion of scandal; to which he answered, that what he did was out of apprehension of the Divine vengeance: whereupon the man offered, for a certain sum, to take the guilt of his apostasy on himself; and the bargain being made, Al Walíd returned to his idolatry, and paid the man part of what had been agreed on; but afterwards, on further consideration, he thought it too much, and kept back the remainder."—*Sale, Baidháwi.*
(36) *Is the knowledge of futurity with him.* "That is, is he assured that the person with whom he made the above-mentioned agreement will be allowed to suffer in his stead hereafter?"—*Sale, Baidháwi.*

his own labour; (41) and that his labour shall surely be made manifest hereafter, (42) and *that* he shall be rewarded for the same with a most abundant reward; (43) and that unto thy LORD *will be* the end *of all things;* (44) and that he causeth to laugh, and causeth to weep; (45) and that he putteth to death, and giveth life; (46) and that he createth the two sexes, the male and the female, (47) of seed when it is emitted; (48) and that unto him *appertaineth* another production, *namely, the raising of the dead again to life hereafter;* (49) and that he enricheth, and causeth to acquire possessions; (50) and that he is the LORD of the dog-star; (51) and that he destroyed the ancient *tribe of* Ád, (52) and Thamúd, and left not *any of them* alive; (53) and also the people of Noah before *them;* for they were most unjust and wicked: (54) and he overthrew the *cities which were* turned upside down; (55) and that which covered *them,* covered them. (56) Which, therefore, of thy LORD's benefits, *O man,* wilt thou call in question? (57) This *our Apostle* is a preacher like the preachers who preceded *him.* (58) The approaching *day of judgment* draweth near: there is none who can reveal *the exact time of* the same, besides GOD. (59) Do ye, therefore, wonder at this new revelation, (60) and do ye laugh, and not weep, (61) spending your time in idle diversions? (62) but rather worship GOD, and serve *him.*

---

(50) *The dog-star.* "Sirius, or the greater dog-star, was worshipped by some of the old Arabs. See Prelim. Disc., p. 38."—*Sale.*

(54) *Cities . . . turned upside down.* "Sodom and the other cities involved in her ruin."—*Sale.* See chap. xi. 81, note.

(57) *Like the preachers who preceded him.* See introduction to chaps. vii., xi., and xxi.

CHAPTER LIV.

ENTITLED SURAT AL QAMR (THE MOON).

Revealed at Makkah.

INTRODUCTION.

THIS chapter owes its title to the statement in ver. 1 that the moon shall be split in sunder as a sign of the approach of the judgment-day.

In style and matter this chapter so closely resembles chapter xi. that it might be called a compend of it. Noëldeke, however, points out that this is the first chapter in chronological order in which the Qurán gives the histories of several prophets together. This being so, we may regard the longer chapter as presenting a more detailed account of the events briefly described here.

The purpose of the revelations of this chapter was to meet the charge of imposture brought by the Quraish against Muhammad. No direct refutation is attempted. The stories of the destruction of other nations and peoples who had rejected their prophets are briefly narrated. Throughout these stories the prophets Noah, Húd, Sálih, Lot, and Moses are represented as messengers of God in all respects like Muhammad, as opposed by unbelievers of the same character as the Quraish, and as charged by the infidels of their day with imposture. The inference from each story is that Muhammad is a true prophet, and that his persecutors are doomed to destruction for their impiety in rejecting him.

After each of the stories related save the last, the following words occur as a sort of refrain: " Now have we made the Qurán easy for admonition, but is any one admonished thereby?" This sad refrain, together with the command to withdraw from the infidels (ver. 6), shows that Muhammad despaired of the conversion of his townsmen.

Probable Date of the Revelations.

This chapter belongs to Makkah. Some Muslim writers, supposing ver. 45 to point to the battle of Badr, and vers. 47–49 to relate to the Christian embassy of Najrán, have thought the whole chapter to be Madínic; but the circumstances of the Prophet, the attitude of his opponents, the matter of the revelations, and the style of composition, all point to Makkah.

As to the date of the revelations, Noëldeke places this chapter at the very beginning of his second period—the fifth year of the call. This seems to me to be too early. It is true that persecution of the Muslims is not positively mentioned in this chapter. If, however, the stories of the prophets reflect the circumstances of the Muslims at the time they were here recorded, we may fairly infer that persecution of the Muslims had already begun. Then the command *to withdraw* and the despair of the Prophet regarding the conversion of the Quraish, point to a later date. Identifying the "withdrawal" with the retirement to the sheb of Abu Tálib, I would fix the date of this chapter at about B.H. 6 or 7. This agrees essentially with Muir, who places it near the beginning of his fourth stage.

Principal Subjects.

	VERSES
The moon shall be split as a sign of the judgment-day	1, 2
Muhammad commanded to withdraw from the infidels	3–6
Infidels shall surely be overtaken suddenly by the judgment	6–8
Noah was charged with imposture by his enemies, who were destroyed by the flood	9–14
Noah's Ark, like the Qurán, a sign to unbelievers who will not be warned	15–18
The Ádites destroyed for calling their prophet an impostor	19–22
The Thamúdites destroyed for rejecting their prophet as an impostor	23–32
The Sodomites destroyed because they rejected Lot as an impostor	33–40
Pharaoh and his people destroyed for rejecting Moses as an impostor	41, 42
The people of Makkah warned by these examples of coming judgment	43–48
God's decree certain and irresistible—illustrated by destruction of former nations	49–51
All actions recorded in the Divine records	52, 53
The pious shall dwell in the gardens of Paradise	54, 55

IN THE NAME OF THE MOST MERCIFUL GOD.

‖ (1) The hour of *judgment* approacheth, and the moon R $\frac{1}{8}$. hath been split in sunder; (2) but if *the unbelievers* see a sign, they turn aside, saying, *This is* a powerful charm. (3) And they accuse *thee, O Muhammad*, of imposture, and follow their own lusts: but everything *will be immutably* fixed. (4) And now hath a message come unto them, wherein *is* a determent *from obstinate infidelity;* (5) *the same being* consummate wisdom: but warners profit *them* not; wherefore do thou withdraw from them. (6) The day whereon the summoner shall summon *mankind* to an ungrateful business, (7) they shall come forth from *their*

---

(1) *The moon hath been split.* "This passage is expounded two different ways. Some imagine the words refer to a famous miracle supposed to have been performed by Muhammad; for it is said that, on the infidels demanding a sign of him, the moon appeared cloven in two, one part vanishing and the other remaining; and Ibn Masúd affirmed that he saw Mount Hará interpose between the two sections. Others think the preter tense is here used in the prophetic style for the future, and that the passage should be rendered, 'The moon shall be split in sunder;' for this, they say, is to happen at the resurrection. The former opinion is supported by reading, according to some copies, *wa kad inshaqqa 'lqamaro, i.e.*, 'since the moon hath already been split in sunder;' the splitting of the moon being reckoned by some to be one of the previous signs of the last day."—*Sale, Baidháwi.*

(2) *A powerful charm.* "Or, as the participle here used may also signify, 'a continued series of magic,' or 'a transient magic illusion.'"—*Sale.*

(3) *They accuse thee ... of imposture.* See notes on chaps. iii. 185, and vii. 203.

Immutably fixed. "Or will reach a final period of ruin or success in this world, and of misery or happiness in the next, which will be conclusive and unchangeable thenceforward for ever."—*Sale, Baidháwi, Zamakhshari.*

(4) *A message, i.e.*, "the Qurán, containing stories of former nations which have been chastised for their incredulity and threats of a more dreadful punishment hereafter."—*Sale.*

(5, 6) This looks like a later Makkan revelation pointing to the withdrawal from Makkah to Madina. It may, however, refer to the withdrawal which took place along with the Ban against the Háshimites.

(6) *The summoner shall summon.* "That is, when the Angel Israfíl shall call men to judgment."—*Sale.*

graves with downcast looks, *numerous* as locusts scattered far abroad; (8) hastening with terror unto the summoner. The unbelievers shall say, This is a day of distress. (9) The people of Noah accused *that prophet* of imposture before *thy people rejected thee:* they accused our servant of imposture, saying, *He* is a madman; and he was rejected with reproach. (10) He called, therefore, upon his LORD, *saying,* Verily I *am* overpowered; wherefore avenge *me.* (11) So we opened the gates of heaven, with water pouring down, (12) and we caused the earth to break forth into springs; so that the water *of heaven and earth* met, according to the decree which had been established. (13) And we bare him on *a vessel* composed of planks and nails; (14) which moved forward under our eyes: as a recompense unto him who had been ungratefully rejected. (15) And we left the *said vessel* for a sign: but *is* any one warned *thereby?* (16) And how *severe* was my vengeance and my threatening! (17) Now have we made the Qurán easy for admonition: but *is* any one admonished *thereby?* (18) Ád charged *their prophet* with imposture; but how *severe* was my vengeance, and my threatening! (19) Verily we sent against them a roaring wind, on a day of continued

---

(9) We here again see how Muhammad represents the former prophets as being like unto himself. See Introduction to chaps. xi. and xxi.

(10) *Wherefore avenge me.* "This petition was not preferred by Noah till after he had suffered repeated violence from his people; for it is related that one of them having fallen upon him and almost strangled him, when he came to himself he said, 'O Lord, forgive them, for they know not what they do.'"—*Sale, Baidháwi.*

The flood is here represented as having been sent for the purpose of avenging Noah, contradicting the former Scriptures both in letter and spirit.

(14) *Under our eyes, i.e.,* "under our special regard and keeping." —*Sale.*

(15) Rodwell thinks that Muhammad owed the statement of this verse, "We left the said vessel for a sign," to a Jewish tradition "as to the collection of pitch from the wood of the ark in the time of Berosus for amulets, and of the wood itself in the time of Josephus (*Ant.* i. 3, 6; c. *Apion,* i. 19)."

(19) *A roaring wind.* "Or a *cold* wind."—*Sale.*

A day, &c., viz., "on a Wednesday." See chap. xli. 15, note.

ill-luck; (20) it carried men away as though they *had been* roots of palm-trees forcibly torn up. (21) And how *severe* was my vengeance and my threatening! (22) Now we have made the Qurán easy for admonition; but *is* any one admonished *thereby?*

|| (23) Thamúd charged the admonitions *of their prophet* R $\frac{2}{9}$. with falsehood, (24) and said, Shall we follow a single man among us? verily we should then be guilty of error and preposterous madness: (25) is the *office of* admonition committed unto him *preferably to the rest* of us? Nay; he is a liar *and* an insolent fellow. (26) *But God said to Sálih,* To-morrow shall they know who *is* the liar and the insolent person; (27) for we will surely send the she-camel for a trial of them: and do thou observe them, and bear *their insults* with patience; (28) and prophesy unto them that the water *shall be* divided between them, and each portion *shall be* sat down to *alternately.* (29) And they called their companion; and he took *a sword* and slew *her.* (30) But how *severe* was my vengeance and my threatening! (31) For we sent against them one cry *of the Angel Gabriel;* and they became like the dry sticks used by him who buildeth a fold *for cattle.* (32) And now have we made the Qurán easy for admonition; but *is* any one admonished *thereby?*

|| (33) The people of Lot charged *his* preaching with R $\frac{3}{10}$.

---

(20) "It is related that they sought shelter in the clefts of the rocks and in pits, holding fast by one another, but that the wind impetuously tore them away, and threw them down dead."—*Sale, Baidháwi.*

(27) See notes on chap. vii. 74–79.

(28) *Between them.* Between the Thamúdites and the she-camel. See note on chap. xxvi. 155.

(29) *Their companion,* namely, "Kídár Ibn Salíf, who was not an Arab, but a stranger dwelling among the Thamúdites."—*Sale.* See also notes on chap. vii. 74–79.

(31) *Dry sticks, &c.* "The words may signify either the dry boughs with which, in the East, they make folds or enclosures to fence their cattle from wind and cold, or the stubble and other stuff with which they litter them in those folds during the winter season."
—*Sale.*

falsehood; (34) but we sent against them *a wind* driving a shower of stones, *which destroyed them all* except the family of Lot; whom we delivered early in the morning, (35) through favour from us. Thus do we reward those who are thankful. (36) And *Lot* had warned them of our severity *in chastising;* but they doubted of that warning. (37) And they demanded his guests of him, *that they might abuse them:* but we put out their eyes, *saying,* Taste my vengeance and my threatening. (38) And early in the morning a lasting punishment surprised them. (39) Taste, therefore, my vengeance and my threatening. (40) Now have we made the Quran easy for admonition; but *is* any one admonished *thereby?* (41) The warning *of Moses* also came unto the people of Pharaoh; (42) *but* they charged every one of our signs with imposture: wherefore we chastised them with a mighty and irresistible chastisement. (43) Are your unbelievers, *O Makkans,* better than these? Is immunity from punishment *promised* unto you in the scriptures? (44) Do they say, We are a body *of men* able to prevail *against our enemies?* (45) The multitude shall surely be put to flight, and shall turn *their* back. (46) But the hour *of judgment is* their threatened time *of*

---

(37) *We put out their eyes.* "So that their sockets became filled up even with the other parts of their faces. This, it is said, was done by one stroke of the wing of the Angel Gabriel. See chap. xi. 80."—*Sale.*

(38) *A lasting punishment.* "Under which they shall continue till they receive their full punishment in hell."—*Sale.*

(41, 42) See notes on chap. vii. 104-136.

(45) "This prophecy was fulfilled by the overthrow of the Quraish at Badr. It is related, from a tradition of Omar, that when this passage was revealed, Muhammad professed himself to be ignorant of its true meaning; but on the day of the battle of Badr he repeated these words as he was putting on his coat of mail."—*Sale, Baidhâwi.*

There is no good reason for supposing these words to have had any reference to the battle of Badr. The "multitude" refers to the Quraish, who were, when compared with the Muslims, a multitude, as were also the enemies of the former prophets described above.

(46) *Threatened time, &c., i.e.,* "the time when they shall receive their full punishment; what they suffer in this world being only the forerunner or earnest of what they shall feel in the next."—*Sale.*

punishment; and that hour *shall be* more grievous and more bitter *than their afflictions in this life.* (47) Verily the wicked *wander* in error, and *shall be tormented hereafter* in burning flames. (48) On that day they shall be dragged into the fire on their faces; *and it shall be said unto them,* Taste ye the touch of hell. (49) All things have we created *bound* by a fixed decree: (50) and our command *is* no more than a single *word,* like the twinkling of an eye. (51) We have formerly destroyed *nations* like unto you; but *is* any *of you* warned *by their example?* (52) Everything which they do *is recorded* in the books *kept by the guardian angels;* (53) and every *action,* both small and great, *is* written down *in the preserved table.* (54) Moreover, the pious *shall dwell* among gardens and rivers, (55) in the assembly of truth, in the presence of a most potent king.

---

(50) *A single word,* viz., "'Kun,' *i.e.*, 'Be.' The passage may also be rendered, 'The execution of our purpose is but a single act, exerted in a moment. Some suppose it refers to the business of the day of judgment."—*Sale, Baidháwi.*

See note on chap. xxxvi. 82.

CHAPTER LV.

ENTITLED SURAT AL RAHMÁN (THE MERCIFUL).

Revealed at Makkah.

INTRODUCTION.

THIS chapter, as indicated by the name given to God in the first verse, from which it receives its title, is a psalm of praise to Allah for his manifold mercies to mankind. This revelation of God is exhibited in his works of creation and providence, but especially in his bountiful provision for the happiness of Muslims amid the gardens and by the cooling fountains and rivers of Paradise.

Among Muslims this is one of the most popular chapters in the Qurán. This is no doubt due partly to its sensual description of Paradise and partly to the "fixed alternating versicle throughout, quaintly addressed in the dual number both to men and genii. To suit the rhyme the objects are introduced in pairs, excepting the damsels, whose number may not thus be limited" (Muir's *Life of Mahomet*, vol. ii. p. 142). This arrangement gives the reading of the chapter in the Arabic language a certain musical ring which is very charming to the ear of an Oriental. In form it resembles Psalm xxxvii., of which, as has been conjectured by Marracci, it is an imitation.

Probable Date of the Revelations.

There can be but one judgment as to the locality in which this chapter originated. "Its fanciful character," says Noöldeke, "shows it to be a later Makkan production." Some Muslim writers hold that the whole chapter is Madínic, or that at least ver. 29 is so; but this opinion is rejected by the better class of commentators. As to the date, the style and contents alike point to the end of the first period, *i.e.*, of the fourth year of the Call.

INTROD.]   (103)   [CHAP. LV.

Principal Subjects.
	VERSES
God taught the Qurán to Muhammad	1
God the creator of all things	2-15
God controlleth the seas and all that is therein	16-25
God ever liveth, though all else decay and die	26-30
God will certainly judge both men and genii	31-40
God will consign the wicked to hell-fire	41-45
The joys of Paradise described	46-78

IN THE NAME OF THE MOST MERCIFUL GOD.

|| (1) The Merciful hath taught *his servant* the Qurán. R ¹ ʟ. (2) He created man; (3) he hath taught him distinct speech. (4) The sun and the moon *run their courses* according to a certain rule: (5) and the vegetables which creep on the ground, and the trees submit *to his disposition*. (6) He also raised the heaven; and he appointed the balance, (7) that ye should not transgress in respect to the balance: (8) wherefore observe a just weight, and diminish not the balance. (9) And the earth hath he prepared for living creatures: (10) therein *are various* fruits, and palm-trees bearing sheaths of flowers; (11) and grain having chaff, and leaves. (12) Which, therefore, of your LORD's benefits will ye ungratefully deny?

|| (13) He created man of dried clay like an earthen Nisf. vessel: (14) but he created the genii of fire clear from smoke. (15) Which, therefore, of your LORD's benefits will ye ungratefully deny? (16) *He is* the LORD of the

---

(1) See chap. liii. 6, note.
(6) *The balance.* · "Or justice and equity in mutual dealings."—*Sale.*
(12) "The words are directed to the two species of rational creatures, men and genii, the verb and the pronoun being in the dual number.
"This verb is intercalated, or repeated by way of burden, throughout the whole chapter no less than thirty-one times, which was done, as Marracci guesses, in imitation of David."—*Sale.* (Comp. Ps. xxxvii.)
(13-14) See notes on chaps. ii. 30, and vii. 12.
(16) *East ... west.* "The original words are both in the dual

east, (17) and the LORD of the west. (18) Which, therefore of your LORD's benefits will ye ungratefully deny? (19) He hath let loose the two seas, that they meet each another: (20) between them *is placed* a bar which they cannot pass. (21) Which, therefore, of your LORD's benefits will ye ungratefully deny? (22) From them are taken forth unions and lesser pearls. (23) Which, therefore, of your LORD's benefits will ye ungratefully deny? (24) His also *are* the ships, carrying their sails aloft in the sea like mountains. (25) Which, therefore, of your LORD's benefits will ye ungratefully deny? (26) Every *creature* which *liveth* on *the earth is* subject to decay: (27) but the glorious and honourable countenance of thy LORD shall remain *for ever*. (28) Which, therefore, of your LORD's benefits will ye ungratefully deny?

R $\frac{2}{12}$.

|| (29) Unto him do all *creatures* which *are* in heaven and earth make petition: every day *is* he *employed* in *some new* work. (30) Which, therefore, of your LORD's benefits will ye ungratefully deny? (31) We will surely attend to *judge* you, O men and genii, *at the last day*. (32) Which, therefore, of your LORD's benefits will ye ungratefully deny? (33) O ye collective body of genii and men, if ye be able to pass out of the confines of heaven and earth, pass forth: ye shall not pass forth but by absolute power. (33) Which, therefore, of your LORD's benefits will ye ungratefully deny? (35) A flame of fire without smoke,

---

number, and signify the different points of the horizon at which the sun rises and sets at the summer and winter solstice."—*Sale*.

See note on chap. xxxvii. 5.

(19) *The two seas*. " Of salt and fresh water (chap. xxv. 55), or the Persian and Mediterranean seas."—*Sale, Baidháwi*.

(29) *Some new work*. " In executing those things which he hath decreed from eternity, by giving life and death, raising one and abasing another, hearing prayers and granting petitions, &c."—*Sale, Baidháwi*.

(33) *To pass out, &c*. " To fly from the power and to avoid the decree of God."—*Sale*.

(35) *A smoke without flame*. " Or, as the word also signifies, *molten brass*, which shall be poured on the heads of the damned."—*Sale*.

and a smoke without flame shall be sent down upon you, and ye shall not be able to defend yourselves *therefrom.* (36) Which, therefore, of your LORD'S benefits will ye ungratefully deny? (37) And when the heaven shall be rent in sunder, and shall become *red as* a rose, *and shall melt like ointment.* (38) (Which, therefore, of your LORD'S benefits will ye ungratefully deny?) (39) On that day neither man nor genius shall be asked concerning his sin. (40) Which, therefore, of your LORD'S benefits will ye ungratefully deny? (41) The wicked shall be known by their marks, and they shall be taken by the forelocks and the feet *and shall be cast into hell.* (42) Which, therefore, of your LORD'S benefits will ye ungratefully deny? (43) This *is* hell, which the wicked deny as a falsehood: (44) they shall pass to and fro between the same and hot boiling water. (45) Which, therefore, of your LORD'S benefits will ye ungratefully deny?

|| (46) But for him who dreadeth the tribunal of his LORD *are prepared* two gardens: (47) (Which, therefore, of your LORD'S benefits will ye ungratefully deny?) (48) planted with shady trees. (49) Which, therefore, of your LORD'S benefits will ye ungratefully deny? (50) In each of them *shall be* two fountains flowing. (51) Which, therefore, of your LORD'S benefits will ye ungratefully deny?

$R \frac{3}{13}$.

---

(37) *A rose, &c.* "Or 'shall appear like red leather,' according to a different signification of the original word."—*Sale.*

(39) *Neither man nor genius, &c.* "For their crimes will be known by their different marks, as it follows in the text. 'This,' says al Baidháwi, 'is to be understood of the time when they shall be raised to life, and shall be led towards the tribunal; for when they come to trial, they will then undergo an examination, as is declared in several places of the Qurán.'"—*Sale.*

(41) See Prelim. Disc., p. 141.

(44) *To and fro, &c.* "For the only respite they shall have from the flames of hell will be when they are suffered to go to drink this scalding liquor."—*Sale.* See chap. xxxvii. 62-65.

(46) *Two gardens, i.e.,* "one distinct Paradise for men, and another for genii, or, as some imagine, two gardens for each person; one as a reward due to his works, and the other as a free and superabundant gift, &c."—*Sale.*

(52) In each of them *shall there be* of every fruit two kinds. (53) Which, therefore, of your LORD's benefits will ye ungratefully deny? (54) They shall repose on couches, the linings whereof *shall be* of thick silk interwoven with gold: and the fruit of the two gardens *shall be* near at hand *together*. (55) Which, therefore, of your LORD's benefits will ye ungratefully deny? (56) Therein *shall receive them beauteous damsels*, refraining their eyes *from beholding any besides their spouses:* whom no man shall have deflowered before them, neither any genius: (57) (Which, therefore, of your LORD's benefits will ye ungratefully deny?) (58) *Having complexions* like rubies and pearls. (59) Which, therefore, of your LORD's benefits will ye ungratefully deny? (60) *Shall* the reward of good works *be* any other good? (61) Which, therefore, of your LORD's benefits will ye ungratefully deny? (62) And besides these *there shall be* two *other* gardens: (63) Which, therefore, of your LORD's benefits will ye ungratefully deny? (64) Of a dark green. (65) Which, therefore, of your LORD's benefits will ye ungratefully deny? (66) In each of them *shall be* two fountains pouring forth plenty of water. (67) Which, therefore, of your LORD's benefits will ye ungratefully deny? (68) In each of them *shall be* fruits, and

---

(52) *Fruit two kinds.* "Some being known, and like the fruits of the earth; and others of new and unknown species, or fruits both green and ripe."—*Sale.*

(54) *Fruit . . . near at hand.* "So that a man may reach them as he sits or lies down."—*Sale.*

(56-58) See note on chap. iii. 15. "This," says Muir, "is the reward of the *highest* class of believers. Another set of gardens and females is immediately after described for the *common* faithful."—*Life of Mahomet*, vol. ii. p. 142.

(62) *Two other gardens.* "For the inferior classes of the inhabitants of Paradise."—*Sale.* See note on vers. 56-58, above.

(64) *Of a dark green.* "From hence, says al Baidháwi, it may be inferred that these gardens will chiefly produce herbs or the inferior sorts of vegetables; whereas the former will be planted chiefly with fruit-trees. The following part of this description also falls short of that of the other gardens, prepared for the superior classes."—*Sale.*

(65-76) See note on chap. ii. 25, and Rodwell *in loco.*

palm-trees, and pomegranates. (69) Which, therefore, of your LORD's benefits will ye ungratefully deny? (70) Therein *shall be* agreeable and beauteous *damsels:* (71) Which, therefore, of your LORD's benefits will ye ungratefully deny? (72) Having fine black eyes, *and* kept in pavilions *from public view:* (73) Which, therefore, of your LORD's benefits will ye ungratefully deny? (74) Whom no man shall have deflowered before *their destined spouses,* nor any genius. (75) Which, therefore, of your LORD's benefits will ye ungratefully deny? (76) *Therein shall they delight themselves,* lying on green cushions and beautiful carpets. (77) Which, therefore of your LORD's benefits will ye ungratefully deny? (78) Blessed be the name of thy LORD, possessed of glory and honour!

CHAPTER LVI.

ENTITLED SURAT AL WÁQÍA (THE INEVITABLE).

Revealed at Makkah.

INTRODUCTION.

THIS chapter forms a single discourse. The first three verses may be regarded as giving the subject of the discourse. In the following verses we have described : (1) the terrors which shall suddenly befall the human race at the judgment-day ; (2) the rewards of the righteous to which they shall then be admitted ; (3) the punishment then to be inflicted upon the wicked, because they had refused to believe in the warnings of the Qurán; and, finally, arguments to prove the possibility of the resurrection of the dead.

Some writers, however, maintain that a new part of this chapter begins with ver. 74'; but since the termination of both parts are alike and ver. 87 *seq.* refer to what is said in the first part, it is only reasonable to regard the chapter as forming a whole.

Probable Date of the Revelations.

A few writers have held this chapter to be Madínic, or that at least vers. 74-81 are so, or ver. 81 only, which they suppose to refer to the hypocrites of Madína ; or vers. 91–96 for the same reason ; or, finally, vers. 1–3, which they suppose to allude to the battle of Badr. The style and matter of the chapter are, however, too clearly in favour of a Makkan origin to admit of any doubt.

As to the date of the revelations, Noëldeke places this chapter immediately after chap. lii. Muir makes it to follow chap. lv., which, considering the similarity of the description of the sensual delights of Paradise and the torments of hell, is the better arrangement.

Principal Subjects.

	VERSES
The coming of the judgment-day inevitable	1, 2
Its terrors described	3-7
Its coming shall separate men into three classes	8-11
Joys of the Muslim heaven described	12-39
The punishment of the wicked in hell depicted	40-56
Arguments for the resurrection of the dead drawn from God's work in creation and providence	57-73
Oath by the stars that the Qurán is divinely inspired	74-81
Men should believe in God since they cannot save the dying from death	82-96

IN THE NAME OF THE MOST MERCIFUL GOD.

|| (1) When the inevitable *day of judgment* shall suddenly come, (2) no *soul* shall charge *the prediction of* its coming with falsehood: (3) it will abase *some* and exalt *others*. (4) When the earth shall be shaken with a violent shock, (5) and the mountains shall be dashed in pieces, (6) and shall become *as* dust scattered abroad; (7) and ye shall be *separated into* three *distinct* classes: (8) the companions of the right hand (how *happy shall* the companions of the right hand *be !*), (9) and the companions of the left hand (how *miserable shall* the companions of the left hand *be !*); (10) and those who have preceded *others in*

R $\frac{1}{14}$

---

(1) *The inevitable*. "The original word, the force whereof cannot well be expressed by a single word, signifies a calamitous accident, which falls surely and with sudden violence, and is therefore made use of here to design the day of judgment."—*Sale*.

(8, 9) *Companions of the right ... and left hand*. "That is, the blessed and the damned; who may be thus distinguished here, because the books wherein their actions are registered will be delivered into the right hands of the former and into the left hands of the latter, though the words translated *right hand* and *left hand* do also signify *happiness* and *misery*."—*Sale, Baidháwi, Jaláluddín*.

(10) *Those who have preceded, &c.* "Either the first converts to Muhammadism, or the prophets, who were the respective leaders of their people, or any persons who have been eminent examples of piety and virtue, may be here intended. The original words literally rendered are, *The leaders, the leaders:* which repetition, as some sup-

the faith shall precede *them to Paradise.* (11) These *are* they who shall approach near *unto God:* (12) *they shall dwell* in gardens of delight. (13) (*There shall be* many of the former *religions,* (14) and few of the last.) (15) Reposing on couches adorned with gold and precious stones, (16) sitting opposite to one another thereon. (17) Youths which shall continue *in their bloom* for ever, shall go round about *to attend* them, (18) with goblets, and beakers, and a cup of flowing *wine:* (19) their heads shall not ache by *drinking* the same, neither shall their reason be disturbed: (20) and with fruits of the *sorts* which they shall choose, (21) and the flesh of birds of the *kind* which they shall desire. (22) And *there shall accompany them* fair damsels having large black eyes; resembling pearls hidden *in their shells:* (23) as a reward for that which they shall have wrought. (24) They shall not hear therein any vain discourse, or any charge of sin; (25) but only the salutation, Peace! Peace! (26) And the companions of the right hand (how *happy shall* the companions of the right hand *be!*) (27) *shall have their abode* among lote-trees free from thorns, (28) and trees of mauz loaded regularly *with their produce* from top to bottom; (29) *under* an extended shade, (30) *near* a flowing water, (31) and *amidst*

---

pose, was designed to express the dignity of these persons and the certainty of their future glory and happiness."—*Sale, Baidháwi, &c.*

(14) *Few of the last, i.e.,* "there shall be more *leaders,* who have preceded others in faith and good works, among the followers of the several prophets from Adam down to Muhammad, than of the followers of Muhammad himself."—*Sale, Baidháwi.*

(16) See note on chap. xv. 47.

(17-25) See notes on chaps. ii. 25, iii. 15, and lv. 46-76.

(28) *Trees of mauz.* "The original word, *Talh,* is the name, not only of the mauz (see chap. xxxvii. 146), but also of a very tall and thorny tree, which bears abundance of flowers of an agreeable smell, and seems to be the acacia."—*Sale.*

Rodwell suggests the *banana* tree.

(30) *Flowing water.* "Which shall be conveyed in channels to such places and in such manner as every one shall desire. Al Baidháwi observes that the condition of the few who have preceded others in faith and good works is represented by whatever may render a city life agreeable, and that the condition of the com-

fruits in abundance, (32) which shall not fail, nor shall be forbidden *to be gathered:* (33) and *they shall repose themselves* on lofty beds. (34) Verily we have created *the damsels of Paradise* by a *peculiar* creation: (35) and we have made them virgins, (36) beloved by their husbands, of equal age *with them;* (37) for *the delight of* the companions of the right hand. (38) *There shall be* many of the former *religions,* (39) and many of the latter.

|| (40) And the companions of the left hand (how miserable shall the companions of the left hand *be!*) (41) *shall dwell* amidst burning winds and scalding water, (42) under the shade of a black smoke, (43) neither cool nor agreeable. (44) For they enjoyed the pleasures of life before this, *while on earth;* (45) and obstinately persisted in a heinous wickedness: (46) and they said, (47) After we shall have died, and become dust and bones, *shall* we

R $\frac{2}{15}$.

---

panions of the right hand, or the generality of the blessed, is represented by those things which make the principal pleasure of a country life; and that this is done to show the difference of the two conditions."—*Sale.*

(33) *Lofty beds.* "The word translated *beds* signifies also, by way of metaphor, *wives* or *concubines;* and if the latter sense be preferred, the passage may be rendered thus, 'And they shall enjoy damsels raised on lofty couches, whom we have created,' &c."—*Sale.*

(34) *We have created, &c.* "Having created them purposely of finer materials than the females of this world, and subject to none of those inconveniences which are natural to the sex. Some understand this passage of the beatified women, who, though they died old and ugly, shall yet be restored to their youth and beauty in Paradise."—*Sale.*

See also Prelim. Disc., pp. 158-163.

(35) *Virgins.* "For how often soever their husbands shall go in unto them, they shall always find them virgins."—*Sale.*

(38, 39) "Father Marracci thinks this to be a manifest contradiction to what is said above (vers. 13, 14), 'There shall be many of the former and few of the latter;' but al Baidháwi obviates such an objection by observing that the preceding passage speaks of the *leaders* only, and those who have preceded others in faith and good works; and the passage before us speaks of the righteous of inferior merit and degree; so that though there be many of both sorts, yet there may be few of one sort, comparatively speaking, in respect to the other."—*Sale.*

(40-56) See chap. xxxvii. 62-65.

surely *be* raised to life? (48) *Shall* our forefathers also *be raised with us?* (49) Say, Verily both the first and the last (50) shall surely be gathered together *to judgment,* at the prefixed time of a known day. (51) Then ye, O men, who have erred, *and* denied *the resurrection* as a falsehood, (52) shall surely eat of *the fruit of* the tree of al Zaqqúm, (53) and shall fill *your* bellies therewith: (54) and ye shall drink thereon boiling water; (55) and ye shall drink as a thirsty camel drinketh. (56) This *shall be* their entertainment on the day of judgment. (57) We have created you: will ye not therefore believe *that we can raise you from the dead?* (58) What think ye? The *seed* which ye emit, (59) do ye create the same, or *are* we the creators *thereof?* (60) We have decreed death unto you *all:* and we shall not be prevented. (61) *We are able* to substitute *others* like unto you *in your stead,* and to produce you *again* in the *condition or form* which ye know not. (62) Ye know the original production *by creation;* will ye not therefore consider *that we are able to produce you by resuscitation?* (63) What think ye? The *grain* which ye sow, (64) do ye cause the same to spring forth, or do we cause *it* to spring forth? (65) If we pleased, verily we could render the same dry and fruitless, *so that* ye would not cease to wonder, (66) *saying,* Verily we have contracted debts *for seed and labour,* but we are not permitted *to reap the fruit thereof.* (67) What think ye? The water which ye drink, (68) do ye send down the same from the clouds, or *are* we the senders *thereof?* (69) If we pleased, we could render the same brackish: will ye not therefore give thanks? (70) What think ye. The fire which ye strike, (71) do ye produce

---

(65) *Ye would not cease to wonder.* "Or *to repent* of your time and labour bestowed to little purpose, &c."—*Sale.*

(66) *We have contracted debts,* or *we are undone.*

Not permitted to reap, &c., or, "*We are unfortunate wretches,* who are denied the necessaries of life."—*Sale.*

(71) See note on chap. xxxvi. 80.

the tree *whence ye obtain* the same, or *are* we the producers *thereof?* (72) We have ordained the same for an admonition, and an advantage to those who travel through the deserts. (73) Wherefore praise the name of thy LORD, the great *God*.

|| (74) Moreover I swear by the setting of the stars, R $\frac{3}{16}$. (75) (and it *is* surely a great oath, if ye knew *it*,) (76) SULS. that this *is* the excellent Qurán, (77) *the original whereof is written* in the preserved book: (78) none shall touch the same except those who are clean. (79) *It is* a revelation from the LORD of all creatures. (80) Will ye, therefore, despise this new revelation? (81) And do ye make *this return for* your food *which ye receive from God,* that ye deny *yourselves to be obliged to him for the same?* (82)' When *the soul of a dying person* cometh up to *his* throat, (83) and ye at the same time are looking on, (84) (and we are nigher unto him than ye, but ye see not *his*

---

(72) *An admonition.* "To put men in mind of the resurrection (chap. xxxvi. 80), which the production of fire in some sort resembles; or, of the fire of hell."—*Sale, Baidháwi.*

(74) *I swear, &c.* "The particle *la* is generally supposed to be intensive in this place; but if it be taken for a negative, the words must be translated, *I will not* or *do not swear*, because what is here asserted is too manifest to need the confirmation of an oath."—*Sale.*

Palgrave, Rodwell, and Savary adopt the latter reading, but the Persian and Urdú translations agree with Sale.

(78) *None shall touch, &c.* "Or, 'Let none touch the same,' &c. Purity both of body and mind being requisite in him who would use this book with the respect he ought, and hopes to edify by it; for which reason these words are usually written on the cover."—*Sale.*

See Prelim. Disc., p. 114, and Muir's *Life of Mahomet*, introd. p. x. note.

(81) *Do ye make . . . your food, &c.* "By ascribing the rains which fertilise your lands to the influence of the stars. (Prelim. Disc., pp. 38-43. "Some copies, instead of *rizqakúm, i.e., your food*, read *shukrakúm, i.e., your gratitude;* and then the passage may be rendered thus, 'And do ye make this return of gratitude for God's revealing the Qurán, that ye reject the same as a fiction?'"—*Sale.*

All copies of the Qurán that I have seen have *rizqakúm*. Rodwell translates thus, "Will ye make it your daily bread to gainsay them?"

(82-86) "The meaning of this obscure passage is, If ye shall not be obliged to give an account of your actions at the last day, as by

true condition,) (85) would ye not, if ye are not to be rewarded *for your action hereafter,* (86) cause the same to return *into the body,* if ye speak the truth? (87) And whether he be of those who shall approach near *unto God,* (88) *his reward shall be* rest, and mercy, and a garden of delights: (89) or whether he be of the companions of the right hand, (90) *he shall be saluted with the salutation,* Peace be unto thee! by the companions of the right hand, *his brethren:* (91) or whether he be of those who have rejected *the true faith* (92) *and* gone astray, (93) *his* entertainment *shall consist* of boiling water (94) and the burning of hell-*fire.* (95) Verily this *is* a certain truth. (96) Wherefore praise the name of thy LORD, the great *God.*

---

your denying the resurrection ye seem to believe, cause the soul of the dying person to return into his body; for ye may as easily do that as avoid the general judgment."—*Sale, Baidháwi, Jaláluddin.*

(87-94) See above in vers. 8, 9, and 14.

CHAPTER LVII.

ENTITLED SURAT AL HADÍD (IRON).

Revealed at Madína.

INTRODUCTION.

THE title of this chapter is taken from the mention of iron in ver 25. The object of the revelations seems to have been to arouse the faithful to greater zeal and energy in warring for the faith. It belongs, therefore, to a period in the history of Islám when Muhammad was in trouble. From ver. 22 *seq.* we infer that that period was the dark time succeeding the defeat at Ohod; comp. ver. 22 *seq.* with chap. iii. 149–154. The latter part of the chapter, vers. 25–29 is addressed to Christians, and therefore probably belongs to a different period. This part is specially interesting, because it set forth Muhammad's prophetic claims in relation to the former prophets and especially in relation to Jesus. We find that all these prophets are recognised as well as the Word of God spoken by them. The "Gospel," by which is intended the New Testament Scriptures, is distinctly mentioned. The prophets and Jesus are all the servants of God, and the books sent down to them are the Word of God; but *now* another Prophet and a new revelation have been sent. It is the duty of Christians to recognise these; failing which they must be regarded as "evil-doers" (ver. 27).

Probable Date of the Revelations.

Muslim authors are quite divided in opinion as to where this chapter belongs. The statement in ver. 10, according to the interpretation of Al Farrá, Al Bagháwi, and Al Bukhári, is quite decisive for Makkah. But, according to others, this statement does not refer to Makkah at all, but to the "victory" at Badr. See Rodwell. Turning to the style and spirit of the composition, we find it on the whole decidedly Madínic.

As to the date of composition, Noëldeke says, "Verse 22 *seq.* implies, if we are not mistaken (comp. ver. 23, with chap. iii. 149 *seq.*), that Muhammad at this time was in distress. We are therefore inclined to place this Sura in the time between the faith of Ohod and the war of the Ditch."

Principal Subjects.

	VERSES
God omniscient and omnipresent	1–6
Muslims exhorted to give alms and help on the holy war	7–11
The wise and the foolish in the judgment-day	12–14
True believers admonished to submit humbly to God	15–17
God will reward the faithful but will punish the wicked	18
The present life a vain show	19, 20
Men exhorted to seek the life to come	21
All things recorded in God's book of decrees	22, 23
God hateth proud and covetous persons (therefore the defeat at Ohod)	24
Apostles sent to former nations	25
Noah, Abraham, the prophets, and Jesus, with the Gospel, sent	26, 27
Christians exhorted to become Muslims	28, 29

IN THE NAME OF THE MOST MERCIFUL GOD.

R 1/7 ‖ (1) Whatever *is* in heaven and earth singeth praise unto GOD; and he *is* mighty *and* wise. (2) His *is* the kingdom of heaven and earth; he giveth life, and he putteth to death; and he *is* almighty. (3) He *is* the first and the last; the manifest and the hidden: and he knoweth all things. (4) *It is* he who created the heavens and the earth in six days, and then ascended *his* throne. He knoweth that which entereth into the earth, and that which issueth out of the same, and that which descendeth from heaven, and that which ascendeth thereto: and he *is* with you wheresoever ye be: for GOD seeth that which

---

(1–6) We have here a striking illustration of the omnipotence and omniscience of God. Such passages show the wonderful superiority of the Makkan preacher over the religious teachers of his idolatrous countrymen.

ye do. (5) His *is* the kingdom of heaven and earth; and unto GOD shall *all* things return. (6) He causeth the night to succeed the day, and he causeth the day to succeed the night; and he knoweth the innermost part of *men's* breasts. (7) Believe in GOD and his Apostle, and lay out *in alms* a part of the *wealth* whereof GOD hath made you inheritors: for unto such of you as believe and bestow alms *shall be given* a great reward. (8) And what aileth you, that ye believe not in GOD, when the Apostle inviteth you to believe in your LORD; and he hath received your covenant *concerning this matter,* if ye believe *any proposition?* (9) *It is* he who hath sent down unto his servant evident signs, that he may lead you out of darkness into light; for GOD *is* compassionate *and* merciful unto you. (10) And what aileth you, that ye contribute not *of your substance* for the defence of GOD's true religion? Since unto GOD *appertaineth* the inheritance of heaven and earth. Those among you who shall have contributed and fought *in defence of the faith* before the taking *of Makkah,* shall not be held equal *with those who shall contribute and fight for the same afterwards.* These shall be superior in degree unto those who shall contribute and fight *for the propagation of the faith* after *the abovementioned success;* but unto all hath GOD promised a most excellent *reward;* and GOD well knoweth that which ye do.

|| (11) Who *is* he that will lend unto GOD an acceptable loan? for he will double the same unto him, and he shall receive *moreover* an honourable reward. (12) On a *certain* day thou shalt see the true believers of both sexes: their

R $\frac{2}{18}$.

---

(7) *Lay out in alms, &c.* See note on chap. ix. 104.

(8) *Your covenant.* "That is, ye are obliged to believe in him by the strongest arguments and motives."—*Sale.*

(10) *The taking of Makkah.* The reference here is to Badr, and not to Makkah.

Not be held equal, &c. "Because afterwards there was not so great necessity for either, the Muhammadan religion being firmly established by that great success."—*Sale.*

light shall run before them, and on their right hands; *and it shall be said unto them,* Good tidings unto you this day: gardens through which rivers flow; *ye* shall remain therein for ever. This will be great felicity. (13) On that day the hypocritical men and the hypocritical women shall say unto those who believe, Stay for us, that we may borrow *some* of your light. It shall be answered, Return back *into the world* and seek light. And a high wall shall be set betwixt them, wherein *shall be* a gate, within which *shall be* mercy; and without it, over against the same, the torment *of hell.* The *hypocrites* shall call out unto *the true believers, saying,* Were we not with you? They shall answer, Yea; but ye seduced your own souls *by your hypocrisy;* and ye waited *our ruin;* and ye doubted *concerning the faith;* and *your* wishes deceived you, until the decree of GOD came, *and ye died;* and the deceiver deceived you concerning GOD. (14) This day, therefore, a ransom shall not be accepted of you, nor of those who have been unbelievers. Your abode *shall be hell-*fire: this *is* what ye have deserved; and an unhappy journey *shall it be thither!* (15) Is not the time yet come unto those who believe, that their hearts should humbly submit to the admonition of GOD, and to that truth which hath been revealed; and that they be not as those unto whom the Scripture was given heretofore, and to whom the time *of forbearance* was prolonged, but their hearts were hardened, and many of them *were* wicked doers? (16) Know that GOD quickeneth the earth after it hath been dead. Now have we distinctly declared *our* signs unto you, that ye may under-

---

(12) *Their light, &c.* "One light leading them the right way to Paradise, and the other proceeding from the book wherein their actions are recorded, which they will hold in their right hand."
—*Sale.*

(13) *Stay for us, &c.* "For the righteous will hasten to Paradise swift as lightning."—*Sale.*

There is a faint resemblance between this passage and the parable of the virgins, Matt. xxv. 1-12.

stand. (17) Verily *as to* the almsgivers, both men and women, and *those who* lend unto GOD an acceptable loan, he will double the same unto them; and they shall *moreover* receive an honourable reward. (18) And they who believe in GOD and his apostles, these are the men of veracity, and the witnesses in the presence of their LORD: they *shall have* their reward and their light. But *as to* those who believe not, and accuse our signs of falsehood, they *shall be* the companions of hell.

|| (19) Know that this present life *is* only a toy and a vain amusement: and *worldly* pomp, and the affectation of glory among you, and the multiplying of riches and children, *are* as the plants nourished by the rain, the springing up whereof delighteth the husbandmen; afterwards they wither, so that thou seest the same turned yellow, and at length they become dry stubble. And in the life to come *will be* a severe punishment *for those who covet worldly grandeur;* (20) and pardon from GOD, and favour *for those who renounce it:* for this present life *is* no other than a deceitful provision. (21) Hasten with emulation to *obtain* pardon from your LORD, and Paradise, the extent whereof equalleth the extent of heaven and earth, prepared for those who believe in GOD and his apostles. This *is* the bounty of GOD: he will give the same unto whom he pleaseth; and GOD is endued with great bounty. (22) No accident happeneth in the earth, nor in your persons, but *the same was entered* in the book *of our decrees* before we created it: verily this *is* easy with GOD: (23) *and this is written* lest ye *immoderately* grieve for the *good* which escapeth you, or rejoice for that which happened unto you; for GOD loveth no proud *or* vainglorious person, (24) *or those* who are covetous, and command men covetousness. And whoso turneth aside *from giving alms;* verily GOD *is* self-sufficient, worthy to be praised.

R $\frac{3}{19}$.

---

(18) *God and his apostles.* See notes on chap. ii. 136, 285.

(25) We formerly sent our apostles with evident *miracles and arguments;* and we sent down with them the Scriptures and the balance, that men might observe justice: and we sent *them* down iron, wherein is mighty strength for war, and *various* advantages unto mankind: that GOD may know who assisteth him and his apostles in secret; for GOD *is* strong *and* mighty.

R $\frac{4}{20}$.   ‖ (26) We formerly sent Noah and Abraham, and we established in their posterity the gift of prophecy, and the Scripture: and of them *some were* directed, but many of them *were* evil-doers. (27) Afterwards we caused our apostles to succeed in their footsteps; and we caused Jesus the son of Mary to succeed *them,* and we gave him the gospel: and we put in the hearts of those that followed him compassion and mercy: but *as to* the monastic state, they instituted the same (we did not prescribe it to them) only out of a desire to please GOD; yet they observed not the same as it ought truly to have been observed. And we gave unto such of them as believed their reward: but many of them *were* wicked doers. (28) O ye who believe *in the prophets,* fear GOD and believe in his Apostle *Muhammad:* he will give you two portions of his mercy, and he

---

(25) *The balance, i.e.*, a rule of justice. "Some think that a balance was actually brought down from heaven by the Angel Gabriel to Noah, the use of which he was ordered to introduce among his people."—*Sale.*

Iron. "That is, we taught them how to dig the same from mines. Al Zamakhsharí adds, that Adam is said to have brought down with him from Paradise five things made of iron, viz., an anvil, a pair of tongs, two hammers, a greater and a lesser, and a needle."—*Sale.*

Wherein, &c. "Warlike instruments and weapons being generally made of iron."—*Sale.*

In secret. That is, sincerely and heartily, not by a mere outward display of loyalty.

(27) *Jesus.* See notes on chaps. ii. 86 and iii. 39.

(28) *O ye who believe, &c.* "These words are directed to the Jews and Christians, or rather to the latter only."—*Sale.*

Two portions of his mercy. "One as a recompense for their believing in Muhammad, and the other as a recompense for their believing in the prophets who preceded him; for they will not lose

will ordain you a light wherein ye may walk, and he will forgive you; for GOD *is* ready to forgive, *and* merciful! (29) that those who have received the Scriptures may know that they have not power over any of the favours of GOD, and that good *is* in the hand of GOD; he bestoweth the same on whom he pleaseth: for GOD *is* endued with great beneficence.

---

the reward of their former religion, though it be now abrogated by the promulgation of Islám."—*Sale, Baidháwi.*

(29) *That those . . . may know, &c.*, *i.e.*, " that they cannot expect to receive any of the favours above mentioned, because they believe not in his Apostle, and those favours are annexed to faith in him ; or, that they have not power to dispose of God's favours, particularly of the greatest of them, the gift of prophecy, so as to appropriate the same to whom they please."—*Sale, Baidháwi.*

CHAPTER LVIII.

ENTITLED SURAT AL MUJÁDALAH (SHE WHO DISPUTED).

Revealed at Madína.

INTRODUCTION.

THIS chapter differs from most of the chapters of the Qurán in that it is addressed entirely to the Muslims. Nothing could better illustrate the change which had taken place in the fortunes of the Makkan preacher. No longer does he appear as "a mere warner;" no more does he strive to win over his adversaries by appeals to the *signs* of God in his works and in his Qurán. Influential enemies and hypocritical allies are alike ignored. Even Muslims are now made to feel the power of their Prophet. Ancient customs are abrogated, with heavy penalties attached to any infringement of the new law. Muslims must henceforth show outward respect, even to the extent of bringing a gift (alms), though this regulation seems to have proved so unpopular as to require speedy abrogation.

We have in the latter verses of this chapter signs of that fanaticism, allied to a proud self-righteousness, which has ever since characterised the followers of Muhammad. "The party of God" is henceforth to be separated from "the party of the devil." Dearest friends and kindred are to be shunned, unless by the formal utterance of the *Kalimah*, they join "the party of God."

Probable Date of the Revelations.

From what has already been said, it is plain that this is one of the latest of the Madína chapters. The opinion of those who regard vers. 1–10 as Makkan is certainly mistaken. Scarcely less mistaken is the opinion that these verses were revealed during the first years of the Hijra.

The several portions of the chapter, though separate revelations, are nevertheless, in point of time, closely connected together. The earlier authorities fix no date to the incident mentioned in vers. 1–5, but later authorities (Weil, 184) fix its date at the end of A.H. 6, or the beginning of A.H. 7, after the return from Hudaibíyah. Noëldeke places this chapter immediately after chap. xxiv., inasmuch as the matters treated of here closely resemble those mentioned there.

Principal Subjects.

	VERSES
An ancient Arab custom of divorce abrogated	1–5
Those who oppose Muhammad threatened	6, 7
Clandestine discourse against Muhammad censured and forbidden	8–11
The prophet of God to be approached with due reverence and honour	12–14
Muslims reproached for keeping company with Jews and infidels	15–21
Nearest relatives, if unbelievers, to be avoided as enemies of Islám	22

IN THE NAME OF THE MOST MERCIFUL GOD.

|| (1) Now hath GOD heard the speech of her who disputed with thee concerning her husband, and made her complaint unto GOD; and GOD hath heard your mutual discourse: for GOD *both* heareth *and* seeth. (2) *As to* those among you who divorce their wives by declaring

TWENTY-EIGHTH SIPARA.

R $\frac{1}{1}$.

---

(1) *Her who disputed.* "This was Khaula Bint Thálaba, the wife of Aus Ibn al Sámat, who being divorced by her husband by a form in use among the Arabs in the time of ignorance, viz., by saying to her, 'Thou art to me as the back of my mother,' came to ask Muhammad's opinion whether they were necessarily obliged to a separation; and he told her that it was not lawful for her to cohabit with her husband any more: to which she replying that her husband had not put her away, the Prophet repeated his former decision, adding that such form of speaking was, by general consent, understood to imply a perpetual separation. Upon this the woman, being greatly concerned because of the smallness of her children, went home and uttered her complaint to God in prayer: and thereupon this passage was revealed, allowing a man to take his wife again, notwithstanding his having pronounced the above-mentioned form of divorce, on doing certain acts of charity or mortification by way of penance."—*Sale.*

(2) Compare chap. xxxiii. 4, and see note there.

that they will thereafter regard them as their mothers, *let them know that* they *are* not their mothers. They only *are* their mothers who brought them forth; and they certainly utter an unjustifiable saying and a falsehood: (3) but GOD *is* gracious *and* ready to forgive. (4) Those who divorce their wives by declaring that they will for the future regard them as their mothers, and afterwards would repair what they have said, *shall be obliged* to free a captive before they touch one another. That *is* what ye are warned *to perform:* and GOD *is* well apprised of that which ye do. (5) And whoso findeth not *a captive to redeem shall observe* a fast of two consecutive months before they touch one another. And whoso shall not be able *to fast that time shall* feed threescore poor men. This *is ordained you* that ye may believe in GOD and his Apostle. These *are* the statutes of GOD: and for the unbelievers *is prepared* a grievous torment. (6) Verily they who oppose GOD and his Apostle shall be brought low, as *the unbelievers* who preceded them were brought low. And now have we sent down manifest signs: and an ignominious punishment awaiteth the unbelievers. (7) On a *certain* day GOD shall raise them all to life, and shall declare unto them that which they have wrought. GOD hath taken an exact account thereof; but they have forgotten the same: and GOD *is* witness over all things.

R ⅔. || (8) Dost thou not perceive that GOD knoweth what-

They only are their mothers, &c. "And therefore no woman ought to be placed in the same degree of prohibition, except those whom God has joined with them as nursing mothers and the wives of the Prophet."—*Sale, Baidháwi.*

But why the wives of the Prophet? See notes on chap. xxxiii. 6. If this "saying" is *unjustifiable* and a *falsehood* for the people, why not for the Prophet?

(4) *Would repair, &c.* "This seems to be here the true meaning of the original word, which properly signifies *to return,* and is variously expounded by the Muhammadan doctors."—*Sale.*

A captive. "Which captive, according to the most received decision, ought to be a true believer; as is ordered for the expiation of manslaughter."—*Sale, Baidháwi.* See chap. iv. 91, and note there.

(8) The omnipresence of a personal God is here very clearly expressed. Compare the words of our Lord, Matt. xviii. 20.

ever *is* in heaven and in earth? There is no private discourse among three persons, but he *is* the fourth of them; nor *among* five, but he *is* the sixth of them; neither *among* a smaller *number* than this, nor a larger, but he *is* with them, wheresoever they be: and he will declare unto them that which they have done on the day of resurrection: for GOD knoweth all things. (9) Hast thou not observed those who have been forbidden to use clandestine discourse, but afterwards return to what they have been forbidden, and discourse privily among themselves of wickedness, and enmity, and disobedience towards the Apostle? And when they come unto thee, they salute thee with that *form of salutation* wherewith GOD doth not salute thee; and they say among themselves, *by way of derision*, Would not GOD punish us for what we say *if this man were a prophet?* Hell *shall be* their sufficient *punishment*: they shall go down into the same to be burned; and an unhappy journey *shall it be!* (10) O true believers, when ye discourse privily together, discourse not of wickedness, and enmity, and disobedience towards the Apostle; but discourse of justice and piety: and fear GOD, before whom ye shall be assembled. (11) Verily the clandestine discourse *of the infidels proceedeth* from Satan, that he may grieve the true believers: but there shall be none to hurt them in the least, unless by the permission of GOD; wherefore in GOD let the faithful trust. (12) O true believers, when it is said unto you, Make room in the

---

(9) *Hast thou not observed those, &c.* "That is, the Jews and hypocritical Muslims, who caballed privately together against Muhammad, and made signs to one another when they saw the true believers; and this they continued to do notwithstanding they were forbidden."—*Sale.*

They salute thee, &c. "It seems they used, instead of *As salám alaika*, i.e., 'Peace be upon thee,' to say, *As sám alaika*, i.e., 'Mischief on thee,' &c."—*Sale, Baidháwi.*

(12) *Make room.* "In this passage the Muslims are commanded to give place in the public assemblies to the Prophet and the more honourable of his companions, and not to press and crowd upon him, as they used to do, out of a desire of being near him and hearing his discourse."—*Sale.*

assembly; make room: GOD will grant you ample room *in Paradise*. And when it is said *unto you*, Rise up; rise up: GOD will raise those of you who believe, and those to whom knowledge is given to *superior* degrees *of honour;* and GOD *is* fully apprised of that which ye do. (13) O true believers, when ye go to speak with the Apostle, give alms previously to your discoursing *with him;* this *will be* better for you, and more pure. But if ye find not *what to give,* verily GOD *will be* gracious *and* merciful *unto you.* (14) Do ye fear to give alms previously to your discoursing with *the Prophet, lest ye should impoverish yourselves?* Therefore if ye do *it* not, and GOD is gracious unto you *by dispensing with the said precept for the future,* be constant at prayer, and pay the legal alms; and obey GOD and his Apostle *in all other matters:* for GOD well knoweth that which ye do.

R ⅔. || (15) Hast thou not observed those who have taken for their friends a people against whom GOD is incensed? They *are* neither of you nor of them: and they swear to a lie knowingly. (16) GOD hath prepared for them a grievous punishment; for it is evil which they do. (17) They have taken their oaths for a cloak, and they have turned *men* aside from the way of GOD: wherefore a shameful punishment awaiteth them; (18) neither their wealth nor their children shall avail them at all against GOD.

---

(13) *Give alms previously, &c.* "To show your sincerity, and to honour the Apostle. It is doubted whether this be a counsel or a precept; but, however, it continued but a very little while in force, being agreed on all hands to be abrogated by the following passage, 'Do ye fear to give alms,' &c."—*Sale, Baidháwi, Jaláluddín.*

(15) *A people, &c., i.e.,* the Jews.
Neither of you nor of them. "Being hypocrites and wavering between the two parties."—*Sale.*

They swear to a lie. "They have solemnly professed Islám, which they believe not in their hearts."—*Sale.*

(16–21) These verses express the intensity of the hatred which Muhammad now felt towards the Jews. They had all along been the keenest of his opponents and the readiest to expose the falseness of his prophetic pretensions. His was a hatred that could not be appeased even by the slaughter of the Bani Quraidha.

These *shall be* the inhabitants of *hell*-fire; they shall abide therein for ever. (19) On a *certain* day GOD shall raise them all; then will they swear unto him as they swear *now* unto you, imagining that it will be of service to them. Are they not liars? (20) Satan hath prevailed against them, and hath caused them to forget the remembrance of GOD. These *are* the party of the devil; and *shall* not the party of the devil *be* doomed to perdition? (21) Verily they who oppose GOD and his apostles *shall be placed among* the most vile. GOD hath written, Verily I will prevail, and my apostles: for GOD *is* strong *and* mighty. (22) Thou shalt not find people who believe in GOD and the last day to love him who opposeth GOD and his Apostle; although they be their fathers, or their sons, or their brethren, or their nearest relations. In the hearts of these hath GOD written faith: and he hath strengthened them with his spirit: and he will lead them into gardens, beneath which rivers flow, to remain therein for ever. GOD is well pleased in them; and they are well pleased in him. These are the party of GOD: and shall not the party of GOD prosper?

CHAPTER LIX.

ENTITLED SURAT AL HASHR (THE EMIGRATION).

Revealed at Madína.

INTRODUCTION.

THE title of this chapter is taken from a word in the second verse, which means, says Sale, "the quitting or removing from one's native country or settlement to dwell elsewhere, whether it be by choice or compulsion." It accords better with the matter of the chapter than titles in the Qurán generally do, nearly the whole chapter being taken up with the expulsion of the Baní Nadhír and matters resulting therefrom.

In the portion of this chapter relating to the distribution of the rich spoils taken from these unfortunate Jews, we see how the Qurán is made to subserve the political interests of Muhammad in providing at once for the replenishment of the war chest (vers. 6 and 7) and for the support of the poor refugees at Madína (vers. 8-10).

The expulsion of the Jews had weakened the party in Madína antagonistic to the Muslims, here styled "the hypocrites." This party is dealt with severely in this chapter. If the closing words (vers. 18-24) belong to Madína, they were probably intended for the instruction of these hypocrites, though addressed to the "true believers."

Probable Date of the Revelations.

The expulsion of the Baní Nadhír occurred in Rabí ul Awwal, A.H. 4. The revelations of this chapter were enunciated soon after that event. "Of vers. 18-24," says Noöldeke, "I cannot say anything definite. Nothing, however, hinders their having originated at the same time as the first portion of the Sura (compare the expression *yúsabbihú laho* in ver. 24 with *sabbaha lilláhi* in the first verse)."

Principal Subjects.

	VERSES
Everything in the universe praiseth God	1
Passage relating to the expulsion of the Baní Nadhír	2–5
Ruling of Muhammad concerning spoils	6, 7
Special ruling for the benefit of the Muhájirín	8–10
Hypocrites in Madína reproved for treachery	11–17
Muslims exhorted to fear God	18–20
Had the Qurán descended on a mountain, it would have split asunder	21
God hath excellent names, and he only to be worshipped	22–24

IN THE NAME OF THE MOST MERCIFUL GOD.

|| (1) Whatever *is* in heaven and earth celebrateth the praise of GOD : and he *is* the almighty, the wise. (2) *It was* he who caused those who believed not, of the people who receive the Scripture, to depart from their habitations at the first emigration. Ye did not think that they would

R $\frac{1}{4}$.

---

(2) *The first emigration.* Rodwell translates, "those who had emigrated previously," meaning the Qainuqáa, to whom the Baní Nadhír (mentioned here) first went after their retiring from Madína.

Sale says, "The people here intended were the Jews of the tribe of al Nadhír, who dwelt in Madína, and when Muhammad fled thither from Makkah, promised him to stand neuter between him and his opponents, and made a treaty with him to that purpose. When he had gained the battle of Badr, they confessed that he was the prophet described in the law ; but upon his receiving that disgrace at Ohod, they changed their note ; and Qáb Ibn al Ashraf with forty horse went and made a league with Abu Sufián, which they confirmed by oath. Upon this Muhammad got Qáb dispatched, and, in the fourth year of the Hijra, set forward against al Nadhír, and besieged them in their fortress, which stood about three miles from Madína, for six days, at the end of which they capitulated, and were allowed to depart, on condition that they should entirely quit that place ; and accordingly some of them went into Syria and others to Khaibar and Hira.

"This was the '*first* emigration,' mentioned in the passage before us. The other happened several years after, in the reign of Omar, when that Khalif banished those who had settled at Khaibar, and obliged them to depart out of Arabia."

Muir (*Life of Mahomet*, vol. iii. p. 216, note) says :—"The commentators interpret the words to mean 'at the first emigration,'

go forth; and they thought that their fortresses would protect them against GOD. But *the chastisement of* GOD came upon them from whence they did not expect; and he cast terror into their hearts. They pulled down their houses with their own hands, and the hands of the true believers. Wherefore take example *from them*, O ye who have eyes. (3) And if GOD had not doomed them to banishment, he had surely punished them in this world; and in the world to come they shall suffer the torment of *hell*-fire. (4) This, because they opposed GOD and his Apostle: and whoso opposeth GOD, verily GOD *will be* severe in punishing *him*. (5) What palm trees ye cut down or left standing on their roots, *were so cut down or left* by the will of GOD; and that he might disgrace the wicked doers. (6) And *as to the spoils* of these *people*, which GOD hath granted *wholly* to his Apostle, ye did not push forward any horses or camels against the same; but GOD giveth unto his apostles dominion over whom he pleaseth: for GOD *is* almighty. (7) *The spoils* of the inhabitants of the towns which GOD hath granted to his Apostle *are due* unto GOD and to the Apostle, and to him

---

alluding, by prophetic foresight, to the *second*, that was to follow when Omar drove the Jews out of the Peninsula. This, however, is an after-thought."

They pulled down their houses, &c. "Doing what damage they could, that the Muslims might make the less advantage of what they were obliged to leave behind them."—*Sale.*

(3) *He had surely punished them.* "By delivering them up to slaughter and captivity, as he did those of Quraidha."—*Sale.*

(6) *The spoils, &c.* "It is remarkable that in this expedition the spoils were not divided according to the law given for that purpose in the Qurán, but were granted to the Apostle, and declared to be entirely in his disposition; and the reason was, because the place was taken without the assistance of horse; which became a rule for the future."—*Sale.*

See notes on chap. viii. 1, 42.

Ye did not push forward any horses, &c. "For the settlement of those of al Nadhír being so near Madína, the Muslims went all on foot thither, except only the Prophet himself."—*Sale.*

God giveth unto his Apostle, &c. We see here how Muhammad made capital out of his military successes.

who is of kin *to the Apostle,* and the orphans, and the poor, and the traveller; that they may not be *for ever divided* in a circle among such of you as are rich. What the Apostle shall give you, that accept; and what he shall forbid you, *that* abstain from: and fear GOD; for GOD *is* severe in chastising.

‖ (8) *A part also belongeth* to the poor Muhájirín, who have been dispossessed of their houses and their substance, seeking favour from GOD and *his* good-will, and assisting GOD and his Apostle. These are the men of veracity. (9) And they who quietly possessed the town *of Madína,* and *professed* the faith *without molestation* before them, love him who hath fled unto them, and find in their breasts no want of that which is given the *Muhájirín,* but prefer *them* before themselves, although there be indigence among them. And whoso is preserved from the covetousness of his own soul, those shall surely prosper. (10) And they who have come after them say, O LORD, forgive us and our brethren who have preceded us in the faith, and put not into our hearts ill-will against those who have believed: O LORD, verily thou *art* compassionate *and* merciful.

‖ (11) Hast thou not observed them who play the hypocrites? They say unto their brethren who believe not, of those who have received the Scriptures, Verily if ye

RUBA.

R $\frac{2}{5}$.

---

(8) *Poor Muhájirín.* "Wherefore Muhammad distributed those spoils among the Muhájirín, or those who had fled from Makkah only, and gave no part thereof to the Ansárs or those of Madína, except only to three of them, who were in necessitous circumstances."—*Sale.*

(9) *Who possessed the town . . . before them.* "That is, the Ansárs; who enjoyed their houses and the free exercise of their religion before the Hijra, while the converts of Makkah were persecuted and harassed by the idolaters."—*Sale.*

Find . . . no want, &c. "And bear them no grudge or envy on that account."—*Sale.*

(10) *They who have come after them.* "The persons here meant seem to be those who fled from Makkah after Muhammad began to gain strength and his religion had made a considerable progress."— *Sale.*

(11) *Those who have received the Scriptures.* "That is, the Jews of the tribe of al Nadhír."—*Sale.*

be expelled *your habitations,* we will surely go forth with you; and we will not pay obedience, in your respect, unto any one for ever: and if ye be attacked, we will certainly assist you. But GOD is witness that they *are* liars. (12) Verily if they be expelled, they will not go forth with them: and if they be attacked, they will not assist them: and if they do assist them, they will surely turn their backs; and they shall not be protected. (13) Verily ye *are* stronger *than they,* by reason of the terror *cast* into breasts from GOD. This, because they *are* not people of prudence. (14) They will not fight against you in a body, except in fenced towns or from behind walls. Their strength in war among themselves *is* great: thou thinkest them *to be* united; but their hearts are divided. This, because they *are* people who do not understand. (15) Like those who lately preceded them, they have tasted the evil consequence of their deed; and a painful torment *is* prepared for them *hereafter.* (16) *Thus have the hypocrites deceived the Jews:* like the devil, when he saith unto a man, Be thou an infidel; and when he is become an infidel, he saith, Verily I *am* clear of thee; for I fear GOD, the LORD of all creatures. (17) Wherefore the end of them both shall be that they *shall dwell* in *hell-*fire, abiding therein for ever: and this shall be the recompense of the unjust.

R ⅖.   ‖ (18) O true believers, fear GOD; and let a soul look

---

(12) *They will not assist them.* "And it happened accordingly; for Ibn Ubbai and his confederates wrote to the Nadhirites to this purpose, but never performed their promise."—*Sale, Baidháwi.*

This prophecy, however, seems to have been written after the event. See ver. 15.

(14) *Their strength ... is great, i.e.,* "it is not their weakness or cowardice which makes them decline a field-battle with you, since they show strength and valour enough in their wars with one another; but both fail them when they enter into the lists with God and his Apostle."—*Sale.*

(15) *Those who lately preceded them, i.e.,* "the idolaters who were slain at Badr, or the Jews of Qainuqáa, who were plundered and sent into exile before those of al Nadhir."—*Sale.*

what it sendeth before for the morrow: and fear GOD, for GOD *is* well acquainted with that which ye do. (19) And be not as those who have forgotten GOD, and whom he hath caused to forget their own souls: these are the wicked doers. (20) The inhabitants of *hell*-fire and the inhabitants of Paradise shall not be held equal. The inhabitants of Paradise are they who shall enjoy felicity. (21) If we had sent down this Qurán on a mountain, thou wouldest certainly have seen the same humble itself, and cleave in sunder for fear of GOD. These similitudes do we propose unto men, that they may consider. (22) He *is* GOD, besides whom there is no GOD; who knoweth that which is future and that which is present: he *is* the most Merciful; (23) he *is* GOD, besides whom there is no GOD: the King the Holy, the Giver of peace, the Faithful, the Guardian, the Powerful, the Strong, the Most High. Far be GOD exalted above *the idols* which they associate *with him!* (24) He is GOD, the Creator, the Maker, the Former. He hath most excellent names. Whatever *is* in heaven and in earth praiseth him: and he *is* the Mighty, the Wise.

---

(18) *The morrow.* "That is, for the next life, which may be called 'the morrow,' as this present life may be called 'to-day.'"—*Sale.*

(21) The allusion here is to the giving of the law on Sinai.

(23) *Holy.* This is one of a very few passages in which God is called holy (*Quddûs*). See also chap. lxii. 1.

(24) *Excellent names.* See note on chap. vii. 181.

CHAPTER LX.

ENTITLED SURAT AL MUMTAHINA (SHE WHO IS TRIED).

Revealed at Madína.

INTRODUCTION.

THIS chapter bears this title, says Sale, "because it directs the women who desert and come over from the infidels to the Muslims to be examined and tried whether they be sincere in their profession of the faith." The incident which is said to have occasioned this revelation is given in the note on the first verse.

The separation of the Muslims from believers, noticed in the Introduction to chap. lviii., is here strictly enjoined. In this case the measure seems to have been a matter of policy to prevent the Quraish from tampering with the loyalty of the refugees, or to prevent their receiving information as to the intentions of the Muslims. See Muir's *Life of Mahomet*, vol. iv. p. 45, note.

Probable Date of the Revelations.

According to the Muslim commentators, the first part of this chapter (vers. 1–9) was revealed in A.H. 8, when the incident occurred which is narrated in the note on the first verse. The remaining verses date from a short time after the treaty with the Quraish at Hudaibiyah (ver. 10, note), A.H. 6.

Principal Subjects.

	VERSES
Muslims forbidden to make friends with the enemies of God	1–3
This precept enforced by the example of Abraham	4–6
Enemies of God may become friends of Muslims by conversion	7
Distinction between enemies and mere unbelievers	8, 9

	VERSES
Female refugees, being true believers, are to be regarded as divorced from their heathen husbands	10
How to recover dowers of Muslim women who apostatise .	11
The confession of faith required of converts from Arab idolatry	12
True believers not to make friends with infidels . . .	13

IN THE NAME OF THE MOST MERCIFUL GOD.

‖ (1) O true believers, take not my enemy and your R ¼ enemy for *your* friends, showing kindness towards them; since they believe not in the truth which hath come unto you, having expelled the Apostle and yourselves *from your native city*, because ye believe in GOD your LORD. If ye go forth to fight in defence of my religion, and out of a desire to please me, and privately show friendship unto them, verily I well know that which ye conceal and that which ye discover: and whoever of you doth this hath already erred from the straight path. (2) If they get the better of you, they will be enemies unto you, and they will

---

(1) *My enemy and your enemy, &c.* "This passage was revealed on account of Hátib Ibn Abi Balpáa, who, understanding that Muhammad had a design to surprise Makkah, wrote a letter to the Quraish, giving them notice of the intended expedition, and advised them to be on their guard; which letter he sent by Sarah, a maidservant belonging to the family of Háshím. The messenger had not been gone long, before Gabriel discovered the affair to the Prophet, who immediately sent after her; and having intercepted the letter, asked Hátib how he came to be guilty of such an action? To which he replied that it was not out of infidelity or a desire to return to idolatry, but merely to induce the Quraish to treat his family, which was still at Makkah, with some kindness: adding that he was well assured his intelligence would be of no service at all to the Makkans, because he was satisfied God would take vengeance on them. Whereupon Muhammad received his excuse and pardoned him; but it was thought proper to forbid any such practices for the future."—*Sale, Baidháwi.*

See also Muir's *Life of Mahomet,* vol. iv. p. 114.

Privately show friendship. "The verb here used has also a contrary signification, according to which the words may be rendered, 'and yet openly show friendship unto them.'"—*Sale.*

stretch forth their hands and their tongues against you with evil; and they earnestly desire that ye should become unbelievers. (3) Neither your kindred nor your children will avail you at all on the day of resurrection, which will separate you from one another: and GOD seeth that which ye do. (4) Ye have an excellent pattern in Abraham and those who were with him, when they said unto their people, Verily we are clear of you, and of the *idols* which ye worship besides GOD: we have renounced you; and enmity and hatred is begun between us and you for ever, until ye believe in GOD alone: except Abraham's saying unto his father, Verily I will beg pardon for thee; but I cannot obtain aught of GOD in thy behalf. O LORD, in thee do we trust, and unto thee are we turned; and before thee shall we be assembled *hereafter*. (5) O LORD, suffer us not to be put to trial by the unbelievers; and forgive us, O LORD; for thou *art* mighty *and* wise. (6) Verily ye have in them an excellent example, unto him who hopeth in GOD and the last day: and whoso turneth back; verily GOD *is* self-sufficient *and* praiseworthy.

R $\frac{2}{8}$. ‖ (7) Peradventure GOD will establish friendship between yourselves and such of them as ye *now* hold for enemies: for GOD *is* powerful; and GOD *is* inclined to forgive, *and* merciful. (8) As to those who have not

---

(4) *An excellent pattern.* The Muhájirín and others leaving Makkah with Muhammad are likened to Abraham and those leaving Chaldea with him. See Rodwell's note *in loco.*

Except Abraham's saying, &c. "For in this Abraham's example is not to be followed."—*Sale.* See notes on chap. ix. 114, 115.

(5) *Suffer us not, &c., i.e.,* "suffer them not to prevail against us, lest they thence conclude themselves to be in the right, and endeavour to make us deny our faith by the terror of the persecution."—*Sale, Baidháwi.*

(7) "And this happened accordingly on the taking of Makkah, when Abu Sufián and others of the Quraish, who had till then been inveterate enemies to the Muslims, embraced the same faith, and became their friends and brethren. Some suppose the marriage of Muhammad with Omm Habíba, the daughter of Abu Sufián, which was celebrated the year before, to be here intended."—*Sale, Baidháwi.*

borne arms against you on account of religion, nor turned you out of your dwellings, GOD forbiddeth you not to deal kindly with them, and to behave justly towards them; for GOD loveth those who act justly. (9) But as to those who have borne arms against you on account of religion, and have dispossessed you of your habitations, and have assisted in dispossessing you, GOD forbiddeth you to enter into friendship with them : and whosoever *of you* entereth into friendship with them, those are unjust doers. (10) O true believers, when believing women come unto you as refugees, try them : GOD well knoweth their faith. And if ye know them *to be* true believers, send them not back to the infidels : they *are* not lawful for the *unbelievers to have in marriage;* neither are *the unbelievers* lawful for them. But give *their unbelieving husbands* what they shall have expended *for their dowers.* Nor *shall it be* any crime in you if ye marry them, provided ye give them

---

(8) *Behave justly towards them.* "This passage, it is said, was revealed on account of Kutaila bint Abdul Uzza, who having, whilst she was an idolatress, brought some presents to her daughter, Asma bint Abu Baqr, the latter not only refused to accept them, but even denied her admittance."—*Sale, Baidháwi.*

(10) *Try them.* "When such women sought an asylum at Madína, Muhammad obliged them to swear that they were prompted only by the desire of embracing Islamism, and that hatred of their husbands, or love of some Mussulmán, had not had any influence on their conduct."—*Savary.*

They are not lawful for the unbelievers. Muslim men may marry unbelievers, if not idolaters, but Muslim women may marry only believers. The practical working of this law has been very favourable to the propagation of Islám.

But give . . . their dowers. "For, according to the terms of the pacification of al Hudaibiyah (chap. xlviii. 15), each side was to return whatever came into their power belonging to the other; wherefore, when the Muslims were, by this passage, forbidden to restore the married women who should come over to them, they were at the same time commanded to make some sort of satisfaction, by returning their dowry.

" It is related that, after the aforesaid pacification, while Muhammad was yet at al Hudaibiyah, Subaia bint al Hárith, of the tribe of Aslam, having embraced Muhammadism, her husband, Musáfir, the Makhzúmite, came and demanded her back; upon which this passage was revealed ; and Muhammad, pursuant thereto, adminis-

their dowries. And retain not the patronage of the unbelieving *women;* but demand back that which ye have expended *for the dowry of such of your wives as go over to the unbelievers;* and let them demand back that which they have expended *for the dowry of those who come over to you.* This *is* the judgment of GOD, which he establisheth among you, and GOD *is* knowing *and* wise. (11) If any of your wives escape from you to the unbelievers, and ye have your turn *by the coming over of any of the unbelievers' wives to you;* give unto those *believers* whose wives shall have gone away, *out of the dowries of the latter,* so much as they shall have expended *for the dowers of the former:* and fear GOD, in whom ye believe. (12) O Prophet, when believing *women* come unto thee, and plight their faith unto thee that they will not associate anything with GOD, nor steal, nor commit fornication, nor kill their children,

---

tered to her the oath thereafter directed, and returned her husband her dower, and then Omar married her."—*Sale, Baidháwi.*

Noëldeke points out that this must have occurred after the return from Hudaibiyah, on the ground of the terms of the treaty, which could not have been infringed at Hudaibiyah itself.

Provided ye give them their dowries. "For what is returned to their former husbands is not to be considered as their dower."—*Sale.*

See also notes on chaps. ii. 229 and iv. 3.

(11) *If any of your wives, &c.* "Literally, 'anything of your wives;' which some interpret, 'any part of their dowry.'"—*Sale.*

And ye have your turn. "Or, as the original verb may be translated, 'and ye take spoils;' in which case the meaning will be, that those Muslims whose wives shall have gone over to the infidels shall have a satisfaction for their dower out of the next booty. This law, they say, was given because the idolaters, after the preceding verse had been revealed, refused to comply therewith, or to make any return of the dower of those women who went over to them from the Muslims; so that the latter were obliged to indemnify themselves as they could."—*Sale, Baidháwi.*

(12) *Plight their faith unto thee.* "See the Prelim. Disc., p. 81. Some are of opinion that this passage was not revealed till the day of the taking of Makkah, when, after having received the solemn submission of the men, he proceeded to receive that of the women."—*Sale, Baidháwi.*

It is best to connect this verse with those preceding. It thus gives the confession of faith required of true Muslim converts from Arab idolatry.

Nor kill their children. See note on chap. lxxxi. 8.

nor come with a calumny which they have forged between their hands and their feet, nor be disobedient to thee in that which shall be reasonable: then do thou plight thy faith unto them, and ask pardon for them of GOD; for GOD *is* inclined to forgive, *and* merciful. (13) O true believers, enter not into friendship with a people against whom GOD is incensed; they despair of the life to come, as the infidels despair of *the resurrection of* those who dwell in their graves.

A calumny. "Jaláluddín understands these words of their laying their spurious children to their husbands."—*Sale.*

(13) *A people against whom God is incensed, i.e.,* "the infidels in general, or the Jews in particular."—*Sale.*

See note on chap. i. 5-7.

They despair, &c. "By reason of their infidelity, or because they well know they cannot expect to be made partakers of the happiness of the next life, by reason of their rejecting of the Prophet, foretold in the law, and whose mission is confirmed by miracles."—*Sale, Baidháwi.*

CHAPTER LXI.

ENTITLED SURAT AL SAF (BATTLE-ARRAY).

Revealed at Madína.

INTRODUCTION.

THIS chapter is an exhortation to Muslims to spend their money and their lives in the defence of Islám. Its title is taken from the words of the fourth verse, "God loveth those who fight for this religion in battle-array."

The circumstances which gave rise to this exhortation were those which resulted from the disobedience and cowardice of some of the Muslims during the battle of Ohod. This he likens to the rebellion of the Israelites against Moses, probably at Kadesh Barnea. The reference to Jesus, introduced here probably by the compilers of the Qurán, was intended to confirm the faith of the Muslims in this time of distress and doubt. Victory over the infidels had not been secured at Ohod, as they had anticipated, but "a speedy victory" over them would yet be secured (ver. 13), because Islám would yet be exalted over every other religion (ver. 9). If by "religion" we understand the Muhammadan faith, this prophecy was only true of its relation to the idolatrous religions of Arabia. It is probable, however, that Muhammad here identified his religion with the religion of God, which had always been upheld against all enemies in the past, and would therefore finally triumph over all other religions.

Probable Date of the Revelations.

From what has been said above we conclude that the probable date of this chapter is about the beginning of A.H. 4. The date of vers. 6-9 is uncertain, but, like the rest of the chapter, is Madínic, "because," says Noëldeke, "Muhammad *before* the Hijra could not have spoken of his religion conquering all others (ver. 9)."

Principal Subjects.

	VERSES
All things in the universe praise God	1
Muslims exhorted to be faithful and to fight for Islám	2–4
This exhortation enforced by the example of Moses	5
Jesus foretells Muhammad by the name Ahmad	6
Jesus was rejected as a sorcerer notwithstanding his miracles	7, 8
Islám to be exalted above every other religion	9
Muslims exhorted to seek wealth by fighting for Islám	10, 11
The rewards of those who fight for the faith	12, 13
Muslims' exhorted to follow the example of the apostles of Jesus	14

IN THE NAME OF THE MOST MERCIFUL GOD.

|| (1) Whatever *is* in heaven and in earth celebrateth R $\frac{1}{9}$. the praise of GOD; for he *is* mighty *and* wise. (2) O true believers, why do ye say that which ye do not? (3) *It is* most odious in the sight of GOD that ye say that which ye do not.

|| (4) Verily GOD loveth those who fight for his religion NISF. in battle-array, as though they *were* a well-compacted building. (5) *Remember* when Moses said unto his people, O my people, why do ye injure me; since ye know that I am the apostle of GOD *sent* unto you? And when they had deviated *from the truth*, GOD made their hearts to deviate *from the right way;* for GOD directeth not wicked people. (6) And when Jesus the Son of Mary said, O children of Israel, verily I *am* the apostle of GOD *sent* unto you, confirming the law which *was delivered* before

---

(2) "The commentators generally suppose these words to be directed to the Muslims, who, notwithstanding they had solemnly engaged to spend their lives and fortunes in defence of their faith, yet shamefully turned their backs at the battle of Ohod. They may, however, be applied to hypocrites of all sorts, whose actions contradict their words."—*Sale.*

(5) *Why do ye injure me?* "By your disobedience, or by maliciously aspersing me."—*Sale.*

See also note on chap. xxxiii. 69. May not the allusion here be to the rebellion of the Israelites at Kadesh Barnea?

me, and bringing good tidings of an apostle who shall come after me, *and* whose name *shall be* Ahmad. And when he produced unto them evident miracles, they said, This *is* manifest sorcery. (7) But who *is* more unjust than he who forgeth a lie against GOD when he is invited unto Islám? And GOD directeth not the unjust people. (8) They seek to extinguish GOD's light with their mouths; but GOD will perfect his light, though the infidels be averse *thereto*. (9) *It is* he who hath sent his Apostle with the direction and the religion of truth, that

---

(6) *An apostle . . . whose name is Ahmad.* "For Muhammad also bore the name of Ahmad, both names being derived from the same root, and nearly of the same signification. The Persian paraphrast, to support what is here alleged, quotes the following words of Christ, 'I go to my Father, and the *Paraclete* shall come' (John xvi. 7); the Muhammadan doctors unanimously teaching that by the 'Paraclete' (or, as they choose to read it, the *Periclyte* or *Illustrious*), their Prophet is intended, and no other."—*Sale.* (See Prelim. Disc., p. 124.)

The reply to "the Persian paraphrast" is that in John xv. 26 this Paraclete is described as "the Spirit of truth which proceedeth from the Father; he shall testify OF ME;" while in chap. xvi. 13 it is written that "when he, the Spirit of truth, is come, he will guide you into all truth;" and in ver. 14 we read, "He shall glorify ME, for he shall receive of MINE and show it unto YOU." If in these passages we substitute "Muhammad" for "Paraclete," we shall see how impossible it is there could be any reference to him whatever.

Even granting, for the sake of argument, that, as Muslims claim, a prophet is here foretold, it does not by any means follow that Muhammad was that prophet. The only ground of the claim is the *meaning of the name* "Ahmad," an unusual form of Muhammad's name, which *meaning* can only be secured by *perverting the words of Jesus* (*i.e.*, by changing *Paracletos* to *Periclytos* and omitting the clause "even the Spirit of truth"). Surely this is "perversion" (*tahríf*) of the Scriptures with a vengeance! (See notes on chap. iv. 44.)

Muhammad probably got the notion that he was the Paraclete from Christian perverts to Islám, who had previously been adherents to some form of the old Manichean heresy, such heretics having sought refuge from persecution by flight to Arabia.

The Urdu and Persian translations of the Qurán render the words "Ismuhu Ahmadu"—"His name *is* Ahmad."

And when he produced . . . miracles. Rodwell and Palmer introduce this sentence with "but," and instead of "miracles" they have "proofs" and "signs."

(9) *Exalt the same above every religion.* See note on chap. xlviii. 28.

he may exalt the same above every religion, although the idolaters be averse *thereto*.

|| (10) O true believers, shall I show you a merchandise R 10/? which will deliver you from a painful torment *hereafter ?* (11) Believe in GOD and his Apostle; and defend GOD's true religion with your substance, and in your own persons. This *will be* better for you, if ye knew *it*. (12) He will forgive you your sins, and will introduce you into gardens through which rivers flow, and agreeable habitations in gardens of perpetual abode. This *will be* great felicity. (13) And *ye shall obtain* other things which ye desire, *namely,* assistance from GOD and a speedy victory. And do thou bear good tidings to the true believers. (14) O true believers, be ye the assistants of GOD; as Jesus the son of Mary said to the apostles, Who *will be* my assistants with respect to GOD? The apostles answered, We *will be* the assistants of GOD. So a part of the children of Israel believed, and a part believed not: but we strengthened those who believed, above their enemy; wherefore they became victorious *over them*.

---

(14) Compare chap. iii. 51, and see note there.

A part believed not. "Either by rejecting him, or by affirming him to be God and the son of God."—*Sale, Jalaluddin.*

CHAPTER LXII.

ENTITLED SURAT AL JUMA (THE ASSEMBLY).

Revealed at Madína.

INTRODUCTION.

THIS chapter consists of two parts; first, vers. 1-8, relating to the enmity of the Jews of Madína towards Muhammad and his prophetic pretensions: second, vers. 9-11, relating to the prayer service of Friday, called here the Day of the Assembly, from which the chapter derives its title.

Probable Date of the Revelations.

The first part of this chapter is thought to belong to the same period as the greater portion of chap. ii., *i.e.*, A.H. 2, because it is aimed at the Jews of Madína. The second part of the chapter, according to the commentators, was revealed when Dahya al Kalbi, before his conversion, entered Madína with a loud noise, at the head of a caravan (ver. 11, note). But Noëldeke points out that this statement gives no exact chronological date, because we know nothing of the date of Dahya's conversion beyond this, that he is said by some to have fought as a Muslim at the battle of the Ditch, and by others at the battle of Ohod. Inasmuch, however, as the Friday prayers were instituted soon after the Hijra, it is probable that this part of the chapter belongs to about the same date as the first part.

Principal Subjects.

	VERSES
A wise, powerful, and holy God sent Muhammad as his apostle to the Arabians	1-4
The Jews rebuked for their opposition to Islám	5-8
Admonition concerning the observance of worship on Friday	9-11

IN THE NAME OF THE MOST MERCIFUL GOD.

‖ (1) Whatever *is* in heaven and earth praiseth GOD, the King, the Holy, the Mighty, the Wise. (2) *It is* he who hath raised up amidst the illiterate *Arabians* an Apostle from among themselves, to rehearse his signs unto them, and to purify them, and to teach them the Scriptures and wisdom; whereas before they were certainly in a manifest error; (3) and others of them have not yet attained unto them, *by embracing the faith; though they also shall be converted in God's good time;* for he *is* mighty *and* wise. (4) This *is* the free grace of GOD: he bestoweth the same on whom he pleaseth; and GOD is endued with great beneficence (5) The likeness of those who were charged with the observance of the law and then observed it not *is* as the likeness of an ass laden with books. How wretched *is* the likeness of the people who charge the signs of GOD with falsehood! and GOD directeth not the unjust people. (6) Say, O ye who follow the Jewish religion, if ye say that ye are the friends of GOD above *other* men, wish for death if ye speak truth. (7) But they will never wish for it, because of that which their hands have sent before them: and GOD well knoweth the unjust. (8) Say, Verily death, from which ye fly, will surely meet you; then shall ye be brought before him who knoweth as well what is concealed as what is discovered; and he will declare unto you that which ye have done.

$R \frac{1}{11}$.

‖ (9) O true believers, when ye are called to prayer on

$R \frac{2}{12}$.

---

(2) *The illiterate.* See note on chap. vii. 158, and Prelim. Disc., pp. 73, 74.

(5) *The likeness of an ass, &c.* "Because these understand not the prophecies contained in the law, which bear witness to Muhammad, no more than the ass does the books he carries."—*Sale.* See Muir's remarks, quoted in note on chap. iv. 44.

(6) *Wish for death, &c.*, i.e., "make it your request to God that he would translate you from this troublesome world to a state of never-fading bliss."—*Sale.*

(7) *Which their hands have sent before.* See note on chap. ii. 94.

the day of the assembly, hasten to the commemoration of GOD and leave merchandising. This *will be* better for you, if you knew *it*. (10) And when prayer is ended, then disperse yourselves through the land *as ye list*, and seek *gain* of the liberality of GOD: and remember GOD frequently, that ye may prosper. (11) But when they see any merchandising or sport, they flock thereto, and leave thee standing up *in the pulpit*. Say, The *reward* which *is* with GOD *is* better than any sport or merchandise: and GOD is the best provider.

---

(9) *The assembly.* "That is, Friday, which being more peculiarly set apart by Muhammad for the public worship of God, is therefore called Yaum al jumá, *i.e.*, the Day of the Assembly or Congregation; whereas before it was called al Arúba. The first time this day was particularly observed, as some say, was on the Prophet's arrival at Madína, into which city he made his first entry on a Friday; but others tell us that Káb Ibn Luwa, one of Muhammad's ancestors, gave the day its present name, because on that day the people used to be assembled before him. One reason given for the observation of Friday preferably to any other day of the week is because on that day God finished the creation."—*Sale, Baidháwi.*

Leave merchandising. The original purpose of Muhammad was to establish a day of rest similar to the Jewish Sabbath, but to be observed less rigidly. Work was to be stopped during the hours of prayer, but might be resumed when the prayers were ended. See on this subject Muir's *Life of Mahomet,* vol. iii. pp. 41, 42.

(10) *And when the prayer is ended.* "By returning to your commerce and worldly occupations, if ye think fit; for the Muhammadans do not hold themselves obliged to observe the day of their public assembly with the same strictness as the Christians and Jews do their respective Sabbaths, or particularly abstain from work after they have performed their devotions. Some, however, from a tradition of their Prophet, are of opinion that works of charity and religious exercises, which may draw down the blessing of God, are recommended in this passage."—*Sale.*

(11) *Leave thee standing, &c.* "It is related that one Friday, while Muhammad was preaching, a caravan of merchants happened to arrive with their drums beating, according to custom; which the congregation hearing, they all ran out of the mosque to see them, except twelve only."—*Sale, Baidháwi.*

CHAPTER LXIII.

ENTITLED SURAT AL MUNÁFIQÚN (THE HYPOCRITES).

Revealed at Madína.

INTRODUCTION.

This chapter was revealed shortly after the expedition against the Baní Mustaliq, in order to rebuke Abdullah Ibn Ubbai and his followers for their treatment of the refugees, and for certain seditious words uttered at the wells of Maraisí when on the march back. See Muir's *Life of Mahomet*, vol. iii. pp. 241, 242. The declaration of ver. 8, that "the worthier shall expel thence the meaner," though intended to convey a threat, was never fulfilled, except by the gradual absorption of the disaffected by the Muslim party, after that military success had made religious and temporal interests in Madína to be identical.

Probable Date of the Revelations.

If what has been said as to the circumstances under which this chapter was enunciated is true, the date of the revelations, excepting vers. 9–11, which may belong to some other period, must be fixed at about the end of A.H. 6.

Principal Subjects.

	VERSES
The treachery of the hypocrites of Madína exposed and rebuked	1–3
Muhammad warned to beware of trusting the hypocrites	4
Hypocrites cursed and declared reprobates	5, 6
They are threatened with expulsion from Madína	7, 8
The duty of almsgiving enjoined	9–11

IN THE NAME OF THE MOST MERCIFUL GOD.

R $\frac{1}{13}$. ‖ (1) When the hypocrites come unto thee, they say, We bear witness that thou *art* indeed the Apostle of GOD. And GOD knoweth that thou *art* indeed his Apostle; but GOD beareth witness that the hypocrites *are* certainly liars. (2) They have taken their oaths for a protection, and they turn *others* aside from the way of GOD: it is surely evil which they do. (3) This *is testified of them*, because they believed, and afterwards became unbelievers: wherefore a seal is set on their hearts, and they shall not understand. (4) When thou beholdest them, their persons please thee; and if they speak, thou hearest their discourse *with delight*. They resemble pieces of timber set up *against a wall*. They imagine every shout *to be* against them. They are enemies: wherefore beware of them. Go curse them: how are they turned aside *from the truth!* (5) And when it is said unto them, Come, that the Apostle of GOD may ask pardon for you; they turn away their heads, and thou seest them retire big with disdain. (6) *It shall be* equal unto them, whether thou ask pardon for them, or do not ask pardon for them:

(1–3) These verses allude to the hypocritical and secretly disaffected inhabitants of Madina. Military success and conscious strength now enable Muhammad to denounce even the powerful Abdullah Ibn Ubbai.

(4) *Their persons please thee.* "The commentators tell us that A dullah Ibn Ubbai, a chief hypocrite, was a tall man of very graceful presence, and of a ready and eloquent tongue, and used to frequent the Prophet's assembly attended by several like himself; and that these men were greatly admired by Muhammad, who was taken with their handsome appearance, and listened to their discourse with pleasure."—*Sale, Baidháwi.*

Pieces of timber. "Being tall and big, but being void of knowledge and consideration."—*Sale.*

They imagine, &c. "Living under continual apprehension, because they are conscious of their hypocrisy towards God and their insincerity towards the Muslims."—*Sale.*

God curse them. Rodwell translates more literally "God do battle with them."

(6) *It shall be equal unto them, &c.* See this applied in the case of Abdullah in chap. ix. 81, note.

GOD will by no means forgive them; for GOD directeth not the prevaricating people. (7) These *are the men* who say *to the inhabitants of Madína,* Do not bestow *anything* on *the refugees* who *are* with the Apostle of GOD, that they may *be obliged to* separate *from him.* Whereas unto GOD *belong* the stores of heaven and earth: but the hypocrites do not understand. (8) They say, Verily, if we return to Madína, the worthier shall expel thence the meaner. Whereas superior worth *belongeth* unto GOD and his Apostle, and the true believers; but the hypocrites know *it* not.

|| (9) O true believers, let not your riches or your children divert you from the remembrance of GOD; for whosoever doth this, they will surely be losers. (10) And give alms out of that which we have bestowed on you, before death come unto one of you, and he say, O LORD, wilt thou not grant me respite for a short term, that I may give alms, and become *one* of the righteous? (11) For GOD will by no means grant further respite to a soul when its determined time is come: and GOD *is* fully apprised of that which ye do.

$R \frac{2}{14}$.

---

(8) *Verily if we return, &c.* "These, as well as the preceding, were the words of Ibn Ubbai to one of Madína, who in a certain expedition quarrelling with an Arab of the desert about water, received a blow on the head with a stick, and made his complaint thereof to him."—*Sale, Baidháwi.*

(10) *Give alms.* See notes on chap. ix. 60, 104. Almsgiving is here made a necessary condition of salvation. See on this point note on chap. iii. 31.

CHAPTER LXIV.

ENTITLED SURAT AL TAGHABÚN (MUTUAL DECEIT).

Revealed at Madína.

INTRODUCTION.

THE title of this chapter is taken from words found in ver. 9, but there is no connection between it and the matter of the composition.

The revelations are hortatory in their character, but exceedingly confused. In the beginning the exhortation is to faith in God and his power to raise the dead. Farther on the subject is faith in the Qurán. Then we have words of comfort for those in distress, who are urged to trust God, since nothing occurs without his permission. The exhortation then turns to the duty of obeying God and Muhammad; and, finally, married Muslims are urged to contribute towards the cause of God, especially by way of almsgiving, not allowing the cares of family and children to interfere with the performance of this duty.

Probable Date of the Revelations.

Neither Muslim commentators nor modern writers are agreed as to whether this chapter belongs to Makkah or Madína. Noëldeke thinks there can be no doubt about vers. 14–18 being Madínic. He thinks this is also probably true of vers. 11–13. Rodwell thinks ver. 7 and the phrase "God and the Apostle" in vers. 8 and 12, together with the subject-matter, confirm the view of those who regard the chapter as Madínic. Weil and Muir regard it as Makkan. Vers. 2–7 are in their form and matter like the ordinary Makkan Suras, and the sentence in ver. 12, "the duty of our Apostle is only a public preaching," looks also towards Makkah.

On the whole, we think the chapter should be regarded as Madínic, though it includes passages imported into it from Makkah, either by Muhammad or the compilers. As to date, Noëldeke places it just before chap. lxii., which would make its date about A.H. 2.

Principal Subjects.

	VERSES
All things in heaven and earth praise God	1
God hath fore-ordained men to be either believers or unbelievers	2
God, the Creator, knoweth all things	3, 4
Former nations destroyed for their unbelief	5, 6
Unbelief will not prevent infidels from rising from the dead	7
Exhortation to believe in God and his Apostle	8–10
God sovereign, therefore should be trusted	11–13
Muslims exhorted to abjure worldly ties and to devote themselves to God	14–18

IN THE NAME OF THE MOST MERCIFUL GOD.

|| (1) Whatever *is* in heaven and earth celebrateth the R $\frac{1}{15}$. praises of GOD: his *is* the kingdom, and unto him *is* the praise *due;* for he *is* almighty. (2) *It is* he who hath created you; and *one* of you *is predestined to be* an unbeliever, and *another* of you *is predestined to be* a believer: and GOD beholdeth that which ye do. (3) He hath created the heavens and the earth with truth; and he hath fashioned you, and given you beautiful forms: and unto him must ye all go. (4) He knoweth whatever *is* in heaven and earth: and he knoweth that which ye conceal, and that which ye discover; for GOD knoweth the innermost part of *men's* breasts. (5) Have ye not been acquainted with the story of those who disbelieved heretofore, and tasted the evil consequence of their behaviour? And for them *is prepared in the life to come* a tormenting punishment. (6) This *shall they suffer*, because their apostles came unto them with evident *proofs of their mission*, and they said, Shall men direct us? Wherefore they believed not, and turned their backs. But GOD standeth in need of no person; for GOD *is* self-sufficient, *and* worthy to be praised. (7) The unbelievers imagine that they shall not be raised again. Say, Yea, by my LORD, ye shall surely be raised again; then shall ye be

told that which ye have wrought; and this *is* easy with GOD. (8) Wherefore believe in GOD and his Apostle, and the light which we have sent down; for GOD *is* well acquainted with that which ye do. (9) On a *certain* day he shall assemble you, at the day of the *general* assembly: that *will be* the day of mutual deceit. And whoso shall believe in GOD, and shall do that which is right, from him will he expiate his evil deeds, and he will lead him into gardens beneath which rivers flow, to remain therein for ever. This *will be* great felicity. (10) But they who shall not believe, and shall accuse our signs of falsehood, those *shall be* the inhabitants of *hell*-fire, wherein they shall remain *for ever;* and a wretched journey *shall it be thither!*

|| (11) No misfortune happeneth but by the permission of GOD; and whoso believeth in GOD, he will direct his heart: and GOD knoweth all things. (12) Wherefore obey GOD, and obey the Apostle: but if ye turn back, verily *the duty incumbent* on our Apostle *is* only public preaching. (13) GOD! there is no GOD but he: wherefore in GOD let the faithful put their trust. (14) O true believers, verily of your wives and your children ye have

---

(8) *God and his Apostle.* See note on chap. viii. 20. Rodwell thinks this expression an argument in favour of the view of those who regard this chapter as Madínic. The style and the matter of all that precedes it, however, count decidedly for Makkah. Indeed it must be admitted that even Makkan chapters may have been emended at Madína, and that expressions, common to Madína chapters, may have occasionally found their way into those of Makkah.

(9) *The day of mutual deceit.* "When the blessed will deceive the damned, by taking the places which they would have had in Paradise had they been true believers, and contrariwise."—*Sale, Baidhāwi, Yahya.*

Expiate his evil deeds. See note on chap. iii. 194.

(12) *Only public preaching.* This is another mark pointing to Makkah as the place where this revelation was given. There he was uniformly a preacher only. See note to chap. ii. 119.

(13) *Wives and children, &c.* "For these are apt to distract a man from his duty, especially in time of distress; a married man caring for the things that are of this world, while the unmarried careth for the things that belong to the Lord (1 Cor. vii. 25)."—*Sale.*

an enemy: wherefore beware of them. But if ye pass over *their offences*, and pardon and forgive *them*, GOD *is* likewise inclined to forgive, *and* merciful. (15) Your wealth and your children *are* only a temptation; but with GOD *is* a great reward. (16) Wherefore fear GOD as much as ye are able; and hear and obey: and give alms for the good of your souls; for whoso is preserved from the covetousness of his own soul, they shall prosper. (17) If ye lend unto GOD an acceptable loan, he will double the same unto you, and will forgive you: for GOD is grateful *and* long-suffering, (18) knowing both what is hidden and what is divulged; the Mighty, the Wise.

If ye pass over, &c. "Considering that the hindrance they may occasion you proceeds from their affection, and their ill bearing your absence in time of war, &c."—*Sale.*

(16, 17) See note on chap. lxiii. 10.

(17) *God is grateful.* See notes on chaps. ii. 159 and iv. 146.

CHAPTER LXV.

ENTITLED SURAT AL TALÁQ (DIVORCE).

Revealed at Madína.

INTRODUCTION.

THIS chapter was probably revealed to supplement the law of divorce given in chap. ii. 226-237; hence the title, found in the first verse.

That this is not the original law of divorce, as the title might suggest, is evident from the statement in the first verse, as well as from the testimony of tradition, which states that it was revealed to correct an abuse of the privilege of divorce by Ibn Omar, who, having put away his wife at an improper time, was hereby obliged to take her again.

The latter portion of the chapter reads very much like a Makkan revelation, and indeed is so regarded by at least one author, Umar Bin Muhammad. However, since it is addressed to true believers, it is probably Madínic. It was intended to impress more deeply the Muslim mind with the solemnity of the law which precedes it.

Probable Date of the Revelations.

If the first verse refers to Ibn Omar, as tradition declares, then we must refer this chapter to a period as late as A.H. 6 or 8, because Ibn Omar was then only eighteen or twenty years of age. But, Noëldeke informs us, another and an accurate tradition declares that Muhammad only *read* this passage from the Qurán, it having been revealed before. Noëldeke places it in his chronological list just after chap. iv., whose date is A.H. 4 or 5.

Principal Subjects.

	VERSES
Certain limitations to the law of divorce	1-7
The apostate and disobedient chastised for their sin . .	8-10
True believers exhorted to faith in Muhammad . .	11
God hath created the seven heavens	12

IN THE NAME OF THE MOST MERCIFUL GOD.

|| (1) O Prophet, when ye divorce women, put them R $\frac{1}{17}$. away at their appointed term; and compute the term *exactly:* and fear GOD your LORD. Oblige them not to go out of their apartments, neither let them go out, *until the term be expired,* unless they be guilty of manifest uncleanness. These *are* the statutes of GOD; and whoever transgresseth the statutes of GOD assuredly injureth his own soul. Thou knowest not whether GOD will bring something new to pass, *which may reconcile them* after this. (2) And when they shall have fulfilled their term, either retain them with kindness, or part from them honourably: and take witnesses from among you, men of integrity; and give *your* testimony as in the presence of GOD. (3) This admonition is given unto him who believeth in GOD and the last day; and whoso feareth GOD, unto him will he grant a *happy* issue *out of all his afflictions,* and he will bestow on him an ample provision from whence he expecteth *it* not: and whoso trusteth in GOD, he *will be* his sufficient support; for GOD will surely attain his purpose. Now hath GOD appointed unto everything a determined period. (4) *As to* such of your wives as shall despair having their courses, *by reason of their age;* if ye be in doubt *thereof,* let their term *be* three months: and *let the same be the term of* those who have not yet had their courses. But *as to* those who are pregnant, their term *shall be* until they be delivered of their burden. And whoso feareth GOD, unto him will he make his command

---

(1) *Their appointed time.* "That is, when they shall have had their courses thrice after the time of their divorce, if they prove not to be with child; or, if they prove with child, when they shall have been delivered. Al Baidháwi supposes husbands are hereby commanded to divorce their wives while they are clean; and says that the passage was revealed on account of Ibn Omar, who divorced his wife when she had her courses upon her, and was therefore obliged to take her again."—*Sale.*

On this whole passage see also notes on chap. ii. 226–237.

easy. (5) This *is* the command of GOD, which he hath sent down unto you. And whoso feareth GOD, he will expiate his evil deeds from him and will increase his reward. (6) Suffer the *women whom ye divorce* to dwell in *some part* of *the houses* wherein ye dwell; *according to the room and conveniences* of the *habitations* which ye possess: and make them not uneasy, that ye may reduce them to straits. And if they be with child, expend on them *what shall be needful,* until they be delivered of their burden. And if they suckle *their children* for you, give them their hire; and consult among yourselves, according to what shall be just and reasonable. And if ye be put to a difficulty *herein,* and another *woman* shall suckle *the child* for him, (7) let him who hath plenty expend *proportionably in the maintenance of the mother and the nurse* out of his plenty: and let him whose income is scanty expend *in proportion* out of that which GOD hath given him. GOD obligeth no man to more than he hath given him *ability to perform:* GOD will cause ease to succeed hardship.

R 2/18. ‖ (8) How many cities have turned aside from the command of the LORD and his apostles! Wherefore we brought them to a severe account; and we chastised them with a grievous chastisement: (9) and they tasted the evil consequence of their business; and the end of their business was perdition. (10) GOD hath prepared for them severe punishment; wherefore fear GOD, O ye who are endued with understanding. (11) True believers, now hath GOD sent down unto you an admonition, an Apostle who may rehearse unto you the perspicuous signs of GOD; that he may bring forth those who believe and do good works from darkness into light. And whoso believeth in GOD and doth that which is right, him will he lead into gardens beneath which rivers flow, to remain therein for ever: now hath GOD made an excellent provision for him. (12) *It is* GOD who hath created seven heavens, and as many

---

(12) *Seven heavens.* See note on chap. ii. 29.

different storeys of the earth; the *divine* command descendeth between them; that ye may know that GOD is omnipotent, and that GOD comprehendeth all things by *his* knowledge.

And as many of the earth. "The earth has seven storeys like unto the seven storeys of the heavens," so says the *Tafsir-i-Raufi*, but what it means it would be difficult to explain.

The command descendeth, &c. "Penetrating and pervading them all with absolute efficacy."—*Sale.*

CHAPTER LXVI.

ENTITLED SURAT AL TAHRÍM (PROHIBITION).

Revealed at Madína.

INTRODUCTION.

THE title of this chapter is taken from the statement of the first verse. According to Sale, who writes on the authority of Baidháwi, Jaláluddín, and Yahya, the occasion of this chapter was as follows: "Muhammad having lain with a slave of his, named Mary, of Coptic extract (who had been sent him as a present by al Muqauqas, governor of Egypt), on the day which was due to Ayesha or to Hafsa, and, as some say, on Hafsa's own bed, while she was absent; and this coming to Hafsa's knowledge, she took it extremely ill, and reproached her husband so sharply, that, to pacify her, he promised, with an oath, never to touch the maid again; and to free him from the obligation of this promise was the design of the chapter."

As, however, such a *contretemps* was looked upon as improper, another ludicrous story is related to explain vers. 1-5 of this chapter. It is alluded to by Sale thus: "There are some who suppose this passage to have been occasioned by Muhammad's protesting never to eat honey any more, because, having once eaten some in the apartment of Hafsa or of Zainab, three other of his wives, namely, Ayesha, Sauda, and Safía, all told him they smelt he had been eating of the juice which distils from certain shrubs in those parts, and resembles honey in taste and consistence, but is of a very strong savour, and which the Prophet had a great aversion to."

This story, Noëldeke thinks, was probably invented by Ayesha, as she was chiefly concerned in this quarrel. Scarcely any portion of the Qurán has been attacked so violently by Christians, or defended so strenuously by Muslims and their apologists as this chapter. In it the character of Muhammad appears in anything but a favourable light. From the Christian standpoint, he appears to have been guilty of breaking a solemn vow, and that in order to gratify unholy passion. This done, he justifies himself by pretending to have the sanction of God for the act. In this light it is difficult to see how he is to be cleared of the charge of imposture. We see here the low and selfish ends which these revelations of the Qurán were now made to subserve. The only parallel to it, and that perhaps an imitation of it, is the pretended revelation by which Smith, the Mormon prophet, sought to justify his adultery.

It appears to me that vers. 6–9, which manifestly relate to other circumstances, and which break the continuity of sentiment between vers. 1–5 and 10–12, were inserted here by mistake, probably by the compilers.

Probable Date of the Revelations.

According to Noëldeke, the first and last portions of this chapter, i.e., vers. 1–5 and 10–12, belong to the year A.H. 7. The remaining verses belong to a later period, when Muhammad was in a position to deal harshly with the infidels and hypocrites.

Principal Subjects.

	VERSE
Muhammad reproved for making a vow to please his wives	1
He is relieved from his vow	2
Muhammad's wives reproved and threatened for their jealousy in the affair of Mary, the Coptic slave	3–5
Exhortation to believers to exercise faith, repentance, &c.	6–8
Muhammad commanded to treat infidels and hypocrites with severity	9
The wives of Noah, Lot, Pharaoh, and the daughter of Imrán examples to Muslim women	10–12

IN THE NAME OF THE MOST MERCIFUL GOD.

|| (1) O Prophet, why holdest thou that to be prohibited $R \frac{1}{10}$. which God hath allowed thee, seeking to please thy wives;

(1) *O Prophet, why holdest thou, &c.* On this verse Sale has the following: "I cannot here avoid observing, as a learned writer has done before me, that Dr. Prideaux has strangely misrepresented this passage. For having given the story of the Prophet's amour with his maid Mary a little embellished, he proceeds to tell us that in this chapter Muhammad brings in God allowing him, and all his Muslims, to lie with their maids when they will, notwithstanding their wives (whereas the words relate to the Prophet only, who wanted not any new permission for that purpose, because it was a

since GOD *is* inclined to forgive, *and* merciful? (2) GOD hath allowed you the dissolution of your oaths; and GOD

---

privilege already granted him [chap. xxxiii.] though to none else); and then, to show what ground he had for his assertion, adds, that the first words of the chapter are, 'O Prophet, why dost thou forbid what God hath allowed thee, that thou mayest please thy wives? God hath granted unto you to lie with your maid-servants.' Which last words are not to be found here, or elsewhere in the Qurán, and contain an allowance of what is expressly forbidden therein (Sale's note on chap. iv. 3), though the Doctor has thence taken occasion to make some reflections which might as well have been spared. I shall say nothing to aggravate the matter, but leave the reader to imagine what this reverend divine would have said of a Muhammadan if he had caught him tripping in the like manner. (But see notes on chaps. iv. 3, 24.—E. M. W.)

"Having digressed so far, I will adventure to add a word or two, in order to account for one circumstance which Dr. Prideaux relates concerning Muhammad's concubine Mary, viz., that after her master's death no account was had of her or the son which she had borne him, but both were sent away into Egypt, and no mention made of either ever after among them; and then he supposes (for he seldom is at a loss for a supposition) that Ayesha, out of the hatred which she bore her, procured of her father, who succeeded the impostor in the government, to have her thus disposed of. But it being certain, by the general consent of all the Eastern writers, that Mary continued in Arabia till her death, which happened at Madína about five years after that of her master, and was buried in the usual burying-place there, called al Baki, and that her son died before his father, it has been asked whence the Doctor had this? I answer, That I guess he had it partly from Abulfaragius, according to the printed edition of whose work the Mary we are speaking of is said to have been sent with her sister Shírín (not with her son) to Alexandria by al Muqanqas: though I make no doubt but we ought in that passage to read *min, from,* instead of *ila, to* (notwithstanding the manuscript copies of this author used by Dr. Pocock, the editor, and also a very fair one in my own possession, agree in the latter reading); and that the sentence ought to run thus: *quam* (viz. Mariam) *unà cum sorore* Shírína *ab* Alexandria *miserat* al Muquuqas." See Prelim. Disc., p. 206, note, Muir's reply to Sale's assertion that cohabitation with slave girls was not permitted. See the whole story of Mary, the Coptic maid, related in Muir's *Life of Mahomet,* vol. iv. pp. 157-167.

(2) *God hath allowed, &c.* "By having appointed an expiation for that purpose; or, as the words may be translated, 'God hath allowed you to use an exception to your oaths if it please God;' in which case a man is excused from guilt if he perform not his oath. The passage, though directed to all the Muslims in general, seems to be particularly designed for quieting the Prophet's conscience in regard to the oath above mentioned; but Al Baidháwi approves not this opinion,

is your master; and he *is* knowing *and* wise. (3) When the Prophet intrusted as a secret unto one of his wives a certain accident; and when she disclosed the same, and GOD made it known unto him; he acquainted *her* with part *of what she had done,* and forbore *to upbraid her with the other part* thereof. And when he had acquainted her therewith, she said, Who hath discovered this unto thee? He answered, The knowing, the sagacious *God* hath discovered *it* unto me. (4) If ye both be turned unto GOD (for your hearts have swerved), *it is well:* but if ye join against him, verily GOD is his patron; and Gabriel, and the good men among the faithful, and the angels also *are his* assistants. (5) If he divorce you, his LORD can easily give him in exchange other wives better than you, *women* resigned *unto God,* true believers, devout, penitent, obedient, given to fasting, *both such as have been* known by other men, and virgins. (6) O true believers, save your souls, and *those of* your families, from the fire whose fuel

---

because such an oath was to be looked upon as an inconsiderate one, and required no expiation."—*Sale.*

See also note on chap. v. 91.

(3) "When Muhammad found that Hafsa knew of his having injured her, or Ayesha, by lying with his concubine Mary on the day due to one of them, he desired her to keep the affair secret, promising, at the same time, that he would not meddle with Mary any more; and foretold her, as a piece of news which might soothe her vanity, that Abu Baqr and Omar should succeed him in the government of his people. Hafsa, however, could not conceal this from Ayesha, with whom she lived in strict friendship, but acquainted her with the whole matter: whereupon the Prophet, perceiving, probably by Ayesha's behaviour, that his secret had been discovered, upbraided Hafsa with her betraying him, telling her that God had revealed it to him; and not only divorced her, but separated him from all his other wives for a whole month, which time he spent in the apartment of Mary. In a short time, notwithstanding, he took Hafsa again, by the direction, as he gave out, of the Angel Gabriel, who commended her for her frequent fasting and other exercises of devotion, assuring him likewise that she should be one of his wives in Paradise."—*Sale, Baidhâwî, Zamakhshari.*

(4) "This sentence is directed to Hafsa and Ayesha, the pronouns and verbs of the second person being in the dual number."—*Sale.*

(6) *Angels fierce and terrible.* See chap. lxxiv. 30, and Prelim. Disc., p. 148.

is men and stones, over which are *set* angels fierce *and* terrible; who disobey not GOD in what he hath commanded them, but perform what they are commanded. (7) O unbelievers, excuse not yourselves this day; ye shall surely be rewarded for what ye have done.

R $\frac{2}{20}$. ‖ (8) O true believers, turn unto GOD with a sincere repentance: peradventure your LORD will do away from you your evil deeds, and will admit you into gardens through which rivers flow; on the day *whereon* GOD will not put to shame the Prophet, or those who believe with him: their light shall run before them, and on their right hands, and they shall say, LORD, make our light perfect, and forgive us: for thou *art* almighty. (9) O Prophet, attack the infidels *with arms*, and the hypocrites *with arguments;* and treat them with severity: their abode shall be hell, and an ill journey *shall it be thither.* (10) GOD propoundeth as a similitude unto the unbelievers the wife of Noah and the wife of Lot: they were under two of our righteous servants, and they deceived them both: wherefore *their husbands* were of no advantage unto them at all in the sight of GOD: and it shall be said *unto*

---

(7) "These words will be spoken to the infidels at the last day."—*Sale.*

(8) *Their light shall run.* See note on chap. lvii. 11.

(10) *The wife of Noah and . . . of Lot.* "Who were both unbelieving women, but deceived their respective husbands by their hypocrisy. Noah's wife, named Wáila, endeavoured to persuade the people her husband was distracted; and Lot's wife, whose name was Wáhila (though some writers give this name to the other, and that of Wáila to the latter), was in confederacy with the men of Sodom, and used to give them notice when any strangers came to lodge with him, by a sign of smoke by day and of fire by night."—*Sale, Jaláluddín.*

Of no advantage, &c. "For they both met with a disastrous end in this world, and will be doomed to eternal misery in the next. In like manner, as Muhammad would insinuate, the infidels of his time had no reason to expect any mitigation of their punishment on account of their relation to himself and the rest of the true believers." —*Sale.*

The *insinuation* is evidently intended specially for his two wives, Ayesha and Hafsa.

them at the last day, Enter ye into *hell*-fire, with those who enter *therein*. (11) GOD also propoundeth as a similitude unto those who believe the wife of Pharaoh, when she said, LORD, build me a house with thee in Paradise, and deliver me from Pharaoh and his doings, and deliver me from the unjust people : (12) and Mary the daughter of Imrán, who preserved her chastity, and into whose womb we breathed of our spirit, and who believed in the words of her LORD and his Scriptures, and was a devout and obedient person.

---

(11) *The wife of Pharaoh*, viz., "Asíah, the daughter of Muzáhim. The commentators relate, that because she believed in Moses, her husband cruelly tormented her, fastening her hands and feet to four stakes, and laying a large mill-stone on her breast, her face, at the same time, being exposed to the scorching beams of the sun. These pains, however, were alleviated by the angels shading her with their wings, and the view of the mansion prepared for her in Paradise, which was exhibited to her on her pronouncing the prayer in the text. At length God received her soul ; or, as some say, she was taken up alive into Paradise, where she eats and drinks."—*Sale, Jaláluddín.*

Rodwell thinks the name Asíah is probably a corruption from that of Pharaoh's daughter, *Bithiah*, 1 Chron. iv. 18.

(12) *Mary.* See notes in chaps. iii. 35, xix. 29, and xxi. 91.

A devout and obedient person. "On occasion of the honourable mention here made of these two extraordinary women, the commentators introduce a saying of their Prophet, 'That among men there had been many perfect, but no more than four of the other sex had attained perfection, to wit, Asíah, the wife of Pharaoh, Mary, the daughter of Imrán, Khadíjah, the daughter of Khuwailid (the Prophet's first wife), and Fátíma, the daughter of Muhammad.'"—*Sale.*

CHAPTER LXVII.

ENTITLED SURAT AL MULK (THE KINGDOM).

Revealed at Makkah.

INTRODUCTION.

THIS chapter receives its title from the mention of the "kingdom" of God in the first verse. "It is also entitled by some," says Sale, "*The Saving* or *The Delivering*, because, say they, it will save him who reads it from the torture of the sepulchre." The contents of the chapter differ little from those of other Makkan Suras. The object of these revelations was to warn the people of the sin of rejecting the doctrine of the Qurán, especially the doctrine of the resurrection and future judgment.

Probable Date of the Revelations.

This chapter is regarded by nearly all authorities as belonging wholly to Makkah. Noëldeke mentions one tradition which declares it to be Madínic, but gives no sufficient reason for that opinion. As to the date, all authorities agree in fixing the date about B.H. 8.

Principal Subjects.

	VERSES
Praise to the Almighty, the Creator and Ruler of all things	1–3
The perfection of the works of God, seen in the heavens, glorify him	3–5
The heavens adorned with shooting stars	5
Torments of hell prepared for unbelievers	6–8
Infidels shall confess in hell their folly in calling Muhammad an impostor	8–11
The righteous shall receive great reward	12
God knoweth all things	13, 14
God shall destroy unbelievers	15–18

	VERSES
Unbelievers ungrateful to the God who sustains them in life	19–24
The Prophet challenged to hasten the judgment-day, but they shall dread its approach	25–28
The Merciful the only protector on that day	29, 30

IN THE NAME OF THE MOST MERCIFUL GOD.

|| (1) Blessed be he in whose hands *is* the kingdom, for he *is* almighty! (2) Who hath created death and life, that he might prove you, which of you is most righteous in *his* actions: and he *is* mighty, *and* ready to forgive. (3) Who hath created seven heavens, one above another: thou canst not see in a creature of the most Merciful any unfitness or disproportion. (4) Lift up thine eyes again *to heaven, and look* whether thou seest any flaw; then take two other views, and thy sight shall return unto thee dull and fatigued. (5) Moreover, we have adorned the lowest heaven with lamps, and have appointed them to be darted at the devils, for whom we have prepared the torment of burning fire: (6) and for those who believe not in their LORD *is also prepared* the torment of hell; an ill journey *shall it be thither*. (7) When they shall be thrown thereinto, they shall hear it bray like an ass; and it shall boil, (8) and almost burst for fury. So often as a company *of them* shall be thrown therein, the keepers thereof shall ask them, *saying,* Did not a warner come unto you? (9) They shall answer, Yea, a warner came unto us; but we accused *him* of imposture, and said, GOD hath not revealed anything; ye *are* in no other than a great error: (10) and they shall say, If we had hearkened or had rightly considered, we should not have been among the inhabitants of burning fire: (11) and they shall confess their sins; but far be the inhabitants of burning fire *from obtaining*

TWENTY-NINTH SIPARA.

R $\frac{1}{1}$.

---

(3) *Seven heavens.* See note on chap. ii. 29.
(5) *Lamps . . . to be darted at the devils.* See note on chap. xv. 17.
(7) *Bray like an ass.* See note on chap. xxxi. 18.

mercy! (12) Verily they who fear their LORD in secret shall receive pardon and a great reward. (13) Either conceal your discourse or make it public; he knoweth the innermost parts of *your* breasts; (14) shall not he know *all things* who hath created *them*, since he *is* the sagacious, the knowing?

R ⅔.

‖ (15) *It is* he who hath levelled the earth for you: therefore walk through the regions thereof, and eat of his provision; unto him *shall be* the resurrection. (16) Are ye secure that he who *dwelleth* in heaven will not cause the earth to swallow you up? and behold, it shall shake. (17) Or are you secure that he who *dwelleth* in heaven will not send against you an *impetuous whirlwind*, driving the sands *to overwhelm you?* then shall ye know how *important* my warning *was*. (18) Those also who *were* before you disbelieved; and how *grievous* was my displeasure! (19) Do they not behold the birds above them, extending and drawing back their wings! None sustaineth them except the Merciful; for he regardeth all things. (20) Or who *is* he that *will be as* an army unto you, to defend you against the Merciful? Verily the unbelievers *are* in no other than a mistake. (21) Or who *is* he that will give you food, if he withholdeth his provision? yet they persist in perverseness and flying *from the truth*. (22) Is he, therefore, who goeth grovelling upon his face better directed than he who walketh upright in a straight way? (23) Say, *It is* he who hath given you being, and endued you with hearing, and sight, and understanding; *yet* how little gratitude have ye! (24) Say, *It is* he who hath sown you in the earth, and unto him shall ye be gathered together. (25) They say, When *shall* this menace *be put in execution*, if ye speak truth? (26) Answer, The knowledge *of this matter is* with GOD alone; for I *am* only a public warner. (27)

---

(22) "This comparison is applied by the expositors to the infidel and the true believer."—*Sale.*

(23) *How little gratitude.* In that ye turn from him to worship dumb idols.

(26) *Only a public warner.* See note on chap. ii. 119.

But when they shall see the same nigh at hand, the countenance of the infidels shall grow sad: and it shall be said *unto them*, This is what ye have been demanding. (28) Say, What think ye? Whether GOD destroy me and those *who are* with me, or have mercy on us, who will protect the unbelievers from a painful punishment? (29) Say, He is the Merciful; in him do we believe, and in him do we put our trust. Ye shall hereafter know who is in a manifest error? (30) Say, What think ye? If your water be in the morning swallowed up by the earth, who will give you clear and running water?

CHAPTER LXVIII.

ENTITED SURAT AL QALAM (THE PEN).

Revealed at Makkah.

INTRODUCTION.

This chapter is also entitled Nún (N), from the letter in the beginning of the first verse, wherein the ordinary title is also found. In its revelation we have indicated a period of strong opposition between Muhammad and his townsmen. The Prophet had been called a madman and an impostor. Slander and defamation had been resorted to even by some of the chief men of Makkah. In reply to the warnings of the seer, they had challenged him to hasten on his judgments.

These charges had not failed to rouse the resentment of Muhammad. He did not now hesitate to call the chief of his opponents "a common swearer," "a transgressor, a wicked person, cruel, and, besides this, of spurious birth." He even threatens him with a mark on a prominent part of his face !

The preacher of Makkah had been rejected, and his unbelieving hearers were ready to treat him with violence (ver. 51).

Probable Date of the Revelations.

This chapter is regarded by ancient Muslim writers as the oldest, or at least the second revelation of the Qurán. There is, however, little to give credence to their dictum. On the contrary, there is good reason to believe that this chapter does not even belong to the very early period of Muhammad's ministry assigned it by Noöldeke and Rodwell. The attitude of the Quraish (vers. 8 and 51), especially of the notable person mentioned in vers. 10–16, is not that of the earliest period of Muhammad's prophetic history. The same is true of the attitude of the preacher towards his townsmen, apparent in vers. 16 and 48. At the same time, the absence of any notice of

INTROD.] (169) [CHAP. LXVIII.

violence towards Muslims (which notice would assuredly have been recorded in a chapter specifying the crimes of the unbelievers), proves Muir's date (fourth stage) to be too late. We would fix the date about the fourth year of Muhammad's ministry.

Principal Subjects.

	VERSES
Muhammad not a madman nor an impostor	1–8
Invective against a prominent enemy of Islám	9–16
The example of certain gardeners a warning to the Makkans	17–34
Unbelievers warned of coming judgment	35–47
Muhammad exhorted not to be impatient, like Jonah	48–50
Extreme hatred of the Quraish towards Muhammad and the Qurán exposed	51, 52

IN THE NAME OF THE MOST MERCIFUL GOD.

|| (1) N. By the pen, and what they write, (2) thou, R $\frac{1}{3}$. *O Muhammad*, through the grace of thy LORD, *art* not distracted. (3) Verily *there is prepared* for thee an everlasting reward: (4) for thou *art* of a noble disposition. (5)

(1) *N.* "This letter is sometimes made the title of the chapter, but its meaning is confessedly uncertain. They who suppose it stands for the word Nún are not agreed as to its signification in this place; for it is not only the name of the letter N in Arabic, but signifies also 'an inkhorn' and 'a fish.' Some are of opinion the former signification is the most proper here, as consonant to what is immediately mentioned of 'the pen' and 'writing;' and, considering that the blood of certain 'fish' is good ink, not inconsistent with the latter signification; which is, however, preferred by others, saying that either the whole species of 'fish' in general is thereby intended, or the fish which swallowed Jonas (who is mentioned in this chapter), or else that vast one called Behemoth, fancied to support the earth, in particular. Those who acquiesce in none of the foregoing explications have invented others of their own, and imagine this character stands for the 'table of God's decrees' or 'one of the rivers in Paradise,' &c."—*Sale, Zamakshari, Baidháwi, Yahya.*

What we write. "Some understand these words generally, and others of the pen with which God's decrees are written on the preserved table, and of the angels who register the same."—*Sale.*

(4) *A noble disposition.* "In that thou hast borne with so much patience and resignation the wrongs and insults of thy people,

Thou shalt see, and *the infidels* shall see, (6) which of you *are* bereaved of your senses. (7) Verily thy LORD well knoweth him who wandereth from his path; and he well knoweth those who are *rightly* directed; (8) wherefore obey not those who charge *thee* with imposture. (9) They desire that thou shouldest be easy *with them*, and they will be easy *with thee*. (10) But obey not any *who is* a common swearer, a despicable *fellow*, (11) a defamer, going about with slander, (12) who forbiddeth that which is good, *who is also* a transgressor, (13) a wicked person, cruel, *and* besides this, of spurious birth; (14) although he be possessed of wealth and *many* children; (15) when our signs are rehearsed unto him, he saith, *They are* fables of the ancients. (16) We will stigmatise him on the nose. (17) Verily we have tried *the Makkans*, as we *formerly* tried the owners of the garden, when they swore that

---

which have been greater than those offered to any apostle before thee."—*Sale, Baidhāwi.*

(8) See notes on chap. xxii. 53.

(9) "That is, if thou wilt let them alone in their idolatry and other wicked practices, they will cease to revile and persecute thee." —*Sale.*

(10-13) "The person at whom this passage was particularly levelled is generally supposed to have been Muhammad's inveterate enemy, al Walíd Ibn al Mughaira, whom, to complete his character, he calls 'bastard,' because al Mughaira did not own him for his son till he was eighteen years of age. Some, however, think it was al Akhnas Ibn Shuraik, who was really of the tribe of Thakíf, though reputed to be that of Zahra."—*Sale, Jalāluddín.*

(15) *Fables, &c.* See note on chap. xxi. 5.

(16) *The nose.* "Which, being the most conspicuous part of the face, a mark set thereon is attended with the utmost ignominy. It is said that this prophetical menace was actually made good, al Walíd having his nose slit by a sword at the battle of Badr, the mark of which wound he carried with him to his grave."—*Sale, Jalāluddín.*

(17) *We have tried the Makkans.* "By afflicting them with a grievous famine."—*Sale.* See chap. xxiii. 65.

As we formerly tried the owners of the garden. "This garden was a plantation of palm-trees, about two parasangs from Sanaa, belonging to a certain charitable man, who, when he gathered his dates, used to give public notice to the poor, and to leave them such of the fruit as the knife missed, or was blown by the wind, or fell beside the cloth spread under the tree to receive it. After death, his sons, who

they would gather the fruit thereof in the morning, (18) and added not the exception, *if it please God:* (19) wherefore a surrounding *destruction* from thy LORD encompassed it while they slept; (20) and in the morning it became like *a garden* whose fruits had been gathered. (21) And they called *the one to the other* as they rose in the morning, (22) *saying,* Go out early to your plantation, if ye intend to gather the fruit thereof: (23) so they went on, whispering to one another, (24) No poor man shall enter *the garden* upon you this day. (25) And they went forth early, with a determined purpose. (26) And when they saw *the garden blasted and destroyed* they said, We have certainly mistaken our way: (27) *but when they found it to be their own garden they cried,* Verily we are not permitted *to reap the fruit thereof.* (28) The worthier of them said, Did I not say unto you, Will ye not give praise unto GOD? (29) They answered, Praise be unto our LORD! Verily we have been unjust doers. (30) And they began to blame one another, (31) *and* they said, Woe be unto us! verily we have been transgressors: (32) peradventure our LORD will give us in exchange a better *garden* than this: and we earnestly beseech our LORD *to pardon us.* (33) Thus *is the* chastisement *of this life:* but the chastisement of the next *shall be* more griev-

---

were then become masters of the garden, apprehending they should come to want if they followed their father's example, agreed to gather the fruit early in the morning, when the poor could have no notice of the matter; but, when they came to execute their purpose, they found, to their great grief and surprise, that their plantation had been destroyed in the night."—*Sale, Baidháwi, Jaláluddín.*

This story is simply an enlargement of the statement in the text.

Gather the fruit. "Literally, 'that they would cut it;' the manner of gathering dates being to cut the clusters off with a knife. Marracci supposes that they intended to 'cut down' the trees and destroy the plantation; which, as he observes, renders the story ridiculous and absurd."—*Sale.*

(27) *We are not permitted.* See note on chap. lvi. 66.

(30) *Began to blame.* "For one advised this expedition, another approved of it, a third gave consent by his silence, but the fourth was absolutely against it."—*Sale, Baidháwi.*

ous: if they had known *it, they would have taken heed.*
(34) Verily for the pious *are prepared*, with their LORD, gardens of delight.

R 2/4. || (35) Shall we deal with the Muslims as with the wicked? (36) What aileth you that ye judge thus? (37) Have ye a book *from heaven* wherein ye read (38) that ye are therein promised that which ye shall choose? (39) Or have ye *received* oaths which shall be binding upon us to the day of resurrection, that ye shall enjoy what ye imagine? (40) Ask them which of them *will be* the voucher of this. (41) Or have they companions *who will vouch for them?* Let them produce their companions, therefore, if they speak truth. (42) On a *certain* day the leg shall be made bare, and they shall be called upon to worship, but they shall not be able. (43) Their looks *shall be* cast down: ignominy shall attend them; for that they were invited to the worship *of God* while they *were* in safety, *but would not hear.* (44) Let me alone, therefore, with him who accuseth this new revelation of imposture. We will lead them gradually *to destruction*, by

---

(35) "This passage was revealed in answer to the infidels, who said, 'If we shall be raised again, as Muhammed and his followers imagine, they will not excel us; but we shall certainly be in a better condition than they in the next world, as we are in this.'"—*Sale, Baidháwi.*

(41) *Companions.* "Or, as some interpret the word, 'idols;' which can make their condition in the next life equal to that of the Muslims."—*Sale.*

The "companions" alluded to were their false gods, represented by their idols. See note on chap. x. 29.

(42) *The leg shall be made bare.* "This expression is used to signify a grievous and terrible calamity; thus they say, 'War has made bare the leg,' when they would express the fury and rage of battle."—*Sale, Baidháwi.*

See a similar expression Isaiah xlvii. 2.

Shall not be able. "Because the time of acceptance shall be past. Al Baidháwi is uncertain whether the words respect the day of judgment or the article of death; but Jaláluddín supposes them to relate to the former, and adds that the infidels shall not be able to perform the act of adoration, because their backs shall become stiff and inflexible."—*Sale.*

(44) *We will lead them gradually, &c., i.e.,* "by granting them long

ways which they know not, (45) and I will bear with them for a long time; for my stratagem *is* effectual. (46) Dost thou ask them any reward *for thy preaching?* But they are laden with debts. (47) *Are* the secrets of futurity with them; and do they transcribe the same *from the table of God's decrees?* (48) Wherefore, patiently wait the judgment of thy LORD: and be not like him who was swallowed by the fish, when he cried *unto God*, being inwardly vexed. (49) Had not grace from his LORD reached him, he had surely been cast forth on the naked *shore*, covered with shame: (50) but his LORD chose him, and made him *one* of the righteous. (51) It wanteth little but that the unbelievers strike thee down with their *malicious* looks, when they hear the admonition *of the Qurán;* and they say, He *is* certainly distracted: (52) but it is no other than an admonition unto all creatures.

---

life and prosperity in this world, which will deceive them to their ruin."—*Sale.*

(47) See chap. lii. 38-41.

(48) *Him who was swallowed by the fish.* Jonah. See note on chap. xxi. 87.

(54) See chap. xxv. 8, 9.

CHAPTER LXIX.

ENTITLED SURAT AL HÁQQAT (THE INFALLIBLE).

Revealed at Makkah.

INTRODUCTION.

THE title of this chapter, understood as referring to the infallible truth of the doctrine of a future judgment, though probably taken at random from the first verse, as in the case of so many other titles, nevertheless expresses the purport of the contents very well. The strong asseveration of the Prophet to the truth of his claims found in the last verses of the chapter must be understood as intended to emphasise the inevitable advent of the dread day. The necessity for such strong language, however, predicates strong opposition to the Prophet and his message on the part of his hearers. Aside from this, there is nothing worthy of special note to distinguish this from other Makkan revelations.

Probable Date of the Revelations.

In his chronological list, Noëldeke places this chapter immediately before chap. li., *i.e.*, about the sixth year of the Call. Muir places it somewhat later.

Principal Subjects.

	VERSES
The judgment of God will infallibly come	1-3
Ád, Thamúd, and Pharaoh destroyed for rejecting their prophets	4-10
As the flood came, so shall the judgment certainly come .	11-16
On the judgment-day God's throne shall be borne by eight mighty angels	17
The good and bad shall receive their account-books and be judged according to their deeds	18-29

| INTROD.] | (175) | [CHAP. LXIX. |

VERSES

Infidels shall be bound with chains seventy cubits in length
and be cast into hell-fire 30–37
With terrible oaths Muhammad asserts the truth of his
prophetic claims 38–39

IN THE NAME OF THE MOST MERCIFUL GOD.

‖ (1) The infallible! (2) What *is* the infallible? (3) And what shall cause thee to understand what the infallible *is*? (4) *The tribes of* Thamúd and Ád denied as a falsehood the *day* which shall strike *men's hearts with terror*. (5) But Thamúd were destroyed by a terrible noise, (6) and Ád were destroyed by a roaring *and* furious wind, (7) which *God* caused to assail them for seven nights and eight days successively: thou mightest have seen people during the same lying prostrate, as though they *had been* the roots of hollow palm-trees; (8) and couldest thou have seen any of them remaining? (9) Pharaoh also, and those who *were* before him, and the *cities* which were overthrown, were guilty of sin: (10) and they *severally* were disobedient to the apostle of their LORD; wherefore he chastised them with an abundant chastisement. (11) When the water *of the deluge* arose, we carried you in the *ark* which swam *thereon;* (12) that we might make the same a memorial unto you, and the retaining ear might retain it. (13) And when one blast

RUBA.
R $\frac{1}{8}$

---

(1) *The infallible.* "The original word, *al háqqat*, is one of the names or epithets of the day of judgment. As the root from which it is derived signifies not only *to be* or *come to pass of necessity*, but also to *verify*, some rather think that day to be so called because it will verify and *show the truth* of what men doubt of in this life, viz., the resurrection of the dead, their being brought to account, and the consequent rewards and punishments."—*Sale, Baidháwi.*

(4) *The day which shall strike.* "Arabic, *al qáriat*, or the striking, which is another name or epithet of the last day."—*Sale.*

(7) *Hollow palm-trees.* Compare chap. lii. 31, 32. See also notes on chap. xi. 50–68.

(9) *Cities, &c.* See note on chap. xi. 81, 82.

(13) *One blast.* See Prelim. Disc., p. 135.

shall sound the trumpet, (14) and the earth shall be moved *from its place*, and the mountains also, and shall be dashed in pieces at one stroke: (15) on that day the inevitable *hour of judgment* shall suddenly come; (16) and the heavens shall cleave in sunder, and shall fall in pieces, on that day: (17) and the angels *shall be* on the sides thereof; and eight shall bear the throne of thy LORD above them, on that day. (18) On that day ye shall be presented *before the judgment-seat of God;* and none of your secret *actions shall be* hidden. (19) And he who shall have his book delivered into his right hand shall say, Take ye, read this my book; (20) verily I thought that I should be brought to this my account: (21) he *shall lead* a pleasing life (22) in a lofty *garden*, (23) the fruits whereof shall be near *to gather.* (24) Eat and drink with easy digestion; because of the *good works* which ye sent before you, in the days which are past. (25) But he who shall have his book delivered into his left hand shall say, O that I had not received this book; (26) and that I had not known what this my account *was!* (27) O that *death* had made an end *of me!* (28) My riches have not profited me; (29) *and* my power is passed from me. (30) *And God shall say to the keepers of hell,* Take him and bind him, (31) and cast him into hell to be burned: (32) then put him into a chain of the length of seventy cubits: (33) because he believed not in the great GOD, (34) and was not solicitous to feed the poor: (35) wherefore this day he shall have no friend

---

(17) *The angels, &c.* "These words seem to intimate the death of the angels at the demolition of their habitation, beside the ruins whereof they shall lie like dead bodies."—*Sale.*

Eight shall bear, &c. "The number of those who bear it at present being generally supposed to be but four, to whom four more will be added at the last day for the grandeur of the occasion."—*Sale, Baidháwi.*

(19–25) See Prelim. Disc., pp. 142, 144.

(32) *Seventy cubits.* "Wrap him round with it, so that he may not be able to stir."—*Sale.*

here; (36) nor *any* food, but the filthy corruption *flowing from the bodies of the damned*, (37) which none shall eat but the sinners.

‖ (38) I swear by that which ye see, (39) and that R $\frac{2}{8}$ which ye see not, (40) that this *is* the discourse of an honourable apostle, (41) and not the discourse of a poet: how little do ye believe! (42) Neither *is it* the discourse of a soothsayer: how little are ye admonished! (43) *It is* a revelation from the LORD of all creatures. (44) If *Muhammad* had forged any part of *these* discourses concerning us, (45) verily we had taken him by the right hand, (46) and had cut in sunder the vein of his heart; (47) neither would we have withheld any of you from *chastising* him. (48) And verily this *book is* an admonition unto the pious; (49) and we well know that there are *some* of you who charge *the same* with imposture: (50) but it *shall* surely *be* an *occasion of* grievous sighing unto the infidels; (51) for it *is* the truth of a certainty. (52) Wherefore praise the name of thy LORD, the great *God*.

---

(38) *I swear*. Or, *I will not swear*. See note on chap. lvi. 74.

(41) *A poet*. Muhammad was so anxious to combat the idea that he was merely a mad poet (chaps. xxi. 5 and xxxvii. 5), that he here brings in the oath of Divinity itself to prove that he is not. This desire no doubt accounts in a measure for the more prosaic style of the later chapters of the Qurán.

(42–52) This passage contains, perhaps, the strongest as well as most impassioned assertions of the Prophet's belief in his own inspiration to be found in the Qurán. Yet the very earnestness and temper in which Muhammad makes this assertion is in strong contrast with the calm dignity of the true prophet. Let it be remembered that the speaker here, as elsewhere in the idiom of the Qurán, is God. The real speaker, however, is Muhammad. One would think that if miracles were ever needed to attest the claims of a prophet, they were needed in this case. But of these there were none.

CHAPTER LXX.

ENTITLED SURAT AL MAÁRIJ (THE STEPS).

Revealed at Makkah.

INTRODUCTION.

THE title of this chapter is taken from ver. 3. The occasion of its composition is mentioned in the first verse. One of the unbelievers at Makkah, whether one of those mentioned by Sale in his note on ver. 1, or some other representative of the infidel Quraish, mockingly asked Muhammad to attest the proof of his prophetic claims by bringing upon them the punishment of the judgment-day. In reply, we have a discourse at once suited to warn the unbelievers and to comfort the Prophet.

In this chapter we have probably the earliest rule of Muslim practice, vers. 22-34. A portion of this, however, vers. 29-34, seems to have been added at a later date, because the law regulating the marriage of Muslims, and especially their practice regarding "the slaves which their right hands possess," is referred to here with too much definiteness to comport with a Makkan revelation. Besides this, the statement in ver. 34 is a mere repetition of that of ver. 23, which is best accounted for by supposing these passages to have been originally separate, but brought together here by the compilers.

The attitude of Muhammad towards his townsmen here is that of despair for their conversion. He now calmly awaits the visitation of divine justice against their unbelief.

Probable Date of the Revelations.

Noëldeke places this chapter immediately after chaps. lvi. and liii., probably because of the allusion of the first verse of this chapter to the beginning of chap. lvi. Muir places it in about the same period of time. This would fix the date at about the fifth year of the call of Muhammad to preach. I would, however, except vers. 29-34, which I would assign to a period as late as A.H. 5.

Principal Subjects.

	VERSES
A man demanded that the day of judgment might come at once	1
The day, whose space is fifty thousand years, will surely come	2–4
Muhammad to bear the insults of the infidels patiently, because judgment is near	5–14
Riches, children, and friends will not save the wicked from hell	12–18
The wicked are niggardly in health, but full of complaint when evil befalleth	19–24
The character of true believers described	25–35
Unbelievers need entertain no hope they shall escape destruction	36–41
Muhammad counselled to permit the unbelieving Makkans to sport themselves, because their damnation is nigh	42–45

IN THE NAME OF THE MOST MERCIFUL GOD.

∥ (1) One demanded and called for vengeance to fall R ¼· on the unbelievers: (2) there shall be none to avert the same (3) from *being inflicted by* GOD, the possessor of the steps (4) *by which* the angels ascend unto him, and the spirit *Gabriel also*, in a day whose space is fifty thousand years: (5) wherefore bear *the insults of the Makkans* with becoming patience: (6) for they see *their punishment* afar

---

(1) *One demanded ... vengeance.* "The person here meant is generally supposed to have been al Nudár Ibn al Hárith, who said, 'O God, if what Muhammad preaches be the truth from thee, rain down upon us a shower of stones, or send some dreadful judgment to punish us.' Others, however, think it was Abú Jahl, who challenged Muhammad to cause a fragment of heaven to fall on them."—*Sale, Baidháwi.*

(3) *The steps.* "By which prayers and righteous actions ascend to heaven, or by which the angels ascend to receive the divine commands, or the believers will ascend to Paradise. Some understand thereby the different orders of angels, or the heavens, which rise gradually one above another."—*Sale.*

(4) *Fifty thousand years.* See note on chap. xxxii. 4.

"This is supposed to be the space which would be required for their ascent from the lowest part of creation to the throne of God, if it were to be measured, or the time which it would take a man to perform that journey; and this is not contradictory to what is

off, (7) but we see it nigh at hand. (8) On a certain day the heaven shall become like molten *brass*, (9) and the mountains like wool of various colours *scattered abroad by the wind:* (10) and a friend shall not ask a friend *concerning his condition*, (11) *although* they see one another. The wicked shall wish to redeem himself from the punishment of that day by *giving up* his children, (12) and his wife, and his brother, (13) and his kindred, who showed kindness unto him, (14) and all who *are* in the earth; and that *this* might deliver him: (15) by no means: for hell-fire, (16) dragging *them* by *their* scalps, (17) shall call him who shall have turned his back, and fled *from the faith*, (18) and shall have amassed *riches,* and covetously hoarded *them*. (19) Verily man is created extremely impatient: (20) when evil toucheth him, *he is* full of complaint; (21) but when good befalleth him, *he becometh* niggardly: (22) except those who are devoutly given, (23) and who persevere in their prayers; (24) and those of whose substance a due and certain portion (25) *is ready to be given* unto him who asketh, and him who is forbidden *by shame to ask:* (26) and those who sincerely believe the day of judgment, (27) and who dread the punishment of their LORD: (28) (for *there is* none secure from the punishment

---

said elsewhere (chap. xxxii. 4), (if it be to be interpreted of the ascent of the angels), that the length of the day whereon they ascend is one thousand years, because that is meant only of their ascent from earth to the lower heaven, including also the time of their descent.

"But the commentators generally take the day spoken of in both these passages to be the day of judgment, having recourse to several expedients to reconcile them, some of which we have mentioned in another place (Prelim. Disc., p. 137), and as both passages seem to contradict what the Muhammadan doctors teach, that God will judge all creatures in the space of half a day (Prelim. Disc., p. 144), they suppose those large number of years are designed to express the time of the previous attendance of those who are to be judged (Prelim. Disc., p. 141), or else to the space wherein God will judge the unbelieving nations, of which, they say, there will be fifty, the trial of each nation taking up one thousand years, though that of the true believers will be over in the short space above mentioned."—*Sale, Zamakhshari.*

(19) See note on chap. xvii. 12.

of their LORD:) (29) and who abstain from the carnal knowledge of *women* (30) other than their wives, or the *slaves* which their right hands possess: (for *as to them* they shall be blameless; (31) but whoever coveteth *any woman* besides these, they *are* transgressors).

|| (32) And those who faithfully keep what they are intrusted with, and their covenant; (33) and who are upright in their testimonies, (34) and who carefully observe *the requisite rights in* their prayers: (35) these *shall dwell* amidst gardens, highly honoured. (36) What aileth the unbelievers, that they run before thee in companies, (37) on the right hand and on the left? (38) Doth every man of them wish to enter into a garden of delight? (39) By no means: verily we have created them of that which they know. (40) I swear by the LORD of the east and of the west, that we are able to *destroy them*, (41) *and to* substitute better than them *in their room;* neither *are* we to be prevented, *if we shall please so to do.* (42) Wherefore suffer them to wade in vain disputes, and to amuse themselves with sport, until they meet their day with which they have been threatened; (43) the day *whereon* they shall come forth hastily from *their* graves, as though they were *troops* hastening to *their* standard: (44) their looks *shall be* downcast; ignominy shall attend them. (45) This *is* the day with which they have been threatened.

R $\frac{2}{8}$.

(29-31) See notes on chap. iv. 3. This passage clearly teaches that a Muslim is not limited to the four lawful wives, but may have as many slave girls as he pleases besides.

(39) *Of that which they know*, viz., "of filthy seed, which bears no relation or resemblance to holy beings : wherefore it is necessary for him who would hope to be an inhabitant of Paradise to perfect himself in faith and spiritual virtues, to fit himself for that place."— *Sale, Baidhāwi.*

(40) *I swear.* "Or, *I will not swear, &c.*"—*Sale.* See chap. lvi. 74, note.

The east . . . the west. "The original words are in the plural number, and signify the different points of the horizon at which the sun rises and sets in the course of the year."—*Sale.*

See note on chap. xxxvii. 5.

(43) *Troops hastening, &c.* Comp. chap. xxxix. 71-73.

CHAPTER LXXI.

ENTITLED SURAT NÚH (NOAH).

Revealed at Makkah.

INTRODUCTION.

THIS chapter records the prophetic experience of Noah, and is therefore rightly named. The Noah of these revelations, however, is no other than the Muhammad of Makkah. The words ascribed to him are those constantly used by Muhammad. This Noah was a *warner;* so was Muhammad. His people rejected him, refused to leave the worship of their idols, Wadd, Suwa, Yaghúth, Yauk, and Nasr, and *plotted* against him. The Quraish rejected Muhammad, refused to leave Wadd, Suwa, Yaghúth, Yauk, and Nasr, and devised a dangerous *plot* against their prophet. We leave the reader to make his own inferences from the facts thus stated, referring him for further instances of a like character to chapter xi. Surely a counterfeit of prophecy like this must have been inspired by a spirit different from that which moved holy men of old.

Probable Date of the Revelations.

On the assumption that the circumstances of Noah detailed in this chapter were the circumstances of Muhammad at the time of writing it, we have to seek a date for it when (1) Muhammad was rejected by the Quraish as a body (vers. 5, 6, and 20), (2) when the Quraish had devised a dangerous plot against him (ver. 21), and (3) when they had taken steps to defend the national idols (vers. 22-24). We think such a combination of circumstances were present to Muhammad about the time when Abu Tálib frustrated the evil designs of the Quraish who plotted to slay him. This would give us B.H. 7 as about the date of this chapter. Noëldeke places it early in his second period, which would be about the fifth year of the Call. This is hardly consistent with his conjecture that this chapter is a fragment of a longer Sura.

INTROD.]   (183)   [CHAP. LXXI.

Principal Subjects.
	VERSES
Noah sent as a warner; his message to his people	1-4
Noah's people refuse to believe him, notwithstanding every effort	5-20
The people of Noah plot against him and are destroyed	21-26
Noah prays for the destruction of the infidels, and for the pardon of his parents and the true believers	27-29

IN THE NAME OF THE MOST MERCIFUL GOD.

|| (1) Verily we sent Noah unto his people, *saying,* R $\frac{1}{9}$. Warn thy people before a grievous punishment overtake them. (2) *Noah* said, O my people, verily I *am* a public warner unto you; (3) wherefore serve GOD, and fear him, and obey me: (4) he will forgive you *part* of your sins; and will grant you respite until a determined time: for GOD'S determined time, when it cometh, shall not be deferred; if ye were men of understanding, *ye would know this.* (5) He said, LORD, verily I have called my people night and day; but my calling only increaseth their aversion: (6) and whensoever I call them *to the true faith,* that thou mayest forgive them, they put their fingers in their ears, and cover themselves with their garments, and persist *in their infidelity,* and proudly disdain *my counsel.* (7) Moreover, I invited them openly, (8) and I spake to them again in public; and I also secretly admonished them in private; (9) and I said, Beg pardon of your LORD; for he is inclined to forgive: (10) and he will cause the heaven to pour down rain plentifully upon you, (11) and will give you increase of wealth and of children; and he

---

(1) *Noah.* See notes on the story of Noah recorded in chap. xi. 26-49. See how Noah is here said to use in his discourses the very words of Muhammad's discourses to the Quraish.

(4) *He will forgive part of your sins, i.e.,* "your past sins, which are done away by the profession of the true faith."—*Sale.*

(11) *Wealth and children.* "It is said that after Noah had for a long time preached to them in vain, God shut up the heaven for forty years, and rendered their women barren."—*Sale, Baidháwi.*

will provide you gardens, and furnish you with rivers. (12) What aileth you, that ye hope not for benevolence in God, (13) since he hath created you variously? (14) Do ye not see how GOD hath created the seven heavens, one above another; (15) and hath placed the moon therein for a light, and hath appointed the sun for a taper? (16) GOD hath also produced and caused you to spring forth from the earth: (17) hereafter he will cause you to return into the same; and he will *again* take you *thence*, by bringing *you* forth *from your graves.*

R $\frac{2}{10}$.   ‖ (18) And GOD hath spread the earth as a carpet for you, (19) that ye may walk therein through spacious paths. (20) Noah said, LORD, verily they are disobedient unto me; and they follow him whose riches and children do no other than increase his perdition. (21) And they devised a dangerous plot *against Noah:* (22) and *the chief men* said *to the others,* Ye shall by no means leave your gods; neither shall ye forsake Wadd, nor Suwa, (23) nor Yaghúth, and Yauk, and Nasr. (24) And they seduced many (for thou shalt only increase error in the wicked): (25) because of their sins they were drowned, and cast into the fire *of hell;* (26) and they found none to protect them against GOD. (27) And Noah said, LORD, leave not

---

(12) *What aileth you, &c, i.e.,* "that God will accept and amply reward those who serve him? For some suppose Noah's people made him this answer, 'If what we now follow be the truth, we ought not to forsake it; but if it be false, how will God accept or be favourable unto us, who have rebelled against him?'"—*Sale, Baidháwi.*

(13) *He hath created you variously.* "That is, as the commentators expound it, by various steps or changes from the original matter, till ye became perfect men."—*Sale.*

See notes on chaps. xxii. 5, and xxiii. 14, &c.

(23) "These were five idols worshipped by the Antediluvians, and afterwards by the ancient Arabs. See the Prelim. Disc. p. 40."—*Sale.*

This explanation of the Muslim authors cannot shield their Prophet from the anachronism into which he has fallen here. The people of Noah were too much like the Quraish in Muhammad's mind to have had any other gods than those of Makkah.

(27, 28) "They say Noah preferred not this prayer for the destruc-

any families of the unbelievers on the earth: (28) for if thou leave them, they will seduce thy servants, and will beget none but a wicked and unbelieving *offspring*. (29) LORD, forgive me and my parents, and every one who shall enter my house, being a true believer, and the true believers of both sexes; and add unto the unjust doers nothing but destruction.

---

tion of his people till after he had tried them for nine hundred and fifty years, and found them incorrigible reprobates."—*Sale*.

See also notes on chap. liv. 10.

(29) *Forgive me and my parents.* "His father, Lamech, and his mother, whose name was Shamkha, the daughter of Enoch, being true believers."—*Sale*.

Muhammad was not permitted to pray for his mother. See note on chap. ix. 114. Observe that Noah is also here represented as a sinner needing pardon. This passage, therefore, also refutes the Muslim conceit as to the sinlessness of the prophets. See note on chap. ii. 253.

My house. "The commentators are uncertain whether Noah's dwelling-house be here meant, or the temple he had built for the worship of God, or the ark."—*Sale*.

This passage illustrates the efficiency of Muhammad's intercession on the judgment-day. For true believers he will pray, though for them his intercession is not needed, and for the infidels he may only ask their condemnation.

CHAPTER LXXII.

ENTITLED SURAT AL JINN (THE GENII).

Revealed at Makkah.

INTRODUCTION.

THIS chapter records the conversion of certain genii, who overheard Muhammad reading the Qurán while on his return from Tayif to Makkah. It is only remarkable for the position which it assigns these imaginary beings, making them along with mankind the recipients of the blessings or curses consequent upon faith or disbelief in the Qurán. We have here what professes to be a divine revelation concerning the nature, character, employment, and religion of these spirits. The Qurán is therefore responsible for perpetuating the superstitious belief of the Arabs regarding the genii among Muslims everywhere.

For a historical statement of the circumstances of the Prophet alluded to here, see Muir's *Life of Mahomet*, vol. ii. pp. 203–205.

Probable Date of the Revelations.

Noëldeke accepts a tradition which ascribes Muhammad's vision of the genii to a journey which he made to Oqátz, and accordingly places this chapter immediately after chap. xliii. We prefer here to follow Muir, who places the scene of the vision in the grove of an idol temple in the valley of Nakhla, where Muhammad slept after his expulsion from Tayif. The date of the revelations would therefore be about B.H. 2.

Principal Subjects.

	VERSES
Certain of the genii converted to Islám by hearing the Qurán	1, 2
The folly of men and genii in ascribing offspring to God	3-7
Genii prying into heavenly secrets are driven away with fiery darts	8, 9
Different classes of genii, some Muslims and others infidels	10-14

	VERSES
Believing genii rewarded in Paradise, the unbelievers punished in hell .	15–18
The genii pressed upon Muhammad to hear the Qurán .	19
Muhammad can only publish what hath been revealed to him	20–24
The judgments of God shall overtake the unbelievers .	25, 26
God revealeth his secrets to his apostles only	27, 28

IN THE NAME OF THE MOST MERCIFUL GOD.

|| (1) Say, It hath been revealed unto me that a company of genii attentively heard *me reading the Qurán*, and said, Verily we have heard an admirable discourse, (2) which directeth unto the right institution; wherefore we believe therein, and we will by no means associate any *other* with our LORD. (3) He (may the majesty of our LORD be exalted!) hath taken no wife, nor *hath he begotten* any issue. (4) Yet the foolish among us hath spoken that which is extremely false of GOD; (5) but we verily thought that neither man nor genius would by any means have uttered a lie concerning GOD. (6) And there are certain men who fly for refuge unto certain of the genii; but they increase their folly and transgression: (7) and they also thought, as ye thought, that GOD would not raise any one

NISF.

R. ١/١.

---

(1) *Genii.* See notes on chap. xlvi. 28, 29. Consult also note 21, introduction to Lane's "Thousand and One Nights."

(3) *He hath taken no wife.* See note on chap. ii. 116.

(4) *The foolish, i.e.,* "Iblis, or the rebellious genii."—*Sale.*

(6) *Certain men, &c.* "For the Arabs, when they found themselves in a desert in the evening (the genii being supposed to haunt such places about that time), used to say, 'I fly for refuge to the Lord of this valley, that he may defend me from the foolish among his people.'"—*Sale, Baidháwi.*

(7) *They thought . . . as ye thought.* "It is uncertain which of these pronouns is to be referred to mankind and which to the genii; some expositors taking that of the third person to relate to the former, and that of the second person to the latter, and others being of the contrary opinion."—*Sale.*

Neither of them refer to mankind alone, but to the unbelieving men and genii; (they) thought as " ye (now believing genii) thought," &c.

to life. (8) And we *formerly* attempted *to pry into what was transacting* in heaven; but we found the same filled with a strong guard *of angels,* and with flaming darts; (9) and we sat on *some of the* seats thereof to hear *the discourse of its inhabitants;* but whoever listeneth now findeth a flame laid in ambush for him, *to guard the celestial confines.* (10) And we know not whether evil be *hereby* intended against those who *are* in the earth, or whether their LORD intendeth to direct them aright. (11) *There are* some among us who are upright; and *there are* some among us who are otherwise: we are of different ways. (12) And we verily thought that we could by no means frustrate GOD in the earth, neither could we escape him by flight: (13) wherefore, when we had heard the direction *contained in the Qurán,* we believed therein. And whoever believeth in his LORD need not fear any diminution *of his reward,* nor any injustice. (14) *There are some* Muslims among us, and *there are others* of us who swerve from righteousness. And whoso embraceth Islám, they earnestly seek true direction; (15) but those who swerve from righteousness shall be fuel for hell. (16) If they tread in the way *of truth,* we will surely water them with abundant rain, (17) that we may prove them thereby; but whoso turneth aside from the admonition of his LORD, him will he send into a severe torment. (18) Verily the places of worship *are set apart* unto GOD: wherefore invoke not any *other therein* together with GOD. (19) When the servant of GOD stood up to invoke him, it wanted little but that *the genii* had pressed on him in crowds, *to hear him rehearse the Qurán.*

(8, 9) See note on chap. xv. 17.
(14) *Some Muslims among us.* See Prelim. Disc., p. 121.
(16) *We will surely water them, &c., i.e.,* " we will grant them plenty of all good things. Some think by these words rain is promised to the Makkans, after their seven years' drought, on their embracing Islám."—*Sale.*
(19) *The servant of God, i.e.,* Muhammad. See reference to Muir's *Life of Mahomet,* at chap. xl. 29.

‖ (20) Say, Verily I call upon my LORD only, and I associate no *other god* with him. (21) Say, Verily I am not able, *of myself*, to procure you either hurt or a right institution. (22) Say, Verily none can protect me against GOD; (23) neither shall I find any refuge besides him. (24) *I can do no more* than publish *what hath been revealed unto me* from GOD, and his messages. And whosoever shall be disobedient unto GOD and his Apostle, for him *is* the fire of hell *prepared:* they shall remain therein for ever. (25) Until they see *the vengeance* with which they are threatened, *they will not cease their opposition:* but then shall they know who *were* the weaker in a protector, and the fewer in number. (26) Say, I know not whether *the punishment* with which ye are threatened *be* nigh, or whether my LORD will appoint for it a distant term. He knoweth the secrets of futurity; and he doth not communicate his secrets unto any, (27) except an apostle in whom he is well pleased: and he causeth a guard *of angels* to march before him and behind him; (28) that he may know that they have executed the commissions of their LORD; he comprehendeth whatever is with them; and counteth all things by number.

R $\frac{2}{12}$.

(21-25) How different the tone of the Prophet, weak, discouraged, and driven from Tayif, from that of the Prophet-general triumphant at Madína!

(26) See note on chap. vii. 188.

(28) *That he may know, &c.* "That is to say, either that the Prophet may know that Gabriel and the other angels, who bring down the revelation, have communicated it to him pure and free from any diabolical suggestions, or that God may know that the Prophet has published the same to mankind."—*Sale, Baidháwi.*

CHAPTER LXXIII.

ENTITLED SURAT AL MUZZAMMIL (WRAPPED UP).

Revealed at Makkah.

INTRODUCTION.

THIS chapter is regarded by some writers as one of the earliest revelations of the Qurán. I can find for this opinion no other reason than that the words with which it begins, and from which it receives its title, have a somewhat striking similarity to those which are found in the first verse of chapter lxxiv., which, on all hands, is admitted to be one of the earliest parts of the Qurán. This theory, however, is disproved by the following facts :—(1) Ver. 10 speaks of enemies of the Prophet, contumelies, and opposition, which did not exist at so early a period ; (2) vers. 10 and 11 exhort the Prophet *to withdraw* from the infidels and to leave them in the hands of God ; moreover, (3), the statements concerning the punishment of hell and the destruction of Pharaoh point to a later date.

The object of the chapter seems to have been the stirring up of the Muslims to more earnest devotion to God in prayer. This was due to the trials they were now called upon to endure. In later times, when the stress of business in the camp at Madína left no time for sleep in the daytime, this law was found to be inconvenient. For this reason ver. 20 was added to abrogate the obnoxious sections of the law in vers. 1–4.

Probable Date of the Revelations.

Noëldeke fixes the date of this chapter at about the middle of the first period, while Muir, with more reason, fixes it at the beginning of the sixth year of Muhammad's mission.

Principal Subjects.

	VERSES
Muhammad and the Muslims bidden to pray during the night	1–4
The Qurán to be pronounced with a distinct sonorous tone	5–9
Muhammad exhorted to bear patiently the contumelies of the infidels	10, 11

	VERSES
God will visit the infidels with dire calamities	11-14
The punishment of Pharaoh a warning to the people of Makkah	15-19
Modification of the law given in vers. 1-4	20

IN THE NAME OF THE MOST MERCIFUL GOD.

|| (1) O thou wrapped up, (2) arise *to prayer, and con-* $R \frac{1}{13}$. *tinue therein* during the night, except a small part; (3) *that is to say, during* one half thereof: or do thou lessen the same a little (4) or add thereto. And repeat the Qurán with a distinct and sonorous voice: (5) for we will lay on thee a weighty word. (6) Verily the rising by night

---

(1) *Thou wrapped up.* "When this revelation was brought to Muhammad, he was wrapped up in his garments, being affrighted at the appearance of Gabriel; or, as some say, he lay sleeping unconcernedly, or, according to others, praying, wrapped up in one part of a large mantle or rug with the other part of which Ayesha had covered herself to sleep.

"This epithet of 'wrapped up' and another of the same import given to Muhammad in the next chapter, have been imagined by several learned men pretty plainly to intimate his being subject to the falling sickness; a malady generally attributed to him by the Christians, but mentioned by no Muhammadan writer. Though such an inference may be made, yet I think it scarce probable, much less necessary."—*Sale.*

(2) *Except a small part.* "For a half is such with respect to the whole. Or, as the sentence may be rendered, 'Pray half the night, within a small matter,' &c. Some expound these words as an exception to nights in general; according to whom the sense will be, 'Spend one-half of every night in prayer, except some few nights in the year,' &c."—*Sale, Baidháwi.*

See on this passage Rodwell *in loco* and Muir's *Life of Mahomet*, vol. ii. p. 188. See also note on chap. xvi. 105.

(3, 4) *Lesson . . . a little or add, i.e.,* "set apart either less than half the night, as one-third, for example, or more, as two-thirds. Or the meaning may be, 'Either take a small matter from a lesser part of the night than one-half, *e.g.,* from one third, and so reduce it to a fourth; or add to such lesser part, and make it a full half.'"—*Sale, Baidháwi.*

(5) *A weighty word,* viz., "the precepts contained in the Qurán, which are heavy and difficult to those who are obliged to observe them, and especially to the Prophet, whose care it was to see that his people observed them also."—*Sale, Baidháwi, Jaláluddín.*

(6) *The rising by night.* "Or, 'the person who rises by night,' or 'the hours,' or particularly 'the first hours of night,'" &c.—*Sale.*

is more efficacious for steadfast continuance *in devotion*, and more conducive to decent pronunciation : (7) for in the daytime thou hast long employment. (8) And commemorate the name of thy LORD; and separate thyself unto him, renouncing worldly vanities. (9) *He is* the LORD of the east and of the west; *there is* no GOD but he. Wherefore take him for thy patron : (10) and patiently suffer the *contumelies* which the *infidels* utter *against thee;* and depart from them with a decent departure. (11) And let me alone with those who charge *the Qurán* with falsehood, who enjoy the blessings of this life; and bear with them for a while : (12) verily with us *are* heavy fetters and a burning fire, (13) and food ready to choke *him who swalloweth it,* and painful torment. (14) On a certain day the earth shall be shaken, and the mountains *also,* and the mountains shall become a heap of sand poured forth. (15) Verily we have sent unto you an Apostle, to bear witness against you; as we sent an apostle unto Pharaoh ; (16) but Pharaoh was disobedient unto the apostle; wherefore we chastised him with a heavy chastisement. (17) How, therefore, will ye escape, if ye believe not, the day which shall make children become grey-headed *through terror?* (18) The heavens *shall* be rent in sunder thereby : the promise thereof shall surely be performed. (19) Verily this *is* an admonition : and whoever is willing *to be admonished* will take the way unto his LORD.

R $\frac{2}{14}$. ‖ (20) Thy LORD knoweth that thou continuest *in prayer and meditation sometimes* near two third parts of

---

Conducive to decent pronunciation. " For the night-time is most proper for meditation and prayer, and also for reading God's word distinctly and with attention, by reason of the absence of every noise and object which may distract the mind."—*Sale.*

(13) *Food ready to choke, &c.* " As thorns and thistles, the fruit of the infernal tree al Zaqqúm, and the corruption flowing from the bodies of the damned."—*Sale.*

(15, 16) See notes on chap. vii. 104–136.

(20) *Thy Lord knoweth, &c.* These hours of the night "were spent by Muhammad in devotion and in the labour of working up

the night, and *sometimes* one half thereof, and *at other times* one third part thereof; and a part of *thy companions, who are* with thee, *do the same.* But GOD measureth the night and the day; he knoweth that ye cannot *exactly* compute the same: wherefore he turneth favourably unto you. Read, therefore, so much of the Qurán as may be easy *unto you.* He knoweth that there will be some infirm among you; and others travel through the earth, that they may obtain *a competency* of the bounty of GOD; and others fight in the defence of GOD'S faith. Read, therefore, so much of the same as may be easy. And observe the stated times of prayer, and pay the legal alms; and lend unto GOD an acceptable loan: for whatever good ye send before your souls, ye shall find the same with GOD. This *will be* better, and will merit a greater reward. And ask GOD forgiveness; for GOD *is* ready to forgive *and* merciful.

---

his materials in rhythmical and rhyming Suras, and in preparation for the public assumption of the prophetic office."—*Rodwell.*

See Muir's *Life of Mahomet*, vol. ii. p. 188.

A part of thy companions. Some of the commentators say the command to spend so much of the night in prayer lasted for one year, when it was abrogated by the milder requirements of the latter portion of this verse. Under cover of this requirement Muhammad and a "part of his companions" might have wrought out the revelations enunciated with so much zeal in the daytime (ver. 7); and a suspicion of this certainly did exist among the unbelieving (chap. xvi. 105), and would account for the "contumelies" noted in vers. 10, 11, above.

Wherefore he turneth favourably unto you. "By making the matter easy to you, and dispensing with your scrupulous counting of the hours of the night which ye are directed to spend in reading and praying; for some of the Muslims, not knowing how the time passed, used to watch the whole night, standing and walking about till their legs and feet swelled in a sad manner. The commentators add that this precept of dedicating a part of the night to devotion is abrogated by the institution of the five hours of prayer."—*Sale, Baidháwi.*

Others fight, &c. Observe ... prayer ... alms, &c. This portion of this chapter is certainly Madínic, and probably added on by Muhammad himself.

A greater reward, i.e., "the good which ye shall do in your lifetime will be much more meritorious in the sight of God than what ye shall defer till death and order by will."—*Sale, Baidháwi.*

CHAPTER LXXIV.

ENTITLED SURAT AL MUDDASSIR (THE COVERED).

Revealed at Makkah.

INTRODUCTION.

THIS chapter is regarded by some writers as the very first which was revealed (Sale's note on ver. 1), but the preponderance of evidence is in favour of chapter xcvi. It is, therefore, given the second place by Noëldeke, Rodwell, and Palmer. This place is not, however, accorded to any but the first seven verses. The interval between the revelation of chapter xcvi. and that of these verses is called by Muslims the *Fatrah* or Intermission, the duration of which "is variously held to have lasted from six months to three years" (Muir's *Life of Mahomet*, vol. ii. pp. 85, 86). The remaining portion of the chapter belongs to a later Makkan period, excepting vers. 31–34, which undoubtedly belong to Madína. We find in these verses allusion to all the parties prominent in Madína Suras; the Jews, or "they to whom the Scriptures have been given;" the Muslims, or "the true believers;" the hypocrites, or "those in whose hearts there is an infirmity;" and the idolaters, or "the unbelievers." Muir gives this chapter the twentieth place in his chronological list of Suras.

Probable Date of the Revelations.

From what has been said above we may safely assign vers. 1–7 to the earliest period of Muhammad's ministry. Vers. 8–30 and 35–55 probably mark the period of early opposition to Muhammad by the Quraish in the third year of his public ministry (see Muir's *Life of Mahomet*, vol. ii. pp. 79, 80). The Madínic section, vers. 31–34, Noëldeke thinks should be assigned to a period soon after the Híjra, owing to the kindly mention of the Jews, whom Muhammad, soon after his arrival at Madína, found to be his most inveterate enemies.

| INTROD.] | (195) | [CHAP. LXXIV.

Principal Subjects.

	VERSES
Muhammad commanded to rise and preach Islám	1–7
The judgment-day shall be a sad day for the unbelievers	8–10
God exhorts Muhammad to leave his enemy in his hands	11–26
The pains of hell described	27–29
Nineteen angels set as a guard over hell, and why nineteen are mentioned	30–34
Oath to attest the horrible calamities of hell-fire	35–40
The wicked shall in hell confess their sins to the righteous	41–49
Infidels shall receive no other warning than that of the Qurán	50–55

IN THE NAME OF THE MOST MERCIFUL GOD.

|| (1) O thou covered, arise (2) and preach, (3) and magnify thy LORD. (4) And cleanse thy garments : (5) and fly *every* abomination : (6) and be not liberal in hopes to receive more in return : (7) and patiently wait for thy LORD. (8) When the trumpet shall sound, (9) verily that day *shall be* a day of distress, (10) and uneasiness unto the unbelievers. (11) Let me alone with him whom I have

R $\frac{1}{15}$.

---

(1) *Thou covered.* "It is related, from Muhammad's own mouth, that, being on Mount Hira, and hearing himself called, he looked on each hand and saw nobody ; but looking upwards, he saw the Angel Gabriel on a throne between heaven and earth : at which sight, being much terrified, he returned to his wife Khadíjah and bid her cover him up ; and that then the angel descended and addressed him in the words of the text. From hence some think this chapter to have been the first which was revealed ; but the more received opinion is that it was the 96th. Others say that the Prophet, having been reviled by certain of the Quraish, was sitting in a melancholy and pensive posture, wrapped up in his mantle, when Gabriel accosted him ; and some say he was sleeping."—*Sale.* See note to the preceding chapter on ver. 1.

See Rodwell *in loco.*

(2) *Preach.* "It is generally supposed that Muhammad is here commanded more especially to warn his near relations, the Quarish, as he is expressly ordered to do in a subsequent revelation."—*Sale.*

See note on chap. xxvi. 214, and Prelim. Disc., p. 76.

(5) *Abomination.* "By the word 'abomination' the commentators generally agree idolatry to be principally intended."—*Sale.*

(11) *Let me alone with him, &c.* "The person here meant is gene-

created, (12) on whom I have bestowed abundant riches, (13) and children dwelling in his presence, (14) and for whom I have disposed *affairs* in a smooth and easy manner, (15) and who desireth that I will yet add *other blessings unto him*. (16) By no means; because he is an adversary to our signs. (17) I will afflict him with grievous calamities: (18) for he hath devised and prepared *contumelious expressions to ridicule the Qurán*. (19) May he be cursed: how *maliciously* hath he prepared *the same!* (20) And again, may he be cursed: how *maliciously* hath he prepared *the same!* (21) Then he looked, (22) and frowned, and put on an austere countenance; (23) then he turned back, and was elated with pride; (24) and he said, This *is* no other than a piece of magic, borrowed from others: (25) these *are* only the words of a man. (26) I will cast him to be burned in hell. (27) And what shall make thee to understand what hell *is?* (28) It leaveth not *anything unconsumed*, neither doth it suffer *anything* to escape; (29) it scorcheth men's flesh: (30) over the same *are* nineteen *angels appointed*. (31) We

---

rally supposed to have been al Walíd Ibn al Mughaira, a principal man among the Quraish."—*Sale, Baidháwi, &c.*

(12, 13) *Riches and children, &c.* "Being well provided for, and not obliged to go abroad to seek their livings, as most others of the Makkans were."—*Sale.*

(14) *A smooth and easy manner.* "By facilitating his advancement to power and dignity, which were so considerable that he was surnamed Riháná Quraish, *i.e.,* 'The sweet odour of the Quraish,' and Al Walíd, *i.e.,* 'The only one,' or 'The incomparable.'"—*Sale, Baidháwi.*

(16) *By no means, &c.* "On the revelation of this passage it is said that Walíd's prosperity began to decay, and continued daily so to do to the time of his death."—*Sale, Baidháwi.*

(17) *Calamities.* "Or, as the words may be strictly rendered, 'I will drive him up the crag of a mountain;' which some understand of a mountain of fire, agreeably to a tradition of their Prophet importing that al Walíd will be condemned to ascend this mountain, and then to be cast down from thence alternately for ever; and that he will be seventy years in climbing up and as many in falling down."—*Sale, Baidháwi, &c.*

(24, 25) See note on chaps. vi. 24, xvi. 105.

have appointed none but angels to preside over *hell*-fire; and we have expressed the number of them only for an occasion of discord to the unbelievers; that they to whom the Scriptures have been given may be certain *of the veracity of this book*, and the true believers may increase in faith; (32) and that those to whom the Scriptures have been given, and the true believers, may not doubt *hereafter;* (33) and that those in whose hearts *there is* an infirmity, and the unbelievers, may say, What mystery doth GOD intend by this *number?* (34) Thus doth GOD cause to err whom he pleaseth; and he directeth whom he pleaseth. None knoweth the armies of thy LORD besides him; and this *is* no other than a memento unto mankind.

|| (35) Assuredly. By the moon, (36) and the night R $\frac{2}{16}$. when it retreateth, (37) and the morning when it reddeneth, (38) *I swear* that this *is* one of the most terrible *calamities*, (39) giving warning unto men, (40) as well as unto him among you who' desireth to go forward, as *unto*

---

(31) *None but angels.* "The reason of which is said to be, that they might be of a different nature and species from those who are to be tormented, lest they should have a fellow-feeling of, and compassionate their sufferings; or else because of their great strength and severity of temper."—*Sale, Baidháwi.*

This passage up to ver. 35, "evidently produced many years after" the above, is interposed "in reply to certain objections raised, as it would appear, by the Jews respecting the *number* of the infernal guard."—*Muir's Life of Mahomet*, vol. ii. p. 78, note.

For an occasion of discord. "Or, 'for a trial of them;'" because they might say this was a particular borrowed by Muhammad of the Jews."—*Sale.*

(32) *Those to whom the Scriptures, &c.* "And especially the Jews; this being conformable to what is contained in their books."—*Sale, Jaláluddín.*

(34) *Armies of the Lord, i. e.,* "all his creatures; or particularly the number and strength of the guards of hell."—*Sale.*

The allusion is probably to the armies of angels said to have assisted the Muslims at Badr and Hunain, of whom the "nineteen" are but a "memento unto mankind."

And this. "The antecedent seems to be 'hell.'"—*Sale.* I should say it was "number," the same being supplied by Sale himself in ver. 33.

him who chooseth to remain behind. (41) Every soul *is* given in pledge for that which it shall have wrought: except the companions of the right hand; (42) *who shall dwell* in gardens, and shall ask one another questions concerning the wicked, (43) *and shall also ask the wicked themselves, saying,* What hath brought you into hell? (44) They shall answer, We were not of those who were constant at prayer, (45) neither did we feed the poor; (46) and we waded in vain disputes with the fallacious reasoners; (47) and we denied the day of judgment, (48) until death overtook us; (49) and the intercession of the interceders shall not avail them. (50) What aileth them, therefore, that they turn aside from the admonition *of the Qurán,* (51) as though they *were* timorous asses flying from a lion? (52) But every man among them desireth that he may have expanded scrolls delivered to him *from God.* (53) By no means. They fear not the life to come. (54) By no means: verily this *is* a *sufficient* warning. (55) Whoso is willing *to be warned,* him shall it warn: but they shall not be warned, unless GOD shall please. He *is* worthy to be feared, and he *is* inclined to forgiveness.

---

(41) *Every soul, &c.* See note on chap. lii. 21.
Companions of the right hand, i.e., "the blessed, who shall redeem themselves by their good works. Some say these are the angels, and others, such as die infants."—*Sale, Baidháwi.*
See note on chap. lvi. 8, 9.
(48) *Death.* "Literally, that which is certain."—*Sale.*
(52) *Expanded scrolls, &c.* "For the infidels told Muhammad that they would never obey him as a prophet till he brought each man a writing from heaven to this effect, viz., ' From God to such a one: Follow Muhammad.' "—*Sale, Baidháwi.*

CHAPTER LXXV.

ENTITLED SURAT AL QÍYÁMAT (THE RESURRECTION).

Revealed at Makkah.

INTRODUCTION.

THE title of this chapter, taken from the first verse, expresses very well the general subject of its contents. The doctrine of the resurrection was rejected by the Quraish of Makkah as incredible, but the preacher declares that he who created every bone of man would have no difficulty in collecting together the scattered bones of the dead on the resurrection-day.

The passage contained in vers. 16-19, which has been inserted probably by the compilers, has no connection with the subject of this chapter. It seems to have been placed here because it could not be placed more appropriately elsewhere. It must therefore be read as a parenthesis.

Probable Date of the Revelations.

All authorities agree in placing this chapter at about the end of the fourth or the beginning of the fifth year of Muhammad's public ministry.

Principal Subjects.

	VERSES
God is able to raise the dead	1-4
Unbelievers may mock, but they shall be overtaken by the resurrection-day	5-11
Man shall be his own accuser on that day	12-15
Muhammad rebuked for anticipating Gabriel in receiving the Qurán	16-19
Men choose this life, but neglect the life to come	20-21
Various thoughts of the righteous and the wicked on the resurrection-day	22-25
Man helpless in the hour of death	26-36
God, who created man, can raise him from the dead	37-40

IN THE NAME OF THE MOST MERCIFUL GOD.

SULS.

R $\frac{1}{17}$.

‖ (1) Verily I swear by the day of resurrection; (2) and I swear by the soul which accuseth *itself*: (3) doth man think that we will not gather his bones together? (4) Yea, *we are* able to put together the *smallest* bones of his fingers. (5) But man chooseth to be wicked, *for the time which is* before him. (6) He asketh, When *will* the day of resurrection *be?* (7) But when the sight shall be dazzled, (8) and the moon shall be eclipsed, (9) and the sun and the moon shall be in conjunction; (10) on that day man shall say, Where *is* a place of refuge? (11) By no means: *there shall be* no place to fly unto. (12) With thy LORD *shall be* the sure mansion of rest on that day: (13) on that day shall a man be told that which he hath done first and last. (14) Yea, a man *shall be* an evidence against himself; (15) and though he offer his excuses, *they shall not be received.* (16) Move not thy tongue, *O Muhammad*, *in repeating the revelations brought thee by Gabriel, before he shall have finished the same,* that thou mayest quickly commit them to memory; (17) for the collecting

---

(1) *I swear*, or *I will not swear*. See note on chap. lvi. 74.

(2) *The soul that accuseth itself.* "Being conscious of having offended, and of failing of perfection, notwithstanding its endeavours to do its duty; or, *the* pious *soul which shall blame others* at the last day for having been remiss in their devotions, &c. Some understand the words of the soul of Adam in particular, who is continually blaming himself for having lost Paradise by his disobedience."— *Sale, Baidháwi.*

(9) *Sun and moon . . . in conjunction.* "Rising both in the west (Prelim. Disc., pp. 131-134); which conjunction is no contradiction to what is mentioned just before, of the moon's being eclipsed; because those words are not to be understood of a regular eclipse, but metaphorically of the moon's losing her light, at the last day, in a preternatural manner. Some think the meaning rather to be that the sun and the moon shall be *joined* in the loss of their light." —*Sale, Baidháwi.*

(13) *That which he hath done.* "Or the good which he hath done, and that which he hath left undone."—*Sale.*

(16-19) See notes on chap. liii. 6. Rodwell remarks that these words show that Muhammad had in mind the promulgation of a written book from the first. Compare chap. xx. 113.

the *Qurán* in thy mind, and the *teaching thee the true* reading thereof, *are incumbent* on us. (18) But when we shall have read the same *unto thee by the tongue of the angel*, do thou follow the reading thereof; (19) and afterwards *it shall be* our part to explain it *unto thee*. (20) By no means shalt thou be thus hasty for the future. But ye love that which hasteneth away, (21) and neglect the life to come. (22) *Some* countenances on that day *shall be* bright, (23) looking towards their LORD; (24) and *some* countenances on that day *shall be* dismal: (25) they shall think that a crushing calamity shall be brought upon them. (26) Assuredly. When *a man's soul* shall come up to his throat *in his last agony*, (27) and *the standers-by* shall say, Who bringeth a charm *to recover him?* (28) and shall think it *to be his* departure *out of this world;* (29) and *one* leg shall be joined with *the other* leg: (30) on that day unto thy LORD shall he be driven.

---

(19) *Our part to explain it.* The Qurán cannot be understood without the Traditions, which, so far as they relate to the text of the Qurán, may be regarded as the words of Muhammad explanatory of his Qurán. This mystery of the Qurán gives rise to that mass of literature comprised within the writings of the Muslim fathers, and to which Muslims invariably refer when any question of doctrine or practice requires an answer. A bann has been set upon free thought and independent investigation in matters of religion so far as the orthodox are concerned. Gabriel explained everything to Muhammad. Muhammad explained what was necessary to the faithful. The faithful handed this down to the collectors of the six received books of tradition. These form the basis of opinion in the commentaries, and the commentaries are the authorities of the Maulvies and Mullahs who teach the people. How different this from the simple teaching of the Old and New Testaments current among Christians—at least among those of the Protestant faith.

(20) *That which hasteneth away, i.e.,* "the fleeting pleasures of this life. The words intimate the natural hastiness and impatience of man (chap. xvii. 12), who takes up with a present enjoyment, though short, and bitter in its consequences, rather than wait for real happiness in futurity."—*Sale.*

(29) *One leg, &c., i.e.,* "when he shall stretch forth his legs together, as is usual with dying persons. The words may also be translated 'and when one affliction shall be joined with another affliction.'"—*Sale.*

R $\frac{2}{18}$.   ‖ (31) For he believed not, neither did he pray; (32) but he accused *God's Apostle* of imposture, and turned back *from obeying him;* (33) then he departed unto his family, walking with a haughty mien. (34) Wherefore, woe be unto thee; woe! (35) And again, woe be unto thee; woe! (36) Doth man think that he shall be left at full liberty, *without control?* (37) Was he not a drop of seed, which was emitted? (38) Afterwards he became a little coagulated blood, and *God* formed him, and fashioned him with just proportion; (39) and made of him two sexes, the male and the female. (40) Is not he *who hath done this* able to quicken the dead?

---

(31) *He believed not.* "Or, 'He did not give alms;' or, 'He was not a man of veracity.' Some suppose Abu Jahl, and others one Abi Ibn Rábía, to be particularly inveighed against in this chapter."—*Sale.*

(34, 35) Rodwell translates this passage, "*That hour* is nearer to thee and nearer. It is ever nearer to thee and nearer still." Palmer agrees with Sale, as do also the Persian and Urdu translators.

CHAPTER LXXVI.

ENTITLED SURAT AL INSÁN (MAN).

Revealed at Makkah.

INTRODUCTION.

IN the Arabic copies of the Qurán the title of this chapter is AL DAHR (A SPACE OF TIME).

Beyond the statement that God has created and directed man, this chapter has very little to say of his career in this world. Almost the whole of the revelation is taken up with a description of the joys of Paradise.

The story recorded by Umr Bin Muhammad (Itqán 28, see Noëldeke), and given by Sale in note on ver. 10, as affording the occasion of this revelation, is entirely unworthy of credence. That story would oblige us to regard the chapter, or at least vers. 8–31, as Madínic, whereas the style and language show it to be Makkan.

The purpose of the chapter seems to have been to encourage and comfort the Muslims amidst the opposition of the unbelievers, by setting before them, in contrast with present poverty and suffering, the riches and joy of the believers in Paradise.

Probable Date of the Revelations.

As already observed, this chapter is without doubt of Makkan origin. Some (Itqán 28 and 37) have thought ver. 24 to be Madínic, but for this opinion there is no good reason given. Noëldeke, with whom Muir substantially agrees, fixes the date about the fifth year of the Call.

Principal Subjects.

	VERSES
Man conceived and born by the power of God	1, 2
Unbelievers warned by the terrors of hell	3, 4
The rewards of the Muslims in Paradise	5–22
The Qurán revealed by degrees	23

		VERSES
Muhammad and the Muslims exhorted to patience and prayer	. . . .	24–26
Unbelievers love the present life	. . . . .	27, 28
Only those saved whom God willeth to save	. . .	29–31

IN THE NAME OF THE MOST MERCIFUL GOD.

R $\frac{1}{19}$.   ‖ (1) Did there not pass over man a *long* space of time, during which he was a thing not worthy of remembrance? (2) Verily we have created man of the mingled seed of both sexes, that we might prove him: and we have made him to hear and to see. (3) We have surely directed him in the way, whether *he be* grateful or ungrateful. (4) Verily we have prepared for the unbelievers chains, and collars, and burning fire. (5) But the just shall drink of a cup *of wine* mixed with *the water of* Káfúr, (6) a fountain whereof the servants of GOD shall drink; they shall convey the same by channels *whithersoever they please*. (7) *These* fulfil *their* vow, and dread the day, the evil whereof will disperse itself far abroad; (8) and give food unto the poor, and the orphan, and the bondman, for his sake, (9) *saying*, We feed you for GOD's sake only: we

---

(1) "Some take these words to be spoken of Adam, whose body, according to the Muhammadan tradition, was at first a figure of clay, and was left forty years to dry before God breathed life into it: others understand them of man in general, and of the time he lies in the womb." See notes on chap. ii. 30.

(2) *To hear and to see.* "That he might be capable of receiving the rules and directions given by God for his guidance; and of meriting reward or punishment for his observance or neglect of them."—*Sale.*

(5) *Káfúr.* "Is the name of a fountain in Paradise, so called from its resembling *camphor* (which the word signifies) in odour and whiteness. Some take the word for an appellative, and think the wine of Paradise will be mixed with camphor, because of its agreeable coolness and smell."—*Sale, Baidhâwi.*

The faithful may not taste wine on earth, but they shall have rivers of it in Paradise. It is said, however, that the wine of Paradise will not intoxicate the blissful inhabitants thereof (chap. lxxviii. 34, 35). This wine (*khamr*) would, however, intoxicate a Muslim here. See note on chap. xlvii. 16.

desire no recompense from you, nor any thanks: (10) verily we dread from our LORD a dismal *and* calamitous day. (11) Wherefore GOD shall deliver them from the evil of that day, and shall cast on them brightness of countenance and joy; (12) and shall reward them for their patient persevering with a garden and silk *garments:* (13) therein shall they repose themselves on couches; they shall see therein neither sun nor moon; (14) and the shades thereof *shall be* near, *spreading* above them; and the fruits thereof shall hang low, so as to be easily gathered. (15) And *their attendants* shall go round about unto them with vessels of silver and goblets: the bottles shall be bottles of silver *shining like glass;* (16) they shall determine the measure thereof *by their wish.* (17) And therein shall they be given to drink of a cup *of wine* mixed with *the water* of Zanjabíl, (18) a fountain in *Paradise* named

---

(10) "It is related that Hasan and Husain, Muhammad's grandchildren, on a certain time being both sick, the Prophet, among others, visited them, and they wished Ali to make some vow to God for the recovery of his sons: whereupon Ali and Fátima, and Fidda, their maid-servant, vowed a fast of three days in case they did well; as it happened they did. This vow was performed with so great strictness, that the first day, having no provisions in the house, Ali was obliged to borrow three measures of barley of one Simeon, a Jew of Khaibar, one measure of which Fátima ground the same day, and baked five cakes of the meal, and they were set before them to break their fast with after sunset: but a poor man coming to them, they gave all their bread to him, and passed the night without tasting anything except water. The next day Fátima made another measure into bread, for the same purpose; but an orphan begging some food, they chose to let him have it, and passed that night as the first; and the third day they likewise gave their whole provision to a famished captive. Upon this occasion Gabriel descended with the chapter before us, and told Muhammad that God congratulated him on the virtues of his family."—*Sale, Baidháwi.*

(13) *Neither sun nor moon.* "Because they shall not need the light of either (see Rev. xxi. 23). The word *Zamharir,* here translated *moon,* properly signifies *extreme cold;* for which reason some understand the meaning of the passage to be, that in Paradise there shall be felt no excess either of heat or of cold."—*Sale.*

(17) *Zanjabíl.* "The word signifies *ginger,* which the Arabs delight to mix with the water they drink; and therefore the water of this fountain is supposed to have the taste of that spice."—*Sale, Baidháwi.*

Silsabíl: (19) and youths, which shall continue *for ever in their bloom*, shall go round *to attend* them; when thou seest them, thou shalt think them *to be* scattered pearls: (20) and when thou lookest, there shalt thou behold delights and a great kingdom. (21) Upon them *shall be* garments of fine green silk and of brocades, and they shall be adorned with bracelets of silver: and their LORD shall give them to drink of a most pure liquor; (22) *and shall say unto them*, Verily this is your reward, and your endeavour is gratefully accepted.

R $\frac{2}{20}$.
|| (23) Verily we have sent down unto thee the Qurán by a *gradual* revelation. (24) Wherefore patiently wait the judgment of thy LORD, and obey not any wicked person or unbeliever among them. (25) And commemorate the name of thy LORD in the morning and in the evening; (26) and *during some part* of the night worship him, and praise him a long *part of the* night. (27) Verily these *men* love the transitory *life*, and leave behind them the heavy day *of judgment*. (28) We have created them, and have strengthened their joints; and when we please, we will substitute *others* like unto them in their stead. (29) Verily this *is* an admonition: and whoso willeth, taketh the way unto his LORD: (30) but ye shall not will, unless GOD willeth; for GOD is knowing *and* wise. (31) He leadeth whom he pleaseth into his mercy; but for the unjust hath he prepared a grievous punishment.

---

(18) *Silsabíl.* "Signifies water which flows gently and pleasantly down the throat."—*Sale.*

(22) The passage beginning with ver. 12 and ending here is to be understood literally. See note on chap. iii. 15.

(23) *Gradual revelation.* See notes on chap. xxv. 34.

(25, 26) "The *times* of prayer are as yet only mentioned generally as morning, evening, and night."—*Muir's Life of Mahomet*, vol. ii. p. 140, note. See also note on chap. lxxiii. 20.

(29–31) Man's freedom of will does not seem to be recognised here. Man wills to take "the way unto his Lord" only because God wills him to do so. The teaching of the text is that even the will of man is subject to God's control.

CHAPTER LXXVII.

ENTITLED SURAT AL MURSALÁT (THE MESSENGERS).

Revealed at Makkah.

INTRODUCTION.

THIS chapter seems to be a sort of philippic denunciatory of the conduct of those unbelievers at Makkah who charged him with being an impostor. The words "Woe be on that day unto those who accused the prophets of imposture" are repeated as a kind of refrain, and occur no less than ten times in the course of the chapter. It is the Prophet's cry of "Woe! woe!" to the unbelievers of Makkah. May not this characteristic have given rise to the opinion expressed by Jaláluddín al Syuti, that this chapter was revealed while Muhammad and Abu Baqr were hidden in the cave during the flight from Makkah to Madína?

Probable Date of the Revelations.

The general style and language of this chapter prove it to be of early Makkan origin. Muhammad appears as a "warner" crying "Woe! woe!" to the idolaters who have rejected him as an impostor. Ver. 39 would seem to indicate that this opposition was more than passive, and now ready to take an active form. These circumstances justify the date assigned by Noëldeke and also by Muir, which is about the fourth year of the ministry.

Principal Subjects.

	VERSES
Oath by the messengers of God that the judgment-day is inevitable	1–7
Woe on that day to those who accuse Muhammad of imposture	8–15
In former times infidels were destroyed for accusing their prophets of imposture	16–19

		VERSES
God the Creator of all things, therefore woe to those who accuse his messengers of imposture	. . . .	20–28
The woe of those who have been cast into hell for calling their prophets impostors	. . . . .	29–40
The joy of those who did not call their prophets impostors	.	41–44
The infidel Quraish soon to be overtaken by the woes of the judgment-day	. . . . . .	45–50

IN THE NAME OF THE MOST MERCIFUL GOD.

R $\frac{1}{2}$T ‖ (1) By the *angels* which are sent *by God*, following one another in a continual series; (2) and those which move swiftly with a rapid motion; (3) and by those which disperse *his commands*, by divulging them *through the earth;* (4) and by those which separate *truth from falsehood*, by distinguishing *the same;* (5) and by those which communicate *the divine* admonitions, (6) to excuse or to threaten: (7) verily that which ye are promised *is* inevitable. (8) When the stars, therefore, shall be put out, (9) and when the heaven shall be cloven in sunder, (10) and when the mountains shall be winnowed, (11) and when the apostles shall have a time assigned to them *to appear and bear testimony against their respective people;* (12) to what a day shall *that appointment* be deferred! (13) to the day of separation: (14) and what shall cause thee to understand what the day of separation *is?* (15) On that day, woe be unto them who accused *the prophets* of

---

(1-6) "Some understand the whole passage of the verses of the Qurán, which continued to be sent down, parcel after parcel, during the space of several years, and which rescind (for so the verb *asafa* may also be translated) and abolish all former dispensations, divulging and making known the ways of salvation, distinguishing truth from falsehood, and communicating admonition, &c. Some interpret the first three verses of the winds, sent in a continual succession, blowing with a violent gust, and dispersing rain over the earth; and others give different explications."—*Sale.*

(7) *That which ye are promised.* "The day of judgment."—*Sale.*

(15) *Woe . . . unto them who accused . . . of imposture.* See introduction to chap. xi. This sentence occurs ten times in this chapter,

imposture! (16) Have we not destroyed the *obstinate unbelievers* of old? (17) We will also cause those of the latter times to follow them. (18) Thus do we deal with the wicked. (19) Woe be, on that day, unto them who accused *the prophets* of imposture! (20) Have we not created you of a contemptible drop *of seed*, (21) which we placed in a sure repository, (22) until the fixed term *of delivery?* (23) And we were able *to do this:* for we are most powerful. (24) On that day, woe be unto those who accused *the prophets* of imposture! (25) Have we not made the earth to contain (26) the living and the dead, (27) and placed therein stable *and* lofty *mountains*, and given you fresh water to drink? (28) Woe be, on that day, unto those who accused *the prophets* of imposture! (29) *It shall be said unto them,* Go ye to the *punishment* which ye denied as a falsehood: (30) go ye into the shadow *of the smoke of hell*, which *shall ascend* in three columns, (31) and shall not shade *you from the heat*, neither shall it be of service against the flame; (32) but it shall cast forth sparks *as big* as towers, (33) resembling yellow camels *in colour*. (34) Woe be, on that day, unto those who accused *the prophets* of imposture! (35) This *shall be* a day whereon they shall not speak *to any purpose;* (36) neither shall they be permitted to excuse themselves. (37) Woe be, on that day, unto those who accused *the prophets* of imposture! (38) This *shall be* the day of separation: we will assemble *both* you and your predecessors. (39) Wherefore, if ye have any cunning stratagem, employ stratagems against me. (40) Woe be, on that day, unto those who accused *the prophets* of

---

illustrating the intensity of the Prophet's feelings. The charge of forgery is no modern invention of the Christian opponents of Islám. See note on chap. vi. 48.

(33) *Yellow camels.* "Being of a fiery colour. Others, however, suppose these sparks will be of a dusky hue, like that of black camels, which always inclines a little to the yellow; the word translated yellow signifying sometimes black. Some copies, by the variation of a vowel, have cables instead of camels."—*Sale.*

imposture! (41) But the pious *shall dwell* amidst shades and fountains, (42) and fruits of the *kinds* which they shall desire: (43) *and it shall be said unto them,* Eat and drink with easy digestion, *in recompense* for that which ye have wrought; (44) for thus do we reward the righteous doers. (45) Woe be, on that day, unto those who accused *the prophets* of imposture! (46) Eat, *O unbelievers,* and enjoy *the pleasures of this life* for a little while: verily ye *are* wicked men. (47) Woe be, on that day, unto those who accused *the prophets* of imposture! (48) And when it is said unto them, Bow down; they do not bow down. (49) Woe be, on that day, unto those who accused *the prophets* of imposture! (50) In what new revelation will they believe, after this?

---

(48) *When it is said, &c.* These words are said by some to have reference to the Thaqífites, who during the last years of the Prophet declared their willingness to accept Islám provided they were exempted from the duty of prayer. For this opinion no good reason can be given, as the passage refers in general to all unbelievers.

CHAPTER LXXVIII.

ENTITLED SURAT AL NABÁ (THE NEWS).

Revealed at Makkah.

INTRODUCTION.

THIS chapter receives its title from ver. 2, where it signifies News of the Resurrection, which news was the burden of the Prophet's message at this period. The whole is a warning to the unbelievers to repent and believe the Qurán ere it be too late, ere he say, "Would to God I were dust."

Probable Date of the Revelations.

The opinion of most writers is that this chapter belongs to the earlier Makkan revelations, though it is admitted that vers. 37–41 were added at a somewhat later date. Believing that ver. 17 presupposes chap. lxxvii. 12 *seq.*, Noëldeke places this chapter immediately after chap. lxxvii.

Principal Subjects.

	VERSES
Unbelievers shall yet learn the truth of the resurrection	1–5
God the Creator and Preserver of all things	6–16
Judgment-day scenes described	17–20
The recompense of unbelievers in hell described	21–30
The joys of believers in Paradise described	31–37
No intercessor except by God's permission	37, 38
Sinners exhorted to flee from the day of wrath	39–41

IN THE NAME OF THE MOST MERCIFUL GOD.

|| (1) Concerning what do *the unbelievers* ask questions THIRTIETH SIPARA. of one another? (2) Concerning the great news *of the*

R ¼. *resurrection,* (3) about which they disagree. (4) Assuredly they shall hereafter know *the truth thereof.* (5) Again, assuredly they shall hereafter know *the truth thereof.* (6) Have we not made the earth for a bed, (7) and the mountains for stakes *to fix the same?* (8) And have we not created you of two sexes; (9) and appointed your sleep for rest; (10) and made the night a garment *to cover you;* (11) and destined the day to the gaining *your* livelihood; (12) and built over you seven solid *heavens;* (13) and placed *therein* a burning lamp? (14) And do we not send down from the *clouds* pressing forth rain, water pouring down in abundance, (15) that we may thereby produce corn and herbs, (16) and gardens planted thick *with trees?* (17) Verily the day of separation is a fixed period: (18) the day whereon the trumpet shall sound, and ye shall come in troops *to judgment;* (19) and the heaven shall be opened, and shall be *full of* gates *for the angels to pass through;* (20) and the mountains shall pass away, and become *as* a vapour; (21) verily hell shall be a place of ambush, (22) a receptacle for the transgressors, (23) who shall remain therein for ages: (24) they shall not taste any refreshment therein or any drink, (25) except boiling water and filthy corruption: (26) a fit recompense *for their deeds!* (27) For they hoped that they should not be brought to an account, (28) and they disbelieved our signs, accusing them of falsehood. (29) But everything have we computed and written down. (30) Taste, therefore: we will not add unto you *any other* than torment.

(6, 7) See note on chaps. xvi. 15, and xxxi. 9.

(8-29) The numerous proofs of God's almighty power cited here have been noticed so frequently in the Makkan Suras as to make further comment unnecessary.

(30) *We will not add . . . other than torment.* "This, say the commentators, is the most severe and terrible sentence in the whole Qurán pronounced against the inhabitants of hell; they being hereby assured that every change in their torments will be for the worse."
—*Sale.*

|| (31) But for the pious *is prepared* a place of bliss: R $\frac{2}{2}$.
(32) gardens planted with trees, and vineyards, (33) and *damsels* with swelling breasts, of equal age *with themselves*, (34) and a full cup. (35) They shall hear no vain discourse there, nor any falsehood. (36) *This shall be their* recompense from thy LORD; a gift *fully* sufficient: (37) *from* the LORD of heaven and earth, and of whatever *is* between them; the Merciful. *The inhabitants of heaven or of earth* shall not dare to demand audience of him: (38) the day whereon the spirit *Gabriel* and the *other* angels shall stand in order, they shall not speak *in behalf of themselves or others*, except he *only* to whom the Merciful shall grant permission, and who shall say that which is right. (39) This *is* the infallible day. Whoso, therefore, willeth, let him return unto his LORD. (40) Verily we threaten you with a punishment nigh at hand: (41) the day whereon a man shall behold *the good or evil deeds* which his hands have sent before him; and the unbeliever shall say, Would to GOD I were dust!

(31–37) One is at a loss how to interpret this of spiritual joy. See note on chap. iii. 15.

(38) *The spirit.* See notes on chap. ii. 86, 253.

Except he only, &c. See notes on chaps. ix. 81, xxxix. 45, and xl. 7.

CHAPTER LXXIX.

ENTITLED SURAT AL NÁZIÁT (THOSE WHO TEAR FORTH).

Revealed at Makkah.

INTRODUCTION.

THIS chapter consists of three parts; vers. 1-14 containing a declaration concerning the certainty of the approach of the resurrection and judgment-day, vers. 15-26, giving a brief account of the call and ministry of Moses, and vers. 37-46, also relating to the doctrine of the resurrection and judgment-day.

The second of these parts is too detailed in its character to belong to the very early Makkan Suras, where Jewish history and legend are alluded to in a vague way. It is probably a fragment of a later Sura inserted here by the compilers.

Probable Date of the Revelations.

Noëldeke places this chapter immediately before chap. lxxvii. Muir places it at a later period, *i.e.*, about the sixth year of the Call. We would follow Noëldeke for the first fourteen verses; vers. 27-46 perhaps belong to a period somewhat later, but from vers. 15-26 we would follow Muir.

Principal Subjects.

	VERSES
Oaths by the messengers of death that there will be a resurrection and judgment-day	1-7
Infidels shall be restored to life notwithstanding their unbelief	8-14
The story of Moses and his mission to Pharaoh	15-26
The Creator can raise the dead	27-33
The righteous and the wicked in judgment, their various condition	34-41
No one knows the time of judgment, but whenever it comes it will be soon for the infidels	42-46

IN THE NAME OF THE MOST MERCIFUL GOD.

‖ (1) By the *angels* who tear forth *the souls of some* with violence; (2) and by those who draw forth *the souls of others* with gentleness; (3) by those who glide swimmingly *through the air with the commands of God;* (4) and those who precede and usher *the righteous to Paradise;* (5) and those who subordinately govern the affairs *of this world:* (6) on a *certain* day the disturbing *blast of the trumpet* shall disturb *the universe;* (7) and the subsequent *blast* shall follow it. (8) On that day *men's* hearts shall tremble: (9) their looks *shall be* cast down. (10) *The infidels* say, Shall we surely be made to return whence we came? (11) After we shall have become rotten bones, *shall we be again raised to life?* (12) They say, This then *will be* a return to loss. (13) Verily it *will be* but one sounding *of the trumpet,* (14) and, behold, they *shall appear alive* on the face of the earth. (15) Hath not the story of Moses reached thee? (16) When his LORD called unto him in the holy valley Tuwá, (17) *saying,* Go unto Pharaoh; for he is insolently wicked: (18) and say, Hast thou *a desire* to become just and holy? (19) and I will

R ⅓·

(1, 2) *The angels who tear forth.* "These are the angel of death and his assistants, who will take the souls of the wicked in a rough and cruel manner from the inmost part of their bodies, as a man drags up a thing from the bottom of the sea; but will take the souls of the good in a gentle and easy manner from their lips, as when a man draws a bucket of water at one pull.

"There are several other interpretations of this whole passage; some expounding all the five parts of the oath of the stars, others of the souls of men, others of the souls of warriors in particular, and others of war-horses; a detail of which, I apprehend, would rather tire than please."—*Sale, Baidháwi.*

(10) *Shall we be made to return, i.e.,* "shall we be raised from the dead and be restored to our former condition?"

(13) *One sounding,* viz., "the second or third blast, according to different opinions."—*Sale.*

(14) *They shall appear alive, &c.* "Or, 'they shall appear at the place of judgment.' The original word, *al Sábira,* is also one of the names of hell."—*Sale.*

(16) See references in chap. xx. 8-10.
(16-26) See notes on chap. vii. 104-136.

direct thee unto thy LORD, that thou mayest fear *to transgress.* (20) And he showed him the very great sign *of the rod turned into a serpent:* (21) but he charged *Moses* with imposture, and rebelled *against God.* (22) Then he turned back hastily; (23) and he assembled *the magicians,* and cried aloud, (24) saying, I *am* your supreme LORD. (25) Wherefore GOD chastised him with the punishment of the life to come, and *also* of this present life. (26) Verily herein *is* an example unto him who feareth *to rebel.*

R ⅔ || (27) *Are* ye more difficult to create, or the heaven which *God* hath built? (28) He hath raised the height thereof, and hath perfectly formed the same: (29) and he hath made the night thereof dark, and hath produced the light thereof. (30) After this, he stretched out the earth, (31) whence he caused to spring forth the water thereof, and the pasture thereof; (32) and he established the mountains, (33) for the use of yourselves, and of your cattle. (34) When the prevailing, the great *day* shall come, (35) on that day shall a man call to remembrance what he hath purposely done: (36) and hell shall be exposed to the view of the spectator. (37) And whoso shall have transgressed, (38) and shall have chosen this present life, (39) verily hell shall be his abode; (40) but whoso shall have dreaded the appearing before his LORD, and shall have refrained *his* soul from lust, (41) verily Paradise

---

(30) *The earth.* "Which had been created before the heavens, but without expansion."—*Sale, Jalāluddín.*

(35) *Purposely done.* Sins committed without intent are not recognised by Muslims.

(40) *Shall have refrained his soul from lust.* "Without going the length of Dr. Prideaux and others, who seem to think that Mahommed thought more of gratifying his lust than anything else, it seems on the whole that he was, judge him by what standard you like, a lustful man, and one who, as the Prophet of God, did not check his passions so much as he ought to have done."—*Brinckman in "Notes on Islám."*

The Muslims will not, however, admit that their Prophet can be charged with immorality, inasmuch as he had the Divine permission for all he did. Looking at this matter from their standpoint, the

shall be *his* abode. (42) They will ask thee concerning the *last* hour, when *will be* the fixed time thereof? (43) By what means *canst* thou *give* any information of the same? (44) Unto thy LORD *belongeth the knowledge of* the period thereof: (45) and thou *art* only a warner, who fearest the same. (46) The day whereon they shall see the same, *it shall seem to them* as though they had not tarried *in the world longer* than an evening or a morning thereof.

Christian will abstain from urging this question against the prophetic claim of Muhammad. Many inspired writers were polygamists.

CHAPTER LXXX.

ENTITLED SURAT AL ABAS (HE FROWNED).

Revealed at Makkah.

INTRODUCTION.

THE story told by the Muslim writers to account for the occasion upon which this chapter was revealed is related by Sale as follows :— "A certain blind man, named Abdullah Ibn Omm Maktúm, came and interrupted Muhammad while he was engaged in earnest discourse with some of the principal Quraish, whose conversion he had hopes of; but the Prophet taking no notice of him, the blind man, not knowing he was otherwise busied, raised his voice and said, 'O Apostle of God, teach me some part of what God hath taught thee;' but Muhammad, vexed at this interruption, frowned and turned away from him, for which he is here reprehended. After this, whenever the Prophet saw Ibn Omm Maktúm, he showed him great respect, saying, 'The man is welcome on whose account my Lord hath reprimanded me;' and he made him twice governor of Madina."

Noëldeke doubts this story, with very good reason. This Ibn Omm Maktúm belonged to one of the most influential families of the tribe of Quraish, whereas the drift of the passage makes us expect a man of the common multitude.

The chapter relates to the obduracy of those unbelievers, who fail to recognise and obey the God who creates and preserves them.

Probable Date of the Revelations.

All authorities agree in regarding this chapter as an early Makkan Sura. Noëldeke places it in the early part of his first period. Muir makes it one of the first Suras enunciated by Muhammad as a public preacher.

INTROD.] (219) [CHAP. LXXX.

Principal Subjects.

	VERSES
Muhammad rebuked for frowning on a poor blind Muslim	1-11
The Qurán written in honourable, exalted, and pure volumes	12-15
Man cursed for turning aside from his Creator	16-23
It is God who provides man with food	24-32
On the judgment-day men will desert their nearest relatives and friends	33-37
The bright and sad faces of the resurrection-day	38-42

IN THE NAME OF THE MOST MERCIFUL GOD.

|| (1) *The Prophet* frowned and turned aside (2) because R $\frac{1}{5}$. the blind *man* came unto him: (3) and how dost thou know whether he shall peradventure be cleansed *from his sins,* (4) or *whether* he shall be admonished, and the admonition shall profit him? (5) *The man* who is wealthy (6) thou receivest respectfully; (7) whereas *it is not to be charged* on thee that he is not cleansed: (8) but him who cometh unto thee earnestly, (9) seeking *his salvation,* and who feareth *God,* (10) dost thou neglect. (11) By no means *shouldst thou act thus.* Verily, *the Qurán* is an admonition (12) (and he who is willing retaineth the same); (13) *written* in volumes honourable, (14) exalted, *and* pure; (15) by the hands of scribes honoured *and* just. (16) May man be cursed! What hath seduced him to infidelity? (17) Of what thing doth GOD create him? (18) Of a drop of seed (19) doth he create him: and he

---

(1-11) Muhammad is justly praised for the magnanimous spirit shown in this passage. Throughout his career we rarely after find him courting the favour of the rich or the great, and he was ever ready to recognise merit in the poorest of his followers.

(13-15) *Written in volumes.* "Being transcribed from the 'preserved table,' highly honoured in the sight of God, kept pure and uncorrupted from the hands of evil spirits, and touched only by the angels. Some understand hereby the books of the prophets, with which the Qurán agrees in substance."—*Sale, Zamakhshari.*

(16) *Man be cursed.* This expression is limited to the unbelievers by what follows. Jesus prayed for his enemies; Muhammad cursed his.

formeth him with proportion; (20) and then facilitateth *his* passage *out of the womb:* (21) afterwards he causeth him to die, and layeth him in the grave; (22) hereafter, when it shall please him, he shall raise him to life. (23) Assuredly. He hath not hitherto fully performed what *God* hath commanded him. (24) Let man consider his food; *in what manner it is provided.* (25) We pour down water by showers; (26) afterwards we cleave the earth in clefts, (27) and we cause corn to spring forth therein, (28) and grapes and clover, (29) and the olive and the palm, (30) and gardens planted thick with trees, (31) and fruits, and grass, (32) for the use of yourselves and of your cattle. (33) When the stunning sound *of the trumpet* shall be heard; (34) on that day shall a man fly from his brother, (35) and his mother, and his father, (36) and his wife, and his children. (37) Every man of them, on that day, shall have business *of his own* sufficient to employ *his thoughts.* (38) On that day *the* faces *of some shall be* bright, (39) laughing, *and* joyful; (40) and upon *the* faces *of others,* on that day, *shall there be* dust; (41) darkness shall cover them. (42) These are the unbelievers, the wicked.

---

(33) See note on chap. lxxix. 13. The first blast, however, is referred to here. See Prelim. Disc., p. 135.

CHAPTER LXXXI.

ENTITLED SURAT AL TAKWÍR (THE FOLDING UP).

Revealed at Makkah.

INTRODUCTION.

THE title of this chapter is taken from the first verse. The only matter worthy of notice here is the allusion it makes to the vision of Gabriel which Muhammad claimed he had in Mount Hira. This vision is here referred to as a Divine attestation to his apostleship. Noëldeke thinks this vision to have been "a night vision," and, from vers. 15-18, he concludes "the revelation took place toward the end of the night, when the light of the stars was waning and the dawn about to break."

Probable Date of the Revelations.

What is said in this chapter of Muhammad's vision is so like the statement of chapter liii. as to suggest that the date is probably the same. The style and language agrees very well with this opinion.

Principal Subjects.

	VERSES
The terrible signs of the judgment-day	1–14
Oaths that the Qurán is the word of God, and that Muhammad is neither a madman nor deluded by the devil .	15–25
The Qurán an admonition to all men	26–29

IN THE NAME OF THE MOST MERCIFUL GOD.

|| (1) When the sun shall be folded up; (2) and when R $\frac{1}{6}$. the stars shall fall; (3) and when the mountains shall be

(1) *Folded up.* "As a garment that is to be laid by."—*Sale.*

made to pass away; (4) and when the camels ten months gone with young shall be neglected; (5) and when the wild beasts shall be gathered together; (6) and when the seas shall boil; (7) and when the souls shall be joined *again to their bodies:* (8) and when the girl who hath been buried alive shall be asked (9) for what crime she was put to death; (10) and when the books shall be laid open; (11) and when the heaven shall be removed; (12) and when hell shall burn fiercely; (13) and when Paradise shall be brought near; (14) *every* soul shall know what it hath wrought. (15) Verily I swear by the stars which are retrograde, (16) which move swiftly, *and* which hide themselves; (17) and by the night, when it cometh on; (18) and by the morning, when it appeareth; (19) that these *are* the words of an honourable messenger, (20) endued with strength, of established dignity in the sight of the possessor of the throne, (21) obeyed *by the angels under his authority,* and faithful: (22) and your companion *Muhammad* is not distracted. (23) He had already seen him in the clear horizon: (24) and he suspected not the

---

(4–6) See Prelim. Disc., p. 135.
(8) *Buried alive* "For it was customary among the ancient Arabs to bury their daughters alive as soon as they were born, for fear they should be impoverished by providing for them, or should suffer disgrace on their account."—*Sale.*
See also note on chap. xvi. 60.
(11) *The heaven . . . removed.* "Or plucked away from its place, as 'the skin is plucked off' from a camel which is flaying, for that is the proper signification of the verb here used. Marracci fancies the passage alludes to that in the Psalms (Ps. civ. 2), where, according to the versions of the Septuagint and the Vulgate, God is said to have 'stretched out the heaven like a skin.'"—*Sale.*
(16) *Which hide, &c.* "Some understand hereby the stars in general, but the more exact commentators, five of the planets, viz., the two which accompany the sun and the three superior planets, which have both a retrograde and a direct motion, and hide themselves in the rays of the sun, or when they set."—*Sale.*
(19) *An honourable messenger.* "Gabriel."—*Sale.*
(20) *Endued with strength.* See note on chap. liii. 6.
(23) See notes on chap. liii. 7–11.
(24) *And he suspected not.* "Some copies, by a change of one letter only, instead of *dhanînin* read *danînin,* and then the words

secrets *revealed unto him*. (25) Neither *are* these the words of an accursed devil. (26) Whither, therefore, are you going? (27) This *is* no other than an admonition unto all creatures; (28) unto him among you who shall be willing to walk uprightly; (29) but ye shall not will, unless GOD willeth, the LORD of all creatures.

---

should be rendered, ' He is not tenacious of, or grudges not to communicate to you, 'the secret revelations' which he has received."
—*Sale.*

(25) *An accursed devil.* "Who has overheard by stealth the discourse of the angels. The verse is an answer to a calumny of the infidels, who said the Qurán was only a piece of divination or magic; for the Arabs suppose the soothsayer or magician receives his intelligence from those evil spirits who are continually listening to learn what they can from the inhabitants of heaven."—*Sale.*

See notes on chap. xv. 17, 18.

CHAPTER LXXXII.

ENTITLED SURAT AL INFITÁR (THE CLEAVING IN SUNDER).

Revealed at Makkah.

INTRODUCTION.

THIS chapter is typical of the Suras first enunciated at Makkah. The burden of the Prophet is the unbelief of man in the doctrine of a future judgment, in which God shall reward the righteous and punish the wicked.

Probable Date of the Revelations.

Nothing more definite can be said as to the date of this chapter than that it is one of the earliest Makkan Suras. Noëldeke places it immediately before chapter lxxxi.

Principal Subjects.

	VERSES
Signs of the judgment-day	1–5
Astonishing unbelief of man in his Creator	6–9
Guardian angels record the deeds of men	10–12
In the judgment the righteous shall be rewarded and the wicked punished	13–16
On the day of judgment there shall be no intercessor	17–19

IN THE NAME OF THE MOST MERCIFUL GOD.

R 7/. ‖ (1) When the heaven shall be cloven in sunder; (2) and when the stars shall be scattered; (3) and when the seas shall be suffered to join their waters; (4) and when

---

(1–4) These are all signs of the judgment-day. See Prelim. Disc., p. 135.

the graves shall be turned upside down: (5) *every* soul shall know what it hath committed, and *what* it hath omitted. (6) O man, what hath seduced thee against thy gracious LORD, (7) who hath created thee, and put thee together, and rightly disposed thee? (8) In what form he pleased hath he fashioned thee. (9) Assuredly. But ye deny the *last* judgment as a falsehood. (10) Verily *there are appointed* over you guardian *angels*, (11) honourable *in the sight of God*, writing down *your actions*, (12) who know that which ye do. (13) The just *shall* surely *be* in *a place of* delight, (14) but the wicked *shall* surely *be* in hell; (15) they shall be cast therein to be burned, on the day of judgment, (16) and they *shall* not *be* absent therefrom *for ever*. (17) What shall cause thee to understand what the day of judgment *is?* (18) Again, what shall cause thee to understand what the day of judgment *is?* (19) *It is* a day whereon one soul shall not be able to obtain anything in behalf of *another* soul; and the command on that day shall be GOD'S.

(6-8) Compare chap. lxxx. 16 *seq.*
(10) See chap. l. 26, and Prelim. Disc., pp. 148, 149.
(18, 19) Compare chap. lxxvii. 11-14.

CHAPTER LXXXIII.

ENTITLED SURAT AL TATFÍF (THOSE WHO GIVE SHORT MEASURE).

Revealed at Makkah.

INTRODUCTION.

THIS chapter opens with a philippic against the use of false weights and measures. Woes are then pronounced against those who charge their prophets with imposture, while the believers are comforted by a description of the joys which await them in Paradise. The infidels may with mocking and jesting taunt the Muslims now, but the time will come when the Muslims shall laugh at the infidels as they look down from the couches of Paradise upon their writhings in hell-fire.

Probable Date of the Revelations.

Muslim authors differ as to the location of this chapter. Some hold (Itqán, 37) that vers. 1–6 only are Madínic, others that the whole chapter is Madínic (Itqán, 28, 55). According to others, this is the last Makkan Sura, or the first Madínic, or revealed between Makkah and Madína. Noëldeke and Muir alike place it among the early Makkan Suras, making the date to be about the fourth year of Muhammad's public ministry.

Principal Subjects.

	VERSES
Denunciation of those who use false weights and measures	1–6
The acts of the wicked are recorded in the book Sajjín	7–9
Woe to those who reject Muhammad and deny the judgment-day	10–18
The acts of the righteous are registered in Illíyún	18–21
The rewards of the righteous in Paradise	22–28
Unbelievers mock at Muslims now, but shall be laughed at in turn	29–36

IN THE NAME OF THE MOST MERCIFUL GOD.

|| (1) Woe be unto those who give short measure or RUBA. weight; (2) who, when they receive by measure from *other* R ⅛ men, take the full; (3) but when they measure unto them, or weigh unto them, defraud! (4) Do not these think they shall be raised again (5) at the great day, (6) the day whereon mankind shall stand before the LORD of all creatures? (7) By no means. Verily the register of *the actions of* the wicked *is* surely in Sajjín. (8) And what shall make thee to understand what Sajjín *is?* (9) *It is* a book distinctly written. (10) Woe be on that day unto those who accused *the prophets* of imposture, (11) who denied the day of judgment as a falsehood! (12) And none denieth the same as a falsehood except every unjust *and* flagitious person, (13) who, when our signs are rehearsed unto him, saith, *They are* fables of the ancients. (14) By no means; but rather their lusts have cast a veil over their hearts. (15) By no means. Verily they *shall be* shut out from their LORD on that day; (16) and they shall be sent into hell to be burned: (17) then shall it be said *unto them by the infernal guards,* This *is* what ye denied as a falsehood. (18) Assuredly. But the register

---

(1-6) This passage, as well as many others in this portion of the Qurán, illustrates the character of the instruction given by the reformer of Makkah. It has a genuine ring about it. A pure morality is insisted on, and enforced by the doctrine of a final judgment.

(7) "*Sajjín* is the name of the general register, wherein the actions of all the wicked, both men and genii, are distinctly entered. *Sajjín* signifies a *prison;* and this book, as some think, derives its name from thence, because it will occasion those whose deeds are there recorded to be *imprisoned* in hell. Sajjín or Sajín is also the name of the dungeon beneath the seventh earth, the residence of Iblís and his host; where it is supposed, by some, that this book is kept, and where the souls of the wicked will be detained till the resurrection. If the latter explication be admitted, the words, 'And what shall make thee to understand what Sajjin is?' should be enclosed within a parenthesis."—*Sale, Baidháwi, Jaláluddín.*

See also Prelim. Disc., p. 129.

(13) See notes on chaps. vi. 24, and xxi. 5.

of *the actions of* the righteous *is* Illíyún: (19) and what shall cause thee to understand what Illíyún *is?* (20) *It is* a book distinctly written: (21) those who approach near *unto God* are witnesses thereto. (22) Verily the righteous *shall dwell* among delights: (23) *seated* on couches, they shall behold *objects of pleasure;* (24) thou shalt see in their faces the brightness of joy. (25) They shall be given to drink of pure wine, sealed; (26) the seal whereof *shall be* musk: and to this let those aspire who aspire *to happiness:* (27) and the *water* mixed therewith *shall be* of Tasním, (28) a fountain whereof those shall drink who approach near *unto the divine presence.* (29) They who act wickedly laugh the true believers to scorn, (30) and when they pass by them, they wink at one another; (31) and when they turn aside to their people, they turn aside making scurrilous jests; (32) and when they see them, they say, (33) Verily these *are* mistaken men. But they

---

(18) *Illíyún.* "The word is a plural, and signifies *high places.* Some say it is the general register wherein the actions of the righteous, whether angels, men, or genii, are distinctly recorded. Others will have it to be a place in the seventh heaven, under the throne of God; where this book is kept, and where the souls of the just, as many think, will remain till the last day. If we prefer the latter opinion, the words, 'And what shall make thee to understand what Illíyún is?' should likewise be enclosed in a parenthesis."—*Sale, Baidháwi.*

(21) *Witnesses thereto.* "Or *are present with* and keep *the same.*"—*Sale.*

(25) *Pure wine.* See note on chap. lxxvi. 5.

(26) *The seal, &c., i.e.,* "the vessels containing the same shall be sealed with musk, instead of clay. Some understand by the seal of this wine its farewell, or the flavour it will leave in the mouth after it is drunk."—*Sale.*

(27) *Tasním.* "Tasním is the name of a fountain in Paradise, so called from its being conveyed to the highest apartments."—*Sale.*

(28) *A fountain, &c.* "For *they* shall drink the water of Tasním pure and unmixed, being continually and wholly employed in the contemplation of God; but the other inhabitants of Paradise shall drink it mixed with their wine."—*Sale.*

(33) *Not . . . keepers, i.e.,* "the infidels are not commissioned by God to call the believers to account, or to judge of their actions."—*Sale.*

are not sent *to be* keepers over them. (34) Wherefore one day the true believers, *in their turn,* shall laugh the infidels to scorn: (35) *lying* on couches, they shall look down *upon them in hell.* (36) Shall not the infidels be rewarded for that which they have done?

---

(34) *Shall laugh . . . to scorn.* " When they shall see them ignominiously driven into hell. It is also said that a door shall be shown the damned, opening into Paradise, and they shall be bidden to go in ; but when they come near the door, it shall suddenly shut ; and the believers within shall laugh at them."—*Sale, Baidháwí.*

CHAPTER LXXXIV.

ENTITLED SURAT AL INSHIQÁQ (THE RENDING IN SUNDER).

Revealed at Makkah.

INTRODUCTION.

THIS chapter begins with very much the same language, and the style and composition throughout is much the same, as that of chapters lxxxi. and lxxxii. We cannot, therefore, err much if we regard the

Probable Date of the Revelations

to be about the same. With this opinion both Muir and Noëldeke seem to agree, as these chapters are brought quite near together in their chronological lists.

Principal Subjects.

	VERSES
Signs of the judgment-day	1–5
The books of the righteous and the wicked given into their hands, and the consequence thereof	6–15
Oaths attesting the doctrine of the resurrection . . .	16–20
The unbelievers denounced and threatened . . .	21–25

IN THE NAME OF THE MOST MERCIFUL GOD.

R 1/6. ‖ (1) When the heaven shall be rent in sunder, (2) and shall obey its LORD, and shall be capable *thereof;* (3) and when the earth shall be stretched out, (4) and shall cast

---

(3) *The earth . . . stretched out.* "Like a skin, every mountain and hill being levelled."—*Sale.*

forth that which *is* therein, and shall remain empty, (5) and shall obey its LORD, and shall be capable *thereof*: (6) O man, verily labouring thou labourest to *meet* thy LORD, and thou shalt meet him. (7) And he who shall have his book given into his right hand (8) shall be called to an easy account, (9) and shall turn unto his family with joy; (10) but he who shall have his book given him behind his back (11) shall invoke destruction *to fall upon him*, (12) and he shall be sent into hell to be burned; (13) because he rejoiced insolently amidst his family *on earth*. (14) Verily he thought he should never return *unto God:* (15) yea, verily, but his LORD beheld him. (16) Wherefore I swear by the redness of the sky after sunset, (17) and by the night, and the *animals* which it driveth together, (18) and by the moon when she is in the full, (19) ye shall surely be transferred *successively* from state to state. (20) What *aileth* them, therefore, that they believe not *the resurrection*, (21) and that, when the Qurán is read unto them, they worship not? (22) Yea, the unbelievers accuse *the same* of imposture; (23) but God well knoweth the *malice* which they keep hidden *in their breasts*. (24) Wherefore denounce unto them a grievous punishment, (25) except those who believe and do good works: for them *is prepared* a never-failing reward.

---

(4) *That which is therein.* "As the treasures hidden in its bowels, and the dead bodies which lie in their graves."—*Sale.*

(6) *Thou shalt meet him.* "Or, *and thou shalt meet thy labour;* whether thy works be good or whether they be evil."—*Sale.*

(9) *His family, i.e.*, "his relations and friends who are true believers; or rather, to his wives and servants, or the damsels and youths of Paradise, who wait to receive him."—*Sale, Baidháwi.*

(10) *Behind his back.* "That is, into his left hand; for the wicked will have that hand bound behind their back, and their right hand to their neck."—*Sale.*

(19) *From state to state, i.e.*, "from the state of the living to that of the dead, and from the state of the dead to a new state of life in another world."—*Sale.*

(21) *Worship not.* "Or, *humble not themselves.*"—*Sale.*

CHAPTER LXXXV.

ENTITLED SURAT AL BURÚJ (THE CELESTIAL SIGNS).

Revealed at Makkah.

INTRODUCTION.

THE first seven verses of this chapter are generally supposed to refer to the persecution of the Christians in Najrán by the cruel king Dhú Nawás. Geiger, however, and after him Noëldeke, adopts the opinion of al Bogháwi that the three men in the furnace (Dan. iii.) are here alluded to.

Vers. 8 and 11, says Noëldeke, " have probably been added later on by Muhammad himself, as they differ from the other verses, with which they are otherwise connected, by reason of a greater length, a more diffuse style, and a somewhat modified rhyme." The term *múminát* (female believers) does not occur in any but the latest chapters of the Qurán.

Probable Date of the Revelations.

The chapter, excepting perhaps vers. 8–11, is of Makkan origin. Noëldeke assigns it to the earlier half of his first period.

Principal Subjects.

	VERSES
Cursed were the persecutors of the believers burned with fire	1–7
The believers persecuted for their faith in God . . .	8, 9
For the infidels is hell-fire, but for believers Paradise . .	10–12
God is Creator and Sovereign Ruler of the universe . .	13–16
Pharaoh and Thamúd examples to warn those who reject the Qurán	17–20
The glorious Qurán is kept in the Preserved Table . .	21

IN THE NAME OF THE MOST MERCIFUL GOD.

|| (1) By the heaven *adorned* with signs; (2) by the promised day *of judgment;* (3) by the witness and the witnessed; (4) cursed were the contrivers of the pit, (5) of fire supplied with fuel; (6) when they sat around the same, (7) and were witnesses of what they did against the true believers, (8) and they afflicted them for no other reason but because they believed in the mighty, the glorious GOD, (9) unto whom *belongeth* the kingdom of heaven and earth; and GOD *is* witness of all things. (10) Verily for those who persecute the true believers of either sex, R $\frac{1}{10}$.

---

(1) *Signs.* "The original word properly signifies 'towers,' which some interpret of real towers, wherein it is supposed the angels keep guard; and others, of the stars of the first magnitude: but the generality of expositors understand thereby the twelve signs of the zodiac, wherein the planets make their several stations."—*Sale.*

See notes on chap. xv. 17, 18.

(3) "The meaning of these words is very uncertain, and the explications of the commentators consequently vary. One thinks 'the witness' to be Muhammad, and 'that which is borne witness of' to be 'the resurrection' or 'the professors of the Muhammadan faith;' or else that these latter are 'the witness,' and the professors of every other religion those who will be 'witnessed against' by them. Another supposes 'the witness' to be the 'guardian angel,' and his charge the person 'witnessed against.' Another expounds the words of the day of Arafát, the 9th of Dhul Hajja, and of the day of slaying the victims, which is the day following, or else of Friday, the day of the weekly assembling of the Muhammadans at their mosques, and of the people who are assembled on those days."—*Sale, Jaláluddín, Baidháwi, Yahya.*

(4) *Contrivers of the pit.* "Literally, 'the lords of the pit.' These were the ministers of the persecution raised by Dhú Nawás, king of Yaman, who was of the Jewish religion, against the inhabitants of Najrán; for they having embraced Christianity (at that time the true religion, by the confession of Muhammad himself), the bigoted tyrant commanded all those who would not renounce their faith to be cast into a pit or trench filled with fire, and there burnt to ashes. Others, however, tell the story with different circumstances."—*Sale.*

See, on this subject, Introduction to Muir's *Life of Mahomet*, p. clxii.

(6) *And were witnesses, &c.* Or, as some choose to understand the words, 'And shall be witnesses against themselves at the day of judgment, of their unjust treatment of the true believers."—*Sale.*

and afterwards repent not, *is prepared* the torment of hell; and they *shall suffer* the pain of burning. (11) But for those who believe, and do that which is right, *are destined* gardens beneath which rivers flow: this *shall be* great felicity. (12) Verily the vengeance of thy LORD *is* severe. (13) He createth, and he restoreth *to life:* (14) he *is* inclined to forgive, *and* gracious; (15) the possessor of the glorious throne, (16) who effecteth that which he pleaseth. (17) Hath not the story of the hosts (18) of Pharaoh and of Thamúd reached thee? (19) Yet the unbelievers cease not to accuse *the divine revelations* of falsehood; (20) but GOD encompasseth them behind, *that they cannot escape.* (21) Verily *that which they reject* is a glorious Qurán; (22) *the original whereof is written* in a table kept *in* heaven.

---

(10) *The pain of burning.* "Which pain, it is said, the persecutors of the 'Christian' martyrs above mentioned felt in this life; the fire bursting forth upon them from the pit, and consuming them."—*Sale, Baidháwi.*

(17, 18) See notes on chaps. vii. 104–136, and xi. 61–68.

(22) *A table kept.* "And preserved from the least change or corruption. See the Prelim. Disc., p. 108."—*Sale.*

CHAPTER LXXXVI.[1]

ENTITLED SURAT AL TÁRIQ (THE STAR WHICH APPEARED BY NIGHT).

Revealed at Makkah.

INTRODUCTION.

ACCORDING to al Wakídí, the first three verses of this chapter, which, by the way, give it a title, were revealed when Abu Tálib was frightened by seeing a shooting star. This story receives some colouring from the mention of the guardian angel in ver. 4, as the shooting stars were supposed to be darts cast at the devils by the angels guarding the gates of heaven. Noëldeke, however, thinks the words point to a planet or fixed star.

This chapter seems to us to be composed of two small Suras or fragments of Suras, vers. 11-17 being the second, belonging to a later period, because of the mention of *plots* against Muhammad, which point to the time preceding the first emigration to Abyssinia.

Probable Date of the Revelations.

The first part of this chapter certainly belongs to the earliest period of Muhammad's ministry. Muir and Noëldeke place the whole chapter there; but, for the reason stated above, we prefer to regard vers. 11-17 as belonging to about the fourth year of the ministry at Makkah.

Principal Subjects.

	VERSES
Oath by the star of piercing brightness	1-3
Every soul has its guardian angel	4
God the Creator, and therefore can raise the dead	5-8
The judgment-day shall reveal secret thoughts	9, 10
Oaths by heaven and earth that the Qurán is God's word	11-14
Muhammad exhorted to bear patiently with the unbelievers plotting his ruin	15-17

IN THE NAME OF THE MOST MERCIFUL GOD.

R $\frac{1}{11}$ ‖ (1) By the heaven, and that which appeareth by night: (2) but what shall cause thee to understand what that which appeareth by night *is?* (3) *it is* the star of piercing brightness: (4) every soul hath a guardian *set* over it. (5) Let a man consider, therefore, of what he is created. (6) He is created of seed poured forth, (7) issuing from the loins and the breast-bones. (8) Verily *God is* able to restore him *to life*, (9) the day whereon *all* secret thoughts and actions shall be examined into; (10) and he shall have no power *to defend himself,* nor any protector. (11) By the heaven which returneth *the rain,* (12) and by the earth which openeth *to let forth vegetables and springs,* (13) verily this *is* a discourse, distinguishing *good from evil,* (14) and it *is* not *composed* with lightness, (15) Verily *the infidels* are laying a plot *to frustrate my designs;* (16) but I will lay a plot *for their ruin.* (17) Wherefore, *O Prophet,* bear with the unbelievers! let them alone a while.

---

(3) *The star, &c.* "Some take the words to signify any bright star, without restriction, but others think some particular star or stars to be thereby intended; which one supposes to be the morning star (peculiarly called 'al Táriq,' or 'the appearing by night'), another Saturn (that planet being by the Arabs surnamed 'al Thakib,' or 'the piercing,' as it was by the Greeks 'Phœnon,' or 'the shining'), and a third, the Pleiades."—*Sale.*

(7) *Loins and breast-bones.* "From the loins of the man and the breast-bones of the woman."—*Sale, Baidháwi.*

(9) *Secret thoughts and actions.* The judgment-day shall reveal all such thoughts and actions, but some Muslims deny a moral character to mere thoughts so long as they are not manifested in words or actions.

(11) *Which returneth rain.* "Or, as some expound it, 'which performeth its periodic motion, returning' to the point from whence it began the same. The words seem designed to express the alternate returns of the different seasons of the year."—*Sale.*

CHAPTER LXXXVII.

ENTITLED SURAT AL ÁLÁ (THE MOST HIGH).

Revealed at Makkah.

INTRODUCTION.

IN some editions the title of this chapter is "Praise." The matter of these revelations is considered to be so precious as to vouchsafe to every reader ten celestial blessings for every letter in the books of Abraham, Moses, and Muhammad!

This chapter professes especially to encourage the Prophet, promising him help to rehearse and remember the revelations, except such portions as it might please God to suppress. Thus early do we find mention of the very convenient law of abrogation. This fact, together with the statement in the last verse that the Qurán is attested by the Scriptures of Abraham and Moses, arouses the suspicion that vers. 7 and 18, 19, have been inserted at a later period; but if so, the additions were made by Muhammad himself.

Probable Date of the Revelations.

Some Muslim writers, comparing vers. 1 and 15, and inferring that the five daily prayers are here alluded to, have concluded this chapter to be Madínic. Ver. 6, referring to Muhammad's purpose to preach the Qurán publicly, together with the style and language of the chapter, shows it to be early Makkan. This can hardly apply to vers. 7, 18, and 19, for reasons given above. Noëldeke places the chapter immediately after chapter lxviii. in his chronological list of Suras.

Principal Subjects.

	VERSES
God, the Most High, praised for his works . . .	1–5
God promises to help Muhammad to proclaim the Qurán .	6–9
The God-fearing only shall be admonished . . .	10, 11
The wicked shall be punished, but the righteous shall be blessed	12–15
Men choose the present life rather than the life to come .	16, 17
The books of Abraham and Moses attest the Qurán . .	18, 19

IN THE NAME OF THE MOST MERCIFUL GOD.

R $\frac{1}{12}$. ‖ (1) Praise the name of thy LORD, the Most High, (2) who hath created (3) and completely formed *his creatures*, and who determineth *them to various ends*, and directeth *them to attain the same;* (4) and who produceth the pasture *for cattle*, (5) and *afterwards* rendereth the same dry stubble of a dusky hue. (6) We will enable thee to rehearse *our revelations;* and thou shalt not forget *any part thereof*, (7) except what GOD shall please; for he knoweth that which is manifest and that which is hidden. (8) And we will facilitate unto thee the most easy *way*. (9) Wherefore admonish *thy people*, if *thy* admonition shall be profitable *unto them*. (10) Whoso feareth *God*, he will be admonished: (11) but the most wretched *unbeliever* will turn away therefrom; (12) who shall be cast to be broiled in the greater fire *of hell*, (13) wherein he shall not die, neither shall he live. (14) Now hath he attained felicity, who is purified *by faith*, (15) and who remembereth the name of his LORD, and prayeth. (16) But ye prefer this present life; (17) yet the life to come *is* better, and more durable. (18) Verily, this *is written* in the ancient books, (19) the books of Abraham and Moses.

---

(3) *Who determineth, &c.* "Determining their various species, properties, ways of life," &c.—*Sale, Baidháwi.*

And directeth. "Guiding the rational by their reason and also by revelation, and the irrational by instinct, &c."—*Sale, Baidháwi.*

(6) See note on chap. lxxv. 16-19.

(7) *Except what God shall please, i.e.,* "except such revelations as God shall think fit to abrogate and blot out of thy memory."—*Sale.* See also notes on chap. ii. 105.

(8) *The most easy way.* "To retain the revelations communicated to thee by Gabriel; or, as some understand the words, 'We will dispose thee to the profession and strict observance of the most easy religion, that is, of Islám.'"—*Sale.*

(12) See note on chap. ii. 38.

(19) Compare chap. iv. 52, 53.

CHAPTER LXXXVIII.

ENTITLED SURAT AL GHÁSHIYA (THE OVERWHELMING).

Revealed at Makkah.

INTRODUCTION.

THE object of the revelations of this chapter seems to have been to inspire reverence for the Prophet and his teachings by describing the tortures of the wicked in hell. The joys of Paradise are described for the comfort of the poor and as yet despised Muslims of Makkah. Muhammad is only a warner, but the very exhortations to use no force against the unbelievers show that the idea of compulsory conversion of the people was now present in his mind.

Probable Date of the Revelations.

The hint that force might have been used to convert the Quraish (ver. 22) implies strong opposition to Muhammad. This, with the somewhat detailed description of the joys of Paradise, points to a period of Muhammad's ministry near to and yet preceding the earliest persecutions of the Muslims. This would be, as Noëldeke has it, about the fourth year of the ministry at Makkah.

Principal Subjects.

	VERSES
The terrible day of judgment	1–3
Description of the torments of hell	4–7
The joyful state of the Muslims on the judgment-day	8–16
God manifests himself in his works	17–20
Muhammad only to warn, not to rule over, the infidels	21, 22
God will himself punish the unbelievers	23–26

IN THE NAME OF THE MOST MERCIFUL GOD.

R $\tfrac{1}{13}$. ‖ (1) Hath the news of the overwhelming *day of judgment* reached thee ? (2) The countenances *of some*, on that day, *shall be* cast down ; (3) labouring *and* toiling, (4) they shall be cast into scorching fire to be broiled : (5) they shall be given to drink of a boiling fountain : (6) they shall have no food, but of dry thorns and thistles : (7) which shall not fatten, neither shall they satisfy hunger. (8) *But* the countenances *of others*, on that day, *shall be* joyful ; (9) well pleased with their *past* endeavour : (10) they *shall be placed* in a lofty garden, (11) wherein thou shalt hear no vain discourse : (12) therein *shall be* a running fountain ; (13) therein *shall be* raised beds, (14) and goblets placed *before them*, (15) and cushions laid in order, (16) and carpets ready spread. (17) Do they not consider the camels, how they are created ? (18) and the heaven, how it is raised ? (19) and the mountains, how they are fixed ? (20) and the earth, how it is extended ? (21) Wherefore warn *thy people ;* for thou *art* a warner only : (22) thou art not empowered to act with authority over them. (23) But whoever shall turn back, and dis-

---

(3) *Labouring and toiling, i.e.,* "dragging their chains, and labouring through hell-fire, as camels labour through mud, &c. Or, ' Employing and fatiguing themselves ' in what shall not avail them." —*Sale.*

(6) *Dry thorns and thistles.* "Such as the camels eat when green and tender. Some take the original word *al Dharí* for the name of a thorny tree."—*Sale.*

(8–16) Compare with these verses chaps. lxxviii. 31–37, iii. 15, and see notes there.

(17) *The camels.* "These animals are of such use, or rather necessity, in the East, that the creation of a species so wonderfully adapted to those countries is a very proper instance, to an Arabian, of the power and wisdom of God. Some, however, think the 'clouds' (which the original word *ibl* also signifies) are here intended, ' the heaven ' being mentioned immediately after."—*Sale.*

(21, 22) See note on chap. ii. 119.

(23) *Whoever shall turn back.* "Or 'except him who shall turn back and be an infidel ; and God shall punish him,' &c. By which

believe, (24) GOD shall punish him with the greater punishment *of the life to come.* (25) Verily unto us shall they return : (26) then shall it be our part to bring them to account.

---

exception some suppose that power is here given to Muhammad to chastise obstinate infidels and apostates."—*Sale.*

See note on chap. v. 59.

CHAPTER LXXXIX.

ENTITLED SURAT AL FAJR (THE DAYBREAK).

Revealed at Makkah.

INTRODUCTION.

THIS chapter, like almost all the earlier Makkan Suras, opens with a number of oaths, which seem to have been uttered as a kind of warning to call special attention to the solemnity of what was to follow. The fourth verse shows us that Muhammad formed these imprecations with deliberate purpose, and uttered them after careful consideration.

The burden of the preacher's warning was levelled against the oppression and greed of the rich in his own town. Perhaps they had already begun to treat harshly the slave converts to Islám. However this may be, they are warned by the examples of Ád, Thamúd, and Pharaoh, who were destroyed for their wickedness and oppression. They are also pointed to the judgment-day, when the wicked shall vainly regret their evil deeds. The chapter ends with a call to the believing soul to enter the joy of Paradise.

Probable Date of the Revelations.

Some Muslim writers (*Itqán*, 29) regard this chapter as Madínic. Noëldeke tells of one author (Hibat Allah) who declares that it was revealed at Makkah in A.H. 8. He, however, regards it as early Makkan, and in his chronological table places it immediately after chapter lxxxviii.

Principal Subjects.

	VERSES
Various oaths by natural objects	1–4
Unbelievers are warned by the fate of Ád, Thamúd, and Pharaoh	5–13
Man praises God in prosperity, but reproaches him in adversity	14–17

INTROD.]   (243)   [CHAP. LXXXIX.

	VERSES
Oppression of the poor and the orphan denounced	18–22
The wicked will vainly regret their evil deeds on the judgment-day	23–25
The believing soul invited to the joys of Paradise	26–30

IN THE NAME OF THE MOST MERCIFUL GOD.

‖ (1) By the daybreak and ten nights; (2) by that which is double, and that which is single; (3) and by the night when it cometh on: (4) *is there* not in this an oath formed with understanding? (5) Hast thou not considered how thy LORD dealt with Ád, (6) *the people of* Iram, adorned with lofty buildings, (7) the like whereof

NISF.

R 1¼.

(1) *Ten nights.* "That is, the ten nights of Dhúl Hajja, or the tenth of that month (whence some understand the day break mentioned just before, or the morning of that day or of the preceding); or the night of the 10th of Muharram; or, as others rather think, the 10th, 11th, and 12th of Dhúl Hajja. All which are days peculiarly sacred among the Muhammadans."—*Sale.*

(2, 3) "These words are variously interpreted. Some understand thereby all things in general; some, all created beings—which are said to have been created by pairs, or of two kinds (chap. li. 49)—and the Creator, who is single; some, of the *primum mobile* and the other orbs; some, of the constellations and the planets; some, of the nights before mentioned, taken either together or singly; and some, of the day of slaying the victims (the 10th of Dhúl Hajja) and of the day of Arafát, which is the day before, &c."—*Sale, Zamakhshari.*

(6) *The people of Iram.* "Iram was the name of the territory or city of the Ádites, and of the garden mentioned in the next note, which were so called from Iram or Aram, the grandfather of Ád, their progenitor. Some think Aram himself to be here meant, and his name to be added to signify the ancient Ádites, his immediate descendants, and to distinguish them from the latter tribe of that name; but the adjective and relative joined to the word are, in the original, of the feminine gender, which seems to contradict this opinion."—*Sale, Baidháwi.*

Lofty buildings, "or 'pillars.' Some imagine these words are used to express the great size and strength of the old Ádites; and then they should be translated, 'who were of enormous stature.' But the more exact commentators take the passage to relate to the sumptuous palace and delightful gardens built and made by Shaddád, the son of Ád. For they say Ád left two sons, Shaddád and Shaddíd, who reigned jointly after his decease and extended their power over the greater part of the world; but Shaddíd dying, his brother became

hath not been erected in the land; (8) and with Thamúd, who hewed the rocks in the valley *into houses;* (9) and with Pharaoh, the contriver of the stakes: (10) who had behaved insolently in the earth, (11) and multiplied corruption therein? (12) Wherefore thy LORD poured on them various kinds of chastisement: (13) for thy LORD *is* surely in a watch-tower, *whence he observeth the actions of men.* (14) Moreover, man, when his LORD trieth him *by prosperity,* and honoureth him, and is bounteous unto him, (15) saith, My LORD honoureth me; (16) but when he proveth him *by afflictions* and withholdeth his provisions from him, (17) he saith, My LORD despiseth me. (18) By no means: but ye honour not the orphan, (19)

---

sole monarch; who, having heard of the 'Celestial Paradise,' made a garden in imitation thereof in the deserts of Aden, and called it Iram, after the name of his great-grandfather. When it was finished, he set out with a great attendance to take a view of it; but when they were come within a day's journey of the place, they were all destroyed by a terrible noise from heaven. Al Baidháwi adds that one Abdullah Ibn Kalábah (whom, after D'Herbelot, I have elsewhere named Colabah, Prelim. Disc., p. 21) accidentally hit on this wonderful place as he was seeking a camel."—*Sale, Baidháwi.*

See Prelim. Disc., pp. 20, 21.

(7) *The like, &c.* "If we suppose the preceding words to relate to the vast stature of the Adites, these must be translated, 'The like of whom hath not been created,' &c."—*Sale.*

(8) "The learned Greaves, in his translation of Abul Fida's 'Description of Arabia,' has falsely rendered these words, which are there quoted, 'Quibus petræ vallis responsum dederunt,' *i.e.,* 'To whom the rocks of the valley returned answer;' which slip being made by so great a man, I do not at all wonder that La Roque and Petis de la Croix, from whose Latin version and with whose assistance La Roque made his French translation of the aforesaid treatise, have been led into the same mistake, and rendered those words, 'A qui les pierres de la vallée redirent réponse.' The valley here meant, say the commentators, is Wádi al Qurá, lying about one day's journey (not five and upwards, as Abul Fida will have it) from al Hajr."—*Sale.*

(9) See note on chap. xxxviii. 11.

(12) *Various kinds.* "The original word signifies a 'mixture,' and also a 'scourge' of platted thongs; whence some suppose the 'chastisement of this life' is here represented by a 'scourge,' and intimated to be as much lighter than that of the next life as 'scourging' is lighter than death."—*Sale, Baidháwi.*

(18) *By no means.* "For worldly prosperity or adversity is not a certain mark either of the favour or disfavour of God."—*Sale.*

neither do ye excite *one another* to feed the poor; (20) and ye devour the inheritance *of the weak*, with undistinguishing greediness, (21) and ye love riches with much affection. (22) By no means *should ye do thus*. When the earth shall be minutely ground to dust: (23) and thy LORD shall come, and the angels rank by rank; (24) and hell, on that day, shall be brought nigh: on that day shall man call to remembrance *his evil deeds*: but how *shall* remembrance *avail* him? (25) He shall say, Would to GOD that I had heretofore done *good works* in my lifetime! On that day none shall punish with his punishment; (26) nor shall any bind with his bonds. (27) O thou soul which art at rest, (28) return unto thy LORD, well pleased *with thy reward, and* well-pleasing *unto God:* (29) enter among my servants; (30) and enter my Paradise.

---

(20) *Ye devour . . . the weak.* "Not suffering women or young children to have any share in the inheritance of their husbands or parents."—*Sale.* See chap. iv. 2-7 and notes there.

(24) "There is a tradition that, at the last day, hell will be dragged towards the tribunal by 70,000 halters, each halter being hauled by 70,000 angels; and that it will come with great roaring and fury."—*Sale, Baidháwi, Jaláluddín.*

(25) *My lifetime.* "Or, 'For' this 'my' latter 'life.'"—*Sale.*

(26) "That is, none shall be able to punish or to bind, as God shall then punish and bind the wicked."—*Sale, Baidháwi.*

(27) *Thou soul, &c.* "Some expound this of the soul, which having, by pursuing the concatenation of natural causes, raised itself to the knowledge of that Being which produced them and exists of necessity, 'rests' fully contented, or 'acquiesces' in the knowledge of him and the contemplation of his perfections. By this the reader will observe that the Muhammadans are no strangers to Quietism. Others, however, understand the words of the soul, which, having attained the knowledge of the truth, 'rests' satisfied and 'relies securely' thereon, undisturbed by doubts; or of the soul, which is 'secure' of its salvation and free from fear or sorrow."—*Sale, Baidháwi.*

CHAPTER XC.

ENTITLED SURAT AL BALAD (THE TERRITORY).

Revealed at Makkah.

INTRODUCTION.

THIS chapter is quoted by Muir in his "Life of Mahomet," vol. ii. p. 65, to show how earnestly Muhammad at first strove after the truth. According to this author, these revelations, along with those of seventeen more of these short Suras, are not to be regarded as having been proclaimed publicly at the time of composition, but as expressing rather the private thoughts of the inquirer after truth, entertained even years before he set up his claim to be a prophet of God. The eighteen chapters thus described are as follows—103, 100, 99, 91, 106, 1, 101, 95, 102, 104, 82, 92, 105, 89, 90, 93, 94, and 108.

The commentators fancy a definite individual to be addressed in this chapter, and, as usual, they suggest the ubiquitous character of Walíd Ibnal Mughaira. It is better to regard the exhortation here to be addressed to men in general.

Probable Date of the Revelations.

All authorities agree in placing this chapter among the earliest Makkan revelations. It is safe to assign it to the first year of the Call, when, even if written before, it was proclaimed as one of the "signs" to an unbelieving people.

Principal Subjects.

	VERSES
Man, though created in misery, yet boasts of his riches	1–7
Captives to be freed and the poor and orphan to be fed	8–16
Description of the companions of the right and left hand	17–20

IN THE NAME OF THE MOST MERCIFUL GOD.

‖ (1) I swear by this territory, (2) (and thou, *O Prophet*, R $\frac{1}{15}$ residest in this territory), (3) and by the begetter, and that which he hath begotten; (4) verily we have created man in misery. (5) Doth he think that none shall prevail over him? (6) He saith, I have wasted plenty of riches. (7) Doth he think that none seeth him? (8) Have we not made him two eyes, (9) and a tongue, and two lips; (10) and shown him the two highways *of good and evil?* (11) Yet he attempteth not the cliff. (12) What shall make thee to understand what the cliff *is?* (13) *It is* to free the captive; (14) or to feed, in the day of famine, (15) the orphan who is of kin, (16) or the poor man who

---

(1) *I swear.* Or, *I will not swear.* See note on chap. lvi. 74.
Territory, viz., "the sacred territory of Makkah."—*Sale.* See Prelim. Disc., p. 181.
(2) "Or, *Thou shalt be allowed to do what thou pleasest in this territory;* the words, in this sense, importing a promise of that absolute power which Muhammad attained on the taking of Makkah."
"This interpretation is a mere fancy of the commentators."—*Sale, Baidháwi.*
(3) "Some understand these words generally; others of Adam or Abraham, and of their offspring, and of Muhammad in particular."—*Sale, Baidháwi.*
(4) *Misery.* "Or, 'to trouble.' The passage was revealed to comfort the Prophet under the persecutions of the Quraish."—*Sale, Baidháwi.*
(5) "Some expositors take a particular person to be here intended, who was one of Muhammad's most inveterate adversaries, as al Walíd Ibn al Mughaira; others suppose Abul Ashadd Ibn Qalda to be the man, who was so very strong, that a large skin being spread under his feet, and ten men pulling at it, they could not make him fall, though they tore the skin to pieces."—*Sale, Zamakhshari, Baidháwi.*
(6) *He saith.* "In a vain and ostentatious manner, or in opposing of Muhammad."—*Sale, Baidháwi.*
(13) *To free the captive.* This passage seems to tell forcibly against those Muslims who pursue the slave-trade. The disposition to free the slave is here said to be a sign of a man's being a true believer. Muhammad himself practised the precept here enunciated. How sad that he should have so far modified this teaching, indefinite as it is, as to make Islám responsible for nearly all the slave-dealing practised at the present day! One might hope for a reform on this subject among Muslims, based on passages like this and the example of the Prophet already alluded to, but unfortunately these precepts

lieth on the ground. (17) *Whoso doth this,* and is *one* of those who believe, and recommend perseverance unto each other, and recommend mercy unto each other; (18) these *shall be* the companions of the right hand. (19) But they who shall disbelieve our signs shall be the companions of the left hand : (20) above them *shall be* arched fire.

---

belong to the earlier chapters of the Qurán, and must therefore be regarded as having been abrogated by the later utterances. The worst of it is that *even in this passage slaveholding is not condemned as a sin* inconsistent with love to our neighbour. It is right to hold the slave, but a great merit to bestow upon him freedom.

(18, 19) See note on chap. l. 16, 17.

(249)

CHAPTER XCI.

ENTITLED SURAT AL SHAMS (THE SUN).

Revealed at Makkah.

INTRODUCTION.

THE first ten verses of this chapter are very similar in style and rhythm to chap. xc., and may with it be numbered among what Muir calls the "Soliloquies." In regard to the following verses, however, we think that, owing to the change in style, they must be relegated to a later period. This illustrates how the Prophet revised and improved the revelations in later years, for we can hardly refer the additions to these short chapters to the compilers.

Probable Date of the Revelations.

The first part of this chapter may well be classed along with the preceding chapter as a revelation of the first year of Muhammad's ministry. The allusion to *imposture* in the latter part of the chapter, however, points to the third and fourth year of the Call.

Principal Subjects.

	VERSES
Oaths that man's happiness and misery depends on the purity or corruption he hath wrought in it	1–10
Thamúd destroyed for rejecting their prophet	11–15

IN THE NAME OF THE MOST MERCIFUL GOD.

‖ (1) By the sun, and its rising brightness; (2) by the R $\frac{1}{16}$. moon, when she followeth him; (3) by the day, when it

---

(2) *When she followeth him, i.e.,* "when she rises just after him, as she does at the beginning of the month; or when she sets after him, as happens when she is a little past the full."—*Sale, Baidháwi.*

showeth his splendour; (4) by the night, when it covereth him with darkness; (5) by the heaven, and him who built it; (6) by the earth, and him who spread it forth; (7) by the soul, and him who completely formed it, (8) and inspired into the same its *faculty of distinguishing and power of choosing* wickedness and piety; (9) now is he who hath purified the same happy; (10) but he who hath corrupted the same is miserable. (11) Thamúd accused *their prophet Sálih* of imposture, through the excess of their wickedness: (12) when the wretch among them was sent *to slay the camel;* (13) and the Apostle of GOD said unto them, *Let alone* the camel of GOD, and *hinder not* her drinking. (14) But they charged him with imposture, and they slew her. Wherefore their LORD destroyed them for their crime, and made *their punishment* equal *unto them all:* (15) and he feareth not the issue thereof.

---

(8) *Wickedness and piety.* Sale's words in italics here destroy the meaning of the original. The translation according to Rodwell is "breathed into it its wickedness and its piety." Instead of "breathed," Palmer has "taught." In any case, God is made the author of man's sin as well as of good.

(11-15) *Thamúd.* See notes on chaps. vii. 74-80, and liv. 19 *seq.*

(12) *The wretch.* Kidár Ibn Salíf. See chaps. vii. 78, and liv. 29, notes.

CHAPTER XCII.

ENTITLED SURAT AL LAIL (THE NIGHT).

Revealed at Makkah.

INTRODUCTION.

"JALÁLUDDÍN," says Sale, "thinks this whole description belongs peculiarly to Abu Baqr; for when he had purchased Bilál, the Ethiopian (afterwards the Prophet's Muadhdhin, or crier to prayers), who had been put to the rack on account of his faith, the infidels said he did it only out of a view of interest; upon which this passage was revealed."

The style and language of this chapter are, however, against this explanation. It is best, therefore, to regard the whole as addressed to Muhammad's hearers generally.

Probable Date of the Revelations.

Muir places this chapter among the "Soliloquies;" but this chapter seems to me to be ruled out of that category by the statements of ver. 14 *seq.*, where Muhammad appears as a warner, and therefore is entered upon his public ministry. The whole must, however, be assigned to an early date.

Principal Subjects.

	VERSES
Oaths by various natural objects	1-4
The obedient blessed and the covetous accursed	5-13
The covetous threatened with hell-fire	14-16
True believers shall be rewarded hereafter	17-21

IN THE NAME OF THE MOST MERCIFUL GOD.

R 1/17. ‖ (1) By the night, when it covereth *all things* with darkness; (2) by the day, when it shineth forth; (3) by him who hath created the male and the female: (4) verily your endeavour *is* different. (5) Now whoso is obedient and feareth *God*, (6) and professeth the truth of that *faith* which is most excellent; (7) unto him will we facilitate *the way* to happiness: (8) but whoso shall be covetous, and shall be wholly taken up *with this world*, (9) and shall deny the truth of that which is most excellent; (10) unto him will we facilitate *the way* to misery; (11) and his riches shall not profit him when he shall fall headlong *into hell*. (12) Verily unto us *appertaineth* the direction *of mankind*; (13) and ours *is* the life to come and the present life. (14) Wherefore I threaten you with fire which burneth fiercely, (15) which none shall enter to be burned except the most wretched, (16) who shall have disbelieved and turned back. (17). But he who strictly bewareth *idolatry and rebellion* shall be removed far from the same; (18) who giveth his substance in alms, (19) and by whom no benefit *is bestowed* on any, that it may be recompensed, (20) but *who bestoweth the same* for the sake of his LORD, the Most High, (21) and hereafter he shall be well satisfied *with his reward*.

CHAPTER XCIII.

ENTITLED SURAT AL ZUHÁ (THE BRIGHTNESS).

Revealed at Makkah.

INTRODUCTION.

A STRIKING peculiarity of this chapter, and also of the next one, is that it is addressed throughout to Muhammad himself. The following is a summary of the reasons assigned by Muslim tradition why it was revealed. "It is related," says Sale, "that no revelation having been vouchsafed to Muhammad for several days in answer to some questions put to him by the Quraish, because he had confidently promised to resolve them the next day, without adding the exception, 'If it please God' (chap. xviii. 23), or because he had repulsed an importunate beggar, or else because a dead puppy lay under his seat, or for some other reason, his enemies said that God had left him; whereupon this chapter was sent down for his consolation."

The traditions, however, are founded on the attempt to explain or illustrate the text. The most that can be said is that the chapter indicates the mental depression of the Prophet in the early and unsuccessful period of his ministry.

Probable Date of the Revelations.

Both Muir and Noëldeke assign this chapter to a very early date, the former placing it after chap. xc., and the latter after chap. xciv. in chronological order.

Principal Subjects.

	VERSES
Muhammad comforted by the assurance that God is with him	1–3
The life to come to be preferred to the present life	4, 5
Muhammad exhorted to care for the orphan and beggar	6–11

IN THE NAME OF THE MOST MERCIFUL GOD.

R ₁⁹ ‖ (1) By the brightness *of the morning;* (2) and by the night, when it groweth dark: (3) thy LORD hath not forsaken thee, neither doth he hate *thee.* (4) Verily the life to come *shall be* better for thee than this present life: (5) and thy LORD shall give thee *a reward* wherewith thou shalt be well pleased. (6) Did he not find thee an orphan, and hath he not taken care *of thee?* (7) And did he not find thee wandering in error, and hath he not guided *thee into the truth?* (8) And did he not find thee needy, and hath he not enriched *thee?* (9) Wherefore oppress not the orphan: (10) neither repulse the beggar: (11) but declare the goodness of thy LORD.

---

(1) *The brightness.* "The original word properly signifies the bright part of the day, when the sun shines full out, three or four hours after it is risen."—*Sale.*

(7) *Wandering in error.* That is, in the idolatry of the Arabs. This passage is conclusive against those Muslims who pretend that Muhammad never sinned. See also notes on chap. iv. 105, ix. 43, xl. 57, and xlvii. 21.

(9, 10) Muhammad seems to have shown kindness to the poor and orphans throughout his life. He ever remembered that he had once been in their condition.

See Rodwell's notes on this chapter.

CHAPTER XCIV.

ENTITLED SURAT AL INSHIRÁH (HAVE WE NOT OPENED ?).

Revealed at Makkah.

INTRODUCTION.

LIKE the preceding chapter, this one is addressed to Muhammad himself. It was probably intended to express the encouragement he received from the sense of God's presence with him.

Probable Date of the Revelations.

Since this chapter seems to be closely connected with the one preceding, it is obviously of about the same date.

Principal Subjects.

	VERSES
God made Muhammad's mission easy to him . . .	1–4
He is exhorted to labour and pray after the mission is ended	5–8

IN THE NAME OF THE MOST MERCIFUL GOD.

|| (1) Have we not opened thy breast; (2) and eased thee of thy burden, (3) which galled thy back; (4) and $R \frac{1}{20}$

---

(1) *Opened thy breast.* "By disposing and enlarging it to receive the truth, and wisdom, and prophecy; or, by freeing thee from uneasiness and ignorance? This passage is thought to intimate the *opening* of Muhammad's heart, in his infancy, or when he took his journey to heaven, by the Angel Gabriel, who, having wrung out the black drop, or seed of original sin, washed and cleansed the same, and filled it with wisdom and faith; but some think it relates to the occasion of the preceding chapter."—*Sale, Baidháwí, Yahya.*

(2) *Thy burden, i.e.,* "of thy sins committed before thy mission; or of thy ignorance and trouble of mind."—*Sale.*

raised thy reputation for thee? (5) Verily a difficulty *shall be attended* with ease. (6) Verily a difficulty *shall be attended* with ease. (7) When thou shalt have ended *thy preaching;* labour *to serve God in return for his favours;* (8) and make thy supplication unto thy LORD.

---

(7) *When thou shalt have ended,* or, "*When thou shalt have finished* thy prayer, *labour* in preaching the faith."—*Sale, Baidháwi.*

CHAPTER XCV.

ENTITLED SURAT AL TÍN (THE FIG).

Revealed at Makkah.

INTRODUCTION.

THIS chapter contains what seems to be one of the earliest notices of the judgment-day in the Qurán. Indeed, if vers. 7 and 8 are rightly understood as addressed to Muhammad himself, we may regard this Sura as giving expression to his own apprehension of the doctrine of the judgment-day taught in the Qurán.

Probable Date of the Revelations.

Some Muslim writers, blindly following traditions manufactured to illustrate the Qurán, have declared this chapter to be Madínic. But the statement of the third verse, to say nothing of language and style, plainly points to Makkah. Noëldeke places it immediately after chap. lxxxv.

Principal Subjects.

	VERSES
Oaths that God created man "a most excellent fabric"	1–4
God has made all men vile except true believers	5, 6
None may rightly deny the judgment-day	7, 8

IN THE NAME OF THE MOST MERCIFUL GOD.

|| (1) By the fig and the olive; (2) and by Mount R $\frac{1}{21}$.

---

(1) *The fig and the olive.* "God, say the commentators, swears by these two fruits, because of their great uses and virtues; for the fig is wholesome and easy of digestion, and physically good to carry off

R

Sinai, (3) and this territory of security; (4) verily we created man of a most excellent fabric; (5) afterwards we rendered him the vilest of the vile: (6) except those who believe and work righteousness; for they shall receive an endless reward. (7) What, therefore, shall cause thee to deny the *day of* judgment after *this?* (8) Is not GOD the most wise judge?

---

phlegm, and gravel in the kidneys or bladder, and to remove obstructions of the liver and spleen, and also cures the piles, and the gout, &c.; the olive produces oil, which is not only excellent to eat, but otherwise useful for the compounding of ointments; the wood of the olive-tree, moreover, is good for cleansing the teeth, preventing their growing rotten, and giving a good odour to the mouth; for which reason the prophets, and Muhammad in particular, made use of no other for toothpicks.

"Some, however, suppose that these words do not mean the fruits or trees above mentioned, but two mountains in the Holy Land, where they grow in plenty; or else the temple of Damascus and that at Jerusalem."—*Sale, Baidháwi, Jaláluddín, Zamakhsharí.*

(3) *This territory.* That of Makkah, see chap. xc. I. See also Rodwell's note *in loco.*

(4, 5) "As the commentators generally expound this passage, 'We created man of comely proportion of body, and great perfection of mind; and yet we have doomed him, in case of disobedience, to be an inhabitant of hell.' Some, however, understand the words of the vigorous constitution of man in the prime and strength of his age, and of his miserable decay when he becomes old and decrepit; but they seem rather to intimate the perfect state of happiness wherein man was originally created, and his fall from thence, in consequence of Adam's disobedience, to a state of misery in this world, and becoming liable to one infinitely more miserable in the next."—*Sale.*

The meaning here seems to be about the same as that given under chap. xci. 8.

(7) "Some suppose these words directed to Muhammad, and others to man in general, by way of apostrophe."—*Sale.*

CHAPTER XCVI.

ENTITLED SURAT AL ALAQ (CONGEALED BLOOD).

Revealed at Makkah.

INTRODUCTION.

THE five first verses of this chapter are generally regarded as the first revelation of the Qurán. Like the first verses of chap. lxxiv., these were connected with a vision of Gabriel. These two visions are referred to in chap. lxxxi. as the ground of Muhammad's assurance that he was truly a prophet of the Lord.

As to the vision in which Muhammad heard these five verses summoning him to the prophetic office, one tradition regards it as a real occurrence, while another tradition, said to have emanated from the same source, declares the whole incident to have been a dream. The former of these traditions is that of Urwa Ibn al Zubair, received from Ayesha, who heard it from Muhammad many years after the event. It is given as follows by Noëldeke :—" The revelation commenced with real dreams, which illuminated Muhammad like the glow of the dawn. Thereupon he retired to the solitude of Mount Hirá. When he had spent some time there in devotion, the angel appeared to him and said, 'Read !' Muhammad answered, 'I cannot read.' Thereupon the angel pressed him mightily, and repeated the command. This was all repeated three times, when at last the angel pronounced these five verses. Muhammad was greatly frightened at seeing this, and hastened to his wife, Khadíja, who comforted him."

The other tradition, which represents this vision as simply a dream, is found in Ibn Hishaám, 151, on the authority of Umar Ibn Qatáda. In this tradition it is said that "when Muhammad woke up, the words of the revelation were impressed upon his heart."

After noticing briefly the views of Weil, who thinks Muhammad received in these verses the direction to read publicly a revelation previously given, and who is followed by Muir,—and of Sprenger, who thinks that Muhammad was here commanded to "read the holy books of the Jews and Christians,"—Noëldeke, "following the import of the text, and keeping in mind the tradition, without considering its embellishment," explains the origin of these verses as follows:— "Muhammad, having for some time led an ascetic life in solitude, and having wrought himself up by means of meditation and inner struggles to that condition which is adapted to apparitions, feels himself at last induced by a dream or vision definitely to undertake the work of proclaiming what he had recognised as the truth—in other words, to proclaim himself a prophet. This call to take up this work assumed in his mind the form of the first revelation, the drift of which is, 'Preach to thy fellow-men that which thou hast learned (above all, the unity of God), in the name of thy Lord, who has raised man from the smallest beginning to a higher level, and who therefore may help also thee. Proclaim to them the truth, since thy Lord is the Mighty One who has taught man the art of writing, formerly unknown to thee, and who thereby has furnished thee with a powerful instrument to spread the faith." Noëldeke rejects the position of Weil and Muir, but both his own explanation and the former of the traditions quoted above, which he regards as the most important, seem to me to require the supposition of a period preceding this vision during which Muhammad felt himself drawn toward the prophetic office. The tradition distinctly mentions dreams which occurred previous to this vision, and that the result of these dreams was the awakening of the spirit of inspiration. Granting, then, that these verses are the first of the Qurán, and that the "Soliloquies" of Muir should follow in chronological order, having now been *proclaimed* in public for the first time, may they not still represent the thoughts of Muhammad during these years of doubt and uncertainty?

As to the remainder of the chapter, it is said to refer to the opposition of Abu Jahl to the Muslim cause, and must therefore have been added by Muhammad at a later date.

Probable Date of the Revelations.

The date of the first five verses of this chapter, being the first part of the Qurán, would be the celebrated Night of Power, which occurred in the month of Ramadhán. The remaining verses are of later origin.

Principal Subjects.

	VERSES
Command to Muhammad to recite the Qurán	1–5
Rebuke of Abu Jahl for hindering the Muslim cause	6–14
Abu Jahl threatened with the pains of hell	15–19

IN THE NAME OF THE MOST MERCIFUL GOD.

|| (1) Read, in the name of thy LORD, who hath created R $\frac{1}{2\frac{1}{2}}$. all things; (2) who hath created man of congealed blood. (3) Read by thy most beneficent LORD; (4) who taught the use of the pen; (5) who teacheth man that which he knoweth not. (6) Assuredly. Verily man becometh insolent, (7) because he seeth himself abound in riches. (8) Verily unto thy LORD *shall be* the return *of all.* (9) What thinkest thou *as to* him who forbiddeth (10) *our* servant when he prayeth? (11) What thinkest thou; if he follow the *right* direction; (12) or command piety? (13) What thinkest thou; if he accuse *the divine revelations* of falsehood, and turn his back? (14) Doth he not know that GOD seeth? (15) Assuredly. Verily, if he forbear not, we will drag him by the forelock, (16) the lying, sinful forelock. (17) And let him call his council *to his assis-*

---

(1) *Read.* Rodwell translates the word *Quráa recite.* See his note *in loco.*
(2) *Congealed blood.* "All men being created of thick or concreted blood except Adam, Eve, and Jesus."—*Sale, Yahya.*
See also note on chap. xxii. 5.
(3) *Read, &c.* "These words, containing a repetition of the command, are supposed to be a reply to Muhammad, who, in answer to the former words spoken by the angel, had declared that he could not read, being perfectly illiterate; and intimate a promise that God, who had inspired man with the art of writing, would graciously remedy this defect in him."—*Sale, Baidháwi.*
On the question of Muhammad's ability to read and write, see chaps. xvii. 47, and xxix. 47, and notes there.
(6) *Man becometh insolent.* "The commentators agree the remaining part of the chapter to have been revealed against Abu Jahl, Muhammad's great adversary."—*Sale.*
(9, 10) *Him who forbiddeth.* "For Abu Jahl threatened that if he caught Muhammad in the act of adoration, he would set his foot on his neck; but when he came and saw him in that posture, he suddenly turned back as in a fright; and being asked what was the matter, said there was a ditch of fire between himself and Muhammad, and a terrible appearance of troops to defend him."—*Sale, Baidháwi.*
(15) *Drag him by his forelock.* See note on chap. xi. 56.
(17) *His council, i.e.,* "the council or assembly of the principal Makkans, the far greater part of whom adhered to Abu Jahl."—*Sale.*

tance; (18) we also will call the infernal guards *to cast him into hell.* (19) Assuredly. Obey him not: but *continue to* adore *God,* and draw nigh *unto him.*

---

(18) *Infernal guards.* See chap. lxxiv. 31-32.

CHAPTER XCVII.

ENTITLED SURAT AL QADR (NIGHT OF POWER).

Revealed at Makkah.

INTRODUCTION.

"THE word 'al Qadr,'" says Sale, "signifies 'power,' and 'honour' or 'dignity,' and also the 'divine decree;' and the night is so named either from its excellence above all other nights in the year, or because, as the Muhammadans believe, the 'divine decrees' for the ensuing year are annually on this night fixed and settled, or taken from the 'preserved table' by God's throne, and given to the angels to be executed. On this night Muhammad received his first revelations, when the Qurán, say the commentators, was sent down from the aforesaid table, entire and in one volume, to the lowest heaven, from whence Gabriel revealed it to Muhammad by parcels, as occasion required."

Muir, in his *Life of Mahomet*, vol. ii. p. 138, note, says that that which was sent down to Muhammad was more likely "a clear and vivid view of divine truth, which that night burst upon his mind."

Probable Date of the Revelations.

All authorities agree that this chapter belongs to the earliest Makkan period. Noëldeke places it immediately after chap. xciii.

Principal Subjects.

	VERSES
The Qurán or a divine illumination vouchsafed to Muhammad on the night of al Qadr	1
The night of al Qadr described and lauded	2–5

IN THE NAME OF THE MOST MERCIFUL GOD.

R $\frac{1}{23}$.   ‖ (1) Verily we sent down *the Qurán* in the night of al Qadr. (2) And what shall make thee understand *how excellent* the night of al Qadr *is?* (3) The night of al Qadr *is* better than a thousand months. (4) Therein do the angels descend, and the spirit of *Gabriel* also, by the permission of their LORD, *with his decrees* concerning every matter. (5) It *is* peace until the rising of the morn.

---

(1) *Al Qadr.* "The Muslim doctors are not agreed where to fix the night of al Qadr; the greater part are of opinion that it is one of the ten last nights of Ramadhán, and, as is commonly believed, the seventh of those nights reckoning backwards, by which means it will fall between the 23d and 24th days of that month."—*Sale, Baidháwi, Zamakhshari.*

See also notes on chap. xliv. 2, 3.

(3) *The night, &c.* Muslims usually spend this whole night in fasting and prayer.

(4) *The spirit.* See notes on chap. ii. 86, 253.

Every matter. See above on ver. 1.

(265)

CHAPTER XCVIII.

ENTITLED SURAT AL BAIYANA (THE EVIDENCE).

Revealed at Madína.

INTRODUCTION.

THIS chapter has been thought by some authors to be of Makkan origin, but this opinion has nothing in its favour beyond the fact that it is found among Makkan revelations. We find herein all three of the Madína parties, Idolaters, Jews, and Christians, mentioned ; while the style, language, and contents all point to Madína.

This chapter tells of the divisions and disputes which arose among the different religious sects at Madína, owing to some individuals from each party having become Muslims.

Probable Date of the Revelations.

The mention of disputes having arisen among the Jews and Christians owing to the proclamation of Islám at Madína, points to an early period at Madína as the date of this chapter. The same may be inferred from that kindly spirit in which allusion is made to the Jews, who were so soon separated from the Prophet by bitterest enmity. For reasons like these, Noëldeke places this chapter immediately after chap. ii. in his chronological list of Suras.

Principal Subjects.

	VERSES
The idolaters stagger at the revelations of the Qurán . .	1, 2
Jews and Christians dispute among themselves since the advent of Muhammad and his new religion . .	3, 4
Unbelievers of all classes threatened with divine judgments	5
Muslims are " the best of creatures ; " their reward . .	6-8

IN THE NAME OF THE MOST MERCIFUL GOD.

SULS.
R $\frac{1}{24}$.

|| (1) The unbelievers among those to whom the Scriptures were given, and *among* the idolaters, did not stagger until the *clear* evidence had come unto them: (2) an apostle from GOD, rehearsing *unto them* pure books *of revelations*, wherein *are contained* right discourses. (3) Neither were they unto whom the Scriptures were given divided among themselves until after the *clear* evidence had come unto them. (4) And they were commanded no other *in the Scriptures* than to worship GOD, exhibiting unto him the pure religion, and being orthodox; and to be constant at prayer, and to give alms; and this is the right religion. (5) Verily those who believe not, among those who have received the Scriptures, and among the idolaters, *shall be cast* into the fire of hell, to remain therein *for ever*. These are the worst of creatures. (6) But they who believe and do good works, these are the best of creatures: (7) their

---

(1) *Did not stagger, i.e.,* "did not waver in their religion, or in their promises to follow the truth, when an apostle should come unto them. For the commentators pretend that before the appearance of Muhammad, the Jews and Christians, as well as the worshippers of idols, unanimously believed and expected the coming of that Prophet; until which time they declared they would persevere in their respective religions, and then would follow him; but when he came they rejected him through envy"—*Sale, Jaláluddín, &c.*

Clear evidence, viz., "Muhammad or the Qurán."—*Sale.*

(3) *Until after, &c.* "But when the promised Apostle was sent, and the truth became manifest to them, they withstood the clearest conviction, differing from one another in their opinions, some believing and acknowledging Muhammad to be the prophet foretold in the Scriptures, and others denying it."—*Sale, Baidháwi.*

See notes on chaps. vi. 20, vii. 160.

(4) *They were commanded, &c.* "But these divine precepts in the law and the Gospel have they corrupted, changed, and violated."—*Sale, Baidháwi, &c.*

This is the right religion, i.e., Islám. We have here another proof of the identity of Islám with Judaism and Christianity in the mind of Muhammad. He has therefore pointed to the evidence of the falsity of his own claim to be a true prophet of God.

reward with their LORD *shall be* gardens of perpetual abode, through which rivers flow; they shall remain therein for ever. (8) GOD will be well pleased in them; and they shall be well pleased in him. This *is prepared* for him who shall fear his LORD.

CHAPTER XCIX.

ENTITLED SURAT AL ZILZÁL (THE EARTHQUAKE).

Revealed at Makkah.

INTRODUCTION.

Owing to the rhetorical style of the first verses, this chapter has been considered by some to be Madínic, but the received opinion is that it is Makkan. It appears to be a mere fragment of a Sura.

Probable Date of the Revelations.

Little can be discovered as to the date of this chapter beyond the fact that it belongs to the earliest period of Muhammad's ministry at Makkah.

Principal Subjects.

	VERSES
The judgment-day shall be ushered in by a great earthquake	1–3
The earth shall be inspired to declare why she trembles	4, 5
Men shall be judged according to their deeds	6–8

IN THE NAME OF THE MOST MERCIFUL GOD.

$R \frac{1}{28}$. ‖ (1) When the earth shall be shaken by an earthquake, (2) and the earth shall cast forth her burdens; (3) and a man shall say, What aileth her? (4) On that

---

(1) *An earthquake.* "This earthquake will happen at the first, or, as others say, at the second blast of the trumpet."—*Sale.* See Prelim. Disc., pp. 135, 136.

(2) *Burdens.* "Treasures and dead bodies within it. See chap. lxxxiv."—*Sale.*

day *the earth* shall declare her tidings, (5) for that day thy LORD will inspire her. (6) On that day men shall go forward in distinct classes, that they may behold their works. (7) And whoever shall have wrought good of the weight of an ant, shall behold the same. (8) And whoever shall have wrought evil of the weight of an ant, shall behold the same.

---

(5) *Will inspire her, i.e.,* " will inform all creatures of the occasion of her trembling, and casting forth her treasures and her dead, by the circumstances which shall immediately attend them. Some say the earth will, at the last day, be miraculously enabled to speak, and will give evidence of the actions of her inhabitants."—*Sale.* See also Prelim. Disc., p. 143.

(7, 8) *Weight of an ant.* See note on chap. iv. 38, 39.

CHAPTER C.

ENTITLED SURAT AL ADIYÁT (THE WAR-HORSES WHICH RUN SWIFTLY).

Revealed at Makkah.

INTRODUCTION.

SOME Muslim writers, imagining that the first verses of this chapter refer to the camels employed by Muhammad in warfare, have erroneously classified it as Madínic.

The purport of the revelations is that God will certainly bring to light the secret thoughts of covetous and worldly men.

Probable Date of the Revelations.

On this subject nothing more can be said than that this chapter belongs to an early period of the ministry of Muhammad at Makkah.

Principal Subjects.

	VERSES
Oaths that man is ungrateful to his God	1–6
Man loves the things of this world	7, 8
Man's secret thoughts shall be discovered in the judgment-day	9–11

IN THE NAME OF THE MOST MERCIFUL GOD.

R $\frac{1}{26}$. ‖ (1) By the *war-horses* which run swiftly *to the battle*, with a panting noise; (2) and by those which strike fire,

---

(1–5) "Some will have it that not horses but the camels which went to the battle of Badr, are meant in this passage. Others in-

by dashing *their hoofs against the stones;* (3) and by those which make a sudden incursion *on the enemy* early in the morning, (4) and therein raise the dust, (5) and therein pass through the midst of the *adverse* troops : (6) verily man *is* ungrateful unto his LORD ; (7) and he *is* witness thereof; (8) and he *is* immoderate in the love of *worldly* good. (9) Doth he not know, therefore, when that which *is in* the graves shall be taken forth, (10) and that which *is* in *men's* breasts shall be brought to light, (11) that their LORD *will*, on that day, *be* fully informed concerning them ?

---

terpret all the parts of the oath of the human soul ; but their explications seem a little forced, and therefore I choose to omit them."— *Sale, Yahya, Baidháwi.*

CHAPTER CI.

ENTITLED SURAT AL QÁRÍA (THE STRIKING).

Revealed at Makkah.

INTRODUCTION.

THE name given to the judgment-day, which is made the title of this chapter, is translated "smiting" by Palmer and "blow" by Rodwell. It describes or designates the great day of assizes, not because it will "strike the hearts of all creatures with terror," as Sale has it, but because on that day the wicked will receive the stroke of justice from an angry God.

Probable Date of the Revelations.

All authorities regard this chapter as of Makkan origin. Nöeldeke and Muir alike assign it a place among the earliest revelations of the Qurán.

Principal Subjects.

	VERSES
The day of judgment a day of striking	1–5
The good and bad shall be judged according to their works	6–9
Háwíyah described	10, 11

IN THE NAME OF THE MOST MERCIFUL GOD.

R $\frac{1}{27}$. ‖ (1) The striking! (2) What *is* the striking? (3) And what shall make thee to understand how *terrible* the

---

(1) *The striking, &c.* Savary translates beautifully thus, "Day of calamities! terrible day! Who is able to depict it unto thee? In that day men shall be like unto scattered locusts."

striking *will be?* (4) On that day men shall be like moths scattered abroad, (5) and the mountains shall become like carded wool of various colours *driven by the wind.* (6) Moreover, he whose balance shall be heavy *with good works,* (7) shall lead a pleasing life : (8) but *as to* him whose balance shall be light, (9) his dwelling *shall be* the pit *of hell.* (10) What shall make thee to understand how *frightful* the pit *of hell is?* (11) *It is* a burning fire.

---

(9) *Pit of hell.* "The original word, Háwíyah, is the name of the lowest dungeon of hell, and probably signifies a deep pit or gulf."— *Sale.*

CHAPTER CII.

ENTITLED SURAT AL TAKÁSUR (THE EMULOUS DESIRE OF MULTIPLYING).

Revealed at Makkah.

INTRODUCTION.

THIS chapter is a sort of philippic directed against the covetousness and self-seeking of the Quraish, so often animadverted on in the Qurán. For this reason, perhaps, the judgment-day is referred to only to warn the wicked, and not, as usual, to comfort the righteous. We have given the explanation of this chapter found in Muslim commentators in Sale's note quoted below, though regarding it as a pure fiction.

Probable Date of the Revelations.

Like chap. ci., this one also belongs to the earliest period of the ministry at Makkah.

Principal Subjects.

	VERSE
Men spend their time seeking the things of this world	1–3
The judgment-day shall reveal their folly	3–5
In consequence they shall see hell-fire	6–8

IN THE NAME OF THE MOST MERCIFUL GOD.

R $\frac{1}{28}$. ‖ (1) The emulous desire of multiplying *riches and children* employeth you, (2) until ye visit the graves. (3)

---

(2) *Until ye visit,* &c., *i.e.,* "until ye die. According to the exposition of some commentators, the words should be rendered thus':

By no means *should ye thus employ your time:* hereafter shall ye know *your folly.* (4) Again, by no means: hereafter shall ye know *your folly.* (5) By no means: if ye knew *the consequence hereof* with certainty of knowledge, *ye would not act thus.* (6) Verily ye shall see hell: (7) again, ye shall surely see it with the eye of certainty. (8) Then shall ye be examined, on that day, concerning the pleasures *with which ye have amused yourselves in this life.*

'The contending,' or vieing 'in numbers wholly employeth you, so that ye visit even the graves,' to number the dead; to explain which they relate that there was a great dispute and contention between the descendants of Abd Manáf and the descendants of Sahm, which of the two families were the more numerous; and it being found, on calculation, that the children of Abd Manáf exceeded those of Sahm, the Sahmites said that their numbers had been much diminished by wars in the time of ignorance, and insisted that the dead as well as the living should be taken into the account; and by this way of reckoning they were found to be more than the descendants of Abd Manáf."—*Sale, Zamakhshari, Baidháwi.*

CHAPTER CIII.

ENTITLED SURAT AL ASAR (THE AFTERNOON).

Revealed at Makkah.

INTRODUCTION.

THIS chapter seems to be merely a remnant of some longer Sura. Muir places it at the head of his chronological list of Suras, and therefore first among Muhammad's soliloquies. As to the

Probable Date of the Revelations,

the most that we can say is that the chapter belongs to the number of the early Makkan Suras.

Principal Subjects.

	VERSES
Men generally seek for gain and find loss . . .	1, 2
The righteous, however, are the exception to this rule .	3, 4

IN THE NAME OF THE MOST MERCIFUL GOD.

R $\frac{1}{29}$. ‖ (1) By the afternoon; (2) verily man *employeth himself* in *that which will prove of* loss: (3) except those who believe and do that which is right; (4) and *who* mutually recommend the truth, and mutually recommend perseverance unto each other.

---

(1) *The afternoon,* "or the time from the sun's declination to his setting, which is one of the five appointed times of prayer. The original word also signifies 'the age,' or 'time' in general."—*Sale.*

CHAPTER CIV.

ENTITLED SURAT AL HAMZA (THE SLANDERER).

Revealed at Makkah.

INTRODUCTION.

THIS chapter is also a philippic against the enemies of Muhammad, who, hearing his pious ejaculations, spoke of him as a madman or as one possessed of an evil spirit. It is probable that some person is specially intended, as the commentators will have it, though the application of the chapter is also general.

Like chap. ii., there is mention of the righteous in speaking of future judgment. The

Probable Date of the Revelations

is about the same as that of the three preceding chapters.

Principal Subjects.

	VERSES
Woes pronounced on slanderers and backbiters	1-4
Al Hutama described	5-9

IN THE NAME OF THE MOST MERCIFUL GOD.

‖ (1) Woe unto every slanderer *and* backbiter, (2) who R 1/30 heapeth up riches, and prepareth the same *for the time to come!* (3) He thinketh that his riches will render him

---

(1) *Slanderer.* "Akhnas Ibn Shuraik, or Walíd Ibn al Mughaira, or Umaiya Ibn Khalf, who were guilty of slandering others, and especially the Prophet."—*Sale, Baidháwi, &c.*

immortal. (4) By no means. He shall surely be cast into Al Hutama. (5) And who shall cause thee to understand what Al Hutama *is?* (6) *It is* the kindled fire of GOD; (7) which shall mount above the hearts *of those who shall be cast therein.* (8) Verily it *shall be as* an arched vault above them (9) on columns of vast extent.

---

(4) *Al Hutama.* The name of one of the apartments of hell (Prelim. Disc., p. 148), which is so called because it will 'break in pieces' whatever shall be thrown into it."—*Sale.*

(6) *Kindled fire of God.* "And therefore shall not be extinguished by any."—*Sale, Baidháwi.*

CHAPTER CV.

ENTITLED SURAT AL FÍL (THE ELEPHANT).

Revealed at Makkah.

INTRODUCTION.

THIS chapter is remarkable for its allusion to an incident in the history of Makkah, as an example of how God deals with His enemies. The inappropriateness of the example, however, will be manifest when we recollect that the army destroyed was an army of "the people of the book," going to avenge an insult offered their holy place by the idolaters, who are here being warned. The story of the commentators, with its embellishments, is given in Sale's note quoted below. The chapter is probably a fragment of a longer Sura.

Probable Date of the Revelation.

Noëldeke places this chapter in the first Makkan period, and in his chronological list of Suras it follows chap. cii.

Principal Subject.

VERSES

The army of Abraha destroyed for attacking the Kaabah . 1–5

IN THE NAME OF THE MOST MERCIFUL GOD.

‖ (1) Hast thou not seen how thy LORD dealt with the R 3¹ɪ masters of the elephant? (2) Did he not make their

---

(1) *How thy Lord dealt, &c.* "This chapter relates to the following piece of history, which is famous among the Arabs. Abraha Ibn al Sabáh, surnamed al Ashram, *i.e.*, the *slit-nosed*, king or viceroy of

treacherous design an occasion of drawing them into error; (3) and send against them flocks of birds, (4) which cast

---

Yaman, who was an Ethiopian and of the Christian religion, having built a magnificent church at Sanâa, with a design to draw the Arabs to go in pilgrimage thither, instead of visiting the temple of Makkah, the Quraish, observing the devotion and concourse of the pilgrims at the Kaabah began considerably to diminish, sent one Nufail, as he is named by some, of the tribe of Kinánáh, who, getting into the aforesaid church by night, defiled the altar and walls thereof with his excrements. At this profanation Abraha being highly incensed, vowed the destruction of the Kaabah, and accordingly set out against Makkah at the head of a considerable army, wherein were several elephants, which he had obtained of the king of Ethiopia, their number being, as some say, thirteen, though others mention but one. The Makkans, at the approach of so considerable a host, retired to the neighbouring mountains, being unable to defend their city or temple; but God himself undertook the protection of both. For when Abraha drew near to Makkah, and would have entered it, the elephant on which he rode, which was a very large one, and named Mahmúd, refused to advance any nigher to the town, but knelt down whenever they endeavoured to force him that way, though he would rise and march briskly enough if they turned him towards any other quarter: and while matters were in this posture, on a sudden a large flock of birds, like swallows, came flying from the sea-coast, every one of which carried three stones, one in each foot, and one in its bill; and these stones they threw down upon the heads of Abraha's men, certainly killing every one they struck. Then God sent a flood, which swept the dead bodies, and some of those who had not been struck with the stones, into the sea: the rest fled towards Yaman, but perished by the way; none of them reaching Sanáa, except only Abraha himself, who died soon after his arrival there, being struck with a sort of plague or putrefaction, so that his body opened and his limbs rotted off by piecemeal. It is said that one of Abraha's army, named Abu Yaqsúm, escaped over the Red Sea into Ethiopia, and going directly to the king, told him the tragical story; and upon that prince's asking him what sort of birds they were that had occasioned such a destruction, the man pointed to one of them, which had followed him all the way, and was at that time hovering directly over his head, when immediately the bird let fall the stone, and struck him dead at the king's feet."—*Sale, Baidháwi, Zamakhshari, Jaláluddín.*

Muir ascribes the destruction of Abraha's army to an outbreak of virulent small-pox (the word translated small stones meaning also small-pox), which resulted in a panic which scattered the army among the valleys, where they, being abandoned by their guides, perished. See *Life of Mahomet*, Introd. vol. i. p. cclxv. Muhammad, however, gives the legend of the idolaters as a veritable piece of inspired revelation. See also Rodwell's note *in loco.*

down upon them stones of baked clay; (5) and render them like the leaves of corn eaten *by cattle?*

---

(4) *Stones of baked clay.* "These stones were of the same kind with those by which the Sodomites were destroyed (chap. xi. 81), and were no bigger than vetches, though they fell with such force as to pierce the helmet and the man through. It is said also that on each stone was written the name of him who was to be slain by it."—*Sale.*

CHAPTER CVI.

ENTITLED SURAT AL QURAISH (THE QURAISH).

Revealed at Makkah.

INTRODUCTION.

LIKE the preceding chapter, this one also appears to be a mere fragment of a longer Sura. Some writers regard it as a portion of chap. cv. In it Muhammad exhorts the Quraish to thank the Lord of the Kaabah for their commercial blessings, connected with the dispatch of the two annual caravans.

Probable Date of the Revelation.

For reasons already given, the date of this chapter must be the same as that of chap. cv.

Principal Subject.

	VERSES
The Quraish exhorted to thank God for commercial privileges	1–4

IN THE NAME OF THE MOST MERCIFUL GOD.

R ¹/₅ ‖ (1) For the uniting of *the tribe of* Quraish ; (2) their uniting in *sending forth* the caravan *of merchants and pur-*

---

(1) *For the uniting, &c.* "Some connect these words with the following, and suppose the natural order to be, 'Let them serve the Lord of this house, for the uniting,' &c. Others connect them with the last words of the preceding chapter, and take the meaning to be, that God had so destroyed the army of Abraha for the uniting of the Quraish, &c. And the last opinion is confirmed by one copy, men-

veyors in winter and summer; (3) let them serve the LORD of this house, who supplieth them with food against hunger, (4) and hath rendered them secure from fear.

---

tioned by al Baidháwi, wherein this and the preceding make but one chapter."—*Sale.*

(2) *The caravan.* "It was Háshim, the great-grandfather of Muhammad, who first appointed the two yearly caravans here mentioned; one of which set out in the winter for Yaman, and the other in summer for Syria."—*Sale.*

(3) *Who supplieth . . . food.* "By means of the aforesaid caravans of purveyors; or, 'who supplied them with food in time of a famine,' which those of Makkah had suffered."—*Sale, Baidháwi.*

(4) *Secure from fear.* "By delivering them from Abraha and his troops, or by making the territory of Makkah a place of security."—*Sale.*

CHAPTER CVII.

ENTITLED SURAT AL MÁÚN (NECESSARIES).

Revealed at Makkah.

INTRODUCTION.

THIS chapter, which is evidently merely a fragment of a longer Sura, deals with those who fail to make their religious practice conform to their profession. The title is taken from the seventh verse. It is also sometimes entitled Dín (Religion), which name is found in the first verse.

Probable Date of the Revelations.

The first part of this chapter is probably Makkan, though Zamakhshari, Baidháwi, &c. (Itqán 30) classify the whole chapter as Madínic. Noëldeke places it very early in the first period. Muir fixes it, with more probability, at about the fifth year of Muhammad's public ministry. Verses 4–7 may also be Makkan, but there is much in favour of their being regarded as Madínic.

Principal Subjects.

	VERSES
Denunciation of the infidels, who deny the Qurán and oppress the orphan	1, 2
Hypocrites rebuked for neglect of prayer and charity .	3–7

IN THE NAME OF THE MOST MERCIFUL GOD.

R 3/3 ‖ (1) What thinkest thou of him who denieth the *future* judgment as a falsehood? (2) *It is* he who pusheth away

---

(1) *Judgment as a falsehood.* Rodwell translates, "who treateth our religion as a lie."

(2) *He who pusheth away the orphan.* "The person here intended,

the orphan; (3) and stirreth not up *others* to feed the poor. (4) Woe be unto those who pray, (5) *and* who are negligent at their prayer: (6) who play the hypocrites, (7) and deny necessaries *to the needy.*

---

according to some, was Abu Jahl, who turned away an orphan, to whom he was guardian, and who came to him naked, and asked for some relief out of his own money. Some say it was Abu Sufián, who, having killed a camel, when an orphan begged a piece of the flesh, beat him away with his staff; and others think it was al Walíd Ibn al Mughaira, &c."—*Sale.*

See notes on chap. xciii.

(7) *Necessaries.* "The original word, al máún, properly signifies *utensils*, or whatever is of necessary use, as *a hatchet, a pot, a dish,* and *a needle,* to which some add *a bucket* and *a hand-mill;* or, according to a tradition of Ayesha, *fire, water,* and *salt;* and this signification it bore in the time of ignorance; but since the establishment of the Muhammadan religion, the word has been used to denote alms, either legal or voluntary; which seems to be the true meaning in this place."—*Sale.*

CHAPTER CVIII.

ENTITLED SURAT AL KAUTHAR (ABUNDANCE).

Revealed at Makkah.

INTRODUCTION.

THESE three verses are said by the best authorities to have been revealed to comfort Muhammad on account of an insult offered him by al Ás Ibn Waíl, who called Muhammad *a tailless man, i.e.,* one having no sons. The opinion of those, who regard the chapter to be Madínic, because they think it refers to the death of Muhammad's son Ibrahím, is wrong. In such a case the taunt would be ridiculous.

Probable Date of the Revelations.

This chapter is one of the oldest in the Qurán, and therefore it must be placed among the early Makkan Suras.

Principal Subject.

                   VERSES
Muhammad comforted with abundance of goods . . 1–3

IN THE NAME OF THE MOST MERCIFUL GOD.

$R \frac{1}{34}$. ‖ (1) Verily we have given thee al Kauthar. (2)

---

(1) *Al Kauthar.* "This word signifies *abundance,* especially of good, and thence the gift of wisdom and prophecy, the Qurán, the office of intercessor, &c. Or it may imply abundance of children, followers, and the like. It is generally, however, expounded of a river in Paradise of that name, whence the water is derived into Muhammad's pond, of which the blessed are to drink before their admission into

Wherefore pray unto thy LORD, and slay *the victims*. (3) Verily he who hateth thee shall be childless.

---

that place. According to a tradition of the Prophet's, this river, wherein his Lord promised him abundant good, is sweeter than honey, whiter than milk, cooler than snow, and smoother than cream; its banks are of chrysolites, and the vessels to drink thereout of silver; and those who drink of it shall never thirst."—*Sale.*

See also Prelim. Disc., p. 153.

This latter interpretation of *Kauthar* as a river of Paradise, though old, is, according to Noëldeke, certainly wrong. The word is in reality an adjective meaning "much, ample, in abundance," and not a proper noun.

(2) *Slay the victims.* "Which are to be sacrificed at the pilgrimage in the valley of Mina. Al Baidháwi explains the words thus: Pray with fervency and intense devotion, not out of hypocrisy; and slay the fatted camels and oxen, and distribute the flesh among the poor; for he says this chapter is the counterpart of the preceding, exhorting to those virtues which are opposite to the vices there condemned."—*Sale.*

CHAPTER CIX.

ENTITLED SURAT AL KÁFIRÚN (THE UNBELIEVERS).

Revealed at Makkah.

INTRODUCTION.

This chapter contains the reply of Muhammad to certain of the Quraish who proposed a compromise between Islám and the ancient religion of Makkah, whereby he would concede to their gods an honourable place. Probably the occasion was like that of the lapse described in the notes on chap. xxii. 53.

Probable Date of the Revelation.

Noëldeke places this chapter near the end of the first period of Muhammad's Makkan ministry, because it predicates a time when the Prophet could have had disputes with the idolaters, and a time after which they could have come to him with an offer of compromise. The date would therefore be about the fourth or fifth year of the Call.

Principal Subject.

	VERSES
Muhammad declines to compromise with idolatry	1–6

IN THE NAME OF THE MOST MERCIFUL GOD.

R $\frac{1}{3\,5}$. ‖ (1) Say: O unbelievers, (2) I will not worship that which ye worship; (3) nor will ye worship that which I

---

(1) *O unbelievers.* "It is said that certain of the Quraish once proposed to Muhammad, that if he would worship their gods for a

worship. (4) Neither do I worship that which ye worship; (5) neither do ye worship that which I worship. (6) Ye have your religion, and I my religion.

---

year, they would worship his God for the same space of time; upon which this chapter was revealed."—*Sale.*

(2-6) "These verses," says Muir, "breathe a spirit of uncompromising hostility to idolatry."—*Life of Mahomet*, vol. ii. p. 141.

CHAPTER CX.

ENTITLED SURAT AL NASR (ASSISTANCE).

Revealed at Madína.

INTRODUCTION.

THIS chapter has all the appearance of being a fragment of a Madína Sura. It may, however, have been composed at Makkah, as stated by Muslim, i. 446, and by Waqkídi, who says it was composed after the battle of Hunain. Noëldeke's opinion is that it was composed when Muhammad was about to march against Makkah, and when he could count with certainty on the successful issue of the campaign. The chapter therefore records Muhammad's anticipation of the success of his religion.

Probable Date of the Revelation.

The date of this chapter, according to the views expressed above, is about A.H. 8.

Principal Subject.

VERSES

Command to praise God for the victory of Islám . . . 1-3

IN THE NAME OF THE MOST MERCIFUL GOD.

R $\frac{1}{36}$. ‖ (1) When the assistance of GOD shall come, and the victory; (2) and thou shalt see the people enter into the

---

(1) *Victory, i.e.,* "when God shall cause thee to prevail over thine enemies, and thou shalt take the city of Makkah."—*Sale.*

See notes on chap. xlviii. 1 and 18. This verse corresponds in sentiment with xlviii. 1-3, and probably belongs to the same date. The style and matter are Madínic.

religion of GOD by troops; (3) celebrate the praise of thy LORD, and ask pardon of him; for he is inclined to forgive.

---

(2) *By troops.* " Which happened in the ninth year of the Hijra, when Muhammad having made himself master of Makkah, and obliged the Quraish to submit to him, the rest of the Arabs came in to him in great numbers, and professed Islám."—*Sale, Baidháwi.*

See a similar expression in chap. xxxix. 71, 73, a late Makkan Sura, containing Madínic passages.

(3) *Ask pardon of him.* " Most of the commentators agree that this chapter was revealed before the taking of Makkah, and suppose it gave Muhammad warning of his death; for they say that when he read it al Abbás wept; and being asked by the Prophet what was the reason of his weeping, answered, ' Because it biddeth thee to prepare for death;' to which Muhammad replied, 'It is as thou sayest.' And hence, adds Jaláluddín, after the revelation of this chapter, the Prophet was more frequent in praising and asking pardon of God, because he thereby knew that his end approached: for Makkah was taken in the eighth year of the Hijra, and he died in the beginning of the tenth."—*Sale.*

Muhammad is here again described as a sinner. See notes on chaps. ii. 253, iv. 105, ix. 43, xl. 57, xlvii. 21, and xciii. 7.

CHAPTER CXI.

ENTITLED SURAT AL ABU LAHAB.

Revealed at Makkah.

INTRODUCTION.

THIS chapter was composed soon after the assembly of the Bani Háshim, called together by Muhammad in order that he might invite them to turn to God and accept of Islám. His uncle, Abd al Uzza Ibn Abdul Muttalib, who was surnamed Abu Lahab, came with others, but discovering the nature of the meeting, cried out, "Let him be damned! Is this all thou hast called us together for?" At these words the whole assembly broke up, as they could see no sense in Muhammad's speech when he told them he was a "warner sent them before a grievous chastisement." The words of this chapter contain the curses of Muhammad uttered against Abu Lahab on this occasion.

Probable Date of the Revelation.

Muir and Noëldeke fix the date of this chapter at a very early period of the Prophet's ministry at Makkah. But surely the intensity of the hatred here manifest between the parties points to a later date. I would say the fourth or fifth year of the Call.

Principal Subject.

	VERSES
The curse of Muhammad against Abu Lahab and his house .	1-5

IN THE NAME OF THE MOST MERCIFUL GOD.

‖ (1) The hands of Abu Lahab shall perish, and he R $\frac{1}{37}$ shall perish. (2) His riches shall not profit him, neither that which he hath gained. (3) He shall go down to be burned into flaming fire; (4) and his wife *also,* bearing wood, (5) *having* on her neck a cord of twisted fibres of a palm-tree.

---

(1) *Abu Lahab.* "Abu Lahab was the surname of Abdul Uzza, one of the sons of Abdul Muttallib, and uncle to Muhammad. He was a bitter enemy to his nephew, and opposed the establishment of the new religion to the utmost of his power.

"By the *hands* of Abu Lahab some commentators, by a synecdoche, understand his person; others, by a metonymy, his affairs in general, they being transacted with those members; or his hopes in this world and the next."—*Sale, Baidhāwi, Jalāluddín.*

He shall perish. "He died of grief and vexation at the defeat his friends had received at Badr, surviving that misfortune but seven days. They add that his corpse was left above ground three days till it stank, and then some negroes were hired to bury him."—*Sale, Baidháwi.*

The readers should remember that the stories related by the commentators relating to the enemies of the Prophet are all open to suspicion, and none should be received as true without careful consideration. See on this point Muir's *Life of Mahomet,* Introd., p. lviii.

(2) *His riches, &c.* "And accordingly his great possessions, and the rank and esteem in which he lived at Makkah, were of no service to him, nor could protect him against the vengeance of God. Al Baidháwi mentions also the loss of his son Utba, who was torn to pieces by a lion in the way to Syria, though surrounded by the whole caravan."—*Sale.*

(3) *Flaming fire.* "Arab *.nár dhát lahab,* alluding to the surname of Abu Lahab, which signifies the 'father of flames.'"—*Sale.*

(4) *His wife.* "Her name was Umm Jamíl: she was the daughter of Harb, and sister of Abu Sufián."—*Sale.*

Bearing wood. "For fuel in hell, because she fomented the hatred which her husband bore to Muhammad; or bearing a bundle of thorns and brambles, because she carried such, and strewed them by night in the Prophet's way."—*Sale, Baidháwi, Jalāluddín.*

CHAPTER CXII.

ENTITLED SURAT AL IKHLÁS (DECLARATION OF GOD'S UNITY).

Revealed at Makkah.

INTRODUCTION.

"THIS chapter," says Sale, "is held in particular veneration by the Muhammadans, and declared by a tradition of their Prophet to be equal in value to a third part of the whole Qurán. It is said to have been revealed in answer to the Quraish, who asked Muhammad concerning the distinguishing attributes of the God he invited them to worship." Whether, as Muir seems to think, this is the confession of faith adopted by Muhammad immediately after his call to the prophetic office or not, it seems clearly to be one of the earliest chapters of the Qurán.

Probable Date of the Revelation.

Muir places this chapter among the earliest Makkan Suras. Nöeldeke places it near the end of the first period, or about the fourth year of the Call. I agree with Muir, inasmuch as a creed of a later date would have been more diffuse in style.

Principal Subject.

	VERSES
The unity of God declared	1–4

IN THE NAME OF THE MOST MERCIFUL GOD.

R $\frac{1}{3\,8}$. || (1) Say, *God* is one GOD; (2) the eternal GOD; (3)

(1, 2) *One God.* See note on chap. ii. 164, and Prelim. Disc., pp. 118, 119, note.

he begetteth not, neither is he begotten ; (4) and there is not any one like unto him.

---

(3) *He begetteth not.* This is directed against the Makkan idolaters, who worshipped angels, whom they called " daughters of God." See Prelim. Disc., pp. 38, 39.

Neither is he begotten. The primary allusion here is to the idolatry of the Quraish, noticed in the preceding note, but afterwards was made to apply to the Jews, who are said to have called Ezra the son of God, and to the Christians who worship Christ, the Son of God. See notes on chaps. ix. 30, and iv. 169.

(4) This verse, with those which precede, expresses a Bible truth. The whole chapter is made up of Scriptural phrases.

CHAPTER CXIII.

ENTITLED SURAT AL FALAQ (THE DAYBREAK).

Revealed at Makkah.

INTRODUCTION.

"THE commentators relate," says Sale, "that Lubaid, a Jew, with the assistance of his daughters, bewitched Muhammad by tying eleven knots on a cord which they hid in a well: whereupon Muhammad falling ill, God revealed this chapter and the following, and Gabriel acquainted him with the use he was to make of them, and of the place where the cord was hidden: according to whose directions the Prophet sent Ali to fetch the cord, and the same being brought, he repeated the two chapters over it, and at every verse (for they consist of eleven) a knot was loosed, till, on finishing the last words, he was entirely freed from the charm."

This chapter with the next are called by Muslims the *al Mauwidhatáni*, or Preservative Chapters. They engrave them upon amulets, &c., as charms against evil influences.

Probable Date of the Revelations.

We cannot do better than give the following from Noëldeke:—

"To fix the date of these two Suras (cxiii. and cxiv.) is a most difficult task. This is due to the grotesqueness of the style adopted in such superstitious productions, which allow of no safe conclusion. Indeed, we cannot even be sure these chapters originated before the Hijra. For granting that Muhammad did utter such magic formula in his last years, it assuredly differed from the usual style of the Madína Suras. It is therefore possible that in the tradition, embellished with marvellous excrescences, there is a certain modicum of truth. Possible, however, it is also, as Wiel thinks, that Muhammad applied incantations already existing in order to free himself from the imaginary spell. To such incantations against Satanic influences allusion seems to be made in chaps. xli. 36 and xvi. 160, and in other places. Be this as it may, there can be no doubt that these two Suras have originated at the same time. How difficult the point of chronology is appears evident from the fact that not even Muir, who otherwise fixes the date of each Sura so definitely, ventures to give a decided opinion. He says, indeed, that the date of these Suras is unimportant, but in this he is certainly wrong. It would be of great importance to know certainly the period whereto we might assign these evidences of Muhammad's superstition."

The exact date of these chapters cannot therefore be determined. Since, however, such formula as this is alluded to in the Makkan chapters xvi. and xli., I cannot agree with Noëldeke in thinking we cannot decide whether these chapters belong to Makkah. I also think the peculiarity of the style a strong argument in favour of Weil's suggestion that these formulæ were adopted by Muhammad from incantations already in popular use among the Arabs. The fear of being called a sorcerer would have forbidden Muhammad from adopting anything grotesque at a late date in his ministry.

IN THE NAME OF THE MOST MERCIFUL GOD.

|| (1) Say, I fly for refuge unto the LORD of the day- R $\frac{1}{3\cdot 9}$. break, (2) *that he may deliver me* from the mischief *of those things* which he hath created; (3) and from the mischief of the night, when it cometh on; (4) and from the mis-

(1) *Daybreak.* "The original word properly signifies a *cleaving*, and denotes, says al Baidháwi, the production of all things in general from the darkness of privation to the light of existence, and especially of those things which proceed from others, as springs, rain, plants, children, &c.; and hence it is used more particularly to signify the breaking forth of the light from darkness, which is a most wonderful instance of the divine power."—*Sale.*

(2) *From the mischiefs, i.e.,* "from the mischiefs proceeding either from the perverseness and evil choice of those beings which have a power to choose, or the natural effects of necessary agents, as fire, poison, &c., the world being good in the whole, though evils may follow from these two causes."—*Sale, Baidháwi.*

(3) *From . . . the night.* "Or, as the words may be rendered, 'From the mischief of the moon when she is eclipsed.'"—*Sale.*

(4) *Women blowing on knots.* Rodwell has "weird women." "That is, of witches, who used to tie knots in a cord and to blow on them, uttering at the same time certain magical words over them, in order to work on or debilitate the person they had a mind to

chief of *women* blowing on knots; (5) and from the mischief of the envious, when he envieth.

---

injure. This was a common practice in former days, what they call in France *Nouër l'eguillete;* and the knots which the wizards in the northern parts tie, when they sell mariners a wind (if the stories told of them be true), are also relics of the same superstition."—*Sale.* On the superstitious fears of Muhammad see Muir's *Life of Mahomet*, vol. iii. pp. 61, 62, and iv. p. 80.

CHAPTER CXIV.

ENTITLED SURAT AL NÁS (MEN).

Revealed at Makkah.

INTRODUCTION.

THIS chapter so much resembles the one preceding it, that I have recorded all there that need be said. The date may also be regarded as the same.

IN THE NAME OF THE MOST MERCIFUL GOD.

‖ (1) Say, I fly for refuge unto the LORD of men, (2) the king of men, (3) the GOD of men, (4) *that he may deliver me* from the mischief of the whisperer, who slyly with- R $\frac{1}{40}$.

(1-4) *The whisperer, &c., i.e.,* "the devil, who withdraweth when a man mentioneth God, or hath recourse to his protection."—*Sale.*

The whisperers seem to have been evil spirits and men, judging by what follows.

See notes on the preceding chapter.

(5, 6) *Evil suggestions . . from genii and men.* This chapter shows that Muhammad felt himself to be in some manner specially moved by evil influences. More than once he offered up special prayer for protection against such; see chap. xxiii. 98. He attributed his mistakes to Satanic influences. See notes on chaps. xxii. 53, and liii. 19, 20. Other prophets are said to have been open to the evil suggestions of demons and men. See chaps. vi. 112, and vii. 200, 201, also note and references at chap. iv. 116.

It should be observed that protection is also sought against the evil suggestions *of men.* He no doubt had in mind the suggestions of the aged Makkan chief Walid Ibn al Mughaira and others of his townsmen, who advised him to a compromise, whereby the true God

draweth, (5) who whispereth evil suggestions into the breasts of men; (6) from genii and men.

---

should be worshipped along with the gods of the Kaabah. These suggestions led to the lapse referred to in some of the passages noted above, and which left an indelible impression upon Muhammad's mind ever afterwards.

INDEX.

A Table Showing the Approximate Chronological Order of the Chapters of the Qurán.

According to Jaláluddín.	According to Noëldeke.	According to Muir.	Jaláluddín.	Noëldeke.	Muir.	Jaláluddín.	Noëldeke.	Muir.	Jaláluddín.	Noëldeke.	Muir.
96	96	103[1]	75	100	110	40	38	37	3	46	16
68	74	100	104	79	85	41	36	30	33	6	13
73	111	99	77	77	83	42	43	26	60	13	29
74	106	91	50	78	78	43	72	15	4	2[12]	7
111	108	106	90	88	77	44	67	51	99	98	113
81	104	1	86	89	76	45	23	46[9]	57	64	114
87	107	101	54	75	75	46	21	72	47	62	98[13]
92	102	95	38	83	70	51	25	35	62	8	2
89	105	102	7	69	109	88	17	36	55	47	3
93	92	104	72	51	107	18	27	19	76	3	8
94	90	82	36	52	55	16	18	18	13	61	47
103	94	92	25	56	56	71	32[8]	27	98	57	62
100	93	105	35	70	67[7]	14	41	42	59	4	5
108	97	89	19	55	53	21	45	40	110	65	59
102	86	90	20	112	32	23	16	38	24	59	4
107	91	93	56	109	39	32	30	25	22	33	58
109	80	94	26	113[4]	73	52	11	20	63	63	65
105	68	108	27	114[5]	79	67	14	43	58	24	63
113	87	96[2]	28	1	54	69	12	12	49	58	24
114	95	113	17	54[6]	34	70	40	11	66	22	33
112	103	74	10	37	31	78	28	10	65	48	57
53	85	111	11	71	69	79	39	14	64	66	61
80	73	87[3]	12	76	68	82	29	6	61	60	48
97	101	97	15	44	41	84	31	64	48	110	60
91	99	88	6	50	71	30	42	28	5	49	66
85	82	80	37	20	52	29	10	23	9[10]	9	49
95	81	81	31	26	50	83	34	22	1[11]	5	9
106	53	84	34	15	45	2	35	21	...	...	...
101	84	86	39	19	44	8	7	17	...	...	...

[1] Muir's first period comprises eighteen Suras, which he calls "rhapsodies."
[2] Muir's second period begins here.
[3] Muir's third period begins here.
[4] Indetermediate.   [5] Intermediate.
[6] Here begin the Suras of Noëldeke's second period.
[7] Here begins Muir's fourth period.
[8] Here begin the Suras of Noëldeke's third period.
[9] Here begins Muir's fifth period.   [10] The last Sura in Jaláluddín's list.
[11] Jaláluddín regards the place of this Sura as indeterminable and yet as belonging to an early period of the ministry of the Prophet.
[12] Here begin the Madína Suras.
[13] Here begin the Madína chapters, according to Muir.

AN INDEX

TO THE

PRELIMINARY DISCOURSE, THE TEXT, AND NOTES ON THE QURÁN.

Aaron. See *Moses*.
Abbás, one of Muhammad's uncles, taken at Badr and obliged to ransom himself, viii. 69 n.; professes Islám, viii. 71 n.; remarkable for his loud voice, ix. 25 n.
Abdullah, the father of Muhammad, P.D. 68.
Abdullah Ibn Ubbai Solúl, the hypocrite, admired for his person and eloquence, lxiii. 14 n.; raises a scandalous story of Ayesha, xxiv. 11 n.; is present at an interview between Muhammad and his adversaries, xxxiii. 1 n.; occasions a quarrel, xlix. 9 n.; promises to assist the Bani Nadhír, but fails to do so, lix. 12 n.; endeavours to debauch Muhammad's men at Ohod, iii. 122 n.; excused from going on the expedition to Tabúk, ix. 43; desires Muhammad's prayers in his last sickness, and to be buried in the Prophet's shirt, ix. 81-85 n.
Abdullah Ibn Omm Maktum, a blind man, occasions a passage of the Qurán, lxxx. introd.
Abdullah Ibn Saad, one of Muhammad's amanuenses, imagines himself inspired and corrupts the Qurán, vi. 94 n.
Abdullah Ibn Salám, a Jew, intimate with Muhammad: his honesty, iii. 74 n.; supposed to have assisted in composing the Qurán, xvi. 105 n.
A'bdast. See *Purifications*.
Abd al Mutallib, the grandfather of Muhammad, P.D. 68.
Abd Manáf, a dispute between his descendants and the Sahmites, cii. 1 n.
Abd-ul-Rahmán Ibn Auf, one of Muhammad's first converts, P.D. 75; an instance of his charity, ix. 80 n.

Abel, the story of Cain and Abel, v. 30–34; his ram sacrificed by Abraham, xxxviii. 107 n.

Abraha, his army destroyed near Makkah, cv. 1 n.

Abraham, the patriarch, an idolater in his youth, vi. 77–84; rejects the idols of his fathers, vi. 76–84 n., xliii. 25–27; demolishes the Chaldean idols, xxi. 59; disputes with Nimrod, ii. 258 n.; escapes the fire into which he was thrown by order of Nimrod, xxi. 69 n.; prays for his father, viii. 115; entertains angels, xi. 69, li. 24–30; called the friend of God, iv. 124 n.; his sacrifice of his son, xxxvii. 101 n.; his religion was that of Islám, ii. 130–132 n.; builder of the Kaabah, ii. 125; his scriptures attest the Qurán, lxxxvii. 18, 19; legend concerning "the place of Abrahám," ii. 125 n.; is compared with Muhammad, xxi. introd., xxix. 17–23 n.

Abraham's place, the stone in it, P.D. 185. See also *Kaabah*.

Abrogation, stated and defined, v. 47–50 notes, xvii. 35 n., xxiv. 2 n., xiii. 39, lxxxvii. introd. and notes, P.D. 110, 111; the number of abrogated verses, ii. 105 n., xvi. 69 n., and 103.

Abu Baqr, is converted to Islám, P.D. 75.

Abu Lahab, Muhammad's uncle and bitter enemy, P.D. 76; his and his wife's punishment, cxi. 1, &c.

Abu Tálib, protects Muhammad against his enemies, P.D. 77; his death, P.D. 79; Muhammad refuses to pray for him on his deathbed, ix. 114 n.

Abul Qásim. See *Mahdi*.

Adam, traditions concerning his creation, ii. 30 n., and xvii. 12; his likeness the likeness of Jesus, iii. 58 n.; worshipped by angels, ii. 34 n., vii. 11; his fall, ii. 35 n., vii. 11–26; meets Eve at Mount Arafát, and retires with her to Ceylon, ii. 35 n.; his posterity extracted from his loins by God to acknowledge him for their Lord, vii. 173; names his eldest son as directed by the devil, vii. 190 n.

Adites, their progenitors, P.D. 20; their prodigious stature, P.D. 22, vii. 70; destroyed on account of their idolatry, P.D. 21, 22, xlvi. 20–27, vii. 73–80 notes. See also *Húd*.

Adoption, creates no matrimonial impediment, xxxiii. 4 n.

Adulterers, Muhammad's sentence against them, iii. 23 n.

Adultery, laws concerning, P.D. 209, iii. 23 n., and xxiv. 2–13 notes; its punishment, iv. 4, 15, 24, and xxiv. 2 and 3.

Affliction, meritorious, ii. 157 n.

Ahl-i-Kitab, who are so called in the Qurán, ii. 61 n.

Ahmad. See *Muhammad*.

Ahqáf, its people destroyed, xlvi. 20–27.

Al Aika. See *Midianites*.

INDEX.

Aila or Elath, the Sabbath-breakers there changed into apes, ii. 64, 65 notes.
Al Aswad, the record of the two liars, P.D. 271, 272, v. 59 n.
Alexander the Great, a prophet of Islám, xviii. 82 n.
Ali, is adopted by Muhammad and becomes his disciple, P.D. 75; veneration of the Shíahs for him, P.D. 226; sent to Makkah to publish part of the Qurán, ix. 63 n.; the charity and abstinence of him and his family, lxxvi. 10 n.
Almsgiving (Ziqát), regulation concerning, P.D. 172, 173, ii. 109 n.; a condition of salvation, lxiii. 10, and iii. 92; comparison between Muslim and Jewish almsgiving, P.D. 174, 175; charity begins at home, ii. 214 n.; motives to give liberally, iv. 37 n., and ix. 104 n.; what should be given, ii. 219, 220; liberal givers rewarded, ii. 261–280.
Amalakites, the tribe, its descent, conquests, and destruction, P.D. 24.
Amar and Arbád, attempt to kill Muhammad, and their punishment, xiii. 14 n.
Amar (Abu), a Christian monk and violent enemy to Muhammad, ix. 108 n.
Amar (Banu), their abstinence on the pilgrimage, vii. 32 n.
Amína, Muhammad's mother, he is not permitted to pray for her, ix. 114 n.
Ammár Ibn Yásar, tortured by the Quraish because of his faith, xvi. 108 n.
Amrán. See *Imrán*.
Ámru Banu, build a mosque at Quba, ix. 108 n.
Ámru Ibn Luhai, the great introducer of idolatry among the Arabs, vi. 143 and 144 n.
Anachronisms, in the Qurán, ii. 48, 49, v. 23 n. and 47–50 notes, vii. 64, 128 and 131 notes, xiii. 39, xvii. 35 n., xxiv. 2 n., and lxx. 23.
Anam, the name of Luqman's son, xxxi. 12 n.
Angel, of death. See *Azrail*.
Angels, their original, vii. 12 n.; impeccable, xviii. 48; of different forms and orders, xxxv. 1 n.; believed by the Arabs to be daughters of God, xvi. 59 n.; they worship Adam, ii. 34; assist the Muslims, iii. 13 n. and 125 n., viii. 9 n., ix. 26 and 40 n.; appear to Abraham and Lot, iv. 116 n.; intercede for sinners, xlii. 3; brought down the Qurán from heaven, xvi. 104; record the deeds of men, x. 22 n., l. 16, 17, lxxxii. 10–12; guard the precincts of hell, lxxiv. 31 n.; Munkir and Nákir, iv. 96 n.; belief in angels necessary, P.D. 118; principal angels, P.D. 119; Muslim doctrine of angels borrowed from the Jews, P.D. 120.

VOL. IV.   U

Animals, irrational, will be raised at the resurrection and judged, vi. 37 n.

Ansárs, term defined, viii. 73 n.; are honoured of God, ix. 20; three excommunicated, ix. 119 n.

Ants, their queen's speech to them on the approach of Solomon's army, xxvii. 18.

Anushirwán, destroys Mazdak and the Manicheans, P.D. 66.

Apostles, were not believed who wrought miracles, iii. 184 n.; were, like Muhammad, called impostors, iii. 185 n., and vi. 33.

Apostles of Jesus, described, v. 111 n.; an example to Muslims, lxi. 14; their faithfulness to Jesus, iii. 51, 52 n.; did not forge their scriptures, xxxvi. 16 n.; ask a table to be sent down from heaven, v. 112 n.; two of them sent to Antioch, xxxvi. 12 n.

Apparel, what kind ought to be worn by those who approach the divine presence, vii. 28-34 notes.

Aqabah, first pledge of, P.D. 81; second pledge of, P.D. 82.

Arabia, its name, P.D. 13; boundaries, P.D. 14; its fabled riches not its own, P.D. 15; productions, P.D. 16; government in pre-Islámic times, P.D. 14-30; how governed after Muhammad's time, P.D. 30-33; never conquered, P.D. 35; accepts Islám, P.D. 94, 95; its political power consolidated by Muhammad, P.D. 67, 68; a refuge for heretics, P.D. 64.

Arabians, ancient tribes, P.D. 20; no reliable history of ancient inhabitants, P.D. 25 n.; modern Arabs descended from Qahtán and Adnán, P.D. 28; the al A'riba and al Mustáriba, P.D. 24, 25; the Cushite Arabs, P.D. 26; their love of liberty, P.D. 33; their religion in pre-Islámic times, P.D. 34-48; two classes of Arabs, P.D. 49; their language, P.D. 49, 50; their learning and accomplishments, P.D. 50-60; their hospitality, P.D. 54-56; national defects, P.D. 56-58; become the chosen people of God, ii. 152 n.; their customs in relation to divorce and adoption, xxxiii. 4 n.; custom of burying daughters alive, vi. 137 n; their superstitions in respect to eating, vi. 109 n., xxiv. 60; in respect to cattle, iv. 118; used to worship naked, and why, vii. 28-34 n.; their injustice to orphans and women, iv. 18-20 notes.

Arabs of the desert, more obstinate, ix. 91 n.

Aráf, the wall of, P.D. 152, vii. 47-50 notes.

Arafát, the mount, P.D. 186; why so called, ii. 35 and 198 notes.

Aram, the inundation of, P.D. 26, 27, xxxiv. 15 n.

Ark, Noah's ark, traditions of, liv. 15 n., xi. 41 n.; the ark of Israel taken by the Amalekites, ii. 248 n.

Arrows, for divination forbidden, v. 4 n.
Al Aás Ibn Wáil, an enemy of Muhammad's, xv. 95 and xix. 80 notes.
Asaf, Solomon's prime minister, xxvii. 40 n.
Asáf and Naila, desecrate the Kaabah, ii. 159 n.
Ashadd (Abu'l), his extraordinary strength, xc. 5 n.
Ashama, king of Ethiopia, embraces Islám, v. 86 n.; prayed for after his death by Muhammad, iii. 199 n.
Asharians, their founder and doctrine, P.D. 251–257.
Ashura. See *Muharram.*
Asía, the wife of Pharaoh, martyred by her husband for believing in Moses, lxvi. 11 n.
Asim, his charity, ix. 80 n.
Aslam, xlviii. 11 n.
Astrology, hinted at, iii. 184 n.
Al Aswad Ibn Abd Yaghúth, Al Aswad Ibn al Mutallib, two of Muhammad's enemies, xv. 95 n.
Atonement, salvation by atonement denied, iii. 90 n. and 194 n., v. 49 n., xxii. 36 n. and 39 n.; use of the word *expiate,* iii. 194 n., v. 13 n., 70 n. and 96 n., xxxvii. 107 n.
Aus and Khazraj, their enmity, iii. 100–109 notes.
A'yat ul Kursi, ii. 255 n.
Ayesha, calumnious report of, xxiv. introd. and 11 n.
Azraíl, the angel of death, why appointed to that office, ii. 30 n.; a story of him and Solomon, xxxi. 34 n.
Azar, the name given to Terah, Abraham's father, vi. 75 n.

Baal, the chief idol of the Chaldeans, xxi. 59 n.
Bába, his sect and their doctrine, P.D. 280, 281.
Babel, the tower of, destroyed, xvi. 28 n.
Bábik, his sect and their history, P.D. 275–277.
Backbiting. See *Slander.*
Badr, Muhammad's victory there, iii. 13 and 121 n.; the angels assisted the Muslims there, iii. 124 n.
Bahaira, described, v. 102 n.
Bairám. See *Feasts.*
Bakhtanasr. See *Nebuchadnezzar.*
Balaam, his punishment for cursing the Israelites, vii. 176 n.
Balám, the ox to be slain for the feast of God, P.D. 156.
Balance, the great, of judgment, P.D. 144, vii. 8 n.
Balqís, the Queen of Sheba, xxvii. 42–45 notes.
Baptism, the baptism of God, ii. 138 n.; of the Sabian religion, P.D. 35.
Baqr (Abu), attends Muhammad in his flight from Makkah, ix. 40 n.; bears testimony to the truth by Muhammad's journey

to heaven, xvii. 62 n.; his wager with Ubbá Ibn Khalf, xxx.
1 n.; strikes a Jew on the face for speaking irreverently of
God, iii. 182 n.; gives all he has towards the expedition of
Tabúk, ix. 80 n.; purchases Bilál, xc. 18 n.; compared to
Abrahám, viii. 69 n.

Baqr I'd, described, P.D. 232 n.

Barnabas, the Gospel of, iii. 53 n., and P.D. 123 and 124.

Barzakh (Al), opinions of Muslims regarding it, P.D. 128, 129.

Basharians, their founder and doctrines, P.D. 247, 248.

Bátinites. See *Ismaïlians*.

Be, the command, *Kun fayakuna*, xxvi. 82 n.

Bedouin Arabs, punished for their treachery, xlviii. 15, 16;
their hypocrisy rebuked, xlix. 14–18, xcviii. 100 n.

Bees, made use of as a similitude, xvi. 71 n.

Believers, the sincere ones described, viii. 2–5, xxiii. 1–10,
their works, ix. 72, xxi. 20; heaven their reward, ix. 73,
xiii. 28, and xxiii. 11. See *Paradise*.

Benjamin, son of Jacob, xii. 69 n.

Birds, omens taken from them, xvii. 14 n.

Bismillah, what it signifies, P.D. 100; of Jewish origin, i.
introd. v. 5 n., vi. 118–121 n., xxiii. 101 n.

Blessed, their future happiness described, xxxvi. 55–58, xliv.
51–59. See *Paradise*.

Blood, forbidden, ii. 174 n.; price of blood, iv. 91 n.; blood-
feuds abolished, iv. 92.

Books, account-books given into the hands of men on the
judgment-day, P.D. 144, 145, and lxxxiv. 6–15.

Bridge, over hell, P.D. 147; this doctrine borrowed from the
Magians, P.D. 147.

Brotherhood, of Muslims, iv. 32 n.

Brutes, in the judgment, P.D. 145, 146.

Buáth, the battle of, iii. 100–109.

Budhail, a dispute concerning his effects occasions a passage of
the Qurán, v. 105 n.

Buhaira, the monk, xvi. 105 n.

Burden, every soul to bear its own, xxxv. 20, 21.

Burkai (Al). See *Hakim*.

Cain. See *Abel*.

Caleb. See *Joshua*.

Calf, the golden, worshipped by the Israelites, ii. 50 n.

Calumny, forbidden, iv. 156.

Camels, an instance of God's wisdom, lxxxviii. 17; appointed
for sacrifice, xxii. 34; Jacob abstains from their flesh and
milk, iii. 93 n.

INDEX. 309

Canaan, an unbelieving son of Noah, xi. 40 n.
Caravans, of purveyors sent out by the Quarish, cvi. 1, &c., n.
Carrion, forbidden to be eaten, ii. 174 n.
Cattle, their use, vi. 138, and xl. 79; superstitions of old Arabians concerning them, v. 102.
Ceylon, the isle of. See *Sarandíb*.
Charity, commended, iv. 35-38 notes.
Chastity, commended, v. 6 n.
Chess. See *Games*.
Children, to inherit their parents' substance, ii. 220 n., and iv. 32 n.
Christ, his gospel attested, lvii. 27; his sonship not understood by Muhammad, ii. 116 n., xxi. 17 n., iii. 5 n., v. 21 n.; his divinity rejected by Muhammad, iii. 2 n., v. 19 n., and 110-117 notes, xix. 91-95 notes, xliii. introd. See also *Jesus*.
Christians, persecuted by Dhu Nawás, P.D. 45, 46, lxxxix. 1-9; dispute among themselves about the Qurán, xcviii. 3, 4; said to worship their priests, ix. 31 n.; called infidels and idolaters, ii. 135, and v. 19 n.; exhorted to become Muslims, lvii. 28, 29; Muhammad helped by them, xvi. 105 n., and xviii. 12 n.
Christianity, progress of, in Arabia, P.D. 45-48; state of, at time of Muhammad, P.D. 61-64; Muhammad's estimate of it, ii. 135 n.
Circumcision, Muslim doctrine and practice in regard to, P.D. 168.
Coffee. See *Things forbidden*.
Collars, to be worn by the unbelievers in the life to come, xiii. 6 n.
Commandments, given to the Jews, xiii. 103 n.
Companions, of God, what, vi. 22 n.
Concubinage, unlimited, lxvi. 1 note, lxx. 29-31; children of concubines legitimate, P.D. 213.
Confession of faith, the earliest, of Islám, cxii. 1, &c.; creed of Muhammad in Makkah, x. 104-109.
Congealed blood, the matter of which man is created, xcvi. 1, &c.
Contracts, to be performed, v. 1.
Covetousness, denounced, xcii. 5-16, cii. introd.
Cow, ordered to be sacrificed by the Israelites, ii. 66 n.
Creation, some account of it, xli. 8-11.
Crime, laws and penalties relating to grave offences, P.D. 210-216; crimes punished with death, xvii. 35 n.; petty crimes and their penalties, P.D. 217.

Cushites, described, P.D. 26.
Customs, relating to Bahaira, Saiba, Wasíla, and Hámí. See *Things forbidden, Purifications,* and *Laws.*

Daughters, hated by the Arabs, yet ascribed to God by them, xliii. introd. and 15–18.
David, kills Goliah, ii. 249 n. and xvii. 6 n.; his extraordinary devotion, xxxviii. 16; the birds and mountains sing praises with him, xxxiv. 10; his repentance for taking the wife of Uriah, xxxviii. 23; his and Solomon's judgment, xxi. 79 n.; receives the Book of Psalms, xvii. 57.
Days, appointed to commemorate God, xxii. 29 n.
Dead body, raised to life by a part of the sacrificed cow, ii. 72 n.
Death, unavoidable, iii. 155; every soul shall taste it, iii. 186 n.
Debtors, to be mercifully dealt with, ii. 278–280.
Decrees, the doctrine of, P.D. 164; everything written in the books of, lvii. 22, 23, and xi. 7 n.; God decrees some to be saved and others to be lost, lxiv. 2, and x. 100 n.
Deceivers, their condition in the judgment, iv. 106, &c.
Demons, beset Muhammad, and are the authors of idolatry, vi. 112, 113 notes.
Devil. See *Iblís* and *Satan.*
Devils, included under the name of genii, vi. 130 n.; the patrons of unbelievers, vii. 28, xxvi. 223, and xliii. 35–38.
Dhu'l Qifl, the prophet, opinions concerning him, xxi. 85 n.; saves a hundred Israelites from slaughter, xxxviii. 48 n.
Dhu'l Nun. See *Jonas.*
Dhu Nawás, described, P.D. 28 and 45; his persecution of the Christians, P.D. 45, 46; his persecutions anathematised, lxxxv. 1–7.
Dhu'l Qarnain, who he was, xviii. 82; builds a wall to prevent incursions of Gog and Magog, xviii. 92–96.
Disputes, to be carried on with mildness, xxix. 45 n.
Ditch, war of the, xxxiii. 9 n.
Divining. See *Things forbidden.*
Divorce, ancient Arab custom of, abrogated, lviii. 1–9; of female converts to Islám, lx. 10; laws of divorce, iv. 18 n., xxxiii. 40 n., ii. 226–237, and P.D. 207–209; original law of Islám modified, lxv. 1–7; regulations concerning it, ii. 226–237 notes, and 241 n.; efforts to prevent, iv. 34 n.
Doctors, the four great Muslim authorities, P.D. 205.
Doctrine, the two sciences of divinity, P.D. 233; points of faith subject to scholastic discussion, P.D. 235.

Dogs, &c., allowed to be trained up for hunting, v. 5 n.
Drink, of the damned, vi. 71.
Duráh (Al), the celestial mode of the Kaabah, li. 4 n.

Earth, its creation, xli. 8–11 n.; remonstrates against the creation of man, ii. 30 n.; is kept steady by the mountains, xvi. 15 n., xxxi. 9 n.
Earthquake, a sign of the approach of the last day, xcix. 1.
Eden, the meaning of the word in Arabic, ix. 73 n.
Education, makes a man an infidel, xxx. 29 n.
Egypt, the plagues on, vii. 134–136.
Elephant, war of the, cv. introd. and 1, &c.
Elias, denounces the worship of Baal, xxxvii. 123–125. See *Al Khidr*.
Elisha, the prophet, vi. 87 n.
Emigration, to Abyssinia, P.D. 77, 78, and xxxix. 13 n.; to Madína, P.D. 85.
Enemy, admissible to slay an, ii. 191–194.
Enoch. See *Idrís*.
Entering, into houses abruptly, forbidden, xxiv. 27 and 57 notes.
Esop. See *Luqmán*.
Eucharist, seems to have occasioned a fable in the Qurán, v. 112 n.
Eve. See *Adam*.
Evil, allowable in self-defence, viii. 60 n., xvi. 108 n. See also *Good*.
Examination, of the sepulchre, viii. 52 n.
Exegesis, rules for, P.D. 113, 114.
Expiation. See *Atonement*.
Ezekiel, raises the dry bones, ii. 243 n.
Ezra, and his ass restored to life after they had been dead a hundred years, ii. 259 n.; called by the Jews the son of God, and why, ix. 30 n.

Faith, defined, ii. 3–32; its evidence in new converts, lx. 12; assurance of faith presumptuous, ii. 4 n.; must accompany good works, xi. 24; the reward of those who fight for it, iii. 140 n. and 170; apostates from it to be put to death, xvii. 35 n.
Famine, afflicts the inhabitants of Makkah, xxiii. 76 n.; ceases at Muhammad's intercession, xliv. 9–15.
Fast, of Ramadhán instituted, ii. 184, 185 n., and P.D. 176–178.
Fasting, the duty required, P.D. 175, and ii. 183, &c.; voluntary fasting, P.D. 178; ordinary customs relating to, vii. 142.

Fatalism, Muhammad's belief in, iii. 145 and 155 notes.
Fátihat, the first chapter of the Qurán, chap. i.
Fátimah, Muhammad's daughter, one of the four perfect women, lxvi. 12 n.
Fatra, defined, v. 22 n., lxxiv. introd.
Feasts, the I'd-ul-Fitr and I'd-ul-Qurbán, P.D. 231; feast of God, P.D. 156.
Fidelity, recommended, ix. 7.
Figs, their virtues, xcv. 1 n.
Fire, the manner of striking it in the East, xxxvi. 180 n.
Fishing, allowed during the pilgrimage, v. 97 n.
Flood. See *Noah*.
Food, what kinds are forbidden. See *Things forbidden*.
Forbidden fruit, what, ii. 35 n.
Forgiveness, to whom it belongs, xxxiii. 36; enemies to be forgiven, why, ii. 108 n.; story of Hassan, iii. 134 n.
Fornication, forbidden, and its punishment, iv. 14 and 23 n., xvii. 35 n. See also *Adultery*.
Fountain, of molten brass flows for Solomon, xxxiv. 11 n.
Fountains, of Paradise, lxxvi. 5, and lxxxiii. 27.
Free-will, man's free-will recognised, iii. 145 n., vi. 12 n.; free-will denied, x. 100 n.
Friendship, with unbelievers forbidden, v. 57 n.
Fugitives. See *Muhájjirín*.
Furqán, one of the names of the Qurán, xxv. 1 n.; applied to inspired writings generally, ii. 52 n.

Gabriel, assists the Muslims at Badr, iii. 13; appears to Zacharias, iii. 38; appears twice to Muhammad in his proper form, liii. 6 n.; appears to the Virgin Mary, and causes her to conceive, xix. 17-22 n.; the dust of his horse's feet animates the golden calf, xx. 91; commanded to assist Muhammad against the Quraish, xv. 95 n.; orders Muhammad to go against the Bani Quraidha, xxxiii. 26 n.; Muhammad receives the Qurán through him, ii. 96 n., liii. 6, xcvi. introd.; generally he reveals himself in human form, vi. 9 n., xix. 17 n.
Games, of chance, forbidden, P.D. 193; the game of chess, P.D. 194-196.
Gaming, forbidden. See *Things forbidden*.
Ganím (Banu), build a mosque with an ill design, which is burnt, ix. 108 n.
Garden, the parable of a garden, lxviii. 17-34; Garden of Eden, see *Paradise*.
Genii, Muslim belief concerning them, P.D. 121, vi. 101 n.;

created of fire, lv. 14; some of them converted to Islám, xlvi. 28–31, lxxii. introd.; fate in the judgment-day, P.D. 146.

Ghassán, the kingdom of, and how founded, P.D. 27, 28; its last Christian king, Jabálah, becomes a Muslim, and afterwards apostatises, P.D. 29.

Ghází, the true fanatic, ix. 20 n.

Ghulites, a sect of the Shíahs, P.D. 266.

Girls, black-eyed, of Paradise, xxxvii. 47.

God, the God of Islám, P.D. 118, 119; he is one God, cxii. 1–4, ii. 22 n., and 164 n.; manifested by his works, xli. 8–11 and 37–39, xlii. 28–33, xlvi. 2–5, li. 20–22; Creator and source of life, xliv. 7; is able to raise the dead, ii. 117, vi. 96–102, xvi. 42 n., xxxvi. 82 n., xlv. 23–25; Sovereign, lxiv. 11 and 18; is eternal, lv. 26–30; his laws and word unalterable, vi. 115 n., xxx. 29; is all-powerful, lvii. 1–6, and lxxviii. 8–29; is everywhere present, lviii. 8; is omniscient, ii. 94 n., iv. 107, and lvii. 1–6; five things known only to him, xxxi. 34 n.; his goodness and love, ii. 166 n., iii. 31 n.; the Author of all good, iv. 78 n.; the Author of evil as well as of good, vii. 179, 180 n., xvii. 14 n., xxxv. 9 n.; a refuge against Satan, cxiv. 1–6; his ninety-nine names, vii. 181 n.; his throne, ii. 255 n.; the Trinity denied, iv. 169 n.; cannot have sons, vi. 102.

Goddesses, called the daughters of God, iv. 116.

Gog and Magog, described, xviii. 92–99 n.; they shall punish the infidels, xxix. 96.

Goliah. See *Jálút.*

Good works, who shall be redeemed by them. See *Salvation.*

Gospel attested by Muhammad and the Qurán, P.D. 126, and xlviii. 29; Muslim use of spurious Gospels, P.D. 124, 125.

Gospel of Barnabas, Muslim use of, P.D. 123 and 124, iii. 53 n.

Greaves (Mr.), a mistake of his, lxxxix. 8 n.

Greeks, overcome by the Persians, xxx. 1 n.

Gudarz, the name of Nebuchadnezzar, xvii. 7 n.

Habíb, his martyrdom, xxxvi. 12 n.

Háfidha, an idol of A'd, vii. 66 n.

Hajj. See *Pilgrimage.*

Hakím Ibn Hásham, his prophetic career, P.D. 273–275.

Hámán, Pharaoh's chief minister, xxviii. 5 and 38 n.

Hámi, described, v. 102 n.

Hamza, his conversion, P.D. 78; is killed at Ohod, iii. 121 n.; his body mutilated, xvi. 127 n.

Hanbalites, their founder and their doctrines, P.D. 240, 241.

Handha Ibn Safwán, a prophet, xxii. 46 n., xxv. 40 n.
Haníf. See *Orthodox*.
Hanífites, their founder and doctrine, P.D. 23, 238.
Hárith (Abu), a Christian bishop, disputes with Muhammad, iii. 60 n.
Hárút and Márút, their story, ii. 101 n.
Háshamians, their founder and doctrines, P.D. 245.
Háshimites, the Ban of, P.D. 78.
Hátib, Ibn Abi Baltaa, sends a letter discovering Muhammad's design against Makkah, which is intercepted, lx. 1 n.
Háwíat (Al), the name of an apartment in hell, ci. 9 n.
Háyátians, their founder and doctrines, P.D. 246.
Heavens, Muslim belief concerning them, xxiii. 17; adorned with stars, lxvii. 5; seven in number, ii. 29, and xli. 11; created in six days, vii. 55, and x. 3; guarded by angels, lxxii. 8; will fall at the last day, xxii. 66 n.
Hell, Muhammad's notions of, borrowed from the Magians, P.D. 150, 151; punishments of, P.D. 149, ii. 38 n., iii. 197 n., xxiii. 105 n., xliv. 43-50, lvi. 40-56, lxxxviii. 4-7; the inmates of hell shall vainly seek for annihilation, xliii. 74-78; no repentance there, xxvi. 91-105; it shall not harm true believers, xix. 72 n.; Muslim culprits finally escape, P.D. 149 and 150, xix. 41 n., xxxii. 14 n.; guarded by nineteen angels, lxxiv. 30-34; its various apartments, ci. 10, 11 n., civ. 4 n.; it shall be filled with men and genii, l. 29, xviii. 102 n.; the sufferings of hell corporeal, xiv. 20; in the judgment-day it shall be dragged towards God's tribunal, lxxxix. 24 n.
Heresy, it finds a refuge in Arabia, P.D. 63.
Higgins (Godfrey), quoted, ii. 174 n., xi. 13 n.
Hijáz, its name and boundaries, P.D. 16; chief cities of, P.D. 16-19; the founder of the kingdom, P.D. 26; phylarchical government of, inaugurated, P.D. 30.
Hijra, the era of, P.D. 87 n. See also *Emigration*.
Hira, the kingdom and its history, P.D. 27-29.
Himyárites. See *Yaman*.
Hobal, the chief idol of the Kaabah, P.D. 42.
Holy Spirit. See *Spirit*.
Honey, an excellent medicine, xvi. 71 n.
Houris. See *Húr al Oyún*.
Húd, the prophet of A'd, P.D. 21; his story, see *A'd*.
Hudailians, their founder and doctrines, P.D. 244.
Hudaibiyah, the treaty of, xlviii. 26 n.; Muhammad's dream there, xlviii. 27 n.
Hulúl (Al), the doctrine of, P.D. 266.
Hunain, the battle of, ix. 25 n.

INDEX. 315

Húr al Oyún, or girls of Paradise, earliest mention of, lii. 20; number allowed to each of the true believers, P.D. 157.

Husband. See *Divorce*, *Wives*, and *Marriage*.

Hypocrites, described, lxiii. 1-4; their perfidy, xli. 49-51, and lix. 11-17; threatened, ix. 52-65 notes, xxxiii. 60-62, lxiii. 1-3, lxvi. 9.

Iblís, refuses to worship Adam, and why, ii. 34, vii. 11-18, xvii. 63-65; is accursed, vi. 13, 18, xv. 34, 35; respited till the judgment-day, vi. 14, 15, xv. 36-38; has no power to injure God's people, xv. 42, xvii. 67. See also *Satan*.

I'd. See *Feasts*.

Idolaters, acknowledge God yet worship the creature, xl. 8-14; choose Satan for their friend instead of God, xviii. 48; will be deserted by their own gods in the judgment-day, x. 29, &c., xli. 47, 48; to be treated harshly, ix. 36, lxvi. 9; not to be prayed for while such, ix. 114; shall be cast into hell-fire, iv. 120, vii. 49 n., xxi. 98-101; not permitted to enter Muslim places of worship, ix. 28; the Arab idolaters slay their daughters, xvi. 61; idolatrous practices among modern Muslims, P.D. 37 n. See *Idols* and *Idolatry*.

Idolatry, Arab idolatry and star-worship, P.D. 36-38; to be restored before the judgment-day, P.D. 134; the heinousness of the sin of idolatry, ii. 216; Muslim idea of, iii. 151 n.

Idols, their insignificancy, xxx. 39; will appear as witnesses against their worshippers, x. 29; famous idols of Makkah, Lát, Uzzah, Mináh, Wadd, &c., described, P.D. 38-43; stones worshipped, P.D. 43, and v. 4 n.

Idrís, supposed to be the same with Enoch, xix. 57 n.; a model of patience, xxi. 85.

Ifríts, how they differ from the genii, xxvii. 39 n.

Ilhíz, a sort of food used by the Arabs in times of scarcity, xxiii. 76 n.

Illíyún, the meaning of the word, lxxxiii. 18-21.

Ilyásín, who, xxiii. 130 n.

I'mám, the meaning of the word, ii. 124 n.

Immodesty, condemned, xxiv. 31.

Immunity, declared to the idolaters for four months, ix. 1-5.

Imposture, charged on all the prophets, xxiii. 35-43; charged on Muhammad, see *Muhammad*.

Imrán, father of the Virgin Mary, and whether confounded with the father of Moses, iii. 33 n.; the wife of Imrán, iii. 35 n.

Infanticide prohibited by Muhammad, P.D. 202-204, xvi. 61 n., vii. 33 n.

Infidels, why the Qurán was sent to them, ii. 6 n.; prospered to secure destruction, ii. 211; would not be convinced by miracles, vi. 7–9, 34 and 109 notes; how they will appear at the last day, vi. 30 n.; will drink boiling water, vi. 71; no friendship with them allowed to Muslims, iv. 88 n. and 139 n.; to be made war upon, ii. 191–193; forbidden to approach Makkah, ix. 28 n.; who die such, not to be prayed for, ix. 114 n.; to be forgiven on conversion to Islám, iv. 85, viii. 40, &c.

Inheritance, laws regarding, P.D. 212, 213; legacies to poor, &c., ii. 180 n.; legacies to wives, ii. 240 n.; inheritance of idiots, &c., iv. 4 n.; old rules affecting women and children abolished, iv. 6 n.; law relating to portions, iv. 10–13 n.

Injury, to forgive the same is meritorious, xlii. 38.

Inspiration, why God reveals his word by inspiration, xlii. 50, 51; who are inspired, iv. 162; as applied to Muslim tradition, iv. 57 n.; claimed by Muhammad, iv. 162, and xi. 13; Muhammad's inspiration, iv. 162, xvi. introd., xvii. 88 n., xx. 112, 113 notes; a bee inspired, xvi. 70.

Intercalation, of a month, forbidden, ix. 36 n.

Intercession, Muhammad no intercessor, ii. 152 n., vii. 188 n.; efficiency of Muhammad's intercession in the judgment-day, vi. 50, ix. 81 n., xx. 108 n., lxxi. 29 n.; none admissible on the judgment-day, v. 108 n., xi. 46 n., xvi. 39 n., xxxix. 45 n., lxxxii. 17–19; angels permitted to intercede, xxi. 29 n.; angels called intercessors by Arab idolaters, P.D. 38; Christian doctrine of intercession inconsistent with Islám, xx. 108 n.

Iram, the city of A'd, lxxxix. 6 n.; the garden of, P.D. 20, 21.

Iron, its usefulness, lvii. 29.

Isaac, promised, xi. 71; his faith, xi. 74; represented in the Qurán as Jacob's brother, xi. 71 n.

Ishaqians, their doctrines, P.D. 267.

Ismaíl, his posterity accounted to be Arabs, P.D. 25; nowhere called the child of promise, xi. 71 n.; is offered up as a sacrifice, xxxvii. 99 n.; numbered among the prophets of Islám, ii. 133, xix. 55. See also *Abrahám*.

Ismaílians, their enmity to Muhammadans, P.D. 279.

Islám, the religion of all the prophets, ii. 136 n., iii. 83 n., vii. 104, 127 n., xvi. 91 n., xxi. 92 n., xlii. 11–13, and P.D. 116 *seq.*; the five fundamental points of, P.D. 117; to be exalted above all religions, ii. 193 n., ix. 33 n., xlviii. 28 n.; its various sects, P.D. 236–290; succeeds as a religion through political weakness of Rome and Persia, P.D. 65; propagated by the sword, P.D. 84, ii. 190–193 n., ix. 1 and 124 notes;

what it owes to Judaism, see *Judaism;* some reasons for its success, ii. 85 n. and 94 n., x. 32-37 n.; its antagonism to Christianity denied, and reply, ii. 89 n., v. 72 n., xxv. 35 n.; why said to be further removed from Christianity than heathenism, iii. 31 n.; incapable of elevating the human race, xxii. 61; never changed, xxx. 29 n.

Israelites, pass the Red Sea, vii. 138; miraculously fed in the wilderness, vii. 161; lust for the herbs of Egypt, ii. 60; worship golden calf, ii. 50; word put into their mouth at Jericho, ii. 58; command to sacrifice a red cow, ii. 66 n.; refuse to enter the Holy Land, and their punishment, v. 25; their transgression, xvii. 4 n.; desire a king, ii. 246; cursed by David and Jesus, v. 82; they inherit the eastern and western shores of the Red Sea, vii. 137 n., xvii. 106 n. See also *Jews.*

Jabarians, their name and creed, P.D. 259-261.
Jacob, bequeaths the religion of Islám to his children, iii. 132; grows blind by weeping for the loss of Joseph, xii. 84; recovers his sight by means of Joseph's garment and goes into Egypt, xii. 93.
Jadd Ibn Qais, his excuse for remaining behind in time of war, ix. 49 n.
Jadís, the tribe destroyed by the Tasmians, P.D. 23.
Jahidhians, their founder and doctrines, P.D. 246.
Jahl (Abu), a great enemy of Muhammad, xxii. 8; his injustice to an orphan, cvii. 2 n.; his advice concerning Muhammad, viii. 30 n.; slain at Badr, viii. 49 n.
Jallás (Al), Ibn Suwaid, ix. 75 n.
Jálút, or Goliah, sent against the Israelites, xvii. 5 n.; slain by David, ii. 251. See also *Saul.*
Jannat. See *Paradise.*
Jásúsa (Al), the beast which will appear at the approach of the last day, xxvii. 84.
Jawádh (Abu'l), the hypocrite, ix. 58 n.
Jawwas Ibn Omaiya, mentioned, xlviii. 18.
Jesus, promised to Mary, his miraculous birth, he is compared to Adam, iii. 58 n.; speaks in infancy, iii. 46; when a child he animates a bird of clay, iii. 48 n.; is called the Spirit of God, iv. 169 n.; his worship compared to the worship of heathen idols, xliii. 57 and 58; not God, v. 19 n., ix. 30 n.; yet called "the word of God," ii. 84 n., iii. 39-45 notes; his miracles, ii. 86 n., iii. 46-53; his miraculous birth, ii. 253 n., iii. 45-50, v. 109, xix. 22 n., xxi. 91 n.; his *sinlessness*, ii. 253 n., xix. 19 n.; causes a table with provisions

to descend from heaven, v. 112 n.; rejected by the Jews, iii.
53; sends two of his disciples to Antioch, who work miracles,
xxxvi. 12; receives the gospel, v. 50; the Jews lay a plot
for his life, but are disappointed, and whether he died or
not, iii. 53, 54 notes; was not crucified, iii. 53 n., iv. 154
n.; yet was to die, iii. 54 n., v. 117 n.; he died and rose
again, iii. 54 n., v. 117 n., xix. 34; only an apostle, ii. 253,
v. 79; a sign of the resurrection, xliii. 61; various opinions
concerning him, xix. 38, his descent from heaven, P.D. 133.
See also *Christ*.

Jethro. See *Shuaib*.

Jews, particularly appealed to, ii. 39 n.; accused of having
corrupted the Scriptures and of stifling passages, ii. 39, 40
notes, iii. 77; they accuse the Virgin Mary of fornication,
iv. 156; plot against Jesus, iii. 53 n.; proof required by
them of a prophet's mission, iii. 184; metamorphosed into
swine and apes for their infidelity, v. 65; their law confirmed
by Jesus and the Qurán, v. 50; dispute with Muhammadans
concerning God's favour, xxii. 19; their power in Arabia,
P.D. 64; had revealed to them the law and the prophets,
xlv. 15, 16; reject Muhammad through envy, ii. 89 n., iii.
19 n.; certain Jews confirm the Qurán, ii. 18 n., xxvi. 197
n., xlvi. 9; dispute among themselves about the Qurán,
xcviii. 3, 4; unfit for Muslim companionship, lviii. 15, 21;
hated by Muhammad, ii. 137 n. to 146 n., iii. 118 n., lviii.
16–21; cursed by Jesus, v. 82 n.; they boast of their crime
in slaying Jesus, iv. 156; Jews and Christians accused of
condemning one another, ii. 112; accused of corrupting their
Scriptures, ii. 41 and 160 notes; to be protected on payment
of tribute, ix. 29 n. See also *Israelites*.

Jihád, primary use of the word, ii. 217 n.; commanded, ix.
13, 14 notes. See *War*.

Job, his story, vi. 85, xxi. 83 n., xxxviii. 43 n.

John, the son of Zacharias, his birth, iii. 38–41; his character,
iii. 39 n., xix. 14; his murder revenged on the Jews by
Nebuchadnezzar, xvii. 5–7 notes.

Jonas, his story, x. 98; is impatient, lxviii. 48–50.

Jorhamites, their origin and fate, P.D. 23, 24, and 29; their
alliance with the Ishmaelites, P.D. 25 and 29.

Joseph, his story, xii. 1–102, xxxvii. 139–147 notes; the
prophet of the Egyptians, xl. 36 n.

Joshua and Caleb, sent as spies into the land of Canaan, v. 26.

Journey, Muhammad's journey to heaven, xvii. 1 n.

Jubbaians, their founder and doctrines, P.D. 245.

Judaism, how introduced into Arabia, P.D. 44; what Islám owes to it, P.D. 120, 121, 127, 150, 160, 165, 171, 174, 177, 210, and 218; Muhammad's estimate of it, ii. 135 n.

Judgment-day, the Muslim tradition concerning it, iii. 25; described, xxv. 24, &c., lii. 1–16; signs of its approach, xxii. 1, xliv. 9, and xlvii. 20 n.; the hour only known to God, xli. 47, xlii. 16, 17; none shall escape it, l. 18–20, lxix. 1–3; the wicked shall be speechless therein, xxxvi. 65 n.; its terrors, lvi. 1–11; judgment shall be according to works, iv. 171, vi. 132, vii. 8, 9; that day shall reveal secret houghts, lxxxvi. 9, 10 n.; length of the day, P.D. 137, xvi. 79 n., lxx. 4; place of judgment, P.D. 140; time of trial, P.D. 143, 144; great day of assizes, P.D. 142–147; books, balance of judgment, P.D. 144, 145; no intercessor therein, xliv. 41, ii. 47, 123, and 254.

Junáda, first practises the intercalation of a month among the Arabs, ix. 37 n.

Kaabah, described, P.D. 179–186; its antiquity, P.D. 182; built by Abraham, xxii. 27; the idols of, P.D. 42; made the Muslim Qibla, P.D. 172, ii. 142–146 notes, xxii. 31 n.; defiled, ii. 159 n.; infidels forbidden to enter it, ix. 28; compassing it (Tawáf), and the import of the same, P.D. 187 and 189; keys of it delivered to Othmán Ibn Tálha, iv. 56 n.

Káb, Ibn Málik, he is punished, ix. 107 n.

Káfúr, that of Paradise, lxxvi. 5.

Kail, sent to Makkah to obtain rain for A'd, vii. 73 n.

Kalima, the creed of Adam, ii. 36 n.

Karamians, their founder and doctrine, P.D. 258, 259.

Karmatians, their founder, doctrine, and practice, P.D. 277–279; their disorders, P.D. 30.

Kauthar, its refreshing waters, P.D. 153, 154, cviii. 1 n.

Keys, of knowledge (the five), iii. 34 n.

Khaibar, the expedition thither, xlviii. 15 n.

Khaitana, a story of him, ix. 14 n.

Khadíjah, the first convert to Islám, P.D. 74; her death, P.D. 79; one of the four perfect women, lxvi. 12 n.

Khálid Ibn al Walíd, puts Muhammad's horse to flight at the battle of Ohod, iii. 152 n.; demolishes the idol of al Uzza, xxxix. 37 n.; drives Akrima and his men into Makkah, xlviii. 24.

Khalífah, Adam a *Khilífah*, ii. 36 n.

Khantala, see xxii. 46 n. and xxv. 40 n.

Khárijites, the first of Muslim heretics, P.D. 242, 263, 264.

Khaula bint Thalába, her case alluded to in Qurán, lviii. introd.

Khidr, the prophet, his adventures with Moses, xviii. 64 n.

Khubaib, his martyrdom, xvi. 108 n.

Khudhaa (the tribe of), held the angels to be the daughters of God, xxi. 26 n.

Kindah, a tribe who used to bury their daughters, vi. 137 n.

Khurram-ud-dín. See *Bábik*.

Kussai, names his son after four idols, vii. 190 n.; Quraish ask Muhammad to raise him to life, viii. 23 n.

Lailat-ul-Qadr, the Qurán sent down during that night, xliv. 1–6 notes, and liii. 6; Muir's opinion, xcvii. introd.

Lapwing, gives Solomon an account of the city of Sabá, and carries a letter from him to the queen, xxvii. 20 n.

Last day. See *Judgment*.

Lát (Al), the idol of the Thakífites, P.D. 39; of the Quraish also, iv. 116 n.

Law. See *Pentateuch*.

Laws, on laws in general, P.D. chap. vi.; distinction between civil and ecclesiastical law, P.D. 217; moral laws enjoined, xlix. 9–13; concerning marriage, see *Marriage;* concerning meats, drinks, games, &c., see *Things forbidden;* concerning polygamy, see *Polygamy;* concerning divorce, see *Divorce;* concerning adultery, see *Adultery;* concerning inheritance, see *Inheritance;* concerning wills, see *Wills;* concerning private contracts, P.D. 214; concerning manslaughter and murder, P.D. 214–216; concerning war, P.D. 220–222; concerning spoils, see *Spoils*.

Letters of the alphabet in the beginning of certain chapters, P.D. 101–102, ii. 1 n., vii. 1 n., xix. 1 n., and xx. 1 n.

Light, the, of prophecy, v. 17 n., xi. 18 n.

Lord's Supper, probably alluded to, v. 112.

Lot, the patriarch, his wife a warning to Muslim women, lxvi. 10–12; his story, vii. 81–85, xi. 69–82.

Lote-tree, in heaven, liii. 14 n.

Lots, forbidden, P.D. 193, ii. 218 n., v. 4 and 92 notes.

Love, proved by obedience, iii. 31, 32.

Lubába (Abu), his treachery, viii. 27 n.

Luqmán, his history, and whether the same as Æsop, xxxi. 11 n.

Lying, sometimes allowable, xvi. 108 n.

Madian, a city of the Hajáz, vii. 86 n.; its inhabitants destroyed for their unbelief, xxvi. 189 n. See *Midianites*.

Madína, its ancient name and situation, P.D. 18; description of it, P.D. 19; its modern governors, P.D. 31, 32; its first converts to Islám, P.D. 80; the pledge of Aqabah, P.D. 81; Islám

INDEX.   321

spreads there, P.D. 80, 81; the second pledge of Aqabah, P.D. 82; its inhabitants reproved, ix. 118 n.

Magian, religion, its influence on Arabia, P.D. 44, 147 and 160.

Magog. See *Gog and Magog*.

Mahdi, his coming, P.D. 134; Shiites believe him to be Abu'l Qásim, P.D. 135.

Mahmúd, pretends to be Moses, P.D. 277.

Makkah, description of, P.D. 16–18; employment of its inhabitants, P.D. 18; how watered, P.D. 17; visited by famine, x. 22 n., xi. 11 n., xxiii. 77 n., xxxii. 21 n.; its destruction foretold, xlvii. 14; spared through compassion, xlviii. 25, 26; captured by Muhammad, P.D. 93, 94; its conquest an attestation of Islám, xlviii. 27–29; its ancient rulers, see *Hijáz* and *Quraish*; its government under Islám, P.D. 31, 32 notes.

Makkans, their idolatry condemned, vi. 135–137; reproached for their ingratitude, xiv. 33; threatened with destruction, xli. 12; hold a council and conspire Muhammad's destruction, viii. 30; chastised with famine and sword, xxiii. 78 n., xxxix. 52.

Málik, the principal angel who has the charge of hell, xliii. 77.

Málik Ibn Ans, his sect and their doctrines, P.D. 238, 239.

Man, his wonderful formation, xxxix. 8; created various ways, xxii. 5; shall be rewarded according to his deserts, iv. 53–55; his ingratitude to God, xxx, 32, 33; why destroyed, xi. 117.

Manicheans, destroyed by Anaushírwán, P.D. 66.

Manna, given to the Israelites, ii. 56.

Manslaughter, laws relating to, P.D. 215.

Marriage, four lawful wives allowed to Muslims besides concubines, iv. 3 n., lxx. 29–31; prohibited degrees, P.D., 211, iv. 21–24 notes; peculiar privileges of Muhammad, P.D. 211, 212, v. 6 n., xxxiii. 6 and 49 notes; Muslims not to marry idolaters, ii. 221; law relating to non-Muslim wives, v. 6 n.; dowry required by Muslim law, iv. 3 and 23 notes.

Martyrs, who they are, P.D. 218; martyrs of Ohod, iii. 140 n., 170 n.; they are not dead but living, ii. 155 n.; the sufferings of two Muslims, xvi. 108 n.

Márút. See *Hárút*.

Mary, the Virgin, descended from Imrán, iii. 35 n.; her birth and nurture, iii. 35–38 notes, xix. 1–34; the Angel Gabriel visits her, iii. 42–50 notes; miraculous conception, xix. 22 n., and xxi. 91 n.; calumniated by the Jews, iv. 156; one of the four perfect women, lxvi. 12. See also *Jesus*.

Mary, the Copt, a slave girl given to Muhammad, lxvi. 1–5.

Marwa. See *Safá* and *Marwa*.
Mashar al Harám (Al), ii. 198.
Masíh al Dajjál, his appearing, P.D. 132.
Masjid, the use of the term, vii. 30 n.; who may enter, ix. 18.
Masjid al Harám. See *Kaabah*.
Mastah, one of the accusers of Ayesha, xxiv. 11 n.
Masúd (Ibn), a tradition of, in relation to Pharaoh, xl. 49 n.
Mazdak, his communism, P.D. 66.
Measure, ought to be just, vii. 86 n.
Messiah, prophecies concerning him applied to Muhammad, iii. 188, 189 notes.
Metempsychosis, the doctrine believed by some ancient Arabs, P.D. 44.
Michael, the friend of the Jews, ii. 96 n.
Midian. See *Madian*.
Midianites, called the inhabitants of Al Aika, xv. 78 n.
Mína, the valley of, ii. 202; stones thrown there, P.D. 187, 188.
Mináh, an Arab idol, P.D. 40.
Miracles, of the Qurán and of Muhammad, ii. 98 n., iii. 69, iv. 78 n., viii. 64 n.; at Badr, iii. 13 n.; of Jesus wrought in childhood, v. 109, 110; Muhammad wrought no miracles, vi. 10 and 109–111 notes, xi. 111 n., xiii. 8 n., xiv. 13 n., xvi. 37 n., xvii. 61 and 92–95 notes, xxi. 5 and 6 notes, xxxiv. 27 n., xl. 78 n.
Miráj. See *Night journey*.
Months, the sacred months of ancient Arabs, P.D. 227, 228; their observance by Muslims, P.D. 228–230, ii. 194 and 216 n.
Moon, split in sunder, liv. 1 n.
Moses, his story, vii. 104, &c., xx. 8, &c., xxvi. 9, &c., xxviii. 29, &c.; miraculously preserved, xx. 59; adopted by Pharaoh's wife, ii. 48 n.; the first true believer, vii. 143 n.; at first rejected by his people, xli. 45; asks pardon for his sins, vii. 151 n.; an impediment in his speech, how occasioned, xx. 28 n.; kills an Egyptian and flees to Midian, xxviii. 14–16 notes; entertained by Shuaib and receives his rod from him, xxviii. 25; sees the fire in the bush, xxvii. 7; sent a prophet to the Egyptians, and receives power to work miracles, vii. 133 n., xvii. 116, &c., xxv. 38, and xl. 24–28; his transactions in Egypt, vii. 116, &c.; brings water from the rock, ii. 59; cleared from an unjust aspersion, xxxiii. 69 n.; receives the tables of the law, ii. 52; is wroth with Aaron on account of the golden calf and breaks the tables, vii. 150; he goes in search of Al Khidr, xviii. 4 n.

Muadhdhin or **Muazzin**, the Muslim crier who calls the faithful to prayers, P.D. 169.

Mubaiyadites, their origin and faith, P.D. 275.

Muhájjirín, defined and described, viii. 73 n., xvi. 43 and 111 notes; to be provided for, iv. 99 n.

Muhammad, promised to Adam, ii. 37, 38; foretold by Jesust lxi. 6; expected by the Jews and Christians, xcviii. 1; sen, at forty years of age, x. 17 n.; commanded to [preach Islám, lxxiv. 1–7, lxxxi. introd.; has visions, liii. 11, and xcvi. introd.; complained of by the Quraish to his uncle Abu Tálib, xxxviii. 5 n.; charged with being a madman, lxviii. 1–8, lxxxi. 15–25; claims to be a prophet of God, iv. 67 n., v. 69 n., xxvii. 93 n., xli. 5, xlviii. 29, lxix. 42–52 n., and introductions to chaps. lxxxi. and xcvi.; likens himself to Abraham, xxi. introd.; likens himself to all the former prophets, ii. 70 n. and 125 n., iii. 11 and 146 notes, vii. introd. and notes on vers. 60, 66, 74, and 104, x. 40 and 77 notes, xi. 32 n., xiv. 7 and 14 notes, xxi. 77 n., xxiii. 35–43 n., xxvi. 26 n., xxvii. 24–26, xxxiv. 46 n., xl. 41–47 n., xli. 45 n., xlvi. 8 n., liv. introd., and lxx. introd.; at first declares himself to be only a preacher, ii. 119 n., iii. 144 n., xlii. 47, l. 44 and 45, lxxxviii. 21 and 22; is called the Illiterate Prophet, vii. 158 n., x. 17 n.; at first ignorant of Islám, xlii. 52, 53; receives the Qurán, xlv. 17–19, liii. 6, and xcvi. introd.; repudiates the charge of being a poet, xxvi. 228 n., lxix. 41 n.; claims to have been inspired, xxxix. 1–3 notes (see also *Inspiration*); his early teachings, lxxxiii. 1–6 n., xciii. 9, 10; was subject to Satanic suggestions, iv. 116 n., xvi. 100 n., xxvi. 222 n., cxiv. 5, 6 n.; charged with being an impostor, iii. 137 and 185 notes, vi. 24 and 48 notes, vii. 203 n., x. 39 n., xxvi. introd., xlii. 23, xlvi. 6 and 7, lxviii. 1–8, lxxvii. 8, &c.; reasons for believing him to have been an impostor, ii. 86, 125, 216 and 246 notes, iii. 93 and 121 notes, v. 26 n., vi. 48, 77–84 notes, vii. 2 and 53 notes, viii. 14, 15 n., ix. 63, 64, 74, 95 and 129 notes, xi. 53 n., xii. introd. vers. 3 and 103 notes, xlviii. 15 n.; his sincerity vindicated, reply, ix. 74 n.; his self-assertion no proof of sincerity, vi. 48 n., xxvii. introd.; his policy, iii. 126 n. and 160 n.; his temporary lapse, iv. 116 n., vi. 55 n., xvii. 75 n., xxii. 53 n., xl. 7 n.; exhorted to be patient, xlvi. 35, and lxviii. 48–50; his patience due to policy, P.D. 83; disclaims all knowledge of future events, vi. 49, and xi. 32; wrought no miracles, ii. 98 and 118 notes, iii. 184 n., vi. 109–111 notes (see *Miracles*); his superstition, chaps. cxiii. and cxiv., introd. and notes; is declared to be a sinner,

ii. 199 n., iv. 105 n., ix. 43 and 118 notes, xl. introd., and notes on vers. 7 and 57, lxxx. 1-11; his personal influence, iii. 100-109 n.; to be implicitly obeyed, iv. 62 n.; to be treated with respect, xlix. 1-5, lviii. 12-14; his charity, lxxx. 1-11 n., xciii. 9, 10; his fondness for women, xxxiii. 36-39 notes, lxxix. 40 n.; his cruelty to enemies, viii. 66-69 n., ix. 129, 130 n., xxv. 29 n.; his journey to heaven, xvii. 1 n.; enters into a league with those of Madína, viii. 30; gains proselytes of the genii by reading the Qurán, xlvi. 28-31; accused of injustice in dividing the spoils, xxxi. 62; foretells the victory at Badr, liv. 45; an account of that victory, iii. 13, and viii. 5 n., &c.; loses the battle of Ohod, where he is in danger of his life, iii. 121; his men swear fidelity to him at Hudhaibiyah, xlviii. 18 n.; his courage at the battle of Hunain, ix. 25 n.; conspiracy to kill him, ix. 75 n., and xxxvi. 8 n.; another attempt on his life, from which he is miraculously preserved, iii. 12 n.; his wives demand a better allowance, on which he offers to divorce them, but they chose to stay with him, and he lays down some rules for their behaviour, xxxiii. 28 n.; his privileges in that and other respects, xxxiii. 6, &c. n.; his divorced wives or widows not to marry again, xxxiii. 53; his amour with Mary, the Egyptian slave, lxvi. introd., and vers. 3-5; he changes the Qibla from Jerusalem to Makkah, ii. 142-145 notes; he is pledged to preserve the Jewish and Christian Scriptures from corruption, xl. 56 n.; commands the sword to be drawn against the enemies of Islám, P.D. 84; sends letters inviting foreign princes to embrace Islám, P.D. 90; he consolidates the political power of Arabia, P.D. 67, 68; he is not allowed to pray for reprobate idolaters, ix. 114 n.; utters blasphemy through inadvertence, xxii. 53 n.; no revelation vouchsafed him for several days, xviii. 23 n.; challenges his opponents to produce a chapter like the Qurán, ii. 23 n.; ignorant of the Jewish and Christian Scriptures, ii. 52, 57, 66, 75, 116, 246, and 252 notes, iii. 66 n., iv. 162 n., vi. 85 n., xvi. 105 n., xvii. 1 n., xviii. introd., and vers. 21-23 n., xix. 31 n., and xxviii. 44-46 n.; refuses to eat with an infidel, xxv. 29 n.; prophesies the defeat of the Persians by the Greeks, xxx. 1 n.; his doctrine compared with that of other prophets, xlvi. 8; demolishes the idols of Makkah, xvii. 83 n.; warned to prepare for death, cx. introd.; curses his enemies, lxxx. 16, civ. introd. and notes, ix. 35 n.; a brief history of his life, P.D. 68-95.

Muhaqqimites, a sect of the Khárijites, P.D. 263.

INDEX.   325

Muharram, regulations concerning it, P.D. 229; the days of Ashura, P.D. 178, and ii. 183 n.
Muhrims, described, v. 96 n.
Mukanna (Al). See *Hakím*.
Mukaukas, presents slave girls to Muhammad, P.D. 91.
Munkir and Nákir, described, P.D. 127, iv. 96 n.
Murder, laws concerning, P.D. 214, ii. 178, iv. 91, v. 35 n.
Murjians, their doctrine and sects, P.D. 261–263.
Musailama, claims to be a prophet, but is destroyed, P.D. 270, 271, v. 59 n.
Musháhbihites, their doctrines, P.D. 257, 258.
Muslims, described, ii. 177, ix. 53, 54 n., xlii. 34–41, li. 17–19, xcviii. 6–8; directions in relation to their manners, xxiv. 27–60, xxx. 37, xxxiii. 53; to forgive unbelievers, xlv. 13, 14; their duty to proclaim Islám, ii. 195 n., xli. 33; to avoid near relations if not Muslims, iii. 118, 119 n., ix. 14, 15 and 23, lviii. 22, lx. 1–6 and 13; should have no friendship with Jews and Christians, v. 56 n.; they should fight for Islám, ii. 190–193 and 215 n., iv. 69 n.; they may feign friendship towards infidels, iii. 28, 29 n.; allowed to eat and drink with Jews and Christians, v. 6 n.; bound to establish the religion of Islám in all their dominions, xxii. 43; they obey God through fear, xxiii. 61 n.; they are the chosen of God, iii. 110 n. (see also *Arabians*); shall be joyful in the judgment-day, lxxx. 8–16; all Muslims to be finally saved, iii. 24 n.; the reward of the sincere believers, xxviii. 54 n.; bound to accept the Old and New Testament Scriptures as well as the Qurán, ii. 136 n., iii. 119 n., and v. 70 n.
Mutannabi (Al), his prophetic career, P.D. 279, 280.
Mutazilites, their founder and doctrines, P.D. 242–251; they reject the doctrine of the examination of the sepulchre, P.D. 127; they disbelieve the doctrine of the bridge over hell, P.D. 147; their belief about Paradise, P.D. 153.
Muzdalífah, the oratory between Safá and Marwá, P.D. 187.
Muzdárians, their founder and doctrines, P.D. 247.

Nadhír, the tribe, expelled, lix. 2–5.
Naila. See *Asáf*.
Najáshi, the king of Ethiopia, receives the refugee Muslims kindly, P.D. 78.
Najd, the province, described, P.D. 19.
Nákir. See *Munkir and Nákir*.
Nazarines, Christians so called, v. 19; their kindness, v. 85 n.;

they recognise the Qurán to be God's word, v. 86 n. See also *Christians*.

Nebuchadnezzar, takes Jerusalem, xvii. 5 n.
Night, part of, spent in prayer, lxxiii. 6.
Night journey, of Muhammad from Jerusalem to heaven, P.D. 80; was only a dream, xvii. 1 n., 95 n.
Nimrod, disputes with Abraham, ii. 258 n.; his tower, xvi. 28 n.; attempts to ascend to heaven and persecutes Abraham, his punishment, xxi. 70 n.
Noah, his story, vii. 60–65, x. 72–75, xxvi. 105–122; his prayer, liv. 10; his wife's unbelief, lxvi. 10; lived 950 years, xxix. 13; was a sinner, xi. 47, lxxi. 29.
Nudhár (Al), one of Muhammad's adversaries, his opinion of the Qurán, vi. 24 n.; introduces a Persian romance as preferable to it, xxxi. 5 n.
Nudhámians, their founder and doctrine, P.D. 246.
Nún, the fish to be slain for the feast of God, P.D. 156.
Nusairians, their doctrine, P.D. 267.

Oaths, by various objects, iv. 63, xv. 72, 92, xxxvi. 1, xxxviii. 1, &c., li. 1–11 and 23; to prove the Qurán to be inspired, lvi. 74–81, lxix. 38–52; uttered after careful deliberation, lxxxix. introd.; they should not be in God's name, ii. 224, 225 notes; yet see iv. 63; when they may be violated, ii. 225, 226 n., v. 91, lxvi. 2; how inconsiderate oaths may be expiated, v. 91 n.; not to be violated, xvi. 93; the penalty of perjury, iii. 76, and v. 91.
Oda Ibn Qais, an enemy of Muhammad, xv. 95 n.
Offerings, to God, recommended, xxii. 34 n.
Ohod, defeat at, alluded to, iii. 121 *seq.* notes.
Okail (Abu), his charity, ix. 80 n.
Okatz, the fair, suppressed by Muhammad, P.D. 53.
Omar, his conversion, P.D. 78; decides a dispute between a Jew and a Muslim, iv. 58 n.
Omm Salma, one of Muhammad's wives, xviii. 131 n.
Orphans, the oppression of them denounced, lxxxix. 18, &c.; to be treated kindly, ii. 220 n., xciii. 9, 10 n.; their rights to be maintained, iv. 2–8 notes.
Orthodox, the sect of that name, iii. 95 n., xvi. 121 n.; who are orthodox Muslims, ix. 85 n.
Othmán Ibn Affán, sent by Muhammad to the Quraish, is imprisoned, xlviii. 18; contributes largely to the expedition to Tabúk, ix. 80 n.
Othmán Ibn Matun, his conversion occasioned by a passage of the Qurán, xvi. 92 n.

INDEX.   327

Othmán Ibn Talha, the keys of the Kaabah returned to him by Muhammad, iv. 56.
Oven, whence the first waters of the Deluge poured forth, xi. 40 n.

Parables, of the Qurán, ii. 261, &c., xi. 25, xiv. 29 n., xvi. 77, 78, xviii. 31 n., xxi. 19–31, xxiv. 35, xxix. 40, xxxviii. 23, lvii. 13.
Paraclete, Muhammad's claim to be the, lxi. 6 n.
Paradise, created before the world, P.D. 153; described, P.D. 153–160, xiii. 35, xlvii. 16, &c.; various names, P.D. 155; where situated, ii. 35 n.; its fruits described, ii. 25; Muslim notions obtained from Magians, P.D. 160; inherited by Muslims and their wives, xliii. 68–73; the rewards of, P.D. 154–160, xliv. 51–57, lv. 46–78, lvi. 12–39; different kinds of happiness, lv. 56–68 notes; the pleasures of Paradise carnal and not spiritual, ii. 25 n., iii. 15 n., 196 and 197 notes, ix. 73 n., xv. 47 n., xxxii. 17 n., xxxix. 74 n., lxxviii. 31–37 and P.D. 158–163; Muslim and Christian Paradise compared, P.D. 161.
Pardon, will be granted to the penitent, ix. 5; God only pardons sin, xiii. 7; obtained by repentance and good works, iv. 30, viii. 29; received on the ground of faith, xxxiii. 73.
Parents to be honoured, xvii. 24, &c., and xlvi. 14.
Patience, recommended, iii. 200; the sign of a true believer, ix. 109 n.
Patriarchs, before Moses, neither Jews nor Christians, ii. 140.
Pen, with which God's decrees are written, lxviii. 1 n.
Penitent, their reward, ix. 113.
Pentateuch, given to Moses, vi. 92; sent down to guide mankind, iii. 3 n.; attested by Muhammad as genuine, P.D. 122 and 126, iii. 93 n., vi. 154 n., xlviii. 70–72; preserved uncorrupted in the days of Muhammad, x. 94, 95, and xi. 18.
Perjury, Muslim opinion, v. 91 n.
Persians, overcome by the Greeks, xxx. 1 n.; their influence in Arabia, P.D. 28; the decline of their empire, P.D. 66, 67.
Peter, the Apostle, his stratagem at Antioch, xxxvi. 12 n.
Pharaoh, his story, vii. 104, &c., x. 76, &c., xxviii. 3; a punishment used by him, xxxviii. 11 n.; his presumption, xliii. 50 &c.; destroyed for rejecting Moses, xliv. 16–32.
Pico de Adam. See *Serendíb*.
Pilgrimage, to Makkah, necessary, P.D. 178, 179, ii. 196 n., xxii. 25 n.; fame of, and ceremonies connected with it, P.D. 185–188, v. 2–5, and 96–98; the practice borrowed from heathenism, P.D. 188–190; object of pilgrimage, P.D. 189; trading

at Makkah allowable for pilgrims, ii. 198 n.; none excused from the duty except the incapable, iii. 97 n., xxii. 25 n.
Pledges, to be given where no contract in writing, ii. 282.
Poetry, style of ancient Arab, P.D. 52; poets honoured and rewarded, P.D. 52, 53.
Poets, used and censured by Muhammad, xxvi. 228 n.
Polygamy, laws regulating, P.D. 205-207, iv. 3 n., xxxiii. 4 n. See *Marriage*.
Pomp, of this life, of no value, xxviii. 60.
Poor, oppression of the, denounced, lxxxix. 18-22.
Prayer, commanded and enforced, ii. 42 and 109, iv. 102, xx. 132, &c.; not to be entered on by him who is drunk, iv. 42; should pray before reading the Qurán, xvi. 100; prayer of the angels for the penitent, xl. 7 n.; ceremonial cleanliness necessary to, iv. 42, v. 7; in time of war, armour may be worn during prayers, iv. 101; a prayer for light, i. 1-7; a prayer for forgiveness, iii. 16; prayer of a believer, ii. 238, iii. 8 and 192-195, x. 10, 11, xvii. 82; a prayer of Abraham, xiv. 38-42; prayers accepted by God, iii. 196; Muslim doctrine of prayer described in detail, P.D. 165-171; stated hours of prayer, P.D. 169-171, ii. 109 and 238 notes, v. 105 n., vii. 205 n., xvii. 80, 81 notes; postures in prayer, iii. 192 n.; prayer for the dead, ix. 85 and 114 notes.
Predestination, the doctrine of, iii. 145 n., xvii. 14.
Pre-existence, of souls, a doctrine not unknown to the Muhammadans, vii. 173.
Preserved Table, contains the eternal decrees of God, x. 62; the Qurán copied from it, xliii. 1-3.
Pride, abominable in the sight of God, xvii. 39.
Prodigality, a crime, xvii. 29 n.
Prophecies, concerning Muhammad, iii. 80 and 188 notes, viii. 158 n., lxi. 6; of victory, viii. 36 n., cx. 1, &c.; Muhammad said to have prophesied he would rise from the dead within three days, iii. 144 n.; other prophecies of Muhammad, v. 59, ix. 42 and 96 notes, xi. 110 n., xxviii. 85 n., xxx. 1 n.
Prophets, distinction between *Nabi* and *Rusúl*, xix. 42 n.; their enemy will have God for his, ii. 96; rejected and persecuted before Muhammad, vi. 33, and x. 40, xliii. 4-7; the *Nabi-ul-a'zim*, ii. 86 n.; they spoke by revelation from God, iv. 162; the guardians of God's word, v. 48; Satan their enemy, vi. 112; the number of prophets, v. 22 n., xiv. 10 n.; one sent to each nation, iv. 40 n., xxviii. 75 n.; Muhammad conceives of them as descendants or successors one of another, the number mentioned in the Qurán, vi. 85 n.; all prophets obliged to make a great slaughter of infidels,

viii. 68 n.; **Muslim false prophets,** P.D. 270-280, v. 59 n.; those of the Old and New Testaments attested by the Qurán, P.D. 125, lvii. 26, 27, ii. 177 n.; all declared to be sinners by the Qurán, iii. 147 n., xiv. 42 n., xxvi. 82 n., lxxi. 29.

Prosperity, or adversity, no mark of God's favour or disfavour, lxxxix. 18 n.

Psalms, the Book of, given to David, xvii. 57; confirmed by the Qurán, P.D. 123.

Punishments, and blessings, of the next life, vii. 36, &c. See *Hell* and *Paradise*.

Purifications, ceremonial, P.D. 165-167; whence practice was derived, P.D. 165, 166; based on cleanliness, P.D. 166; sand used instead of water, P.D. 167. See also *Prayer*.

Purgatory, Muslims only suffer for a short time in, iii. 24 n., ix. 114 n.

Qáb, Ibn Asad, persuades the Jews to desert Muhammad, xxi. 26 n.

Qáb, Ibn al Ashraf, a Jew, Muhammad's inveterate enemy, iii. 71 n.; Muhammad causes him to be slain, lix. 2 n.

Qadarians, their founder and doctrine, P.D. 248-250.

Qárún, his story and fearful end, xxviii. 76 n., xxix. 38.

Qibla, how to find the direction of, P.D. 170; the Jewish Qibla for a time adopted by Muhammad, P.D. 172; reason why no Qibla is wanted, ii. 115 n.; the Kaabah in Makkah adopted instead of Jerusalem, ii. 142-145 notes; the Kaabah the true Qibla, ii. 125. See also *Kaabah* and *Makkah*.

Quails, given the Israelites, what kind of birds they were, ii. 56 n.

Quarrels, between the true believers to be composed, xlix. 9; to be avoided on the pilgrimages, ii. 294.

Quraidha, their destruction, xxxiii. 26 n.

Quraish, chief tribe of Makkah, P.D. 30; their nobility, iii. 165 n.; not guardians of the Kaabah, viii. 34 n.; their hatred towards Muhammad, vi. 24 n., lxviii. 51, 52; their anger at the flight of Muslims to Madína, P.D. 85; Muhammad commanded to leave them, xliii. 88, 89; they conspire to kill Muhammad, P.D. 85, viii. 30, xxxviii. 10 n.; the claim that they are the children of Abraham, ii. 129 n.; plagued with famine, xxiii. 65 n.; threatened with destruction, xi. 110 n., xvii. 78 n.; demand miracles of Muhammad, xiii. 30 n.; propound three questions, xvii. 87 n.; make a truce with Muhammad at Hudaibiyah, xlviii. 24 n.; violate truce and lose Makkah, xlviii. 1 n.

Qurán, meaning of the word, P.D. 96; other titles, P.D. 97, xv. 9 n.; divisions of, P.D. 97-100; letters at the beginning of the chapters, P.D. 100–102; language, style, and composition, P.D. 102–104; design, doctrine, and relation to the former Scriptures, P.D. 105, 106; declared to be given by revelation from God, xli. 1–3 and 41, 42, xlii. 1, 2, lxix. 38–52, xcvi. introd., and iv. 163; why revealed in the Arabic language, xli. 44, xlii. 5, xliv. 58, xii. 2 n.; copied from the Preserved Table, P.D. 108, i. introd., xiii. 39, xliii. 1–3, l. 2 n., lxxxv. 22; believed to be eternal, P.D. 111, 112, xxxvi. 82 n.; other opinions in regard to, P.D. 112, 113; punishment of those who reject it, xlv. 6–10; the author of the Qurán was Muhammad, P.D. 106, 107; composed by him during the night-time, lxxiii. 20 n.; revealed to Muhammad by God, xlv. 17–19, liii. 6; regarded as a forgery by the Jews, v. 11 n., xvi. 105 n., xlvi. 10 (see also *Muhammad*); regarded from the first as a complete volume, ii. 152 n., vi. 19 n., vii. 53 n., xv. 1 n., lxxv. 16–19 n.; explained by tradition, lxxv. 19 n.; confirms the Pentateuch, iii. 83 n., v. 50 n., xxviii. 48, 49 n., xlvi. 11; confirmed by the former Scriptures, xx. 133 n., lxxxvii. 18, 19; contains everything necessary to be known, xvi. 92 n.; imperfect, ii. 17 n., iii. 26, 27, and 130 notes, viii. 75 n., xv. 9 n., xvii. 2 n., xxx. 1 n., xliii. 88 n.; twenty-three years in completing, xxv. 34 n.; contrast between Makkan and Madína chapters, xlvii. introd.; Othmán's recension described, P.D. 109; Muslim reverence for the Qurán, P.D. 114; doubt cast on its being from God by its own self-assertion, ii. 2 n., vii. 2 n.; none can write a book like it, ii. 23 n., vi. 94 n., xi. 14 n., xvii. 90; Arabs not convinced of its inimitable style, viii. 31 n., xxi. 5 n.; its influence due to its teachings, ii. 45 n.; said to be the Word of God, ii. 88 n.; claims to attest former Scriptures, ii. 90 n., xii. 111; it attests the Jewish and Christian Scriptures, ii. 40, 91, 96 and 100, iii. 2 and 80, iv. 45–49, 135 and 161, v. 47–52, 72, vi. 90, 93, and 154, ix. 112, x. 38, xi. 18, xii. 111, xxi. 105, xxv. 37, xxviii. 43, xxxv. 23 and 28, xxxvii. 116, xl. 56, xlvi. 11, lvii. 27; Muslim scruples to preserve the text pure, ii. 210 n., xxii. 38 n.; its contradictions of the teachings of the former Scriptures, ii. 243 n., 246–249 n., 259, 271 notes, iii. 2, 35, 148 notes, iv. 169 n., v. 53 n., vii. 81, 85, and 136 notes, ix. 112 n., x. 79 n., xi. 40 and 82 notes, xii. *throughout*, xiv. 13 n., xvi. 95 and 125 notes, xix. 8 and 23 notes, xx. 31–35, xxii. 36 n., xxviii. 23 and 29 notes, xxiv. 13 n.; classification of its revelations, iii. 7 n.; its interpretation known wholly only to God, iii. 7 n., vii. 55 n.; claims to be free from self-contradiction, iv. 81; contradicts itself, iii. 13

n., iv. 81 n., viii. 45, 46 n., ix. 40 n., xvi. 93 n., xx. 91 n., xxv. 53 n., xxvi. 94 n., xxvii. 8 and 10 notes, xxxii. 4 n., xxxix. 24 n.; contradicts science, xv. 19 n., xviii. 59 n., xxxi. 9 n.; not eternal, xxxvi. 82 n.; it is pledged to keep the former Scriptures from corruption, xl. 56 n.

Rahún. See *Sarandíb*.
Raina, a word used by the Jews to Muhammad by way of derision, ii. 103.
Raqún (Al), what, xviii. 17 n.
Ramadhán, the month appointed for a fast, P.D. 175–177, ii. 184–187 note.
Ransom, of captives, disapproved, viii. 69 n.
Rass (Al), various opinions concerning it, xxv. 40, 41 n.; dwellers at, xi. 26–100 notes, l. 12.
Rationalism, its relation to Islám, vi. 19 n.
Rázika, an idol of A'd, vii. 66 n.
Relationships, in the order of hereditary rights, iv. 10–13 notes.
Religion, originally but one, ii. 212 n.; the true religion is Islám, iii. 19 n.; ancestral religion no excuse for idolatry, ii. 171 n., xliii. 19–24; the religion of the ancient Arabians, P.D. 36–43; the character of true religion, ii. 177 n.; not to be propagated by violence, ii. 256 n., iv. 94 n., xi. 29 n.; Islám to be propagated by the sword, ii. 190–193, viii. 40 n., ix. 1–6, 28, 29 and 124 notes; various sects, xxiii. 55.
Religious leaders, the fate of false teachers, xli. 29.
Repentance, necessary to salvation, ii. 16 n., xxxix. 55, 56; its evidence, ix. 11 n.; repentance after the judgment of no avail, xlii. 46.
Reprobates, the doctrine of reprobation, P.D. 164; God reprobates whom he will, xvi. 9 n., 39 n., and 109 n.; the miserable condition of reprobates, vi. 125 n., xlii. 42–45.
Resurrection, the doctrine asserted, xvii. 52, &c., l. 19, &c.; denied by the ancient Arabians, P.D. 43; one of the five fundamental doctrines of Islám, P.D. 126; Muslim opinions concerning it, P.D. 130–141; the doctrine ridiculed by the Quraish, vi. 28; proof of the doctrine, l. 6–11, and lvi. 57–73; the object of the resurrection, P.D. 140; the state of those raised pending judgment, P.D. 140–142; the time known only to God, xxxii. 17; signs of its approach, P.D. 131–137, lxxv. 7, &c.; to be general, P.D. 138; manner of the rising of the dead, P.D. 138–140, xxiii. 102, &c., lxxx. 33–42.

Retaliation, the law relating to, P.D. 216, ii. 178 n.; mutual retaliation of the judgment-day, P.D. 145, 146.

Revelation, the character of Muslim, iv. 162, 163 notes; revelations in writing given to several prophets, ii. 4 n. See also *Inspiration*.

Revenge, allowed, xxii. 61 n.

Rewards, bestowed on the ground of God's mercy, P.D. 156; granted in accordance with justice, iii. 164 n.; described, P.D. 157.

Riches, will not gain a man admission to Paradise, xxxiv. 36; they employ a man's whole life, cii. 1.

Right way, what the Muhammadans so call, i. 5–7 n.

Righteous, their reward. See *Paradise*.

Righteousness, wherein it consists, ii. 177, &c.; that which is required in dealing, ii. 188 and 282.

Rites, appointed in every religion, xxii. 68.

Rock, whence Moses produced water, ii. 59 n.

Romans, decline of their empire, P.D. 65.

Ruh-ul-Amín, a name of Gabriel, xxvi. 193 n., liii. 6.

Saad Ibn Abi Waqqás, mentioned, viii. 1 n.

Saad Ibn Muádh, his severity, viii. 69 n.; dooms the Bani Quraidha to destruction, xxxiii. 26 n.

Sabá, queen of. See *Balqís*.

Saba, the wickedness of his posterity, and their punishment, xxxiv. 15; the city of, and its destruction, P.D. 27.

Sabians, their religion described, P.D. 34; called the Christians of St. John the Baptist, P.D. 35, and ii. 61 n.

Sabbath, the transgression of, punished, vii. 164; the Sabbath of Islám, xvi. 125 n., lxii. 9 n.

Sacred animals, described, v. 102.

Sacred territory, described, P.D. 181, v. 96–98.

Sacrifices, appointed for all nations, xxii. 36; at the Ashura, P.D. 178; at the pilgrimage, P.D. 188; not to be regarded as a mere form, xxii. 39; never offered by Muslims as *a sin-offering*, ii. 82 n., iii. 194 n.; Muhammad not ignorant of the Jewish practice, ii. 66–70, and iii. 194 n.

Sadaqa. See *Almsgiving*.

Safá and Marwá, mountains and monuments of, ii. 159 n.; description of rites at these places, P.D. 187.

Safía, one of Muhammad's wives, xlix. 11 n.

Sáhira, one of the names of hell, lxxix. 14 n.

Saiba, a sacred animal, v. 102.

Saints, Muslim worship of, iii. 63 n.

Sajáj, the prophetess, P.D. 273, v. 59.
Sákia, an idol of A'd, vii. 66 n.
Sakínat. See *Shechinah*.
Sakhar, a devil, gets Solomon's signet and reigns in his stead, his punishment, xxxviii. 32 n.
Sálih, the prophet, his story, P.D. 22, vii. 74 n. See also *Thamúd*.
Salima, an idol of A'd, vii. 66 n.
Salsabíl, the fountain of, P.D. 154, lxxvi. 18.
Salutation, mutual, recommended, iv. 85 n.; form of, among Muslims, iv. 85 n., xxv. 18 n.
Salvation, who will be saved, ii. 61, v. 73, xi. 12, xxiv. 52; by faith, ii. 3–5, 37 and 38, iii. 194, iv. 55 and 174; by grace and works, ii. 81, 111, and 161 notes, iii. 31 n., vii. 44 n., xxxv. 48 n., xl. 17 n.; by repentance, faith, pilgrimage, and warring for the faith, ii. 217, iii. 196, &c.; salvation by atonement rejected by Muhammad, xvi. 34 n. (see also *Atonement*); by grace only, xxxvii. 39 and 55.
Samairi, makes a golden calf for Aaron, ii. 50 n., xx. 96 n.
Saráb, what, xxiv. 39, 40 n.
Saracens, the name, P.D. 13.
Sarah, wife of Abraham, her laughing, xi. 71 n.
Sarandíb, the isle on which Adam fell when cast out of Paradise, his footprint shown there, ii. 35 n.
Satan, Muslim belief concerning him, P.D. 120, 121, ii. 34, &c., vii. 216; his wife and family, xviii. 48 n.; tempts Muslims to apostatise, ii. 207 n.; how he influenced Muhammad, iv. 116 n., liii. 9 n.; God the refuge of Muhammad and his people against his evil suggestions, xli. 36; deceives Adam and Eve, and is punished, vii. 18; he assisted the Quraish, viii. 50 n. See also *Iblís*.
Saul, his story, ii. 247, &c.
Science, what it owes to Muslim learning, P.D. 58–60; scholastic divinity, P.D. 233; Muslim jurisprudence, P.D. 234.
Scriptures, of the Old and New Testament; the teaching of the Qurán *in re*, P.D. 122–125; Muhammad commanded to believe them, iii. 119 n., xlii. 14; Muhammad's knowledge of them acquired from others, ii. 46 n., xxviii. 11 n., xxxvii. 146 n.; current in the days of Muhammad, ii. 40, 77, 90, 100, 112 notes, iii. 23, 64, 77 notes, iv. 45 n., v. 77, 86 notes, x. 38 and 94 notes, xii. 111 n., xvi. 45, xxi. 7 n., xxviii. 49 n., xxix. 45 n.; the text not corrupt in Muhammad's estimation, ii. 41, 78 and 121 notes, iii. 77 n., iv. 44 n., v. 47, 48 n., xviii. 26 n.; if those now current are corrupt, Muhammad and his followers are responsible, v. 86 n., xvi.

45 n., xl. 56 n.; they are not abrogated in the Muslim sense, ii. 105 n.
Sects, the orthodox sects of Islám, P.D. 236–241; the heretical sects, P.D. 241–290; sects of Jews and Christians alluded to, iii. 105 n.
Sennacherib, alluded to, xvii. 5 n.
Sepulchre, the examination of, P.D. 127, iv. 96 n.; this doctrine borrowed from the Jews, P.D. 127.
Sergius, the monk, xvi. 105 n.
Serpent, his sentence for assisting in the seduction of man, vii. 18.
Service, of danger, described, iv. 100, 101 notes.
Seven sleepers, story of, xviii. 15 n.; the only story but one from church history found in the Qurán, xxxvi. 12 n.
Seventy Israelites demand to see God, are killed by lightning, and restored to life at the prayer of Moses, ii. 54 n.
Sháffites, their founder and doctrines, P.D. 239, 240.
Shamhozai, a debauched angel, his penance, ii. 101 n.
Shás Ibn Qais, a Jew, promotes a quarrel between Aus and Khazraj, iii. 100 n.
Shechinah, allusion to it, ii. 248 n., ix. 26 n.
Sheddád, son of A'd, makes a garden in imitation of Paradise, and is destroyed in going to view it, lxxxix. 6 n.
Shedim, Jewish faith in them compared with Muslim faith in genii, P.D. 121.
Shíahs, their distinguishing doctrines, P.D. 264–270.
Shuaib, the prophet, his story, vii. 86–94 n., xii. 83, &c., 176–191.
Sifátians, their founder and sects, P.D. 250 and 253.
Sijíl (Al), the angel who takes an account of men's actions, xxi. 104 n.
Sijjín, lxxxiii. 7–9.
Simon, the Cyrenian, supposed to be crucified instead of Jesus, iii. 53 n.
Sin, great and small, iv. 30 n.; the unpardonable sin, ii. 80 n., iv. 46 n., xiv. 39 n.; defined to be a wilful violation of known law, ii. 284–286 n., ix. 116 n., lxxix. 35 n., lxxxvi. 9 n.; the sins of believers are expiated, xlvii. 2, 3.
Sinai, Mount, lifted up over the heads of the Israelites, ii. 62 and 92; the souls of all the prophets present there at the delivery of the law to Moses, iii. 80 n.
Sinners, the first was Adam, ii. 35; their portion is hell, xviii. 51, xix. 89, and xx. 76.
Sirius, or the greater dog-star, worshipped by the old Arabs, liii. 50 n.

Slander, forbidden, xlix. 12; the punishment of those who slander the prophets, ix. 66, civ. 1 n.

Slavery, freeing of slaves commended, xxiv. 33 n., xc. 8–16 n.; slaveholding not a sin, iv. 24 n., xxiv. 33 n., xc. 13 n.; its moral influence, iv. 3 n.; Muhammad's responsibility for slavery, iv. 24 n.

Smoke, of the judgment-day, P.D. 133, xliv. 9 n.

Sodom, destroyed, vii. 85 n., xl. 80, &c., li. 31–37.

Sodomy, iv. 15 n.

Solomon, succeeds David, xxvii. 16; his power over the winds, xxi. 81, xxxviii. 35; his and David's judgment, xxi. 79 n.; his manner of travelling, xxvii. 20 n.; what passed between him and the Queen of Sabá, xxvii. 23, &c.; a trick of the devils to blast his character, ii. 101 n.; orders several of his horses to be killed because they had diverted him from his prayers, xxxviii. 30 n.; deprived of his signet and his kingdom for some days, xxxviii. 33 n.; his death concealed for a year, in what manner, xxxiv. 13 n.

Somnáth, the idol of, P.D. 41.

Son of God, the Christian doctrine concerning him misunderstood by Muhammad, ii. 116 n.; Muhammad's declaration that if God had a son he would be the first to worship him, xliii. 81 and 82.

Sorcerers, those of Egypt believe in Moses, vii. 111, &c., xxvi. 33, &c.

Soul, its origin, xvii. 87; state of the soul after death, P.D. 127; examined in the sepulchre, P.D. 127.

Spirit (the Holy), the Angel Gabriel so called, ii. 86 and 253 notes, xvi. 2 and 104 notes, xviii. 87 n., xxxii. 8 n.

Spoils, laws relating to, P.D. 222–226, viii. 1, &c., notes; given as a reward of faithfulness, iii. 152 n., ix. 75 n., xlviii. 18 and 19; special ruling in regard to them, lix. 6–10; Muslims slain for the sake of spoil, iv. 93 n.; spoils of Badr, viii. 1 n.; a quarrel over them, viii. 48 n., ix. 58, 59 n.

Stars, shooting stars thrown by the genii, lxxxvi. introd.

Star-worship. See *Idols* and *Idolatry*.

Stoning, as a punishment, iii. 23 n.

Stones, worship of. See *Idols* and *Idolatry*.

Strategy, justified, viii. 60 n.

Sulát. See *Prayer*.

Sufián (Abu), commands the army of the Quraish at Ohod, iii. 121 n.; and the convoy of the caravan at Badr, viii. 5 n.; challenges Muhammad to meet him at Badr a second time, iii. 151 n.; but fails to do so, iii. 173 n.; embraces Muham-

madanism on the taking of Makkah, lx. 7 n.; expostulates with Muhammad, xxiii. 76 n.
Sufís, their pantheism, P.D. 267, 268.
Suhaib, flies to Madína, ii. 206 n.
Suhail, Ibn Amru, treats with Muhammad on behalf of the Quraish, xlviii. 26 n.
Sunnís, a sect of the Muslims, P.D. 237.
Supererogation, xvii. 81.
Superstitions, of the ancient Arabs, P.D. 43, 44; heathen Arab superstitions conserved in Islám, P.D. 178-190.
Sura, or chapter of the Qurán, i. introd., ix. 65 n.; chronological order of the, see table at p. 302, vol. iv.
Suráqah Ibn Málik, the devil appears in his form, viii. 50 n.
Sun and moon, not to be worshipped, xlvii. 37.
Swines' flesh. See *Things forbidden.*

Tabála and Jorash, inhabitants thereof embrace Islám, ix. 28 n.
Tables, of the law, vii. 145 n.
Tabúk, the expedition of, ix. 38 n.
Taghút, an Arab idol, ii. 256 n., iv. 58 n., xvi. 38 n.
Taháma, its boundaries, climate, &c., P.D. 19.
Tasm, the tribe, almost destroyed, P.D. 23.
Tasním, a fountain in Paradise, P.D. 154-157, lxxxiii. 27 n.
Tayif, the inhabitants of, reject Muhammad, P.D. 79.
Tawáf, the march around the Kaabah, ii. 198, 199.
Temple, of Makkah, see *Kaabah;* of Jerusalem, built by genii, xxxiv. 13 n.; the idol temples of ancient Arabians, P.D. 38.
Testimony, law of, v. 105-107.
Thakíf, the tribe of, demand terms of Muhammad, which are denied, xvii. 75 n.
Thálaba, grows suddenly rich on Muhammad's prayer for him, but refusing to pay alms, is again reduced to poverty, ix. 76 n.
Thamámians, their founder and doctrine, P.D. 248.
Thamúd, the tribe of, their story, P.D. 22, vii. 74, &c., xi. 61, and xxvi. 141, &c.
Theft, laws relating to, P.D. 216, v. 42.
Things forbidden, laws for meats and drinks, P.D. 191 and 197, v. 2-5 n.; why wine was forbidden, P.D. 193; question of coffee and tobacco, P.D. 192; games forbidden, P.D. 193-196; divining by arrows forbidden, P.D. 196, 197; blood and swine's flesh forbidden, P.D. 198; usury forbidden, P.D. 199, ii. 275 n.; infanticide forbidden, P.D. 202-204; sacrificing of children forbidden, P.D. 204; flesh of sacred animals for-

bidden, vi. 143, 144; silk clothing forbidden, xxii. 23 n.; meats offered to idols forbidden for food, P.D. 198.

Throne, of God, ii. 255; will be borne by eight angels on the day of judgment, lxix. 17.

Thur, a mountain, in a cave of which Muhammad concealed himself in the flight from Makkah, P.D. 86.

Tíma Abu Ubairak, his theft, iv. 104 n.

Time, computed by the sun and moon, vi. 97.

Titian, the name of the person supposed to have been crucified instead of Jesus, iii. 53 n.

Tobacco. See *Things forbidden*.

Tradition, when relating to genealogies, copied from that of the Jews, P.D. 25 n.

Translations, of the Qurán, P.D. 115.

Tree, of knowledge of good and evil, confounded in Qurán with the tree of life, vii. 21 n.

Tribute, its imposition, ix. 29 n.

Trinity, the doctrine according to Islám, iii. 2 n., iv. 169 n.; doctrine rejected by Muhammad, iii. 2 n., iv. 169 n., and v. 116 n.

Trump, of the resurrection, P.D. 135, 136, xxvii. 89, xxxix. 68.

Túba, the tree of Paradise, P.D. 153, 154.

Tubbá, descended from Qahlán, P.D. 26; they are destroyed, xliv. 33-37.

Tulaiha, a false prophet of Islám, P.D. 272, 273, v. 59 n., xxxiii. 9 n.

Turks, their rule in Arabia, P.D. 31-33 and notes.

Tuwa, the valley where Moses saw the burning bush, lxxix. 16.

Ummi, a title assumed by Muhammad, vii. 158, lxii. 2.

Ummat, what, iii. 64 n., 110 n., x. 20, xlv. 25 n.

Unbelievers, described, xxxiv. 42, &c.; they oppose the truth with blasphemous levity, xli. 25-28 n.; they shall not escape in the judgment, xli. 8-22, 40, 52-54, xlvii. 9-17, l. 12, 13; their punishment, ii. 162, iv. 54.

Unity, of God, asserted, cxii. 1, &c.

Usury. See *Things forbidden*.

Uzza (Al), an idol of the Quraish, P.D. 39, iv. 116, xxxix. 37 n.

Various readings, of the Qurán, P.D. 110, iii. 115 n., and 165 n., vi. 62 n., xxx. 1 n.

Victory, of the Greeks over the Persians, foretold by Muhammad, xxx. 1 n.

Virgin Mary, was worshipped by Christians in the days of Muhammad, P.D. 64.

VOL. IV.   Y

Wahábis, their founder and doctrine, P.D. 281–283; defeated by Ibrahim Pasha, P.D. 32 n.; they repeat the "Amen" in a loud voice, xx. 6 n.

Wahi. See *Inspiration* and *Revelation.*

Wáidians, their name and peculiarities, P.D. 264.

Walíd, Ibn al Mughaira, a great enemy of Muhammad, was a bastard, invective against, lxviii. 9–16 n.; derides Muhammad for calling God al Rahmán, vii. 181 n.; his prosperity and decay, lxxiv. 11, &c., notes; his death, xv. 95 n.; constituted a typical enemy of Islám, xc. introd.

Walíd, Ibn Uqba, xlix. 6 n.

War, against infidels, commanded, P.D. 218, iv. 83, viii. 62–68, xlvii. 4 and 5; how war should be conducted against infidels, P.D. 220–222, xlvii. 4, 5; forbidden in the month of Ramadhán, ii. 16; Muslims bound to help in holy war (Jíhád), ii. 190–193, 217, 244–246 notes, xlvii. 37–40, lvii. 7–11; who may be excused from fighting in holy warfare, ix. 92; rewards of those who fight, xlvii. 6–8; those slain in holy war counted martyrs, iii. 140 and 158.

Waraqa, confirms Khadíjah's faith in her husband, P.D. 75.

Wasíla, described, v. 102.

Water, produced from the rock by Moses, ii. 59.

Weight, to be just, and false weights denounced, vii. 86, lxxxiii. 1–6.

Whoredom, laws concerning, iv. 14, xxiv. 4.

Wicked, their sentence, x. 71, xiv. 50, &c., lxxvii. 16, &c. See also *Unbelievers.*

Widows, to be provided for, ii. 240; laws relating to them, ii. 234.

Wills, laws concerning them, P.D. 213, iv. 6–32; not to be tampered with, ii. 181, 182, v. 105 n.

Winds, their use, xxx. 45, &c.; subject to Solomon, xxi. 81 n., xxxviii. 35.

Wine, the drinking of, forbidden, P.D. 191, ii. 218 n., iv. 42 n., v. 92, 93 n.; rivers of, in Paradise, xxxvii. 44, &c., xlvii. 16 n., lxxvi. 5 n.

Witchcraft, used against Muhammad, cxiii. 1, &c.

Witnesses, laws relating to them, iv. 133, v. 9; necessary in bargains and to secure debts, ii. 283.

Wives, number allowed by the Qurán, iv. 3 n.; their duty to their husbands, ii. 228; their position in relation to their husbands, iv. 33 n.; may be chastised, iv. 33 n. See also *Adultery, Divorce, Marriage,* and *Women.*

Women, to be respected, iv. 1; requirements of Islám in regard to them, ii. 221–223; if converted to Islám, they are *ipso facto* divorced from unbelieving husbands, lx. 10; how married if twice divorced, ii. 230; their apparel in time of prayer, P.D. 171; the wives of ancients an example to them, lxvi. 10-12; they ought to have part of their relations' inheritance, iv. 6; not to be inherited against their will, iv. 18; to be subject to the men, iv. 33; some directions for their conduct, xxiv. 31, &c.; punishment of those who falsely accuse them of incontinence, xxiv. 4, &c.; their rewards in Paradise, P.D. 163, iii. 196 n., iv. 123; their degradation under Islám, ii. 282 n., iv. 15, 33 and 127 notes, xxiv. introd. 13 n.

Works, of an infidel, will appear to him at the last day, vi. 30 n.

Writing, the art, in Arabia, P.D. 50, 51; known to Muhammad, x. 17 n., xxix. 47 n.

Yajúj and Majúj. See *Gog and Magog*.

Yamáma (Al), the province described, P.D. 19; the city of Musailama, the false prophet, P.D. 19; its people warlike, xlviii. 16 n.

Yaman, described, P.D. 14, 15; climate and productions, P.D. 15, 16; founder of the kingdom, P.D. 26; its Himyár and Qahlán princes, P.D. 26; conquered by the Ethiopians, P.D. 28; Persian supremacy established, P.D. 28; Muslim rulers of, P.D. 30, 31 n.; the inhabitants of it slay their prophet, xxi. 10.

Yathrib, the ancient name of Madína, xxxiii. 13.

Zabír (Al), Mount, vii. 143 n.

Zacharias, his story, iii. 38, &c., xix. 7, &c.; praying for a son, is promised John, iii. 38, 39; educates the Virgin Mary, iii. 44; is numbered among the prophets, vi. 86 n.

Zaid, Ibn A'mru, acknowledges one God before the mission of Muhammad, iv. 82 n.

Zaid, the husband of Zainab, his story, xxxiii. 36-40 notes; divorces his wife in favour of Muhammad, xxxiii. 37 n.; the only person of Muhammad's company named in the Qurán, xxxiii. 37.

Zainab. See *Zaid*.

Zakát, described, P.D. 89, ii. 42 n.; rules concerning it, P.D. 172-174, ix. 60 and 104.

Zamharir, the cold of, vi. 128 n.

Zamzam, the well described, P.D. 185; taste of its water. P.D. 17.

Zanjabíl, a stream in Paradise, lxxvi. 17.

Zaqqúm, the tree of hell, xvii. 62 n., xxxvii. 60.
Zendicism, its influence in Arabia, P.D. 48; its professors in the resurrection, P.D. 139.
Zulaikha, Joseph's mistress, xii. 21, &c.
Zulkifl. See *Ezekiel.*
Zulqarnain. See *Alexander the Great.*

THE END.

PRINTED BY BALLANTYNE, HANSON AND CO
EDINBURGH AND LONDON.

www.ingramcontent.com/pod-product-compliance
Lightning Source LLC
Chambersburg PA
CBHW020313240426
43673CB00039B/791